THE
GOBI DESERT

Other Volumes in the Virago/Beacon Traveler Series

THE
GOBI DESERT

MILDRED CABLE
with
FRANCESCA FRENCH

with a new introduction by
MARINA WARNER

'Very full of dreams that desert, . . .'

Beacon Press   Boston

Beacon Press
25 Beacon Street
Boston, Massachusetts 02108

Beacon Press books
are published under the auspices of
the Unitarian Universalist Association of Congregations.

First published by Hodder and Stoughton Ltd in 1942
©1942 by the Estate of Mildred Cable
Introduction ©1984 by Marina Warner
First published as a Beacon paperback in 1987
by arrangement with Virago Press Limited
Printed in the United States of America

94   93   92   91   90   89   88   87   1   2   3   4   5   6   7   8

Cover photograph of Mildred Cable
reproduced by kind permission of the Overseas Missionary Fellowship.

Library of Congress Cataloging-in-Publication Data

Cable, Mildred.
The Gobi Desert.

(Virago/Beacon travelers)
First published in 1942.
1. Gobi Desert (Mongolia and China) 2. Mongolia—Description and
travel. 3. Cable, Mildred—Journeys—Gobi Desert (Mongolia
and China) 4. Cable, Mildred—Journeys—Mongolia. 5. French, Francesca,
1871–1960—Journeys—Gobi Desert (Mongolia and China)
6. French, Francesca, 1871–1960—Journeys—Mongolia.
I. French, Francesca, 1871–1960— Journeys—Mongolia. I. French, Francesca,
1871–1960. II. Title. III. Series.
DS793.G6C3   1987   951'.73   87-47526
ISBN 0-8070-7033-5 (pbk.)

CONTENTS

THE PEOPLE OF THE WAYSIDE

THE KING OF THE GOBI

THE INTERCOURSE OF THE GOBI

THE GREAT TURFAN DEPRESSION

REVOLT IN THE GOBI

HIGHWAYS AND BY-WAYS

CONTENTS

ILLUSTRATIONS

ILLUSTRATIONS

Note: The original Hodder and Stoughton edition of THE GOBI
    DESERT contained three colour plates which we have not been
    able to include in this edition.

IX

ACKNOWLEDGMENTS

I am indebted to the authors of the following books for numerous data of geographical, historical and scientific research:

Barthold. *Turkestan down to the Mongol Invasions.*

Carruthers (Douglas). *Unknown Mongolia.*

Couling (Samuel), M.A. *Encyclopaedia Sinica.*

Czaplicka (M. A.). *The Turks of Central Asia in History and at the Present Day.*

Hedin (Sven). *Through the Gobi Desert.*
The Old Silk Road.
Riddles of the Gobi Desert.

Julien (Stanislas). *Histoire de la vie de Hiouen-Thsang.*

Le Coq (Albert von). *Auf Hellas Spuren in Ost-Turkistan.*
Von Land und Leuten in Ost-Turkistan.

McGovern (W. M.). *The Early Empires of Central Asia.*

Paquier (J. B.). *Le Pamir.*

Prjevalski (N.). *From Kulja across the Tian Shan to Lop Nor.*

Shaw (R. B.). *A Sketch of the Turki Language.*

Stein (Sir Mark Aurel). *Serindia.* 5 vols.
Innermost Asia. 3 vols.

Skrine (F. H.) and Ross (E. Denison). *The Heart of Asia.*

Stewart (Rev. John). *Nestorian Missionary Enterprise.*

P. Vidal de la Blache et L. Gallois. *Géographie Universelle.*

Younghusband (Sir Francis). *Heart of a Continent.*

Yule (Sir Henry). *The Book of Ser Marco Polo.*

INTRODUCTION

The traveller through whose eyes we see the many peoples and the empty vastness of the Gobi desert in this book is not single but three-fold. Mildred Cable was the chief author and the dominant personality, but she was only a member of 'three-in-one venerable teachers of righteousness', as the Chinese put it. Her companions were two sisters, Francesca, with whom she wrote almost all her many works, and Evangeline French, seven years older than Mildred, two years older than Francesca. The friendship began when Eva and Mildred met, in Hwochow (Huozhou) in Shansi (Shanxi) province in 1901, when Mildred was twenty-two and had just arrived as a missionary, and it lasted till the women's deaths, after half a century together, spent divided between nomadic encampments in the desert and Willow Cottage, Shaftesbury, Dorset.

In a photograph of them taken in China when they were in their forties, they look like the Victorian founders of women's colleges. Staunch, stout, with thin wispy buns, all three of them wore granny specs. (The Chinese would exclaim at the speed with which they wrote and read and then sigh, 'They have worn out their eyes with so much learning.') They also exude good-nature, especially Eva, who is beaming over a book; Francesca is sitting beside her, the corners of her mouth dimpling, even though she is not actually smiling. Mildred stands behind both of them, with a rather sterner air, her eyebrows slightly puckered, and she rests her elbow lightly on Francesca's shoulder. Friends agreed that Mildred was the 'father figure' of the 'Trio', Francesca the mother, and Eva the strongwilled, puckish and wonderful child. Certainly Mildred unselfconsciously assumed the authoritative role in this photograph.

Although the Trio have that serene, cerebral, pioneering quality that tells us that they possessed what Henry James, writing around their time, would have called 'beautiful' natures, they strike a much more original note; they are dressed, after all, in Chinese clothes, bundled up in wadded jackets down to their knees over cotton tunics and cloth shoes with white spats-like socks, and their bodies have the soft, rounded, loose look of the Oriental, in exact reversal of the corseted, hard, tormentingly encased bodies of their sisters in Europe

INTRODUCTION

at that time. They were conventional women who had staged a grand escape from convention, and unless the huge amounts of writing they poured out about their lives are distorted beyond the limits of probability, they were remarkably happy. In their autobiography, *Something Happened*, which went through seven editions between 1933 and 1938, they looked back on their joint venture with an enviable sense of fulfilment:

> They have often seen themselves depicted in the similitude of the mule team, which has drawn them over so many mountains, through such dangerous rivers, and across such burning desert plains. The alert beast in the traces gets the first flick of the whip when there is difficulty ahead. She responds with a bound, but before the impetus of her pull has slackened, the driver has touched the steady reliable mule in the shafts, which can be counted on to brace itself to bear the strain. Then the two pull together to one purpose and one end, but without the third mule, hitched so as to get an equal share of the weight, the mountain pass would never be crossed, nor the exhaustion of the wearisome plain endured. The beasts of the team do not select each other, that is the driver's business, as it is his also to give the signals.

Mildred Cable first felt the signal of the 'driver' and received the call to missionary work when she was still in her teens. Born in 1878 and brought up in Guildford, where she chafed against the restrictive social niceties, and the prejudices that set one sect of Christianity at loggerheads with another, she was overwhelmed when she first heard an antidenominational preacher from the evangelical Keswick Movement. 'The tremendous truth "All One in Christ Jesus",' she wrote later, 'was sounded through the town.' The Cables were partners in a shop in the High Street, and Mildred was receiving a traditional education. She was clearly a high-spirited girl, and she champed at the lack of outlet for her energies, especially for her love of adventure, nourished by stories about far-travelling missionaries and martyrs. After hearing another preacher talk of the Chinese, in the summer of 1893, when she was fifteen, Mildred Cable decided that China was where she was called. Her parents were dismayed, as is probably only natural, but allowed her to spend holidays from school in the Women's Candidates' Home of the China Inland Mission in North London. The mission had been established by Dr Hudson Taylor after the First Opium War, when privileges of travel and entry were first wrested from the Chinese, by the unequal treaties of 1842 and 1843, and it despatched men and women, now protected by rights

INTRODUCTION

of extraterritoriality from Chinese justice, into the interior to preach the gospel.

In the Candidates' Home, Mildred Cable was taken care of by Henrietta Soltau (1843-1934), another determined convert to God's service who began by running a home and school for the children of missionaries who'd gone to China, and was then transferred to become superintendent of the first stage of the girl volunteers' training school. Henrietta Soltau was spellbinding to an impatient, gifted and unchannelled spirit like the sixteen-year-old Mildred Cable. (Later, she wrote her biography, *The Woman who Laughed*.) Though Mildred was taken travelling round Europe by her father – a frequent remedy for obstinate daughters – she persisted in her vocation, refused to study music as it would not be useful for missionary work, and instead learned pharmacy, anatomy, surgery, midwifery.

Mildred Cable was the only one of the Trio it seems who nearly married, and she had plans at this time to work in China with her future husband. But the engagement was broken, by a *lettre de rupture*, which she writes about, in *Something Happened*, in the manner of a Victorian heroine:

> In the midst of this welter of hopes and plans there was one more blow, and that a soul-shattering one. On a beautiful May morning, when the lilac was in bloom, there was put into her hand a letter in which that was written which made a goblin of the sun. Unless she take a devious course, and deny her vocation, she must pursue her pathway alone. In one hour the brightest things of life burnt themselves to ashes, and joy removed itself so far from her that it took years to court it back. . .

She saw her disappointment in love in those terms, and they are the terms of her education and background.

In 1901 she set off for China. Her father went with her as far as New York, and she proceeded alone. When Eva French first saw her step down from the cart in the courtyard of her mission house in Hwochow in Northwestern China, she first thought 'What possessed them to send such a frail child to our hard inland conditions?' But on a second look, she changed her mind, as well she might. Mildred Cable could stand a great deal, and in great helpings, and she was temperamentally given to the pleasures of being tried and tested. As this book, *The Gobi Desert*, reveals, she had an ascetic's love of experience stripped to the bone, mixed with a sensuous imagination's delight in the refinement of empirical sensation.

Eva French had been out in China since 1893, and she had been caught up in the Boxer turmoil of 1900 and seen many of her fellow missionaries and their Christian converts tortured and even killed. Shansi was one of the most violent provinces during that uprising against the foreigners – politicians, traders, speculators and Christians who were greedily carving up China in their own interests – and its Governor, Yü-hsien, was executed afterwards for his support of Boxer atrocities. Eva had been reported dead in the newspapers, but though captured and manhandled, she had survived.

Mildred Cable does not have a taste for polemics, and she does not discuss here the reasons behind Boxer xenophobia. Nor does she face the issue of Christianity's fundamental subversiveness. For Christianity of its essence challenged Chinese society, based on Confucian family pietas, arranged polygamous marriages, and ancestor worship. The presence of a foreign mission in a town could cause division; nor were the missionaries always sensitive to the discord their own separate rights and the protection they offered converts could arouse. They did, however, also perform good works, as they were sent out to do. Eva French, for instance, ran a school for young women and an opium smokers' refuge as well as trying to convert Chinese to Christianity.

Mildred Cable began by settling with a Chinese family in order to learn the language, and then she re-opened the girls' school, which grew rapidly. In 1909, on leave back home, Mildred and Eva gathered up Francesca, who had stayed behind in Portsmouth to nurse her mother. She had since died, and Francesca was free to complete the Trio and travel to China. In their autobiography, they describe this change with engaging candour:

> Francesca observed, and saw that there was a greater intimacy between Eva and Mildred than she had ever yet met between two friends. She could not see them together without detecting a deep and subtle understanding which indicated oneness of instinct and purpose. Mildred knew Eva so well as to completely understand her feelings towards Francesca... She watched them both and determined that so far as in her lay, nothing should be allowed which would cause pain to either sister. "If our friendship reveals an exclusive element it will bring unhappiness to both, but if there be nothing of the kind, the relationship between the three of us might develop and grow into something better than we have yet known." ... From the first moment all three behaved with complete honesty, simplicity and truthfulness. Fortunately for their future happiness no one sentimentalised, and no one pretended anything at all... Three lives . . . . were to be twisted by His (God's) hands into a three-fold cord, which would not easily be broken.

INTRODUCTION

Francesca, Mildred Cable's co-author in over a dozen books, was fluent in French as well as English, as she had been born in Bruges, Belgium and educated in Geneva, like Eva, who had been born in Algeria. She had taken a nurses' training course in Dublin before coming out to China, but of the three, she was at her own estimate the most cultivated, and artistic. She wrote of herself:

> Books were among the strongest character forming influences of Francesca's life, but none so definitely moulded her thought as the story of the Brontë family, combined with the portrait which Charlotte gave of herself in her own novels. Looking back it seems that Francesca's first realisation of moral strength was bound up in the picture of this woman, in whom the forces of life worked so violently, yet always under such a disciplined and quiet exterior.

Francesca, it is agreed by many of their friends, supplied the style in their collaborative literary attempts, as well as many French touches, while Mildred provided the energy and the industriousness.

After Francesca joined Eva and Mildred in Hwochow, the school grew to over 200 pupils. Women and their predicament in Chinese society remained the Trio's chief concern. Although footbinding was abolished by the Republican government in 1912, the custom clung on in the remote provinces, and besides, women already crippled could not have their feet restored, only eased. The Trio's mission, like all Christian missions in China, banned the custom, and introduced a novel concept of womanhood to the Confucian Chinese, for whom footbinding was the prime symbol of their elevation as fetishes and degradation as chattels. Mildred Cable, at mission conferences throughout the early part of the twentieth century insisted on the need for teachers of this broader concept of Christianity, to make open the way to a new social order. 'Womankind,' wrote Mildred, needed 'Education, training and emancipation in every form.' We are more aware today of the dangers of arrogance in such an approach to another society's difference; but the lessons of colonialism and its destructiveness should not make us dismiss the China missionaries' interference as imperialist altogether, however prejudiced and superior some of their attitudes were.

There are practices – footbinding, female circumcision – that should be judged by universal principles: every human being shares the common right not to be mutilated. Women like Mildred Cable and the French sisters were justified in seeing women's position in China from the point of view of Western women's freedom and to want to change it.

The irony is that missionaries had little impact on religion, but a profound effect on politics. The Western principles of egalitarianism, free speech, democracy which they also represented made them crucial contacts for the emerging generation of Republicans after the turn of the century. The ideas that had provoked revolt in 1900 were spreading as a new political faith in 1920. Mildred Cable was in China at a historic moment, when the last imperial dynasty fell, and the last Emperor was deposed, in 1911. He was only a child, and the last effective ruler, Tz'u-hsi (Cixi), the formidable and narrow-minded Empress Dowager, had died three years before. The first President of the Republic, Sun Yat-sen, had been educated abroad and was a twofold convert – to Christianity and Western self-determination. But in the Gobi desert the repercussions of these great events were felt only lightly.

The trio set out in 1923, a year before the last eunuchs in the Forbidden City in Peking were driven out, and four years before Chiang Kai-Shek became China's leader. The station at Hwochow was flourishing, and Mildred Cable declared that a missionary should wander, and carry the word where it had never before been heard. Friends worried for them. Three women taking up the nomad's life in the dangers of the most famously harsh desert in Asia was unthinkable. But a woman friend wrote and convinced them: 'I feel the urgency of the currents of spiritual forces set into motion by your message to that provinces . . .' Her prophecy was believed, and turned out to be accurate: the Trio were the first Christians in the region since Nestorians in the sixth century, and they were the last. They were swept out in 1936, during the Sino-Japanese war, by a decree against all foreign nationals. They travelled for the last time through China, not in a mule cart with a baggage train in a slow caravan, but, as a sign of the times, by aeroplane to Sian (Xi'an) and then by train.

The region is legendary for fearsome dangers; it is one of the hottest, dryest places on earth, so landlocked that only one river straggles to the sea at all, the others drain away into the earth. Noonday devils, sand spouts, hurricanes of pebbles, brackish wells, mirages and other prodigies and horrors all contribute to the pull of this wondrous frontier territory, and Mildred Cable, Eva and Francesca French were in a grand tradition of foreigners who had submitted to the wilderness' charm. They mention here some of the

INTRODUCTION

early travellers who made the slow march, in stages, from ancient waterhole to waterhole: Hsüan Tung, the Buddhist magus who crossed into India in the seventh century AD to bring his religion's sacred scriptures back to China, and later, at the turn of our century, the knowledgeable Aurel Stein, who rediscovered the same texts in the caves of Tunhuang (Dunhuang) and brought them back (some say stole) to become part of the British Museum's rich Oriental collection. Mildred Cable provides description of archaeological sites that later historians have found useful, for the fortifications of ancient Karakho have since been dismantled, while the cave sculptures of the Thousand Buddhas at Tunhuang are now mutilated. The tracks Mildred Cable and her companions followed form the easterly arm of the long Silk Road that carried trade between central China and its principal city Sian, the old T'ang capital, to the ports of the Eastern Mediterranean and thence to the whole of luxury–loving Europe. It is a historic road, and few women outsiders have travelled it, with the notable exception of the Chinese Princess who was sent as a political bride to sweeten the King of Khotan and smuggled out silk worms, and the necessary mulberry seeds to feed them, in her elaborate hair in order that, even among barbarian nomads, she could continue to wear silk.*

The authors of this book were the first Englishwomen to cross and recross the Gobi. The dauntless Trio, in carts laden with provisions, carefully avoiding contact with the flea-infested clothing of their carter, wandered for fifteen years on and off, in the country described with such fascinating detail and observation in this book. Mildred's knowledge of medicine and of flowers' and plants' properties and characteristics emerges clearly, as does the threesome's irrepressible enjoyment of desert pleasures, the celebrated melons of Hami, the sweet perfume of the sand-jujube flower. *The Gobi Desert* is the fruit of long experience of a region even more remote in geography and climate and customs today than it was in the 'twenties and 'thirties, and the picturesque and entertaining account given here also constitutes an invaluable repository of research about the people of the desert – the Mongols, Turki, Tungan, the Buddhist pilgrims, the Lamas, the Islamic tribes whose lives have been transformed by the geo-political realities of today.

The Gobi Desert was first published in 1943, and proved popular, as

*For more on this see Peter Hopkirk: *Foreign Devils on the Silk Road* (London 1980).

INTRODUCTION

did many of Cable and French's joint works, running through nine editions in only four years. It was by no means their first book together, nor their first comment on their desert experiences, but the fruit of a decade's contemplation of the world they had left behind. The manuscript was nearly destroyed by a doodle bug that hit the flat in Hampstead they had rented, but they salvaged it and continued work on it in a new flat in West End Lane. As authors, they were extremely prolific. Mildred had started, on her own, in 1917, with a biography of Pastor Hsi, a reformed opium smoker who had become the vicar at the Hwochow mission. Her first book with Francesca was *Despatches from North-West Kansu* (Gansu) (1925), followed by, among others, *Something Happened* (1933). In *Through Jade Gate* (1927) and *A Desert Journal* (1934), the edited collection of their letters home from the Gobi, they wrote what amounts to drafts for the present volume. They also published together several biographies of other China missionaries: *The Making of a Pioneer, Percy Mather of Central Asia* (1935), *George Hunter, Apostle of Turkestan*, 1948, and handbooks for others who might follow them – *Ambassadors for Christ* (1935) and *Towards Spiritual Maturity* (1939). They told the stories of two little girls whom they had adopted, in books for children which show traces of the martyr moralities Mildred liked when she was young. In *Grace, Child of the Gobi* (1938), a slave girl whose foot has gone gangrenous after attempted footbinding and maltreatment by her owners, has to have it amputated. The Trio take her in, and bring her up, as a Christian, and she eventually marries, a destiny that would have been closed to a crippled slave by Confucian norms. *The Story of Topsy, Little Lonely of Central Asia* (1937), is composed rather uneasily in the same simple, sickly, edifying style, but it documents a most interesting aspect of the Trio's lives. Topsy was a Mongolian foundling, who was deaf and dumb. They adopted her and taught her to communicate through writing. When they returned to England, Topsy came too and lived with them in Dorset until their deaths. She was their sole beneficiary, with the provision that their estates should go, after her death, to The Bible Society of London.

The Gobi Desert was Mildred Cable's *magnum opus*, and the apogee of her literary output. She followed it up with the story of her travels, with Francesca and Eva, at advanced ages, to Australia, New Zealand and India, (1950). Their very last publication gave an account of the work for the Bible Society they had undertaken since their return from China. It came out after Mildred's death. In the foreword, Francesca remembered her friend's energy: 'Mildred always thought of Christianity as a dynamic force which must burst every bond that attempted to hinder its expanding power.' The metaphors are justly chosen: Mildred Cable, rooting herself in Christianity, gave herself the chance which she would not otherwise have had to express her often extravagant, potent character.

She was the youngest, and she had died the first, aged 74, on April 30 1952. Eva and Francesca died six years later, within three weeks of each other. After twenty years' rigour and more trekking in the arid wastes of the Gobi, they had lived to reach ninety and eighty-eight years respectively. Francesca French the author fell silent after Mildred, her animating literary genius, had gone.

The lives of Mildred Cable and Francesca French raise important questions for us now. They most probably epitomised the 'frightful old battleaxes' who are so commonly laughed at and shunned in English society. (Mildred was nicknamed 'Napoleon' at the Bible Society). Readers could jump to the conclusion that they were lesbians as well. Probably, once their stories and achievements gain wider audiences, they will be claimed as lesbian feminists and become participants in the argument that reaches backwards through time and intertwines the history of women with the history of lesbian sexuality. They might qualify for a place in the pantheon that has enshrined Willa Cather and Virginia Woolf, for instance, as role models and foremothers, according to some of today's increasingly influential radical feminist thinkers.

They certainly achieved lives of plenitude, living together as female friends who seem never to have kept company with men other than hired muleteers and innkeepers. They conducted their lives in a spirit of independence, enterprise and autonomy that was masculine in gender for their own period and background; they were women who refused the normal lot of women of their sort and by the standards of their day – and perhaps even by ours today – they were unusual if not actually anomalous. But a masculine life does not entail homosexuality, no more than a 'feminine' man need desire men either. The Chinese wondered at them. Husbandless, childless, parentless women travelling alone were to be pitied, if not rejected. They were stoned on one occasion, they tell us here, in passing. But the Chinese accepted them as representative of the Westerners' ways, little realising that in their own country they were hardly run of the mill. Indeed, without their missionary status, they would never have won their own society's approval. It was their faith and their calling that made them acceptable.

Is it possible that the missionary work served Mildred and the French sisters, and the other women like them, as a pretext to escape from the stultifying 'feminine' lives Guildford and Portsmouth held out to them? Protestant missionary work provided a legitimate framework in which independence could find an outlet, be expressed without censure. Their proselytising work hardly dominates these pages; only occasionally are we given glimpses of their methods: they present a copy of the New Testament to the Mohammedan brigand chief, Ma Chung-ying – ('General Thunderbolt') – after they have been inducted to nurse his wounds and his soldiers', and held captive in Tunwhang for several weeks; they write the words of the Gospels in stones on the desert sands, and leave these inscriptions beside a Bible weighted with stones; they pin up in a desert inn a non-denominational image of a lotus flower opening towards heaven with words of wisdom taken from an unnamed oriental text.

The meditations that close *The Gobi Desert*, on the spiritual discipline of the empty spaces, and the imagery of narrow tracks, purity of water and cooling, lifting breezes that the authors develop with intense lyricism as they remember the Crescent Lake, show that they could be eloquent preachers and spiritual counsellors if given the opportunity. But it must be said that this book leaves an impression of admirable broad-mindedness and respect for others' religious faith. After so many decades in China, they were even less bigoted than they had been when they set out, and they were already disgusted then with rigid denominationalism. Experience had perhaps softened their prosletysing zeal. Like the Jesuits who had worked for the Emperors in Peking in the sixteenth and seventeenth centuries, Mildred Cable, Eva and Francesca French hoped to turn the minds of the people of China to the Christian God by showing that his servants were healers, scientists, teachers, honest dealers and trustworthy rather than speech-makers and theologians.

As God's ambassadors, as they called themselves, they were able to lead very exciting lives without incurring much criticism, but rather praise. Although they prove the potential and the strength of female friendship, it may distort social history to claim them as lesbian, if we define lesbian as love between women involving physical love-making. In the cases of many lives like theirs, we cannot unseal the privacy of the past in this way. I think that 'lesbian' is the wrong label for the type that Mildred Cable and the French sisters represent in Victorian and Edwardian English life, because it assumes cultural and historical perspectives that formed no part of their consciousness, and might even have shocked them. It seems to me that sexual identity is bound up with that personal viewpoint and its intricate relations with what is customary and what is permitted. (A polygamist in Saudi-Arabia is not the same as a Don Juan in England; nor a 25-year-old virgin woman in London the same as another in Peking. But psychosexual definitions wrenched out of all historical context are becoming increasingly common.) While seeking to understand the wellsprings of Mildred Cable and Francesca French's remarkable lives, we should respect their understanding of themselves, as missionaries and loving friends.

There is a danger too, in expanding the meaning of the word lesbian to include women who adopted 'masculine' roles or undertook 'masculine' adventures, that their signal achievements are attributed to their homo-erotic leanings and not to the restrictions on women's lives that made male gender behaviour acceptable, and not female.

Mildred Cable, and Francesca French – and Eva – have given us here, and in other works and in their lives, their testimony to the plurality of pleasure and the range of experience that can bring women to fulfilment. *The Gobi Desert*, a book of travellers' tales and observations, is also a work of imagination, because it tells the story of three women's uncommon programme for happiness.

Marina Warner, London, 1984

PROLOGUE

AFTER living for more than twenty years in the province of Shansi in North China, I took the old trade-route and, with my companions Eva and Francesca French, trekked north-west past the Barrier of the Great Wall and into the country which lies beyond. For many years we travelled over the Desert of Gobi and among its oases as itinerant missionaries, and we came to know the country and its people intimately.

We found the desert to be unlike anything that we had pictured. It had its terrors, but it also had its compensating pleasures; it subjected us to many and prolonged hardships, but it also showed us some unique treasures. The oasis dwellers were poor but responsive; the caravan men were rugged but full of native wit; the outstanding personalities of the oases were men of character and distinction; the towns were highly individualistic and each small water-stage had some unique feature. Even the monotonous outlines of the desert, when better known, wore a subtly changing aspect, and landscapes which were similar in broad outline became highly distinctive as their detail was scrutinised. Even the stony flooring of the Gobi varied so much from stage to stage that pebbles picked up on the wide expanse could be located to the actual spot where they were collected.

Once the spirit of the desert had caught us it lured us on and we became learners in its severe school. The solitudes provoked reflection, the wide space gave us a right sense of proportion and the silences forbade triviality. The following record of what we saw and found in the Desert of Gobi may help others to appreciate its unique charm. These experiences were shared by three people, but for obvious reasons the record is written in the first person singular.

"The word Gobi is not the proper name of a geographical area, but a common expression used by Mongols to designate a definite order of geographical features. These are wide, shallow basins of which the smooth rocky bottom is filled with sand, pebbles or, more often, with gravel. . . . The Gobi Desert measures nearly one thousand two hundred miles from north to south, near the 104° meridian, and two thousand miles following the length of the 44° parallel. To the east it reaches nearly five hundred miles beyond the central Khingan, to the west its extent is only limited by the use of the word Gobi. Actually it lies in an uninterrupted stretch over the Dzungarian wilderness and the wastes of Eastern Turkestan, separated from each other by the hilly and fertile belt of the Tienshan. Thus from the Pamirs to the confines of Manchuria it covers a distance of three thousand six hundred miles."

Géographie Universelle: P. VIDAL DE LA BLACHE et L. GALLOIS.

ON THE THRESHOLD OF THE DESERT

I

First Impressions

A RAY of the rising sun touched the scalloped ridge of ice-fields in the Tibetan Alps and threw a veil of pink over their snowy slopes, but the great mass of the mountain range was still in the grip of that death-like hue which marks the last resistance of night to the coming day. The morning star was still visible, but it was grey dawn on the plain below, and light was gaining rapidly. There was a strange sense of vibration in the air, for the world was awakening and all nature responded to the call of a new day.

At the foot of the mountain range lay the old travel road, wide and deeply marked, literally cut to bits by the sharp nail-studded wheels of countless caravan carts. The ruts parted and merged, then spread again, as the eddies of a current mark the face of a river. Over this road myriads of travellers had journeyed for thousands of years, making of it a ceaselessly flowing stream of life, for it was the great highway of Asia, which connected the Far East with distant European lands.

That morning the road was deserted, save for two heavy carts covered with matting and drawn by mules. The beasts stood for a rest while two Chinese carters, dressed in blue cotton, squatted on their heels and each one stuffed the bowl of his long-stemmed pipe with a pinch of tobacco from the leather pouch hanging at his waist.

The land around was arid and the scene desolate but, toward the west, the outline of a mighty fortress and a long line of battlemented wall was silhouetted against the morning sky.

"Another ten *li*[1] and we shall be at the fortress of Kiayükwan," said the head carter, looking toward it. "Let us push on."

The cart bumped mercilessly over the loose stones of the dismal plain, and each slow mile brought the outline of the fort into clearer relief. It was an impressive structure. To the north of the central arch was a turreted watch-tower, and from it the long line of the wall dipped into a valley, climbed a hill and vanished over its summit. . Then a few poplar trees came in sight, and it was evident from the shade of green at the foot of the wall that here was grass and water. Farther on a patch

[1] *li*—a Chinese mile, and equivalent to one-third of an English mile.

13

of wild irises spread a carpet of blue by the roadside, just where the cart passed under an ornamental memorial arch and lurched across a rickety bridge over a bubbling stream.

The massive monument now towered overhead, and, impressive as it was by its own dignity, it made a yet further appeal to the imagination, for this was Kiayükwan (Barrier of the Pleasant Valley), the barrier which marks the western end of that amazing and absurd structure known as the Great Wall of China, dating back to 214 B.C., and built as a protection against Tatar enemy tribes. The length of wall which outlined the crest of the hill to the north would continue, irrespective of difficulties caused by mountains and valleys, rivers and deserts, until it reached the sea 1400 miles away.

Were this a clumsy, grotesque structure it would be a blot on northwest China, but its beauty and dignity redeem it from criticism, and since, in her unique way, China has ordained that her great western outlet should be controlled by a single door, she has made of that door such a striking portal as to be one of the impressive sights of the East. This fortification China calls her "mouth," and in colloquial speech those who have passed beyond it are "outside the mouth," while those still within are "inside the mouth." She thus makes the shame of compulsory exile doubly bitter by the offensive suggestion that an unwanted son has been ejected from her mouth.

The heavy cart shook the loose planks of the unsafe bridge, and the carter with a final shout turned the mules toward the stone-paved approach to the main entrance. The last pull up the ramp was an effort to man and beast. Both were weary with the long night stage, but each carter urged on his team with yells, lashing the air with his whip and cutting circles over his head. One sharp turn to the right, another pull through a further arch, and the carts were in the street of the inns, which was built against the fortress wall.

Then the innkeepers came out to secure custom.

"Turn in, turn in," each man called, and the carter questioned them as he went past: "Have you grass enough for our beasts?"

"Plenty," was the answer.

"What price?"

"A fair price, and no more."

So the caravan swept through the wide portal of the Inn of Harmonious Brotherhood. It took all the drivers' skill to bring the carts round till they stood with shafts facing the entrance. Then the mules were unhitched, the carts unladen, the tired men gathered to a drink of boiling water, and the street relapsed once more into its atmosphere of stagnation.

It was thus that I and my two companions first came to the western portal of the Great Wall of China, now called Kiayükwan (Barrier of the Pleasant Valley), but known to men of a former generation as Kweimenkwan (Gate of the Demons).

*   *   *

The old citadel had three gates, one facing north, one south and another west. Each was symbolic of the particular class of inhabitant whose life demanded its constant use. One was the low Door of Necessity through which the old residents passed each day carrying water from the spring at the foot of the hill. Occasionally they took a longer journey when three families joined together to drive a dozen donkeys to the coal-mines hidden in the foot-hills, and bring them back laden with fuel.

There was also the larger gate made of heavy wood and studded with nails. Each night that gate was locked and the great iron key deposited at the *yamen*.[1] It looked toward the distant green oasis of Suchow (Spring of Wine), and every day soldiers were galloping through the gate and over the plain to fetch supplies of pleasant food for the Governor and his ladies. Their horses clattered through the little crooked street, but the old residents, sitting at their counters, exchanged not a word with the youthful riders. News of matters outside their own gates meant nothing to them, nor had they any requirements which were not met by their own meagre supplies. Even the opium from the poppy patch by the side of the stream was sufficient for their dope.

The most important door was on the farther side of the fortress, and it might be called Traveller's Gate, though some spoke of it as the Gate of Sighs. It was a deep archway tunnelled in the thickness of the wall, where footsteps echoed and re-echoed. Every traveller toward the north-west passed through this gate, and it opened out on that great and always mysterious waste called the Desert of Gobi.

The long archway was covered with writings, and anyone with sufficient knowledge to appreciate Chinese penmanship could see at once that these were the work of men of scholarship, who had fallen on an hour of deep distress. There were lines quoted from the Book of Odes, poems composed in the pure tradition of classic literature, and verses inspired by sorrow too heavy for the careful balance of literary values, yet unbearable unless expressed in words.

[1] *yamen*—official residence of the City Magistrate.

Who then were the writers of this Anthology of Grief? Some were heavy-hearted exiles, others were disgraced officials, and some were criminals no longer tolerated within China's borders. Torn from all they loved on earth and banished with dishonoured name to the dreary regions outside, they stood awhile within the tomb-like vault, to add their moan to the pitiful dirge of the Gate of Sighs.

The men of the garrison shunned that gate, and the old inhabitants never used it. It was only the traveller who must needs pass the grim portal, and he always did so with some dread, for this was a door leading to the unknown, and to man the unknown is ever the fearful.

Unlike those who never looked beyond the gate until they must, I wished to prepare myself for the great adventure, so I set out on foot to view the land. Two men of the patrol joined me, forcing their way, as I did, against the head-wind which fiercely resisted us. Just outside the gate was a high stony mound which blocked the view. It had been thrown up to act as a barrier against the elemental and inimical spirits of the Gobi, for the simple-minded men of the garrison would never credit the goblins with sense enough to find their way round the mound and into the fortress.

We climbed it, and from the summit came into full view of the plain. Stretching as far as eye could see was the arid plateau from which the driving winds had swept away all the finer sand and left nothing but dull, grey grit.

"A place of desolation," murmured one of my companions.

I was fully aware of the acute terror with which the Chinese regard the Gobi regions, and I determined to get a better understanding of their outlook from these men who lived on the very edge of the desert yet always turned away from it with a shudder, and hurried toward the noisy clatter of the drill-ground and the barrack-room.

"It is desolate," I said, "but in the silence and solitude God is still there."

The youth stared, then shook his head. "Demons," he said, "they are the ones who inhabit the Gobi. This place is full of them, and many have heard their voices calling."

"How do they call?" I asked.

"From among the sand-mounds," he answered. "They call out just as a man would shout if he wanted help, but those who turn away from the track to answer them never find anyone, and the next call is always a little farther from the true path, for those voices will lead a man on, but they will never call him back to the right way."

16

"Do many get lost in this desert?" I enquired.

"Very many," he said. "Some miss their way and die of thirst, and others are frozen to death in winter blizzards. You do not yet know, Lady, the terrors of that journey. Must you go out into the Gobi? You have come from Suchow. That is a good place with many people and plenty to eat, but out yonder . . . Must you go?"

"Yes," I said, "I must, for I seek the lost, and some of them are out there."

"Ah!" he said. "You seek the lost; now I understand. There are many like you who go across the Gobi to seek a lost relative. Boys leave home to go out there, and never even send a word back to say where they are. Then the old parents are always unhappy until a second son goes in search of the first. Very often he comes back without finding that lost brother. Perhaps you have some clue as to where the lost ones are, and where you should go to look for them?"

"I have a clue and I know that I shall surely find them, even though the demons of the Gobi try to keep me from reaching them. God Who is their Father and mine will lead me to where they are."

The young soldier stared, dimly feeling that I was speaking of things which concerned the gods, and were outside his ken: "People like you are not in peril as we are," he concluded, "for the spirits cannot hurt them. When there is danger you know how to pray to your God."

We turned back to the great gate and, sordid as the fortress enclosure was, I felt glad to be safe within its walls again, for the howling gale blew grit and sand into my face, and when I reached my tumbledown room at the Inn of Harmonious Brotherhood I was thankful for its shelter. Before another week has passed, I thought, that great gate will have closed behind our caravan. We shall be out on the Gobi, and once we have started on that journey there can be no turning back.

II

Life in the Fortress

Inside the fortress, life was divided into three distinct sections, each of which had an existence quite different from the others. All the inns and shops were in the suburb. The people who owned them were descendants of a long line of old residents who took pride in the very exclusiveness which was imposed by their isolation. Few of them ever left the place, and many had never even seen the neighbouring town of

Suchow. Business could not be made an excuse for always staying at home; the takings were too paltry to count. For the night's lodging a traveller would give two pence, and for that small sum have room enough to stretch himself on the *kang*,[1] get his dinner cooked for him at the kitchen fire, and have unlimited boiling water to drink. Custom required, however, that where the innkeeper could supply it, the traveller should buy the flour or millet needed for his dinner from him, even if the price were high. In the shops he could purchase tobacco, cigarettes, matches and rough paper made from the pulped leaf of the dwarf iris, small screws of red pepper mixed with coarse salt as condiment to the tasteless inn food, strong hand-woven braid for tying a man's trousers round his waist and ankles, and leather thongs for mending harness. Nothing else was regarded as a necessity or worth stocking, except sticks of incense to burn at the shrine so that the traveller might seek the favour of the gods as he journeyed on.

The only really busy place was the blacksmith's shop, which was always lively. In front of it a strong construction of wooden posts, ropes and pulleys looked like a mediaeval instrument of torture, but it was only a contrivance used for slinging difficult beasts who would not be quiet during the process of shoeing. With some mules it was sufficient to tie the hair of the tail to the tongue in order to quell the rebellious spirit, but others had to be lifted from the ground and thoroughly incapacitated before they would stop kicking.

The blacksmith was, incidentally, the veterinary surgeon of the place, and there was constant entertainment for carters in watching the dosing of desert-tried beasts, the ramming of needles into the tongue of a sick mule, and the more delicate operation of cutting the cartilage of the nostrils to cure spasms.

An inner gate led to the military section of the fortress, where life was entirely different. The *yamen*, built in traditional Chinese style, was the centre of garrison life, and here the General and his family lived, guarded day and night by sentries. Officers marched in and out, and much official business was done, for this was an important military centre and the officer in command held a high rank.

Unlike the old residents, the military hated the place and seized every chance of being away from it, bitterly resenting the appointment to such a lonely outpost, and longing to be transferred elsewhere. Nothing would have induced them to walk outside the North-West Gate where that fateful Gobi Desert stretched, and their eyes always turned long-

[1] *kang*—a mud bed warmed by a fire.

ingly to the city where, twenty miles away, there was solace, gaiety and life.

If the men disliked Kiayükwan, the women hated it. "There is nothing to do here all day but sit and listen to that howling wind," they would say fretfully.

The ladies of the *yamen* would gather in each other's rooms, play *ma-jong* for small stakes, sip tea and gossip. Often the game was prolonged until midnight, with interludes for drawing on the opium pipe, but the next morning's reaction brought a fierce hatred of this place where desert demons hid themselves in dust-clouds and whistled through every crevice of the crazy buildings. The little slave girls learnt to dread the days of blizzard when their mistresses' nerves were taut and blows were dealt out irritably for the slightest offence.

Each festival of the year was the occasion for a welcome social function, and during the summer months life was made brighter by the frequent exchange of visits with the officials from Suchow. Twice each year a theatrical troupe visited the fortress, and for the three days of its performance all the inhabitants enjoyed themselves and made merry. But it was soon over, and when the properties were packed and carts carried both actors and their belongings elsewhere, life in the fortress relapsed into desolating stagnation.

The third category of human beings to be met in Kiayükwan were the travellers who came, lodged for a night or two at the inns, and forthwith went their way. Every sunset and every sunrise they arrived, some taking night stages and some travelling by day, but all were travel-worn and weary. They hailed from every part of China's dominion and were bound for her remotest frontiers. For one day or one night they used the place like masters, commanded the innkeeper's time and resources, fed their beasts in his stable and visited the shops, turning over the poor goods, always looking for something new though never finding it, till in disgust they would take a packet of cigarettes or a box of matches, fling down a few coppers and go their way.

These formed the stream of living men and women who moved up and down the great road, acquainted with life and full of knowledge about distant places. They were familiar with the large cities and the great waterways of China, and had traversed her wide plains by the "iron track" at a speed which seemed fabulous to the owners of these little shops. The static inhabitants saw them come, heard them talk, watched them go, but failed to understand the matters of which they spoke, for, to them, everything which they had never seen was unreal, vague, remote and seemed to bear no relation to daily life. Enough for them that to-day they had sold three boxes of matches, two packets of cigarettes and a handful of salt. They cared little for travellers' tales and probably believed none of them, and I was scarcely more advanced in my outlook than they were, for while all which lay behind was real and tangible, the new life across the desert seemed weird and illusory. With many of the travellers we shared past experience, for we, as they, had crossed China on her broad waterways and far-flung railroads, but we, too, were baffled by strange ultra-Gobi tales. Some told of rushing rivers cutting their way through sand, of an unfathomable lake hidden among the dunes, of sand-hills with a voice like thunder, of water which could be clearly seen and yet was a deception. We listened incredulously and, equally with the rough boys of the garrison town, found ourselves giving credence only to that which was confirmed by our own experience.

The restless soldiers of the garrison rushed to and from the large town, but the old inhabitants cared for none of these things, and when the fortress gates were closed each night they put up the shutters of the little shops and crept under miserable coverlets to lie on the mud *kangs*, fill their opium pipes and escape into the land of illusion and dreams, which was the only wider horizon that they knew.

We were in no hurry to leave the Barrier of the Pleasant Valley, for the days spent there were full of interest. We often walked out through the small gate and took the sharp downward path to where the springs bubbled up. The stretch of grass down there was always cool and damp, from the water which welled up and filtered through it in tiny rivulets. These formed a cheerful brook, which in turn joined the larger stream at the foot of the fortress. Here we met most of the "odd-and-end" boys from the inns, for all the drinking-water of the citadel was carried from here in wooden boxes laid across the backs of small donkeys. The "odd-and-ender's" job is the first rung of the ladder which leads to any post of oasis dignity. His work is exactly described by his title. He leads the overheated horse to and fro on a patient stroll until it is safe to water it, he runs about with kettles of boiling water, he wields the guillotine knife which chops sorghum [1] leaves for fodder, he fetches and carries for carters, and is the rich man's servant's servant. He works the box-bellows which fan the coal-dust fire, and wipes out the big iron food pot while his master eats its scrapings. There is little he does not see and he is proverbially communicative. Through listening to their chatter we came to know all about the different households in Kiayükwan.

[1] sorghum—cereal plant known also as Indian millet, Guinea corn, durra.

They told how Merchant Chang's son had stolen sixty dollars of his father's savings and had joined the famous robber chief White Wolf, how Liu the miller had beaten his young wife and how she had killed herself by eating a whole box of matches, how Li the blacksmith's son was so profligate that his father took a sledge-hammer and crushed his head as he lay asleep. The gossip of that sleepy township was one long string of tragic happenings.

We often sat on the customer's bench at the shop doors and talked with the old residents, who liked to recount the past glories of the fortress, and many hours were spent with all sorts and conditions of women, sometimes in hovels, sometimes in back-shops or in private houses, as well as in official residences. Such talk was always interesting and we learnt a great deal from it; we all enjoyed each other's company so that when the time came to move on there was already a root let down which it hurt to tear up. On the last days there were many good-byes to be said, and an exchange of small presents left us provided with a variety of road necessities such as candles, sugar, cakes, crisp sun-dried rusks, and even a handful of fresh green vegetable from someone's little cabbage plot.

One evening before sunset our carts clattered noisily through the echoing arch, plunged through the awkward double gates, swung aside to avoid the spirit mound, pulled up a short steep ascent and drew up on the level plain just where the great stone tablet stood which bore the inscription: "Earth's Greatest Barrier."

The two friendly soldiers were there to see us off. "Look here, Lady," one of them said excitedly, "you cannot start without throwing a stone at our old wall."

They led us to where a portion of the brick facing of the fortress wall had been broken away, leaving a rough hollow, and near by lay a large heap of small stones.

"It is the custom that every traveller as he goes outside the wall, should throw a stone at the fortress. If the stone rebounds he will come back safe and sound, but if not . . ." he left the doom unuttered.

We each picked up a few small stones and threw them. Rebounding from the wall they skipped back with a sharp sound, and the two boys grinned with pleasure.

"What a strange noise!" I said. "It is like the cheeping of chicks."

"That is the echo of this spot," they said proudly. "It is lucky to have heard it. Your journey will be prosperous."

As the sun was now nearing the horizon the carter shouted, "We must be off," and the soldier boys saluted and said, "We shall meet again." Then they quickly turned and re-entered the fortress, for the trumpet was calling all men to barracks. The gate swung to, and we heard them shoot the heavy bar. We were irrevocably launched on the long trek.

*   *   *

We had all lived for many years in the East and were used to the leisurely pace of Oriental life. We had followed many of the trunk roads of China and were familiar with the varied life of the Chinese people. We knew their language, were at home with their customs and habits, and in matters of food and dress had become one of themselves. We had no nostalgia left for Western life and had long been detached from European lands. The Far East had become our home, and our thoughts, occupations and interests were focussed there. In so knowing the Chinese people we had learnt to love them, and it was perhaps this very understanding of them which imparted the dread we all felt in facing this desert isolation. The carter's burdened sigh found an echo in my own heart.

Life in China is always unhurried, and I, for one, had outgrown the hasty impatience which makes the Westerner such a trial to the Easterner. I had even developed the art of concentrating into the faculty of observation the whole mental activity of travel days, when for twelve hours, almost motionless, I watched the passing scene slowly unroll itself, observing every feature of the landscape and seeking to fathom each aspect of human life that we met and passed on the long road. Although the journeys which lay behind had often seemed long, slow and tedious, yet they always led to a kindly shelter for the night, toward a goal which lay within measurable distance, and gave certain promise of a return to a welcoming home. In China the wayside inn had had its unfailing atmosphere of cordiality and pleasant intercourse, but this place had none of these amenities. The life of China's main roads was one of stirring activity, with something happening every moment to interest or to amuse. What faced me here might be the burden of boundless monotony. Should I ever distinguish one stage from the other? Might I not even die, not, as some had done, of thirst or fatigue, but of boredom? In the end, should I make good my quest, or would the desert prove too much for me? Where would it all end? How would it end? Anything might happen and it might end anywhere.

All this went through my mind as I walked ahead of the carts for a few miles of that first Gobi journey. The loose stones hurt my feet and cut them through my Chinese cotton shoes. Soon the landscape faded in the falling night and I could no longer distinguish the detail of the road. I began to stumble among the stones, and fearful of losing my way I climbed up on the cart beside my companions, trusting the beasts, who could see in the dark, to find the track.

The wind had dropped, all was still, and darkness soon spread over the plain. The evening star appeared, then one by one the stars came out and hung like golden lights in the velvety depths of the sky. I watched the expanse of the heavens throughout the whole night and the glory of it amazed me. The polar star unerringly pointed the way, and the constellations swung slowly overhead. The only sound was the steady quiet tramp of the animals' feet and the soft tread of the carter's cloth shoes. We were all conscious of passing through a great silence and instinctively interrupted it as little as might be.

At midnight a light haze on the horizon showed that moonrise was near. Soon the scene was bathed in clear soft light. The stillness intensified. I had previously known great silences, but in comparison with this it seemed that they were noisy. There was not even a blade of grass to rustle, a leaf to move, a bird to stir in its nest, nor an insect on the wing to fly past. No one spoke, we only listened intently and it seemed as though every vibration was stilled. When the moon rode high in the heavens and the hour was nearing three in the morning, the carter spoke once: "That, yonder, is Gold Washer's Halt," he said.

I stared among the undulating gravel-ridges and detected the sharper outline of a man-made structure and then a wall such as might enclose a village. Now that the spell was broken I wanted to speak and ask what this strange place was, and whether it held human inhabitants behind that sheltering wall. The carts came up slowly, and then stood still. Chilled and cramped, I alighted to stretch my limbs. I found a breach in the wall, and walking through it saw in the bright moonlight an old street with ruined buildings, and the remains of what had once been human homes. It was a city of the dead, yet it was impossible to throw off the feeling that the place was still used during the night hours by some ghostly inhabitants, and that I was being watched by vigilant eyes though I could not see them. I felt that I was an intruder.

This was all I saw that night, but later, when the desert road had become familiar by reason of many journeys, I was able to locate the deep well now choked with sand where the long-dead inhabitants had once drawn water. Slowly but surely the level of that water had sunk until the people had fled lest they should die of thirst. The shell of a temple was still standing where vanished gods of mud and stone had once guarded the tank in which gold-washers had carefully scanned the grains of sand, in their search for fragments of the precious metal.

At a certain season of the year a small quantity of evil-coloured water collected in a hole near by, and then an old man would come to stay in a hovel he had built from débris. He sold an infusion of desert herbs which he called "tea," and it sometimes happened that a gang of men bent on plunder joined the old man, so that every traveller was happier when, as now, there was neither water nor human inhabitant.

The gold-dust washers were not the first settlers in this place, for long before their day primitive man had made his abode here. Anyone who climbed the gravel ridges and searched among the stones which littered the ground would be likely to pick up a scraper or other stone implement made, used and discarded by prehistoric man. How strange it seemed that human beings should have used this place for so long and yet allowed the desert to reconquer it. With all his ingenuity man had not been able to hold his own against the all-devouring sands.

I was called back to the immediate by a summons from the carter: "On!" he said. "Let us be off! This is no place for delay."

"Let us get on!" I echoed.

The place was terrifying and even more inimical than I had feared.

III

A Wayside Halt

At sunrise the dreary stage came to an end, and we drove into the short street of a village where already there were signs of life. We met a few people fresh from sleep who were taking on the normal occupations of the day. During the hours of darkness they had been steeped in unconsciousness, and now they faced a new day, restored and vigorous. The weary beasts, the tired carters and the jaded travellers moved wraith-like among them, for all through the night they had been as living creatures who walked among the dead and surprised their secrets, and now they in turn felt like ghosts in this clear bright world, which was the inheritance of those who were refreshed and renewed. They had no part in the life of the new day, since for them it must be turned into night.

We all welcomed the windowless rooms of the dingy inn. Its doors were dilapidated, but a boulder rolled across the opening would prevent intrusion by these lusty, noisy, daylight people, so we spread coverlets on the mud bed, flung ourselves down and fell into deep sleep. I was awakened by flies alighting on my face, and looking upwards saw in the centre of the mat roof the *tunuk* [1] through which the midday sun directed a vertical ray which had reached my cheek. On the roof near the hole there was a large flat stone with which to close it, and, had I shouted, the fodder boy would have scrambled up and pushed it over the *tunuk*, excluding both light and air, and leaving only one small crack sufficient for the flies to use in making their exit to a brighter world. But I was now awake and even a few hours of sleep had reinvigorated me, so that I wished to take my part again in the world of men.

I walked out into the village street to look around. A clear stream somehow found its way here from distant snow-mountains and ran through the village, so dividing it that everyone must needs constantly cross and recross it on stepping-stones. A little general shop faced me, and on its small counter stood the inevitable heap of tobacco, the few boxes of cigarettes and matches, the bundles of incense sticks, the half-dozen screws of red pepper mixed with coarse salt and, hanging from a nail, were twists of hand-woven braid, home-made string and leather thongs.

There was something different here, however, for, in addition to the dull stock of the oasis shopkeeper, this man had a variety of articles made from a fine-grained, light-grey stone which was found near at hand. There were slabs on which to rub down the hard sticks of Chinese ink, and little pots to hold water with which to moisten them. The chief demand, however, was for small pieces to be used as whetstones for knives, razors or scissors, and many a carter passing that way added a hone to his small outfit of traveller's necessities.

In order to encourage business I bought a few stone articles, one of the small screws of red pepper and a box of matches, then sat down and talked with the owner of the shop. After answering all his enquiries concerning myself, my age, my journey and my relatives, I took the lead and, in turn, questioned him about himself, his home and this village where he lived.

Concerning the oasis he had much to tell me. "This place," he said, "is famous for two things. One is its sweet, clear water which flows direct from the snow-fields. When you have been farther among the salt-water stages you will often long for a drink from our stream; but

[1] *tunuk*—a circular hole in the roof which admits light and air.

let me warn you, that when the sun is high and you water your beasts, the carter must either stand the pails in the sun, or pour a little hot water into them. The stream is rapid and the bed stony, so the water has no time to become sun-warmed, and many a horse goes sick in this place through drinking a draught of such chilly water. You too must be careful, but for sweetness there is no water like ours."

"Thank you for telling me," I said; "I will take your advice and be careful. But you spoke of some other things for which this place is renowned. What are they?"

"Our great tomb," he said. "This is the village of the Moslem Tomb (Huei-huei-pu), which is famous everywhere. Surely you have heard of it. Go and see it. A few steps beyond the temple is a wall, and behind the wall lies the Tomb of the great Moslem pilgrim."

I turned to go, and just as I was leaving I noticed on his counter a jar of coarse grey sand. Taking some of it in my hand I rubbed it between my fingers testing the quality of the grains, and as I did so I felt there was something unusual about it. "What do you keep sand for?" I asked. "Is there not enough of it by the roadside?"

"This is special sand, Lady," he said. "It comes from near here, but is not found elsewhere in the Gobi. It is so heavy that the wind does not blow it about, and it is the only sand which can be used for one process in the polishing of jade. Though it is hard enough to use even on jade, yet it never scratches the surface. It is very highly valued, and jade polishers send here to get it."

"Does each oasis have some special product?" I asked.

"More or less," he replied. "If you go straight across there," pointing to the north, "you come to the village of Tien-tsin-wei, and in summer you can find your way there by the melon skins on the sand. The melons are sweeter and more juicy there than elsewhere, and every traveller buys them and eats them as he goes. If you travel one stage farther on the main road, you will see all the houses surrounded with stacks of liquorice root. Traders from "within the mouth" all go there to buy it, and nowhere else is the quality so fine."

"Liquorice and melons are both good things," I said, "but Moslem Tomb supplies sand for the rare beauty of polished jade, and inkslabs for the writer's art, so it counts second to none for its products."

Parting from the friendly merchant with the customary "*tsai chien*" ("we shall meet again"), and joined by my companions, I walked into the little village in search of the pilgrim's tomb, and found it almost immediately. It was enclosed with an outer mud wall, the door through which was locked, but the man in charge saw me try the bolt and came over to open it and take us in. The plot of land held one building only, and this stood in the very centre of the ground: a small, square, mud-built tomb, with domed roof and a crenated border. As we walked round it the old Moslem fitted the key to the heavy lock and we followed him inside.

It was an empty room, but in the centre of the floor was a slightly raised opening covered over with a red satin pall, embroidered in Arabic characters. We were struck by the cleanliness, the order and the tidiness which the Moslem shows in regard to his sacred places. This mud-built tomb was many centuries old, but, thanks to the dry climate and constant attention to repairs, it stood intact.

We questioned the guardian concerning the pilgrim whose body lay buried there, and learnt from him that he was one of three companions who journeyed toward China from distant lands in the west. They overcame all difficulties until they reached the rocky ravine called Hsing-hsing-hsia (Ravine of Baboons), which is at present the frontier of Chinese Turkestan. There one of them died, and only ten stages farther his companion also died and was buried here, leaving the third to travel on alone.

"I suppose that the body of this pilgrim lies in a vault," I said. "Is there any stone slab under that satin pall?"

"No, indeed," was the indignant reply, "for when the angel calls the dead man of Islam by his name, he must sit upright and respond. How could he do that if he were held down by coffin-boards or by stone slabs? When you reach Hsing-hsing-hsia," he continued, "you will find the tomb where the body of the first holy man lies. It is a deep rock sepulchre and you must be sure to see it."

"What happened to the third pilgrim?" I asked.

"He travelled on right through China, and in the end died in Canton. His tomb is there and these graves are always spoken of as 'The Graves of the Three Pilgrims,' but," he added with some pride, "this is the only tomb which gives its name to a locality."

Many legends have grown up round the tradition of the three renowned pilgrims, and later we were assured that the body of the first one had already risen from the cave tomb in Hsing-hsing-hsia. Miracles are also freely quoted in connection with the other burying-sites, but through all the legendary lore the basic fact persists, of three companion pilgrims whose bodies are buried respectively at Hsing-hsing-hsia, at Huei-huei-pu and in Canton.

From the Moslem burying-place we walked on a few steps to the temple which overlooked it. An old Chinese priest lived there, who received us with kindliness, and we sat talking for a long time. To all that we said he nodded approval, murmuring, "Those are true words," and before leaving we handed him a scroll of paper on which the fundamental commands of God were printed in clear ideographs. He read them through, expressed his approbation and immediately rose to fix the paper to the door of the central shrine, well pleased that the people who entered it should read "good words," from whatever source they came.

IV

Gobi Merrymakers

All through the hot afternoon of the day on which we left Moslem Tomb Halt I was aware of a reiterated phrase woven by the carter into a lilting tune, and sung in a nasal falsetto as he went about the business of overhauling harness and trappings.

> "Eighteen hills ahead I see,
> Eighteen hills to climb they'll be;
> Mules will sweat, and men waste strength,
> All because of the steep hills' length."

The terse monosyllabic Chinese phrases subconsciously arrested my attention and I began to wonder what were these eighteen hills about which he was lilting so insistently. Without addressing me he had captured my attention and without a single direct word he was telling me what he wished me to know. Great people these Chinese carters! Finally I could no longer ignore his tale and he had it his own way, for I was questioning him.

"Carter Li," I said, "what is tonight's stage like?"

"A stage to be remembered," he said. "Eighteen hills between here and Pure Gold Hollow."

I had pictured the Gobi as a flat expanse, but that night showed me how it varied from place to place, and before morning we had gone over eighteen steep hills in succession. I do not know which the animals found harder, the pull up or the jog down; uphill was heavier for the beasts in the traces, but the descent was cruel on the shaft mule, for the cart was brakeless and its whole weight fell on the creature's haunches, as, step by step, he resisted its downward course.

As we left the last slope of the eighteenth hill behind us the carter's quavering falsetto was raised again, and this time he sang about the village just ahead :

> "Pure Gold Pond tonight we'll see,
> At Pure Gold Rise then soon we'll be;
> South we'll turn to Pure Gold Fort,
> And round we'll come to Pure Gold Halt."

This opened up a new subject of conversation, and we found that the district of Chihkin (Pure Gold), to which we were coming, was surprisingly extensive and included all the localities of which the carter sang. It spread over the whole area reaching from the bare volcanic hills on the south to three separate stages on the main road which were fully twenty miles apart. The ideographs which composed the name Chihkin stood for Pure Gold and connected the oasis with many other places in the South Mountains which bore this character *kin* (gold) incorporated in their names. We were evidently entering the land of gold dust.

It was a wide basin almost surrounded by hills and fertilised by the water which ran down from them. This basin, like every Gobi oasis, was cultivated to capacity, and besides a large number of isolated farmsteads it held many small hamlets. The farms were rich, and fortified with high crenellated walls, on which stones suitable for throwing at invaders were stored, and below there was a runway for the stone-throwers. A heavy wooden door, strengthened with iron nails, closed the one and only entrance to each farm, and this door was guarded by fierce Tibetan mastiffs, ready to tear a man to pieces if he attempted to force his way past them.

Standing alone on this plain was one small fortified town called the Citadel. About five hundred families lived there permanently, but when an enemy swept down on the fruitful plain all the farmers crowded into the fort for shelter. Secret stocks of provisions were carefully laid up and the people believed themselves able to sustain a long siege.

The outside world scarcely existed for the people of Pure Gold. They married within their own area, they seldom travelled outside it, and decisions of the clan on any point were never questioned within the community. Men and women born and bred in such conditions of monotony and isolation inevitably develop intensified characteristics of exclusiveness, distrust and rigidity. They are unable to mix with any circle other than the one into which they were born, or to have intercourse with any people who think differently from themselves. Should any daring spirit venture to question a local habit, or to suggest that in other places things were done otherwise, the answer with which he was silenced was brief and conclusive: "It is our custom." No discussion which might open the door to another view-point was tolerated. The people of Chihkin were so convinced that their way was the only right one, that their minds were barricaded as effectively by prejudice as their citadel was by stone walls. The opening of a fissure through which a new thought might find entrance to the mind would be more terrifying than a sudden crack and collapse of the stone battlement which safe-guarded them from the enemy.

We wandered for long among this group of oases and tapped its resources in food and in other commodities. We found these sufficient, but absolutely limited to local products, yet Pure Gold, like Moslem Tomb Halt, boasted one special product which was not to be found elsewhere. This was a thick crude mineral oil, drawn from local wells. The oiling of axles on hot desert sands is a great care to carters, and the linseed-oil bottle, generally in use both for cooking and greasing purposes, is a source of perpetual contention between master and man. The oil is bought in order to grease the axle, but the carter covets it as a condiment. The axle is dry and thirsty and requires constant lubrica-tion, but the man s food is tasteless, unless he can flavour it with garlic crushed in oil. The mineral oil of Pure Gold was both inexpensive and totally unsuitable for food, therefore in that area peace reigned in the caravan as the carter was never tempted to add it to his bowl of *mien*.[1]

A few buyers of mineral oil came regularly to the wells from other oases. We talked with one of them whose donkey, saddled with two five-gallon tins stamped with the mark of the Standard Oil Company, spent the whole of its life walking to and fro between Pure Gold and another oasis. The journey took eight days and the net profit made on each trip was the sum of one dollar, at that time worth one shilling and eightpence.

The people's clothes were made of stout, hand-woven cotton cloth, and were very clumsy and old-fashioned, but the contents of the pawn-shops, which are the best indication of a district's riches, revealed big stocks of silk, satin and fur garments. These handsome clothes were most carefully stored by the pawnbrokers and were only redeemed by their owners on such occasions as weddings, funerals and the New Year festivities. After being worn for a few days they were returned to the safe shelves of the pawnbroker's shop until they should be needed again. Sometimes we stayed in the homes of the people and sometimes we

[1] *mien*—home-made macaroni, often called dough-strips.

camped on their threshing-floors. They were all immensely proud of
the locality where they were born, and considered Pure Gold to be a
prime oasis of the desert. They still boasted of the gold-mines once
very plentiful there, but built great hopes on the oil-wells because rumour
had it that these might yet be of more value than even the gold had been.
There was yet another unusual product found in the mountains, described
vaguely as a substance which could go into the fire and come out unburnt.
We talked about it a good deal and I came to the conclusion that what
they spoke of might be asbestos.

It was at the Temple of Pure Gold that we first saw some gay side
to the desert dweller's life. It was a boisterous but pathetic attempt at
hilarity, and its occasion was the celebration of the fifth day of the fifth
moon, a very old festival connected with the historical annals of the
Chinese people. Such commemorations date from very ancient times
and some recurring feasts, such as the Spring Festival and the Feast of
the Moon, have an origin which is lost in the dimmest antiquity.

All over China there is a special and traditional way of celebrating
each festival, and even in far-away Gobi oases the pasteboard cow is
dragged forth at the birth of spring, and each time his anniversary comes
round the old dragon curls and twirls through the sandy streets of
dusty villages. Moon cakes appear at the full moon of the eighth month,
and on the correct day the Boat Festival is remembered.

This fifth day of the fifth moon demands special recognition. In
happier climes it is the Dragon-boat Festival, but Gobi folk have never
seen a boat, so must find some other way of merry-making than sailing
small river craft, and therefore celebrate the event with a theatrical
performance.

The historic incident which is commemorated on that day dates
back to the third century B.C. There was at that time a virtuous and loyal
Minister of State named Chu-yüan. So long as his counsel was sought
and followed by the Prince all was well, but the time came when the
machinations of a jealous rival prevailed and Chu-yüan was dismissed
from office. Knowing that under the new conditions the ruin of the
country must ensue, he wandered out to the bank of the Mi-lo River
with the intention of ending his life. There he met a fisherman and the
following conversation took place: "Are you not His Excellency the
Minister?" asked this man. "Why then should you weary of life?"

"The world," replied Chu-yüan, "is foul and I alone am clean,
men are drunk and I alone am sober, therefore I am dismissed from
office."

To this the fisherman replied: "The true sage does not quarrel with his environment, but adapts himself to it. If, as you say, the world is foul, why not leap into the tide and make it clean? If all men are drunk, why not drink with them, yet by example teach them to avoid excess?"

Having said this the fisherman moved away, and Chu-yüan, clasping a large stone in his arms, plunged into the river and was seen no more. The Dragon-boat Festival commemorates the search made by the people for the body of this virtuous and courageous Minister of State who preferred death to compromise.

The Chinese are a laughter-loving people and regard the theatre as one of the best forms of entertainment, therefore troupes of actors move up and down the trade-routes of the Gobi giving performances as they go, and the Temple of Pure Gold had engaged one of them for a gala performance on the fifth day of the fifth moon. To see the actors arrive was an entertainment in itself. First of all two bullock carts appeared laden with roughly made stage properties and some simple scenery, and with the carts came thirty men dressed in shabby clothes. They walked with a light springy step and carried large wooden boxes slung from a pole between each two men. These boxes held their precious costumes —faded, ragged, embroidered dresses, elaborate tinsel headgear, flowing beards made from the soft white tail of the Tibetan yak, and the mock implements of war which take a large place in Chinese historic drama. The stage was part of the temple structure and only needed the addition of mat roofing for an immediate performance. In a very short while after arrival the players and musicians appeared dressed for their parts, and the musicians' band of cymbals, pipes, flutes and drums crashed out the most hideous din that mortal ears ever heard.

The effect on the oasis dwellers was almost hypnotic, and the noise and show held them spellbound. They had come in their bullock carts from every oasis within reach of the temple, and the crowd was composed of men and women, old and young, and children of every age. The men stood massed in front of the stage, the women, dressed in clothes of the brightest colours, sat in their carts which formed a semicircle a little farther back, while the children ran to and fro indefatigably. The performance was soon in full swing. Each time an actor left the stage and returned he explained to the audience what he was going to do and what he was supposed to have done during his absence. The play was continuous and, though there was no clapping or other expression of appreciation, the rapt attention of the audience evidenced its enjoyment.

There was no admission fee, for the richer people had provided the entertainment and were satisfied to have gained prestige with both gods and men by their generosity. Each performance lasted eighteen hours out of the twenty-four, and during that time was only suspended for the brief space needed for actors and audience to cook a meal and eat it. Immediately after, the play was resumed and continued by torch-light until after midnight.

At Pure Gold Temple there was an unusual and picturesque crowd. The most important person present was an old abbot named Li. He was eighty years old and had entered on his novitiate as a child, when he was dedicated by his parents to a priestly life. Since boyhood his hair had been neither cut nor combed. It now formed a matted rope which he proudly compared with the tail of a cow. This "cow's tail" was, in some way, symbolic of virtue. He wore it twisted round his head, but when let down it reached his knees.

Several priests from neighbouring temples had come to help, as there were many shrines and a priest was required to read the rituals in each. Everyone who came to the theatre visited all the shrines, and at each altar took a few sticks of incense, lighted them at a vegetable-oil lamp which burned perpetually before the god, and then stood them upright in the ash of the large incense-burner. As each worshipper did so the priest's voice rose to a higher pitch, and he beat rhythmic strokes on the crab-shaped wooden clapper at his side. The worshipper prostrated himself in a profound obeisance, then threw down a few coppers and passed out.

While the theatre supplied the prime entertainment, and incense-burning was a good diversion, there were still those who derived their chief enjoyment from the food-market. It was no easy business to supply this hungry crowd with seasonable dainties, yet in spite of all difficulties there were pork dumplings, both boiled and fried according to taste, and cauldrons of chitterling broth in which to soak the dry bread which was brought from home. Substantial doughnuts had the advantage of being very filling at small cost, and steamed rolls of bread with their little centre of black sugar were a nice change.

The special dish connected with the Dragon-boat Festival, however, is made of rice. In old times rice was cast into the river on the anni-versary of Chu-yüan's death, but now the revellers eat cakes made of the rice. These cakes are made of sticky, glutinous rice and are stuffed with the fruit of the jujube [1] tree, then wrapped in reeds and steamed.

In the large oases which lie in deep declivities there are often wide

---

[1] The common jujube—*zizyphus vulgaris*.

ponds where reeds grow abundantly. These reeds are picked and carried all over the Gobi by itinerant cooks who use them in making the three-cornered rice cake for the fifth of the fifth moon. The floor space round the open-air stage is always littered with reed wrappings, stripped from the sticky sweetmeat and flung around.

At dark the children refused to stay awake any longer and there was a general spreading out of wadded quilts. Each family secured a corner of a temple verandah and made itself at home there for the three days of the performance. The men folk stood till after midnight watching the play, but tired women, on foot since dawn, were glad to make their children the excuse for an early bed.

Even the voracious appetite of the Chinese for crowds, din and display must have been satisfied by the time the third day was over and the actors brought their long and exhausting performance to a close. Food vendors abandoned the mud fireplaces, actors packed their properties and tramped off to the next fair, and the desert dwellers drove their bullock carts back to their poor farms, where each would take up again the round of his monotonous and dreary existence.

It was then that Abbot Wang, visiting priest from a famous rock temple, asked us to visit the cave shrines of which he was guardian.

"Few travellers ever come our way," he said, "but the shrines are very ancient and belong to the line of Thousand Buddha Temples which lies along the base of the South Mountains."

"Abbot," we said, "before many moons have passed we hope to pitch our tent in the shade of your temple walls. You will be more leisured then, and you shall tell us all you know of the Thousand Buddha Shrines, and we will tell you all we know of the Way of man's approach to God."

"I shall see you again," he said, then bowed and left us.

THE LURE OF THE GOBI

I

The Desert Dweller's Flair

THE Gobi holds many surprises, and perhaps none is more unexpected than the frescoed caves which it has hidden for centuries and jealously preserved in some of its inner and more inaccessible cliffs. The traveller who would discover them must make long and diligent search, for he may well be in the neighbourhood of some beautifully decorated shrine and yet be unaware of the fact, because the ingrained suspicious nature of the desert dweller makes him unwilling to speak of it.

It is most natural that the villager should question the presence of a stranger, for the only outsiders he sees are men who come and go with a definite object, at regular intervals. He is accustomed to use a traditional saying which fixes his inborn habit of caution, and he applies it to all who come his way: "First time raw, second time ripe." Every new acquaintance who enters his sphere is "raw" and creates suspicion, but let him appear a second time and the simple mind of the oasis man opens to him in a different way. This is a "ripening" acquaintance, and each time he returns he is riper and riper, until the whole desert colony beams with pleasure at his arrival. Nevertheless, the visitor can never become intimate in such a circle until he shows himself able to share its outlook on life, and for this he must be familiar with the language, sayings, customs and traditions of the people.

There is a Gobi secret service which never fails to warn a community of the approach of any treasure-hunter who might wish to carry off booty. Every obstacle is quietly thrown in his way, and in answer to indiscreet enquiries village elders will deny knowledge of local treasures which actually are their chief pride; but once a traveller is accepted on the footing of friendship the whole community becomes as eager to help him as it formerly was to hinder.

It was long before we traced out and visited the whole line of cave temples which lie among the foothills of the Richthofen Range. They begin south of Kanchow in the province of Kansu, and continue as far as the border of the Lob Desert. Chinese scholars assured us that caves with this same style of decoration could be traced across the mountains toward India, and marked out a road traversed by pilgrims from early

35

times, but there is no verification of this statement by travellers. We visited eight separate groups of ancient shrines.

The first we saw were the rock caves of Matishi (Horseshoe Temple). It was a place of great beauty, for water flowed down from the Tibetan Hills above, and underfoot the grass was soft and green. We walked with delight on the cool green carpet, stopping to pick flowers as we went. The first building to appear was a Tibetan *chorten* [1] built high on the slope against a background of pine trees, and a steep rise in the ground brought us to a high place from which we saw many small openings in the perpendicular face of a bright-hued sandstone cliff. These, we knew, must be the windows of the rock shrines, for a little farther on a wide stairway led from ground-level to a broad terrace, from which the temple was entered.

The sandstone cliff was hollowed into a series of shrines rising to the height of five storeys and communicating by means of inner, rock-hewn stairways, with an occasional wooden gallery linking one cave with the other. Each cell was lighted by means of a small window, and inside each were figures peculiar to Indian shrines, wearing draperies and anklets never seen in a Chinese temple. The Buddha carved in wood was generally enshrined in a trefoil-arched niche, flanked by elephants which lifted their trunks in homage over his impassive form. The walls of many of the shrines were decorated with innumerable small moulded plaques representing him in the attitude of contemplation.

The carvings had never been damaged, for the lamas were careful guardians and never allowed the careless public to wander at will among the caves. They were anxious to show us the place and led us from one cool, twilit shrine to another. When we emerged again into the glaring sunlight, and felt the reflected heat of the sandstone cliff, it was an over-powering contrast with the shelter and coolness of the deep grottoes. On the ground floor were other excavated caves, but they had no remaining façade and lay open wide to the valley. They held, however, some gigantic figures whose gleaming bronzed surface glowed in the half-darkness of the deep recesses.

Farther along the road was the rock which has given its name to Horseshoe Temple. It was marked with a shallow impression in the shape of a huge horseshoe, which is supposed to have been left by the fabulous steed of a supernatural rider when he alighted on the spot to indicate the site of the lamasery. Among the treasures were a chased

---

[1] *chorten*—a sacred pyramidal building, originally a sepulchre, but now erected as a cenotaph : considered as a holy symbol of the Buddhist doctrine.

and jewelled saddle and a royal robe, both of which had been presented to the temple by the Emperor Chien Lung (1710-1799). They were beautiful and artistic properties, and preserved with the greatest care, but their value was not to be compared with the silk-woven and embroidered dresses which were part of the lamasery treasury. Some of the voluminous robes, which were in sets of ten, represented various periods of ancient Chinese history and were completed by very interesting sets of head-dresses, some of which were lacquered and shaped like pagodas, and others, made of satin stretched over fantastically shaped frames, were tasselled at the corners. There were other magnificent garments for use in dances symbolic of the four seasons, and apart from these a collection of masks and accessories needed for the devil-dancing. Some masks represented birds of prey, grotesque and horrible, others symbolised elemental powers, such as the god of thunder, and were black and threatening, but the most realistic head-dress was shaped like a skull and was worn with a gown which depicted a skeleton when the wearer took part in the famous Dance of Death. All these were stored in a secret grotto and only used on special occasions when the evil, suggestive and devilish performance took place.

The Valley of the Myriad Buddhas was several stages farther west, and reached by a road which followed a steep and deeply cut watercourse, rising to high ground near the old town of Ta-hsi. In these caves the frescoes presented the same style of decoration as is associated with the dignified form of art characteristic of the Tang period (A.D. 618-907), and the natural beauty of the site added greatly to the charm of that most interesting group of shrines.

There is one monastery which we visited many times before we even discovered the existence of some decorated caves which were its true art treasure. There were about one hundred and fifty modern shrines, built on the jagged points of a rocky mountain, and for one week of each year hundreds of worshippers crowded to the annual festival. The modern idols were crude effigies carved in semi-realistic style and coloured with gaudy paints. Their forms were repulsive, degraded and terrifying, yet some worshipper bowed before each grotesque figure and incense rose in a cloud within each shrine. Even the small-footed women scrambled up precipitous paths and staggered across tumbledown bridges to reach those shrines which were most difficult of access.

It was a Christian companion who revealed the existence of a few small caves here which belonged to a much earlier and better period of Chinese art. The steep pathway by which we climbed the hill was partly obliterated, for no one now ever worshipped at these shrines and it was difficult to reach them at all. When we stepped inside we seemed to be in almost total darkness, but after a while our eyes became accustomed to the gloom, and when we lighted the candles which we had brought we saw clearly that here was an authentic piece of early frescoed decoration. Some of the walls were covered with representations of those typical scenes of Olympian delight where graceful women in flowing draperies stand on light bridges, walk in beautiful gardens or look down from terraced walks on gay pageants below.

On another occasion this same friend took us to another temple which was hidden in a fold of some barren volcanic hills. The guardian priest, an old acquaintance of our guide, received us cordially, expressing surprise that visitors from a distant land should even know of his temple and care to visit it, for it was remote and few pilgrims came there. There had, however, been an incident connected with our friend's conversion to Christianity which was much discussed in temple circles. The members of his clan had always been devout Buddhists and generous contributors to temple funds. He himself had presented a handsomely carved tablet to be hung on the walls of this very temple in recognition of a favour asked of the gods and granted to him. One day this tablet, seemingly unaccountably, crashed from its place on the wall and fell to the ground. It was a terribie omen, and the priests feared that it might be a portent of calamity for him or his family. No misfortune followed, but, strange to relate, the accident happened on the very day that our friend, in a distant town, first made contact with the Christian group which he later joined.

The ceremony of replacing the tablet would have required some exacting ritual on the part of the donor, but, when the messenger who reported the disaster wished to discuss the matter, the Christian man's answer was quite definite, and word went back to the temple that he could have nothing more to do with idols or with idolatrous customs. According to expectation, trouble and disaster should have dogged his path, but nothing of the kind happened, and the priest was curious to hear about this new religion which so changed a man's outlook as to make him indifferent to omens.

This visit gave opportunity for the temple priest to ask all he wished to know, and there was long talk between the two men. Later on our friend asked leave to take us into the dark apse which lay behind the

shrine, like a built-in alcove. The entrance was very small and incon-
spicuous, but when we had lighted our candles we saw that once again
we were in a Gobi art gallery. This time we did not find many frescoes,
but beautifully carved figures which were the reverent work of some
great artist. One in particular represented a cherub with bowed head
and folded wings, whose whole form and attitude carried no suggestion
of idolatry. Not even an incense-burner was placed before the figure.
It stood as a work of art, not asking for a place in any pantheon of
the gods.

We were taken to yet another Hall of Antiquities, by a Chinese
schoolmaster in whose house we received the hospitality which is
characteristic of village life. He was a man of unusual culture and
had a discriminating appreciation of true art. He had spent his whole
life in a locality of great historic interest and was nurtured on the verbal
traditions of the place, but the narrowness of his circle can only be
understood by those who know the circumscribed conditions of oasis
life. His pupils were carefully trained in the precepts of Confucian
ethics, and daily recited the Rules for Disciples:

"Your room must be clean, the walls neat and the stands and tables
without dust.

"Your brushes and inkslab must be in good order.

"If your inkstick is more used on one side than the other, your
heart is not evenly balanced.

"If you show disrespect for the written character, your heart is
not correct.

"Every doctrinal saying commands respect. Do not pretend to
understand them quickly nor superficially.

"Avoid deceitful words, bad talk and idle gossip.

"An empty vase must be handled as carefully as though it were
filled; an empty room must be entered with the same dignity as though
it were full of people.

"The princely man is careful of himself when he is alone."

He owned one shelf of old paper-bound books which had been
handed down by the successive generations of a culture-loving ancestry.
This library he valued as an irreplaceable treasure, and re-read its volumes
constantly. In it were books of ancient Asian history and accounts
of the traditional origins of its peoples. It held commentaries on the
classics, and illustrated lists of old Chinese ideographs, many of which
are no longer in use, tracing them to their most remote sources. No

doubt much was mythical, but the old tomes created an atmosphere in which this man's appreciation of beauty and sense of antiquity grew and developed.

No inscription on a coin baffled him, and when he brought out some old pot which had been dug up on the site of a deserted city, his fine, sensitive fingers handled it and felt the quality of its glaze with an appreciative understanding such as could never have been acquired. His father, grandfather, great-grandfather and many generations behind him, had breathed the atmosphere of connoisseurship, and his instinct was more reliable than the knowledge which comes with years of training.

He was not a rich man, and the meal we ate in his home was necessarily of the simplest, but it was carefully prepared and served unaffectedly, with the knowledge that it was the best he could offer. At a word from him his wife opened the old lacquered cupboard with great brass hinges and took from it a porcelain dish of the Ming period (A.D. 1368-1644). On it she laid a pile of hot steamed bread, and placed four blue-and-white saucers around it, on which she served such common vegetables as the village produced. For hundreds of years his forebears had been handling these dishes, but they were neither cracked nor chipped.

When the meal was over our host said, "This village hall has some very old wall paintings, and if you would care to see them I would like to show them to you."

He took us to a large empty building inside a temple enclosure. It was light and airy, and the walls were covered with frescoes of extreme beauty depicting processions of large, stately, regal beings, draped in flowing robes and with haloes framing their heads. I was amazed at the strength of the free sweeping lines, the charm of graceful movement and the beauty of the pigments which had preserved their intense hues fadeless through the centuries.

Among the Chinese such inherited connoisseurship is not infrequently to be met in the most unlikely places, and the porcelain so often seen in a Chinese home, the value of which is so simply referred to by the family as "the heritage of the older generations," may well have come into those ancestors' hands by way of a very ancient line of commerce. In the early centuries of the Christian era the porcelain trade between China and the nations of the West was transacted by means of the camel caravans plying between Central Asia and Bactria. From time to time disaster inevitably befell some precious cargo which failed to reach its destination, and the goods were scattered among the oases, finally coming to rest in those homes which most appreciated them.

We often visualised the distant happenings which had brought the handwork of some famous craftsman to a squalid hamlet of the Gobi Desert, and as we did so we picked scraped carrot from the polished glaze and sipped herb tea from a delicately patterned cup with some reverence, for these vessels may well have been intended to grace the palace of an Emperor. We shared the oasis man's pride that when pedlars, travelling on behalf of a rich collector, sometimes traced down these treasures, their offers of money were resolutely refused by humble folk who regarded "the heritage of the older generations" as part of a cultural expression which they were responsible to hand on and must not exchange for money.

A brief stay in some small village has often been made delightful because a resident has sought us out and with simplicity, kindness and courtesy invited us to his own home. Such a wayside host has, in his turn, often been surprised to see how easily women from foreign lands fitted in with his own unlettered womenfolk; there was no mistaking the easy ways which showed long and intimate familiarity with Chinese home life. The women were pleased when they were addressed and answered in the local *patois*, and the word went round among the neighbours: "Come and see them. They are just like ourselves. They wear our clothes, they eat our food and they too have fathers and mothers, brothers and sisters. There is no difference at all."

In the dusty oasis so aptly called River of Sand we went to such a home, and after some conversation were taken to an inner room in which a wonderful collection of porcelain and stone-ware vases was displayed on a long table. It is not easy to show off such a collection to best advantage, and this was where the art of our host was seen. It seemed as though nothing could have been improved in the manner of setting out these treasures, so that the delicacy of the Ming was accentuated by the simplicity of the Sung, the purity of the Tang and the nobility of the Kang-hsi.

Each piece stood on a suitable carved stand, and it was evident that the man's whole artistic nature found expression in the arranging of this collection. Outside of that room there was nothing in River of Sand to satisfy his craving for aesthetic beauty. The village consisted of mud shacks, a few shops which never sold anything but screws of red pepper or tobacco, matches and rope. The people were wretched and the conditions of life were of the very lowest. His house outwardly differed but little from those of his neighbours, but in that inner room he stored his own treasury of art.

"Where did you collect these lovely things?" we asked him.

"Just anywhere," he said. "My forebears left me some in my inheritance, and now and again a farmer is glad to sell something which came to him in the same way. Poor harvests, pressure of debt and opium-smoking bring a man to the point of selling anything that he has. They do not really value these things, and I have often bought a dish so caked with dirt that it was only by holding it in my hand that I could detect its quality."

On another occasion, and in another oasis, we were in a tumbledown farmstead talking with its owner, who was shabby, ragged and unkempt. Yet when conversation had revealed the fact that we had some appreciation of works of art he said, "I will show you my pieces of jade if you care to see them." We were quite unprepared for the objects of beauty he produced from a hiding-place at the back of the family bedding, a mass of filthy wadded coverings which were of the most revolting description. He drew out two of the choicest jade bowls that can be imagined. The darker one was a feast for the eyes, but the paler was a masterpiece. The jade was so carved that a delicate outer trellis stood clear of the chaste translucent cup, to which it was only attached by a few tendrils of the vine which spread leaves and fruit over the trellis-work. The contrast with its filthy surroundings seemed to make the vase more noble. "How did this beautiful thing come into your possession?" I asked. "Both bowls were found together, hidden in a cave of the hills," he said. "It must have been in time of danger and the man who hid them was probably killed. It was a long while ago."

He spread the ragged cloth in which he wrapped the bowls, refolded them, and laid them again in the filthy recess of his verminous *kang*.

II

The Caves of the Thousand Buddhas

There is one art gallery in the Gobi which has become world-famous. Not many travellers have seen the Caves of the Thousand Buddhas, for they lie far from any main track, hidden behind wide-spreading dunes. The nearest oasis is Tunhwang (Blazing Beacon), which is marked on many maps as Shachow (City of Sands). The latter name is appropriate to a town standing among towering sand-hills, and the former is equally suitable, for at a short distance from Tunhwang there are several of the desert landmarks called *tun* by the Chinese. These old erections were used to convey messages by fire-signal across desert spaces, hence the name Blazing Beacon for the town and tower placed at this strategic point. When Shachow was destroyed the new town was built on the old site and the ancient name of Tunhwang, which dates from the Han dynasty (206 B.C.-A.D. 220), was revived. The locality is one which figures prominently in Chinese history by reason of its geographical position, for it stands at the point where the oldest trade-route connecting China with the West is crossed by the road which leads from India through Lhasa toward Mongolia and Southern Siberia.

Here the volcanic range which has formed the foothills of the South Mountains meets the first sand-hills of a line which stretches westward through the Desert of Lob. These dunes form the most characteristic feature of this landscape. Their height is from three to five hundred feet, and the ridge of the summits and slopes varies according to season and weather, as each prevailing wind alters the outline. Each clean-cut edge of sand-hill presents a striking contrast of light and shade, for one side of the projecting angle reflects the brilliant sunshine in warm tones, while the surface which lies in the shade has a lustreless cold hue.

This remote and apparently insignificant area is of great geographical, historic and archaeological interest. Old Chinese annals often refer to Tunhwang both as a military outpost and as an important business centre on the old Silk Road which connected Cambaluc (Peking) in China with Rome in the Western world, even before the days of the Han dynasty, and of which the total length is said to have been equal to one quarter of the Equator. It holds two sites which travellers have come from other parts of the world to see. One is the Lake of the Crescent Moon, and the other is the Caves of the Thousand Buddhas.

We were urged by many of our Tunhwang friends to see both the lake and the caves, but we were busy and it was some weeks before we could spare time to make either excursion. At last, however, we began to feel the need of a break from the ceaseless demands made upon us, and when the question of a visit to the caves was again brought up, we gladly responded to it.

"How far from the city are these caves?" we enquired.

"Only forty-five *li*," was the answer.

"What kind of road is it?"

"Passable. You have good mules. They will manage it all right, and at the caves you will find guest-house, stabling and kitchen, and the Abbot Wang knows about you and will see that all is done for your comfort."

"Are the caves hard to find?"

"Some one will go with you," said a young teacher, "then you cannot miss the road."

Every difficulty seemed to be smoothed away, and in due course the promised guide arrived at the inn door and we started out with the pleasant feeling of being on holiday. We left the oasis on its south border, travelling over roads which through centuries of traffic had gradually become deep cuttings between high banks, the tops of which were level with the fields.

At the exact limit of the area of irrigation we stepped out on to the gravel plain and faced desert once more. The line of dwindling sand-hills showed the direction, but the track itself was hard to trace, and on the various occasions when we went to the Caves of the Thousand Buddhas I do not think we ever followed the same course twice.

We were on our way to see something that was very ancient, a place where men of one age make contact with those of another. A thousand years and more lay between them and their work and us and ours. It was fitting that a few hours of silence and solitude should be imposed on us, for to pass, without transition, from any restless or noisy life to this reliquary would be to offer it an insult.

Midday found us still plodding our patient way through the grey grit. There were only two outstanding landmarks. The first was a quaint building with a little round tower, below which was a courtyard and some small rooms where two lamas were sheltering for a few days before taking to the passes which led to their lamasery in Tibet. They quickly boiled a kettle of water, and then shared our pot of tea and the new bread we had brought from town. Not till three hours later did we sight the second landmark. It was a ruin and stood at the point where the sand-hills finally yielded to a low ridge of conglomerate formation. Here we turned our backs on the wide plain and followed the foot of the ridge until it grew to a towering cliff overhead, from which the caves were hollowed. It was heavy going, and the fifteen miles of uncompromising sterility seemed abnormally long, but as we followed the rising bank a trace of moisture appeared in the grit, then a tiny trickle moved among some pebbles and grew to a small stream.

Nothing is so healing to the desert traveller as a trace of water in the sand, and our weariness was instantly relieved. Following the stream, which was without depth, and so narrow as to be easily crossed at any point, we saw the tender green of foliage ahead, a most unexpected and charming sight in this arid waste.

One more hour of toil and we reached the shade of a plantation of young poplars. It was obvious that someone who loved the place was caring for it and using the water to best possible advantage, for such a plantation was made possible only through skilful irrigation. Among the trees stood a guest-house which consisted of one spacious hall from which several large sleeping-rooms opened, each one furnished with a good table, two chairs and a *kang*. In the upper portion of the hall was a handsome shrine, and at the lower end a door led into a kitchen which was as clean and tidy as the guest-hall itself.

The presiding genius of this place was the Abbot Wang, a native of the province of Hupeh. In the course of his extensive wanderings this man came to visit the shrines of the Thousand Buddhas, and, finding them uncared for, he determined to devote his life to the cultivation of this stony waste. The little rill which came from the hills enabled him to fulfil his dream of bringing into being this small but charming oasis. To this end he diverted the water from the hills into a channel which follows the foot of the cliffs, and on its borders planted rows of young poplars over which he watched most tenderly.

A guest-house for pilgrims was his next care, but though material and labour were cheaper in Tunhwang than almost anywhere else, such a house could not be built without a considerable outlay of money. In order to obtain this he went on a series of begging tours, visiting wealthy townsmen and rich farmers to solicit their help. No one sent him away empty-handed, and he always returned to his beloved caves with enough money to proceed with his modest plans.

In the year 1908 fortune favoured the diligent Wang, for it was in that year that Sir Aurel Stein arrived at Tunhwang. He had worked his way through Central Asia and across the Lob Desert from India investigating and exploring all the sites of archaeological interest which lay on that route. While at Tunhwang he heard of a sealed library which had recently been found at the Caves of the Thousand Buddhas, and which was reported to contain a large collection of ancient manuscripts, many of which were written in languages which no Chinese scholar could read. A find of such interest could not remain uninvestigated, and Sir Aurel started out with the determination that, if it were possible, he would open up that library, rescue some of the precious manuscripts, have them deciphered by experts and lodge them safely in a National Museum. The City Magistrate of Tunhwang was a very enlightened man and gave him permission to visit and explore the caves. Thanks to patience, courtesy and diplomacy, this visit finally led to the reopening of the recess in which the old books and many rolls of precious Tibetan paintings had been walled up.

Under his guest's persuasive pressure the Abbot himself carried the rolls of manuscript out of the recess, and piled them up in the outer cave, where Sir Aurel Stein and his Chinese secretary examined their contents. By a most fortunate coincidence, among the first rolls which came to light were some which the Buddhist pilgrim Hsüan Tsang had brought back from India in the seventh century. This holy man was the patron saint of the Abbot, so Wang could but feel this to be a sign of favour, and it encouraged him to go on with the good work of permitting the examination of the treasures.

The first to be brought out were thick rolls of paper which, though they had obviously been well handled and much read, were in an excellent state of preservation. There were also paintings on gauzy scrolls and a variety of decorative pieces. "Nowhere, in all the bundles," says Sir Aurel, "could I trace the slightest effect of moisture."

By far the most valuable discoveries were made among the manuscripts and block prints. These proved to be a veritable treasure-house of historic data, and among other things showed that in olden times Tunhwang was a centre of learning where men of varying faiths met. There were examples of Uighur script, which is a derivative of Syriac writing and is known to have been used before the spread of Mohammedanism in Central Asia. Studying these writings, Sir Aurel observed that the script used in some of them was distinctly less cursive and of a firmer shape than the Uighur text to which he was accustomed; these were found to be examples of Sogdian, which is an Iranian dialect derived from Aramaic, used in early translations of Buddhist literature. There were also rolls written in Sanskrit, in Asian Brahmi, in Manichaean-Turkish and in Tibetan. Other manuscripts showed writing in the most ancient known languages of Central Asia, such as Khotanese or Saka, and Kuchean or Tocharish, which was once spoken in Turfan, and was more nearly related to the Italic and Slavonic branches of the Indo-European languages than to those spoken in Asia.

Professor Thompson, who deciphered the script known as Runic Turkish from its resemblance to the Runic alphabets of Northern

Europe, found with the scrolls a book of stories for use in divination, which he declared to be "the most remarkable, comprehensive and also the best preserved of the relics which came from this early literature." One large block-printed roll which bore a date corresponding to A.D. 868 was the oldest specimen of a printed book so far known, and the total number of manuscripts and rolls of printed matter in this hidden library amounted to no less than nine thousand.

In addition to this the caves contained many choice specimens of silk, woven in beautiful patterns, which showed to what a high standard the art of silk-weaving had attained long before the time of the Han dynasty. All was carefully examined and finally twenty-four cases of manuscript treasures and five additional boxes of paintings and art relics were removed from the caves, carried across Asia and deposited in the British Museum.

The business transaction with the old priest was done honourably, and after this there was no more shortage of money at Chien-fu-tung (Caves of the Thousand Buddhas), but a goodly store of silver with which to carry on. This money was spent on still further beautifying the place, and the traveller on arriving now passes from the shade of leafy trees into the cool, restful, spacious guest-hall, where a clean room awaits him and everything necessary to comfort is at his disposal. From the heat, glare, fatigue and drought of the desert stage we passed into this quiet building and sat down to rest for a few moments before the welcome sound "*Shui-ta-kai-liao*" warned us that the kettle was boiling over.

The unique quality of this great museum of the centuries, unguarded by any suspicious watchman and open to the heavens, drew me with an irresistible fascination. Very soon I slipped out by the small side-door, crossed the stream on a narrow plank-bridge and stood on sand-drift in the darkening shadow of the high cliff, facing the open door of the nearest grotto shrine. From its depths came the faint reverberating sound of a metal disc struck with a heavy wooden clapper. I stepped into the gloom and saw an assistant priest burning the evening incense and sounding the nine strokes of the sunset office. Here, deep within the cliff, was no remaining sign of day, and the only glimmer came from the bead of light rising from a brass saucer-lamp. I stood waiting in the stillness while that solitary figure, unconscious of my presence, moved, bowed, sank to its knees, rose and finally trimmed the lamp and turned to leave the shrine.

*   *   *

Early next morning, standing at the foot of the cliff, we looked up at the great façade, pierced with innumerable openings, each one of which was the entrance to a temple or shrine. These openings lay in irregular lines, rising to three or four tiers; the doorways of the lower caves were generally blocked by sand-drift, but we could look straight into the upper shrines and see frescoed walls and carved figures. The warm-tinted sand underfoot, the grey face of the cliff and the gay tints of the old frescoes were in joyous harmony with the deep tone of the blue sky and the tender green of young poplar trees. The coloured walls showed arabesques, stencilled patterns and figured landscapes in deep red, warm brown ochre and a peculiarly lovely shade which can only be compared with the blue-green bloom which lies on the surface of the young lotus leaf. On the frontage of the caves were many niches, in which stood carved figures; but the most striking of these, and one which immediately caught my attention, was a cherub form with folded wings, standing apart, and resembling the carved figure in the apse of the temple hidden away among the foothills of the Richthofen Range.

The highest caves had become inaccessible, but a lama told us that he once watched a party of young Russians exploring some of them. That was in 1917, during the time of the Russian Revolution, when crowds of White Russians, men who refused to bow to Bolshevik rule, poured over the Siberian border into Turkestan. The Chinese Government treated these refugees very kindly, providing them with food and transport and, among other privileges, allowing a number of them to rest for a time at Chien-fu-tung before travelling across China to Peking or to Shanghai. They spent their time wandering among the caves, and having made an entrance into all which could possibly be reached from below, they climbed the high cliff and took it in turns to lower each other by ropes to the more inaccessible openings. The lama told me that they found many strange things there, including human skeletons.

The Russians left evidence of their visit in long lists of their names written on any available wall-space which they could find. This passion for recording the trivial was in striking contrast with the dignified reticence of the unnamed artists who, having made of these caves a unique reliquary of art, asked for no personal recognition or that any man should remember them by name. The scrawled hieroglyphics of the Russian script seemed rather pitiful alongside the master-touch of those great anonymous artists.

We spent many days wandering among the silent and deserted halls.

The upper cells had small windows which framed the landscape most delightfully, adding a touch of intimacy to the scene. Looking through them, we saw first a fringe of waving young poplar trees, and behind them the arid glacis rising in terraces on which were scattered tombs of forgotten monks. Beyond these terraces the steep hill rose abruptly, marked with the faintest suggestion of a foot-path used by the lamas on their pilgrimages.

When we looked away from the window it was to see walls covered with beautiful pictures, or to look on majestic carvings. Even the smallest *cellas* were fully decorated, and there was not one wall in the whole series of caves which did not hold a frescoed pattern. Where there was no landscape or panel the space was filled with the Thousand Buddha decoration, which consists of stencilled or moulded rows of small figures of the Buddha, varying in colour but alike in pose. In many caves we traced the incidents of Prince Gautama's early life painted on the walls—the miracles of his childhood, the scenes of his youthful pleasures and the tragic encounters which called him to higher things and to his great renunciations.

The ceilings were highly decorative; each rose in the centre to a truncated cone of which every side was covered with elaborate designs. They were shaped like an inverted *dou*, which is the vessel used by the Chinese for measuring grain. It was very difficult to secure a good photograph of such ceilings, as it was only for a very brief time in the morning that the light was sufficient to take a picture. The accompanying picture was photographed by means of a very long exposure at the hour when light was brightest, and with a camera placed on the floor in the centre of the cell. The walls were often covered with scenes so interesting that we stayed for long looking at them. Many were symbolic of the forces which seek to bind men in the realm of the material, as, for example, one which represented a monarch caught in the gale of passion and illusion. He was depicted as a traveller being swept off his feet by a desert sand-storm, and he was fighting for his life. It has been suggested that the terrible *buran* [1] which devastates Tunhwang during the winter months may well have given the artist inspiration for such a scene.

We got inside the lower halls by climbing over the loose sand which was blocking the entrance. When we had slid down into the caves we were in an outer or ante-room, small and unadorned, and before us lay a wide passage beyond which was a shadow-filled cave. The walls

---

[1] *buran*—desert sand-storm.

of the passage were frescoed in rich and harmonious colours, the design being a procession of those large, strong, haloed figures in Graeco-Buddhist style which we had first seen in a village hall in Kansu. We walked between these vigorous figures whose faces all looked toward the vast gloomy grotto from the depths of which a few colossal moulded forms gradually emerged from the darkness. These were raised high on a horseshoe-shaped dais which stood away from the wall, and behind them a dark, encircling passage was vaguely distinguishable. We followed the hollowed path worn by the feet of countless pilgrims, and, as our eyes became more used to the darkness, saw that all the walls were covered with most charming paintings. There was a narrow door leading from this grotto into an inner cave, and here darkness was almost complete, but candle-light revealed that even this innermost recess was carefully decorated with the medallion-patterned figure of the Buddha. The silence was absolute, and although outside the cave the day was intensely hot and glaring, here was chill gloom and deathly stillness. One cave had a small entrance to which a door had been fixed. Seeing that it was closed I, of course, wanted to go inside, but a lama warned me not to do so, saying that one man who had tried to enter had been met by a black creature which flew out and knocked him down. "That cave," he said, "is possessed by demons, do not go near it."

It must have been the unbroken quiet of this place, the remoteness of the oasis and its great solitude, which produced an eerie sense that the caves were guarded by the presence of those who once worked here so busily. Generation after generation, century after century, they had lived the absorbed life of creative artists, handing on, when their own time came to die, that great tradition of a production in which no individual artist is glorified, but in which an unnumbered crowd of craftsmen make their humble contribution toward the whole.

On a much later visit to the Caves of the Thousand Buddhas we found the craftsmen busy again. They no longer handled the chisel and brush as did the men of the Han, Tang and Ming periods. This time they were chipping away the face of the cliff to make a great recess to house the colossal sitting Buddha, which is eighty feet high and which can now be seen from afar. A number of newer caves, at the farthest end of the cliff, had been given up to active idol worship, and the spirit of evil brooded over the grotesque and malevolent figures which they enshrined. There were gods of war, forms of hatred, and even an effigy of the spirit of suicide, among these horrors.

The guest-house was still the hospitable shelter for pilgrims, but a fresh guardian acted as host. Outside, on the stony glacis, a new tomb had been erected, and in it lay the body of the old Abbot Wang; now others carried on his tradition of cheerful service. His successor was a stranger to us, but he welcomed us kindly and, throwing open the door of his own cell, said, "You remember that this was his room. He was a good man." I found it hard to realise that Abbot Wang would not step out as of old, rosary in hand, saying: "You have all come back again. Welcome. That is good."

The young trees had grown and now hid a good deal more of the façade. Other and deeper things must also have changed, for when I commented on this fact to the new priest-in-charge, saying, "The caves seem farther away since the growing trees conceal them," his enigmatic answer was: "That matters not at all; those are dead things, but the trees are alive. Let them grow."

III

The Abbot's Patron Saint

The old Guardian, in his lifetime, had always been eager to relate the mythical incidents which were so beautifully represented in the frescoes, and to talk of the deified characters which they pictured, but his personal allegiance was reserved for Hsüan Tsang, the seventh-century pilgrim, to whom he always referred as "Master of the Law," and whom he had chosen as his own patron saint. In the caves there was a shrine which represented the Master as an *arhat* (Buddhist saint), and every pilgrim who would follow his footsteps and cross the Gobi Desert toward the elusive "Land of the Setting Sun" offered incense at his shrine and craved his protection from the dangers of the way.

In the guest-house, under the Abbot's personal supervision, some of the walls had been decorated with pictures showing the more legendary incidents of the great traveller's life. One of these depicted him returning from his long pilgrimage to India, leading a horse laden with precious Buddhist manuscripts. Standing on the bank of a torrent, the unwilling animal was refusing to plunge into the water, but a great turtle appeared to convey him safely across. On another panel a huge and inimical dragon was seen; the creature had swallowed the horse, but the dauntless pilgrim's attitude showed such authority and fearlessness that the beast was compelled to return it to the holy man.

Hsüan Tsang was certainly a remarkable figure in Chinese history. He belonged to a period of militarism, for the Emperor in whose reign he lived was a great conqueror and war-lord. It has been observed that "The ages of the sword are often the ages of faith," and simultaneously with its political expansion a tide of mysticism swept over China, leading men's minds to ponder the transcendental. While the Emperor Kao Tsu planned the military campaigns which made his name famous, a young Buddhist monk was also making history by his determination to reach India, explore the sources of the Buddhist religion and collect such manuscripts as would settle many matters still imperfectly understood in the Chinese monasteries.

Born in A.D. 602, Hsüan Tsang was the fourth and youngest son of his parents. He was a thoughtful and precocious child, and became absorbed in the study of the Sacred Books of Chinese literature at an early age. Incidentally, such an occupation necessitated familiarity with many thousands of ideographs and an understanding of their use.

The second son of the family had already become a Buddhist priest at a Loyang monastery, and, attracted by his brother's example, young Hsüan Tsang, at the age of twelve, knocked at the Black Gate of the same monastery and begged admittance as a novice of the Order. Monastic life proved to be completely to his taste, and he settled down happily to its studious and abstemious routine. A year later he was already recognised as a teacher and is reported to have "expounded the principles of religion profoundly." While he was still a mere boy a royal mandate was proclaimed ordering the election of fourteen priests to be supported free of charge at the temple, and young Hsüan Tsang, though under age, was chosen to be one of the number on account of his great ability.

The transcendentalism of Buddhistic teaching so fascinated him that he cared for nothing else, and finding meditation difficult among the disturbances of a war zone, he fled for quiet to the western province of Szechwan where he was admitted to full orders at Chengtu, but after ordination he made his way to Hangchow, where he retired to the Temple of Heavenly Radiance. He did not, however, stay there long, but walked the long road to Chang-an (Sian), which is the present capital of the province of Shensi. Here he lived, at the Temple of Great Learning, with a community of monks who devoted their lives to the translation and elucidation of the Sacred Books. They soon realised that there was a young Master of the Law among them, and acknowledged his ability, saying: "Master, the ancient saying is true; you are like 'a courier who travels a thousand *li* a day.' None of us can keep pace with you." The Chang-an monks with scholarly humility acknowledged the superiority of their young companion, but they themselves fell into the inevitable snare of theologians and were in constant dispute with one another on matters of dogma. Listening to the variety of their interpretations young Hsüan Tsang conceived the bold plan of gaining accurate knowledge by a visit to India and by bringing back, not only a first-hand interpretation of the matters under dispute, but a library of Buddhist Sacred Books. He sent a petition to Kao Tsu, the reigning Emperor, asking to be granted a permit to leave China by its north-west frontier, but this was firmly refused. Although, for the moment, his hopes were frustrated, he had no intention whatever of abandoning his plan, and he retired to a tower to meditate, "to reveal his intention to the saints and to pray for their protection." Here the young monk had a strange dream in which he saw a sacred mountain in the midst of a wide sea. Determined to reach it he flung himself into the waves, and immediately a mystic lotus formed itself beneath his feet and carried him to the foot of the mountain. This he would have climbed, but the steepness of its sides made it impossible; a whirlwind, however, caught him and lifted him to the summit, from whence he looked out over a vast expanse which he recognised to be symbolic of "the countless lands that his faith was about to conquer."

After this vision there could be no more hesitation, and in a few days Hsüan Tsang, without waiting for the Imperial permit, started on the pilgrimage which was to take him over the Pamirs to India on a search for spiritual knowledge. Several other monks, fired by his enthusiasm, had earlier purposed to accompany him to India, but on meeting with the Imperial rescript had abandoned the project, and he alone remained firm in his determination to push through. He travelled to the province of Kansu in company with one priest as companion who was returning to his home, and with whom he parted at Chinchow.

As far as Liangchow he was contravening no order, but from there on he knew he must travel secretly, for, the Emperor having refused him a permit, political frontiers were forbidden to him, and he must face a constant risk of being turned back. He needed great courage for the journey which lay before him. On the physical plane he was to suffer intense fatigue, hunger and thirst, and to face danger through the treachery of false guides. He was as yet unaware of the psychic perils which awaited him in the desert, through the illusions of mirage, by deceptive voices, and by the sense of inimical presences.

After passing Kwachow he met a "foreign greybeard, riding a lean red horse," who offered to guide him past Jade Barrier where the military outpost kept a sharp watch on travellers. Hsüan Tsang's guide proved to be a traitor, for at a certain point he stopped and said: "Your disciple can go no farther; he has great family concerns to attend to, and, moreover, is not willing to transgress the laws of his country." So they parted and the pilgrim went on alone, but he gave his own horse to the greybeard and rode the "rusty red nag" himself because it had already done the journey to distant I-ku (Hami) fifteen times and was therefore inured to fatigue and the brackish desert water.

As he approached China's extreme outpost, Hsüan Tsang knew that if he were seen he would be turned back, so by day he hid in an unused canal and only after nightfall did he attempt to reach the spring and fill his water-bottle. As he stealthily crept forward, he heard the whistle of one arrow followed by another, and realising that he had been seen, he came into the open and shouted with all his might: "I am only a monk from Chang-an. Do not shoot me." Thereupon the soldiers seized him and took him to the captain of the fortress. This officer was himself a Buddhist and welcomed the pilgrim, treating him with kindness. He strongly urged the young monk not to press on, but to turn off toward Tunhwang and end his pilgrimage at a monastery, presided over by an abbot who was full of wisdom. Hsüan Tsang, however, had not purposed such a tremendous undertaking in order to stop half-way and become the disciple of any wise abbot. His answer was: "If you insist on detaining me I will allow you to take my life, but Hsüan Tsang will not take a single step backward in the direction of China."

Seeing that he was not to be persuaded, the captain resolved to help the pilgrim on his way, and not only supplied him with provisions but gave him an introduction to the officer at the next frontier station, warning him, however, to avoid the last watch-tower of the line, as the captain in command was hostile to Buddhism and would certainly detain him. In order to avoid this catastrophe Hsüan Tsang left the main foot-track and made a *détour*, which brought him to a place so wild that no vestige of life could be found there. There was "neither bird, nor four-legged beast, neither water, nor pasturage." This digression nearly cost him his life, for he not only missed the path but lost his direction and could only attempt to guide himself by the line of his own shadow. Now, at last, the demon of doubt overcame him. He turned, and for the space of eight miles retraced his steps toward the

Chinese frontier. Then he recovered himself, courage revived, and he turned his horse's head once more toward the goal, saying, "I would rather die with my face toward the West than return and live in the East." He still could not find water, and was almost at the point of final exhaustion when the lean red horse turned off in another direction and, following its animal instinct, led him to a place where there was both water and pasture.

His life was saved, and a few days later the Master of the Law entered Hami, where he found a Buddhist monastery and a community of three Chinese monks who received him with joy and showed him the greatest respect. Here he rested himself in the congenial atmosphere of monastic life, but the news of his arrival soon spread and reached Kaochang, which was a great city near Turfan. The King of Kaochang, who was a pious Buddhist as well as a powerful monarch, sent an escort of ten mounted officers to invite Hsüan Tsang to his dominion. The pilgrim had planned to travel by another road and visit the famous town of Beshbalik (Urumchi), but on the arrival of the escort he felt compelled to abandon his own plans and obey the King's command. He and the escort, therefore, set out for Turfan by the South Road, which was the more direct way.

The people of Turfan, like other Central Asians at this time, professed Buddhism, and the educated classes were deeply steeped in Sanskrit culture. Hundreds of monks spent their lives translating the Sacred Books of India from Sanskrit into Tocharish, which was the Central Asian language of that period. The King, whose name was Chu Wen-tai, heaped honours on Hsüan Tsang, and tried to detain him at his Court indefinitely. The pilgrim was a man of great determination, but he only gained his point by refusing to take food for days at a time. Finally it was the King who yielded, and this he did handsomely, for he not only gave Hsüan Tsang letters of introduction to other rulers, but sent him on toward Kuche laden with presents and road provisions. At this town he was again received with royal honours, but once more had to force his way onward, against strong pressure to detain him and prevent him from reaching India; in spite of all, he determinedly pressed westward, and not even the great difficulties of travel across the Pamirs daunted him. On reaching India he was rewarded by an ample opportunity to study Buddhism and was able to collect a large number of books which were to be the foundation of authoritative teaching of that religion in China.

Fifteen years later Hsüan Tsang reappeared on the northern side of the Great Mountains, with his face turned toward China. During the intervening years political events had moved apace in Central Asia. The Kingdom of Kaochang had fallen under the displeasure of the Chinese Imperial Court and had been sacked and pillaged by Imperial troops. Chu Wen-tai was dead, and the pilgrim was obliged to take another route. This time he travelled through the Kingdom of Khotan, whose monarch came out to meet and escort him to the town, heaping honours on him. In crossing a dangerous river the Master had lost a load of precious books and must needs send back to Kashgar in order to replace them. While awaiting these he wrote ahead begging a royal permit which would enable him to proceed on his journey, and in the course of eight months the messenger returned bringing the required permission. Between Khotan and Tunhwang lay the dread Desert of Lob, "a desert of drifting sand without water or vegetation, burning hot and the haunt of poisonous fiends and imps. There is no road, and travellers, in coming and going here, have only to look for the deserted bones of man and cattle as their guide."

Coming safely across this dread waste, Hsüan Tsang reached Tunhwang and deposited some of his precious manuscripts in the monastic library at the Caves of the Thousand Buddhas, where he probably sheltered while he waited for an answer to a further memorial which he had forwarded to the Emperor himself. When the answer came it was favourable, for his Imperial Majesty condescended to over-look his former disobedience and promised him an honourable reception at Court.

When at last the Emperor met the Master of the Law face to face, he enquired of him concerning the matter of that early disobedience. To this Hsüan Tsang diplomatically replied, "I did indeed request your gracious permit three times over, but, receiving no favourable answer and knowing myself to be so insignificant a subject, I could not suppose that you even knew of my request."

The Emperor was pleased to graciously accept this excuse, and allowed Hsüan Tsang to retire to a monastic life where he might study undisturbed and translate into Chinese some of the six hundred and fifty-seven Buddhist books which he had brought back from India, and also make appropriate use of the one hundred and fifty precious relics which he had collected.

The Master of the Law now had leisure to revise and enlarge the valuable records he had made during the long years of pilgrimage, thus adding a valuable contribution to our accurate knowledge of Central

Asian life in the seventh century. He was there before the close of a period during which the land east of Kashgar had attained a high degree of artistic and scholastic culture. He moved slowly and with long delays through countries which were enjoying a respite from warfare, he sheltered in their halls of learning which were the monasteries, he saw the translators and the transcribers of old libraries at work, and he was the honoured guest of kings who sat at his feet as disciples. The utter loneliness in which he met the Gobi terrors and faced solitary death in the wilderness bred a strength and endurance which carried him through every ordeal, and the long silent desert stages taught him the ways of meditation better than any monastic rule could have done. Now as an elderly and honoured recluse he looked back over it all and knew that the disciplines of life had little more to teach him, and that the understanding of the Sacred Books, which had been his ambition, was near attainment.

IV

The Treasures of the Sands

In the course of years we paid several long visits to Tunhwang and made friends with many of its inhabitants. Among them was a schoolmaster who was a born antiquary, and from whom we learnt a great deal. On one occasion, hearing that we were in the town, he came round at once to tell us of a recent discovery in the neighbourhood.

"I want you to see our new Caves of the Thousand Buddhas," he began.

Thinking that he referred to new excavations on the old site, we were eager to enquire concerning them, but it was not as we had thought.

"These caves are in a different direction altogether," he said; "they are hollowed from the cliff overhanging the Tang River, and are half-way between here and Nan-hu (South Lake)."

"Are the caves new?" we asked.

"They are very old, but newly rediscovered," he answered, "and they belong to the same period as all the shrines along the foot of the South Mountains."

"How were they located and excavated? Do tell us all about it."

I was eager to hear, for I knew that any information from this man would be both reliable and accurate.

"It is a strange story," he said. "A priest well known to us here was travelling back toward Tunhwang from South Lake, and as he crossed the lonely Gobi which stretches out westward, a great blizzard blew up just as darkness fell. The air was full of dust, no stars were visible, and he completely lost his bearings. As he peered about, seeking shelter, he thought he saw a glimmer which he described as the light of a double lantern. Walking toward it, he found himself at a place where there are three small monuments. According to him, the light still moved on, and he followed it through an opening in the cliff, and down a steep path, which led him toward the river. Just there it flows in a very deep bed, and the path he took is so difficult to descend, even by day, that I cannot think how he got down in the dark, and in such rough weather. However, he safely reached a ledge on the bank and felt his way to an opening like the mouth of a cave, which was a welcome shelter from the wind. There he lay down and slept. When he awoke it was daylight, and from the walls of the cave he saw paintings of holy men looking down on him. He tells us that he got up, explored farther, and found various other small openings leading into caves hollowed from the cliff. He pushed on to Tunhwang and immediately reported the matter. Some of us went out to see the place, and found that it was as he said, and that a quantity of loose gravel, recently washed from the bank, had left these caves exposed. Their walls were covered with frescoes, very much like those at Chien-fu-tung. The old priest now lives there with a friend, and the two men are gradually clearing away the rubble from the entrance of other caves. You certainly must see the place, and if you are planning a visit to South Lake, the road would take you quite close to these new caves."

It so happened that we were discussing the possibility of a trip to Nan-hu. It was only two days' journey away, but it had no hostelry of any description, and there was no apparent means of buying the necessities of life for man or beast. As regards ordinary wayfarers, the ramifications of Chinese family life are such that every oasis dweller can move about in the Gobi and always find some relative, or at any rate relative's relative, who will receive and welcome him as a member of the clan. Hospitality of the same kind had often been extended to us, and again a friendly neighbour came forward with a suggestion.

"My cousins from Nan-hu were here yesterday," he said. "When they heard that you were going there they asked if you would stay at their farm. Their land is just by the lake and they have a good threshing-floor where you could pitch a tent if you prefer. I just said they might expect you any day, so you will find the place all ready."

With the way made so easy, there was nothing to delay us, and a few days later our carts rolled over the wooden bridge which spanned the city moat, passed the crumbling earth-works of old Shachow and struck out across the oasis toward the gravel plain which overlooked the river. On the first evening we reached the foot of the three *stupas* [1] of which our friend had spoken, and camped there. They formed a conspicuous landmark on the bare plain, which was completely exposed to all weathers, and as we lay in our canvas tent we were grateful that no blizzard blew up that night.

Next morning we set out to investigate the caves. The river rushed far below, and the glacis on which we stood formed the top of a high conglomerate cliff. At the edge of the cliff was a rough opening, and from it a very precipitous path led down to a narrow ledge from which the new caves opened. Space was restricted and the grottoes were few in number, but as regards the style of decoration and quality of work, they were comparable to the better known Thousand Buddha Grottoes. Here, as there, the figures were free and stately, with flowing lines and elegant draperies, and the frescoes showed the same clear warm tints. There were some processions of rather darkly coloured figures with long white streamers flowing from their head-dresses, and one picture of a very interesting old cart of a peculiar shape, which the Abbot called a phoenix cart (*fei-chae*). The intervening spaces were filled with stencilled figures of the Buddha in contemplation, and in one cave there was a painting in which the figure lay enfolded like a larva in a cocoon, suggesting a transient stage of metamorphosis and reincarnated life.

The priest was very proud of his discovery, and purposed to follow the example of Abbot Wang in his work at Chien-fu-tung. He hoped to raise enough money by begging tours to meet the expenses of further excavation, and thus, in time, to make of this stony ledge a well-known and famous shrine.

On leaving the caves we trekked due west, following the course of the Tang River until it suddenly took a sharp turn to the south and we saw it no more. The direction of South Lake was indicated by a long straight ridge of gravel. Following this ridge we came to a place where there were circular, stony heaps about three to four feet high, many of which were curiously complemented by a straight line of stones giving the impression of a handle. Some of the heaps faced small rectangular enclosures, outlined with large pebbles, and suggested a primitive burial-ground. However, Sir Aurel Stein, who investigated

---

[1] *stupa*—a Sanskrit word used for ancient Buddhist monuments.

the heaps, found that they did not cover the openings of any graves, but were merely mounds of coarse gravel and loose stones heaped on the desert floor. They were clearly not accidental and must have had a definite meaning for those who raised them, but it was hard to conjecture what that meaning was.

In the late afternoon we saw the straight line of the plateau broken by a fringe of vegetation, and the carter's whip shot out: "We have arrived. There it is," he said, and though we knew that we had at least another hour of grind over gravel, we were all relieved when vegetation came in sight.

Cousin Wang had risen to the occasion and was prepared to be the perfect host to our party. His wife had rolled and chopped a stack of dough-strings sufficient to feed us all, and young cabbage shoots and chopped chives were ready to be thrown into the heavy iron frying-pan and tossed in the best linseed oil. Over the fireplace was a cauldron of water ready to make tea, and one of the children was bringing it to the boil by working the "wind box," which he did by pulling a wooden shutter in and out and causing a strong draught to play upon the smouldering sheep-dung with which the fire was fed.

It was a beautiful welcome which supplied lodging, food and service—all offered with simplicity and generous liberality. We, on the other hand, did not arrive as uncouth barbarians who accept favours without return, but brought some delicacies from the town such as are not obtainable in farm life. There were parcels of cakes in scarlet wrappings marked with the words *Tien sin*, which means "a fragment of my heart," two packets of Russian lump sugar, and candied jujube fruits for the children.

Bed-time never comes too soon either for the traveller or for the farmer, for both are up at dawn, but before we went to our tent the household and neighbours gathered in the large living-room and for the first time there were family prayers in South Lake.

Like every other oasis, Nan-hu had its own individuality. Lovely, fertile and luxuriant, it was yet the gateway to the formidable Desert of Lob. Only a few miles off utter desolation began, but the inhabitants of the oasis were shut off from its terrors by sandstone hills and, living at the very edge of a howling wilderness, yet felt complete satisfaction with their surroundings. Uncertainty of crops was unknown to them, for their water-supply came from distant melting snows which never failed to filter into their own clear lake, and this was distributed through irrigation canals all over the land. They knew the secrets of good farming and never allowed any exhaustion of the soil. The traditional rotation of crops was never questioned, and leguminous plants were sown round the margin of each field as their fathers' fathers had ordained that they should be.

Each farmhouse granary had a store of wheat and millet, both hard and glutinous, bins overflowing with peas and sorghum for the beasts' fodder, and festoons of yellow and red Indian corn mixed with bunches of scarlet chillies, which made every storehouse gay with colour, while drops of linseed oil oozed lazily from the oil-press. Jars of poppy-seed and vats of mild home-made vinegar stood in the corners, and hanging from the beams were long-handled brooms made from the desert plant which grows in the shape of a besom. There were always baskets of cotton waiting to be seeded, and jars of indigo ready for dyeing the home-spun cloth. These Nan-hu people relied on no outsider for the necessities of life. What they needed they grew, and what they grew sufficed them.

Our host devoted his time to taking us about and introducing us to his friends, at the same time showing us all that was of interest in the locality. As the oasis was about two miles long and nearly as wide, we were walking most of the day, and only at sunset came home to our evening meal. It was then that he said, "Tomorrow I must take you over to see the 'Barrier of the Sun.'"

This Barrier was an ancient and historic site, the importance of which dates back to more than a century B.C. It is known from old documents that, "When the Emperor Wu-ti (140 B.C.) had ousted the Huns from their grazing-grounds at the northern foot of the South Mountains, he immediately established military colonies in that passage land which was to serve his forward policy toward Central Asia." This Barrier was one of those celebrated military outposts and was intended for guarding the road to the Tarim Basin.

We left the village of Nan-hu and wandered across a tract of coarse sand until we came to the foot of an old clay wall where the tearing blizzards had swept up the sand and piled it high. To stand on the top of the wall was to dominate the outlook over a great area, and to gaze over a scene of utter devastation, for the wells which in olden days must have supplied the garrison with water had disappeared and nothing but barrenness remained.

To the children of South Lake these historic sites were nothing but a grand field for picking up odds and ends. They called them "The Old Treasure Haunts," and after each big wind-storm they went hunting for things which the blizzard had brought to the surface of the dunes and always came away with some spoil, a copper coin, a few beads, an old shoe, or even a piece of brick made of fired clay which was very large, very black and very heavy. "In the days when those bricks were made, men were giants," the small boys said, "and nowadays people could not even lift them to lay them in place." Occasionally they dug out a pot of strong earthenware, and this was a greater find than the other things because it was immediately useful. Many homely and intimate articles of daily use, such as a comb, a wooden lock, a key, a dipper or a bowl which had been found and brought home by the children, could be seen in South Lake farms, and it was quite in keeping with the immobility of this place that the housewives should store their oil, their crushed pepper and their coarse salt in pots which were made by men of the Han dynasty. When I saw a brush which came out of the sand, I noticed that it had the same twist as Cousin Wang was giving to the one he made as he sat busy at our tent door, and the shape of the wooden lock on his granary was identical with one which was a thousand years old.

In the course of investigations in this area Sir Aurel Stein unearthed a foot-rule, with the string by which it hung to the wall still fastened to it. It was like a bootmaker's measure and was "divided into ten inches, with further subdivisions on the decimal principle." Later on Sir Aurel was able to apply the measure to specimens of silk which he unearthed from three widely distant sites in Central Asia, and thereby established the fact that the silk "exported from China to Central Asia and thence to the classical West during the centuries immediately before and after Christ retained a uniform width, corresponding approximately to one foot ten inches British measure, while the measuring standard in China underwent a considerable alteration during that period."

I, myself, began to drift into the spirit of this unchanging place, and to find a strange release from the illusion of passing time. When I stooped to pick up a coin, it was one which had been dropped a thousand years before, and the string of beads in my hand was the ornament of a woman of the Han period. Here the centuries passed and left scarce a trace behind. In the calm of this detached, monotonous life, the passing of an age made less impression than does the flight of a day in the restless, changing West. The people of South Lake remained unaffected by the turmoil of an agitated world, and to them its rapid changes would appear to be both unseemly and unworthy.

V

The Lake among the Dunes

The constant hurricanes which sweep the sandy plains have piled up a long line of dunes stretching from Tunhwang away to the Desert of Lob. The range is so long, and the hills are so lofty, and so massed one behind the other, that it seemed incredible such a mighty rampart could be composed wholly of shifting sand. From season to season the contour of the dunes changes, for under the breath of even the lightest breeze the shifting surface runs like sand in an hour-glass, and every wind lifts the clear-cut ridge like spray, though the solid body of the sand-mountain resists the fiercest winter storms.

Behind the great rampart death reigns, and there is not so much sign of life as the track of a passing antelope. Not even a beetle or a lizard would find sustenance in that sterility, yet it was in search of a lake that we first explored the desolate region.

"The skill of man made the Caves of the Thousand Buddhas, but the Hand of God fashioned the Lake of the Crescent Moon," is a popular saying at Tunhwang, and when I asked where to find this Lake of the Crescent Moon, the answer was:

"It lies behind the first range of those sand-hills."

"Is it so very beautiful?" I enquired.

"More beautiful than words can tell," was the answer.

"How far off is the lake?" I asked, remembering the fatigue of toiling through loose sand.

"It is barely four miles from the town, and once there you will find fresh sweet water, a small temple with clean guest-rooms, and a quiet place in which to rest."

This was an encouraging answer, and a few days later we left the city gate with faces turned toward the dunes. Within an hour we were standing at the base of the outermost hill, and where the range was at its lowest we started to climb the steep side, ploughing upwards through sands which buried our feet to the ankle at each step. Near the top, where the slope was almost perpendicular, exhaustion overcame us and every few steps we sank to the ground. All around us we saw tier on tier of lofty sand-hills, giving the lie to our quest, yet when, with a final desperate effort, we hoisted ourselves over the last ridge and looked down on what lay beyond, we saw the lake below, and its beauty was entrancing.

Small, crescent-shaped and sapphire blue, it lay in the narrow space dividing us from the next range like a jewel in folds of warm-tinted sand. On its farther shore stood a small temple surrounded with silvery trees, and on the surface of the lake a flotilla of little black-headed divers were swimming. The downward stretch of the soft slope was an irresistible inducement to slide, and we all came down with a rush, bringing the sand with us like a cataract. Then, for the first time, we experienced the strange sensation of vibrant sands, for as we slid, a loud noise came from the very depths of the hill on which we were, and simultaneously a strong vibration shook the dune as though the strings of some gigantic musical instrument were twanged beneath us. We had, unknowingly, chosen for our slide one of the resonant surfaces of the hill, for, curiously enough, only a few of the dunes are musical and most of them are as silent as they are dead.

The long descent landed us on the edge of the lake and a short distance from the temple door, where the priest received us and led us to a pleasant room in the guests' courtyard.

"You heard the *lui-ing* (thunder-roll) of the hills as you came down," he said. "The sound reached us here, for you chose the right spot to set the sands thundering. Had you been a little farther to east or west, the noise would have been much fainter, and had you come down that farther hill, nothing would have been heard."

"I never knew sands with a 'thunder voice' before," I said.

"You will hear it often while you stay here," was his answer.

This was true, and whenever the wind blew in a certain quarter a roaring came from the dunes. Once, at midnight, we were awakened by a sound like a roll of drums. On that occasion there were brigands in the neighbourhood, and I jumped up in alarm, fearing an attack, but the priest heard me and called out:

"Don't be anxious, Lady. It is only the drum-roll of our sand-hills. Rest your heart."

The old man was quite satisfied to attribute the mysterious noise to the action of the gods whose shrine he tended so carefully, but we were curious to know more about it and began to study the subject. Marco Polo passed this way nearly seven hundred years ago, and he reported desert sand-hills which emitted a sound like distant thunder. These very dunes must have been the "rumbling sands" to which he referred. We also read of "singing sands" in the Arabian desert where Dr. Bertram Thomas and his companions heard a loud noise, which he describes as being like the sound of a ship's siren, coming from some steep sand-hills of which the wind was lifting the crest with a curl like a centurion's helmet. The Arab desert dwellers were familiar with the sound and called that dune "the bellowing sand-hill" because its voice reminded them of the loud bellow of a bull camel. In the Sinai Peninsula, also, travellers have spoken of a locality called "the Hill of the Bell" where a clanging noise is sometimes heard.

The musical sands which are found in these various localities all present special features of dryness and smoothness, for in deserts the transport of sand is effected solely by the wind, and the grains are so constantly rolled to and fro along the ground that each particle becomes smooth, rounded and polished. No such easy explanation, however, is forthcoming of the undoubted fact that one slope "sings" when another, close by, remains silent, and that one course will give a much louder sound than the other. The sands of the Tunhwang dunes are composed of the tiniest fragments of multi-coloured quartz, blue, green, red, purple, grey and white, and this blend of colours gives an iridescent sheen to the sand-hills which responds to every change of light and shade. The sand-girt lake is referred to in many Chinese books as one of the beauty spots of Central Asia, and an envoy sent to Khotan from the Imperial Court in A.D. 938 spoke of its charm and of the towering dunes, which he estimated as five hundred feet in height. A modern explorer quotes this calculation as evidence of the careful, reliable observations made by these early travellers.

All the temple buildings were on the south side of the lake and terraced down to a flight of steps which led to the water's edge. The shrines were neither very large nor very noteworthy, but they filled the narrow level space between the water and the second range of sand-hills. A grove of trees shaded the courtyard, and the lake water lapped the narrow shore at the foot of some steps which led to a *loggia*. All was bathed in peace, silence and utter restfulness. The hostel was seldom without a pilgrim guest. There were no rules for visitors, but the enclosure was instinct with quiet, and the atmosphere of pervading peace exercised its own control. There were no loud voices and no hasty movements among those who came and went, for the lake was regarded as a place of peculiar sanctity, and was commonly referred to as the "back door of Paradise." Sick people sometimes came from the city to seek healing of the body at the sacred spring, and renewal of the mind in the quiet of meditation.

One of the most frequent pilgrim visitors was a fantastic figure who spent most of his time travelling among Tibetan lamaseries and constantly spoke of an impending journey to Lhasa on which, according to him, the fortunes of the world depended. Two mirrors were fixed above his forehead, and in them he liked to think that he could discern the past and gaze into the future. A passport to Lhasa was draped round his broad-brimmed hat, and his pretensions to occult knowledge were considerable. Very devout in all religious observances, he declared himself to have been appointed "Messenger of Peace to all nations." He said that at a given signal he must rally the peoples of the world to unity and concord, but until that hour there would be strife and tumult. In the course of our many long talks he professed to be deeply impressed by what he heard, and he certainly read the gospels carefully, and carried them when he went on pilgrimage. "I must tell all this to the lamas," he would often say, but he remained convinced that the issues of world peace were committed to his keeping, and that the hour for action would only be revealed to him through the reflections in his magic mirrors.

The guardian priest was a self-respecting, hard-working man who lived a quiet retired life in this hidden oasis. He was helped by two acolytes, and there was plenty of work for them all. The elder was a lame youth who realised to the full the prestige which he had acquired in being admitted to the temple staff. He liked his present work much better than his former occupation, which was that of shepherd boy, as he was always at a disadvantage with the flock on account of his deformed foot and limping gait. The junior helper was a deaf-mute child who did all the odd jobs and searched the sands daily, basket on arm, for fragments of fuel to feed the kitchen fire. Between them they kept the temple land in good order, grew a few rows of cabbages, tended the shrines, sounded the bells, burned incense and observed all the required ceremonies, besides welcoming and caring for the pilgrims. Every guest who came brought some contribution to the store of food, and generous hospitality was the law of the house.

We once claimed that hospitality at mid-winter when the lake was a sheet of grey ice swept by bitter winds. A brigand band had commandeered our town quarters and we were left shelterless, but the guardian welcomed us as old friends and placed part of the guest-house at our disposal, for at that season pilgrims were few. In January when the blizzards blew up, or winter sand-storms blotted out the sun, the dunes were terrifying in their desolation. To be lost among them would be certain death, yet one stormy day, standing on the summit of the "thunder-sound slope," I saw a short string of camels appear between two ridges and descend toward the plain.

"Where have those camels come from?" I asked the guardian.

"They come from the charcoal-burners' camp," was the reply.

"Charcoal-burners!" I said with amazement. "Where do they get the wood for burning charcoal?"

"From dried-up tamarisk plantations," he said. "All through the winter there are people up there, but they can only stay between the eleventh and the second moons (November to February). The camels you saw had carried up blocks of ice for the men's water-supply and were coming back laden with charcoal."

I thus learnt that far back among the hills was a place where once there had been water. None now remained, but clumps of desiccated tamarisk and saksaul (*Anabasis ammondendron*) were still there. In this place a family of charcoal-burners spent four of the winter months each year. Every week the string of camels went to them laden with flour and blocks of ice, and returned to Tunhwang with a load of charcoal. At the first sign of thaw the traffic ceased, and all moved back to the city.

In early summer the borders of the lake were made even more delightful by the exquisite fragrance of the sand-jujube (*Eloeagnus latifolia*). Hidden among its silver leaves are small flowers which embalm the air with their perfume. The people of Turkestan always associate this scent with a story which is told in every home. It is related that among the prisoners of war who were carried away to Peking in the eighteenth century, from the lands beyond the Gobi Desert, was a beautiful Kashgarian girl who won the love of the Emperor Chien Lung. He lavished on her all that wealth could supply, yet still she sighed for her distant home. He built up a Kashgarian landscape in the palace grounds, and constructed a mosque within sight of her windows. In her own garden he erected a pavilion called the "Homeward-Gazing Tower" from which she might look beyond the mosque and picture far-distant Kashgar. Yet all his trouble was in vain and he could never make the exile happy. Her longings have been expressed in verse:

> "'Tis very like my home. From yonder tower,
> Breaking the stillness of the twilight hour,
> In the soft accents of my native tongue,
> I hear the ballads of my country sung.
> But that is all, there the resemblance ends
> That only makes me grieve and crave for more;
> I long for other voices, those of friends;
> 'Twould then be like the home I had before.

'Tis very like my home. But yet its walls
Too oft and much my other home recalls;
Filling my breast with many a vain regret,
With recollections I would fain forget.
'Twas built in kindness, yet 'tis mockery;
It makes me pine, when he would have me gay;
Why do I look? O! that my home should be
So very near and yet so far away."[1]

What more could she need? the Emperor asked himself, and one day she told him: "I long for the fragrance of that tree whose leaves are silver and whose fruit is gold." Messengers were dispatched to Kashgaria, where they found the silver-leaved sand-jujube with its golden fruit, and when this tree was planted in her garden and the wind wafted its exquisite fragrance through her pavilion windows, her distant home seemed nearer than before, and her heart found solace in the illusion.

It is said that musical sands will give out a sound even in a laboratory far from their native dunes. It may be, yet sometimes in my London home I take up a handful of Crescent Lake sand and try to make it sing, but I listen in vain for the echo of the thunder-roll of its voice. Between the leaves of a book I have pressed a small branch of sand-jujube flowers, and whenever I catch its subtle but fading fragrance, I, like the Kashgarian exile, long for a place that seems so near and is yet so far away. Sick with longing I walk among the crowds while my spirit flees to the quiet which is found by the hidden lake among the dunes.

[1] " The Captive Maiden," by G. C. Stent.

WHERE MEN AND DESERTS MEET

I

The People of the Oasis

THE people of Tunhwang viewed themselves as the *élite* of Gobi land, and were abnormally proud of their oasis. They had plenty of money to spend and opened their markets freely to goods from other places, but prided themselves on being a self-supporting community, not only in respect of food, but also in regard to brides and bridegrooms, and they did not approve of marriages arranged between their own children and those of other towns. The market-place was always busy with merchants coming and going, the professional story-teller took his stand each day to amuse the moving crowd, and gaily dressed women came in carts from the farms for a day's shopping and to see their friends. The granaries overflowed with wheat, and the town reckoned itself to be the safest and most prosperous place imaginable, priding itself on its trade-route nickname of "little Peking."

One sign of its deep-seated conservatism was the backward system of money exchange which it retained. Long after the silver dollar had become the common basis of coinage on the main road, Tunhwang business men looked askance at it, and preferred the shoe of silver which was chipped down, weighed up and exchanged for copper coinage. Here again Tunhwang set its own standard by allowing one hundred worn and valueless cash to be introduced into each string of a thousand. It became therefore worth while to collect these useless coppers in other towns, cart them to Tunhwang and dispose of them there. When the reluctance to admit the silver dollar was finally overcome, merchants still discriminated between different issues and refused one or other according to fancy. The coin stamped with the dragon was depreciated in favour of one designated as the "standing man" which was Hong Kong currency. The dollar bearing the head of Yuan Shih-kai found favour, and for some reason the third-year issue was more highly valued than any other, but when a new coin, stamped with the head of Sun Yat-sen, appeared, this Gobi town absolutely refused to recognise it because the new president's effigy was small and unimpressive. No other explanation was offered than the words "The head seems small," but no one would use it. In this little backwater town large business deals were effected, but each roll of dollars received for payment was opened, the contents carefully examined, and the individual coins valued a little higher or a little lower according to the Tunhwang standard.

The oasis has great natural beauty. It is old and mature, and all the land which is available for agriculture has been brought under cultivation for many centuries. The landowners are mainly Chinese whose ancestors were established here very long ago; there is also a colony of Moslem merchants from Turkestan who came to the town along the trade-routes of Central Asia and have remained there for business purposes.

During the spring the fruit orchards show masses of pear, peach and nectarine blossom; all the fields are green with sprouting corn and every bank is covered with blue desert iris. A little later, when the fruit blossom has disappeared, the opium poppy bursts into flower, covering a wide acreage as with a veil of gossamer, sometimes shaded from the faintest touch of pink to deep rose, and at other times scarlet streaked with silver-grey. All through the summer the land yields a succession of crops which include wheat, Indian corn, millet, sorghum, hemp and field peas, with a profusion of vegetables such as aubergines, scarlet capsicum, potatoes, many kinds of beans, carrots, celery, onions, leeks, golden pumpkins and green cucumbers. At different seasons, fields are gay with patches of blue flax, pink buckwheat and yellow colza.

Fruit harvest in Tunhwang is a thing to be remembered, for it is scarcely ever known to fail. In each farmyard there are piles of apricots and plums, then peaches and nectarines, followed by the early "long-stemmed" pear, grapes and finally the large late pear which is carefully kept and stored to be eaten at mid-winter. The market stalls show piles of juicy melons, and late peaches of the kind that has been grafted on to the willow tree and which bears large, green, juicy fruit, handsome but flavourless. The rich brown jujubes and freshly gathered walnuts are so abundant that any one may help himself freely to them. The sight of such plenty is refreshing to the hungry and desert-weary traveller. Even in early spring, when other oases have no green vegetables to offer, the stalls at Tunhwang are covered with little bunches of the first shoots of lucerne, and this *primeur* is followed by branches of flowering elm, the blossom of which, rolled in flour and cooked in a special earthenware steamer, is served as a spring delicacy.

The River Tang flows below the north wall of Tunhwang, and on its farther bank are the ruins of old Shachow, which flourished one thousand three hundred years ago. It is no longer inhabited, but the space enclosed by its massive earthen walls is ploughed and sown by peasants whose little mud houses lean against the outer battlements of the old fort.

The extreme length of the oasis, from north to south, is more than twelve miles, and its farmsteads are dotted over the area, each standing in the centre of its own land and each at a considerable distance from any other. The larger farms are surrounded by a high wall which is a small fortification, and inside the wall is a substantial house made of sun-dried bricks and excellent timber. All the farms are spacious and built to accommodate large numbers of people, for it is customary that all the members of a clan should live together in their generations.

The South Street of Tunhwang led in a vague and desultory fashion to the entrance of a quarter which was as compact and tidy as the remainder of the town was formless and irregular. This was the quarter called Granary Town, and in it were streets, cross-roads and alleys, but no dwelling-houses and no inhabitants. The buildings were of a peculiar character and presented none of the amusing irregularities of the other streets, for they were all built on one pattern.

They were windowless yet did not belong to that style of architecture which presents a blank wall to the street with all its windows opening on to an inner courtyard. The walls were pierced with many openings for ventilation, and each was surmounted by a small latticed turret. The doors were very wide, and where one of them stood open it showed that the interior of the house was one wide space around which were many sliding doors marked on different levels with a Chinese numeral. These were the Municipal Granaries, and behind those sliding doors enormous quantities of grain were stored and the amounts accurately checked.

Grain storage is a vital part of oasis administration, and a wise ruler, knowing how easily money becomes useless and food alone is of value, will build granaries which seem to be quite out of proportion to the needs of the population. At Tunhwang, wheat may be kept for many years without deterioration, and at Ansi, a town four days distant, the soil is so dry that farmers can, in times of trouble, bury their store of grain in deep pits and dig it up unhurt when peace is restored. In the northern parts of the Gobi, however, grain supplies cannot be preserved even from one year to another. For this reason the price of wheat can never seriously rise in those localities, as each year's supply must be cleared before it becomes useless.

A few miles outside Tunhwang there are the ruins of an old building of magnificent proportions. It holds the remains of three adjoining halls, each measuring one hundred and thirty-nine feet in length and forty-eight and a half feet in width. When Sir Aurel Stein saw the huge enclosures, he was greatly puzzled as to what might have been their use. Only after long search did his excavations result in the discovery of some bamboo slips, one of which bore a date corresponding to 52 B.C. Some of these were granary accounts and gave the clue which solved the mystery of the curious construction of the halls, for they proved that these buildings were the ruins of an ancient, colossal oasis granary.

Another interesting feature of the Tunhwang oasis is the fact that it is divided into as many sections as there are prefectures in the whole of the province of Kansu. Its colonisation brought men from all areas, who were anxious to honour the cities which they represented, by erecting temple buildings. The result is that the traveller wanders through the oasis as through a replica of the whole province of Kansu, stepping from the section called after the town of Chingchow to that called Liangchow, from Kaotai to Pingfan, or from Pingliang to Titao, in the course of an afternoon stroll. Near one of these temples was a very old carved stone figure of a man, which was not an idol but was said to represent a historic personage. By it stood a tablet of which the inscription was engraved in a very ancient form of Syriac script.

II

Life in a Moslem Inn

At Tunhwang we temporarily exchanged tent life for inn life. From half a dozen possible hostelries we chose a *serai* where a wooden sign, in the shape of a teapot, swung at the main entrance. This sign bore the inscription "Pure and True Religion," which indicated to passers-by that it was a Moslem inn and offered lodging more particularly to followers of the prophet.

Chinese travellers avoid any such inn because of the rudeness to which they may be subjected when using it. Even though they abstain from eating pork during their stay, every pot and pan which they possess is considered unclean, and will not be allowed inside the kitchen. This is not conducive to good feeling between host and guest, and may at any time lead to high words and even to blows.

The attitude toward our party was different, because, though we were styled *kaper* (infidel), we were known to keep a "clean" kitchen, which is to say that pork, lard and every produce of the pig was rigidly excluded from our menu. We were "infidels of the book," for the Bible and not the Koran was our guide, but we were not "infidels of the pig," which was an insult reserved for eaters of unclean food. The closest watch was kept upon us as we journeyed, and any lapse or laxity would have been reported to every mosque on our route, so that "pure religion" inns would have been closed to us. Moslems acknowledged that we were as free from idolatry as themselves, but openly stigmatised us as blasphemers, for we called the prophet Jesus "Son of God," and the innkeeper turned aside to spit whenever he heard the word.

Like nine out of every ten of his co-religionists, his name was Ma in deference to the first syllable of Mahommed's name. Morning and evening he knelt in his own room, in response to the distant call to prayer, and each midday he walked with grave dignity to the mosque, where he met other prosperous merchants like himself. Stroking their straggling beards they greeted each other in solemn tones, then entered, in strict precedence, by order of wealth.

In his house, the outer court was given up to guests, but the inner one, which led out of it, was his own home, and a rather short cotton *portière*, which hung at the door, warned visitors that this entrance led to women's quarters and was forbidden to men.

Our host was of medium height and wore a thin beard. On his head was a cap made of black silk and shaped like a pork pie. His stocky figure was clothed in a black overcoat folded across the front. He was a Tungan, that is to say, a China-born Moslem. He hailed from Hochow in South Kansu, and when talking with his own people he dropped into a dialect incomprehensible to the Chinese around. The name of Allah rang through the courtyard all day long, spoken sometimes in anger, sometimes in imprecation, and when Mr. Ma drove a bargain he always called on Allah as witness to the word of the righteous and in vindication of his own cause.

Mr. Ma was an obliging man and appreciative of our constant efforts to uphold a certain standard of cleanliness in difficult circumstances. Like other Tungan landlords to whose houses we had the *entrée*, he left us with a sense that he was very wealthy and that his apparent trade of innkeeping was simply a cover for another and more lucrative business. His own quarters were well furnished. The *kangs* were spread and stacked with wadded silken quilts and red satin pillows. The side-table was resplendent with handsome crimson teapots and gay bowls, and an elegant brass ewer, with a thin curved spout, stood near the

73

cooking-stove. The water it held was always tepid and served for purification purposes such as hand-washing before meals. To wash in running water was part of Mr. Ma's creed. It would have been a contamination for him to dip his hands in a wash-hand basin. It was too far to go down to the river for his ablutions, but water which flowed from the spout of a pot could not technically be called stagnant, and, therefore, ritual requirements were satisfied.

Life behind the curtain was far from ideal. At the age of forty Ma's wife was a creature for whom he had no longer any use, and she only held her place of authority by fierce determination and tenacity. Her eldest child was a boy of eighteen with a wife of the same age and an infant one year old. This young woman waited on her mother-in-law and was obliged to submit to her every whim, but there were other and younger women in the *ménage*, whose status was never defined. Their number steadily increased, and the last comer was always the favourite. They spoke of each other as sisters, but eyed each other as rivals. The work of the house, the preparation of meals, all the needlework and the grinding of wheat, devolved on them. The person with most power in the whole group at that moment was a girl of sixteen, for she completely swayed the master of the house. She enjoyed her brief hour of power to the full, but knew that any day some other young girl might come to take her place. She was therefore pitifully anxious to bear a son, as this, and this only, would assure her some kind of position when she was no longer the master's favourite.

The lord of the household came and went, issued his orders, ate the meals which were so carefully prepared for him, and gave no account of himself to any one. Several children ran about the courtyard, but, as discreet visitors, we never enquired concerning the various relationships. We moved in and out of that women's court as enigmatic and inexplicable beings who were independent and unattached, celibate yet satisfied, childless yet happy. There was no son to mourn for us when we should die, and no one to secure us continuity of existence through coming generations, yet we were serene and unafraid. All these women watched us and marvelled. To them continuity of life was bound up with that prolongation of existence which a son secured, one who carried on the life which he owed to his mother, and thus, through the successive generations of her descendants, she would live on. In answer to the many questions which they asked me, I spoke quite otherwise. "Life after death is God's gift," I told them, "and does not depend upon a son and his worship at my shrine. I shall never be an orphan spirit seeking shelter, for Christ has secured me immortality and has planned all my future."

We talked often of these things, but it was hard for them to understand what I told them, and they would turn it off with one excuse or another. "She is different from us," they said, "her life is given up to good works and her merit will secure her an entrance to Paradise." Some envied, some pitied, some just stared and made no effort to understand. Others summed it up in these words: "Eastern ways are for the East, Western ways are for the West." But here and there was one who caught a gleam which lifted her for ever above the sordidness of the life to which so strange a fate had bound her.

III

Gobi Carters—"there's ne'er a good one"

When it became known in the bazar [1] that we needed a carter for a trek across Gobi to Turfan, applications poured in and both officials and merchants sent us word concerning men who had once served them and were now out of a job. As employers we had a good name, for we always paid wages on the day they were due, but on the other hand it was often said that our rigid notions concerning the honesty and good conduct of our servants were hard to comply with.

Cart transport is the most practical way of conveying a traveller and his goods over the main trade-routes of Gobi, but unfortunately it necessitates the use of a carter and, as the Chinese proverb has it, "As to carters, there's ne'er a good one." They are always hired through a middle-man, for no one can with impunity ignore the Chinese custom of doing all such business through an intermediary who guarantees the good behaviour of his man. This arrangement also makes it possible for employer and employed to say unpleasant things to each other, without necessitating such direct speech as would cause loss of face and consequent lifelong enmity. The responsibilities of a middle-man are heavy, and one who acts in that capacity takes care to know the man he recommends, otherwise the employer might too often be on his doorstep demanding redress. If, however, the carter is going to take a long journey the situation is easier, for many months will elapse before the caravan returns, and when it does so, the general

---

[1] bazar—a market in the East.

atmosphere of happiness at a safe home-coming will certainly never be marred by reference to past unpleasantness.

The cook, who was our most responsible factotum, appeared in the living-room and announced in a low confidential tone that Carter Li, recommended by Mandarin Pu, wanted to speak about driving the cart to Turfan.

A tall, strongly built man with a long face like a mule was called into the room. His appearance bore the stamp of what is considered stylish in carter circles; he wore a good suit of black cotton with white calico socks, and the woven band which held in his trousers at the ankle was finished off with a smart knotted fringe. A length of black material was wound round his waist as a girdle, and a white kerchief was twisted round his shaved head. His trousers were well made by a good seamstress and fitted snugly round his middle. Experience enabled us to place him unfailingly in his own carter category. This was a self-respecting man, without the carter's too common vices of opium-smoking, gambling or fast living, and there would certainly be a limit to the squeezes he would expect. The beasts would never be neglected in his hands, for he would always place their requirements before the convenience of his master. His referee was reliable and his own home was only a few streets away. On the other hand, he would certainly be disobliging, unadaptable and rude, and the other servants would find him exacting and overbearing. His voice had a rasping sound like a coffee-grinder, and would inevitably shatter the harmony of caravan life, as he used it to assert his own rights or preferences. The thought of that voice rousing us at two a.m. for early starts made us unwilling to engage him, for the misery of zero hour was bad enough without hearing the grumblings of a disagreeable carter. He answered to the name of Li Kao-teh (Li of the High Virtues), but even this failed to attract us.

A few hours later the cook was back with another man whom a friend of his was prepared to personally recommend. This carter was rather short but very strongly built. He wore a suit of blue cotton much the worse for wear, there were patches on his socks and coat, and his shoes were shabby. His trousers were so baggy as to have no relation to the size of his body. He was an easy talker and there was the swing of a first-class walker in his gait. Anyone with knowledge of the breed would know that this man would be popular with fellow-servants, a jovial road companion, and liked by the innkeepers because of his easy-going ways and lavish generosity with his master's goods. His family name was Wang and he was always called by his nickname of Quick

Stepper. He had been everywhere on the desert trade-routes and knew them thoroughly.

The question under consideration was which of the two carters was the least undesirable. The good-tempered, easily pleased man would certainly help himself to a share of everything which he handled, but pay back in extra service. The disagreeable grouch would do his work well but take control of his employer's team, refuse to yield an inch on his rights, and bring an atmosphere of ill-temper into the whole caravan. During this interview we might have been deceived concerning the proverb, "There's ne'er a good one," for the answers given to the questions we asked were so disarming as to give it the lie. Quick Stepper assured us that he quite understood our demand for scrupulous honesty and the rule that opium-smoking and gambling were not allowed. He heartily concurred in the point of view that, the purpose of our journey being to declare the word of righteousness, it would be most inconvenient if our own people did the very things which we condemned. "Smoke opium!" he said. "Why, I do not even know how to smoke tobacco! Gamble?" He turned to the cook: "*You* would know if I gambled." The cook kept a steady eye and said nothing.

As a matter of fact, the two men were being judged not so much by anything they said as by the cut of their clothes. We knew that every man with the snug fit and careful outline of Li was a disagreeable rascal, while every carter with the baggy breeches and loose coat of Wang was a pleasant rogue. The faults of each one, in turn, became so intolerable that the only relief was to engage the two kinds alternatively. Unfortunately for himself, Quick Stepper confided to the cook, at the close of the interview, that he had a small debt to pay off before leaving the town, and must therefore ask for two months' wages in advance. Experience teaches that a servant paid in advance is a perpetual nuisance; he will certainly run into debt at the inns and probably not be allowed to leave until the account has been settled, so this time Li of the High Virtues, later nicknamed Grouch, got the job.

One of the middle-man's necessary concessions to the carter he recommends is that he will call on the new employer the day before the journey should begin, and say that the man's old mother (or some other female relative for whom he is entitled to feel concern) has suddenly fallen ill and is gripped with a mysterious internal pain. It would certainly not be right for him to leave her at this crisis, and he therefore cannot fulfil his engagement. The inexperienced traveller is distressed, as he sees all his plans turned upside down. He probably shows annoy-

ance and agitation, and fetches doses from his medicine-chest for the
sick person. Before long the middle-man will certainly reappear, suggesting that a small rise in wages, if paid in advance, would perhaps
enable the carter so to arrange home affairs that he himself could leave.
The traveller, eager to be off, agrees, the money is given, the carter
pays his outstanding debts, the illness is never mentioned again, and all
start happily, but the carter never loses the advantage he has gained.

The experienced desert hand has learnt to remain unmoved by any
such tales of woe, and merely says, "Very well, we will postpone
departure, and if the old mother is not soon better I must find another
man." This evident understanding of the situation always hastens
recovery far more effectively than any dose of medicine, and probably
within twenty-four hours the caravan is off on its long journey and there
is no further hold-up.

Months later, when the carter returns to his home-town and drives
his team through the city gate, some youngster will certainly spot him and
run to his wife with the report, "Your child's father is back." The
woman scarcely seems to notice what is said and goes on with her work,
then slowly and deliberately prepares the best meal that she knows how
to cook. An hour later, when her husband walks in, she looks up with
the brief greeting, "Back again?" and takes no further notice of him.
He picks up his small child and holds it while neighbours crowd in and
talk, but husband and wife say nothing more to each other.

In relation to their homes, carters are both sensitive and suspicious,
and reports are handed from one to another on the road as to how the
wife is behaving while her husband is away. During the time he spends
at home her duty is to stitch strong shoes and socks ready for use on
his next journey. Carters' footwear is a most important item, because
the man must expect to walk thirty miles each day over sandy, stony
or gritty roads. On leaving home he may face a journey of a thousand
miles outward and the same distance homeward, and a good carter's
wife will see to it that his supply of home-made shoes and socks carries
him through. The shoes have soles half an inch thick made of hand-
woven cotton, stitched through and through with home-made string
which she herself has twisted from strands of hemp, and packed with
fragments of soft rag which she has saved up most carefully. The uppers
are of strong cotton cloth lined with equally good material and interlined with coarse paper, and she uses many clever devices to strengthen
them. There are two strips of leather piping over the toes, and a strongly
stitched patch at the back of the heel. Socks are no less important than

shoes, and are made of homespun white cotton carefully cut and fitted to the foot. No carter likes wearing leather soles or shop-made shoes, and given suitable footgear, his walking powers are such that he can tramp these enormous distances without being footsore.

On that two-thousand-mile walk he has to face both intense heat and bitter cold and must be inured to real hardship of all kinds. If overtaken by blizzard, he will turn his cart to back the wind and, tying his sheepskin coat round him, will crawl under the cart and stay there until the blizzard has abated. At the end of each day's stage he can neither rest nor eat until the beasts are stalled, fed and watered. He is responsible for watching the wooden wheels and watering them daily lest they become brittle and break under the strain of bad roads, and he must know how to dose and bleed his beasts if they show the least sign of illness. Any animal with a sore back is a personal disgrace to the carter, and he must carefully examine each one every day to see that the saddle is not pressing unduly in any place. It will often take him hours to pad and repad the felt lining of the wooden saddle so as to secure even pressure everywhere. These Gobi transport men are a class to themselves. Every traveller realises what he owes to their endurance, yet every traveller concurs in the truth of the saying: "Carters—there's ne'er a good one."

IV

Ansi, where the Great Winds Blow

The nearest town to Tunhwang lies four days' journey to the north-east on the main trade-route connecting China and Turkestan. It is called Ansi, and there is not even a village between the two places, but only isolated inns which offer a meagre shelter at the close of each stage. The track follows the foothills of the South Mountains, and it is necessary to keep to the path, because soggy deposits of salt efflorescence make the waste land impossible for even a camel to cross.

Ansi is a place of real importance, though this would never be guessed from its shabby appearance. It is the southern bridge-head of the high road to Turkestan, and its position at a junction of the great trade-routes gives it significance. Geographers place it at the very centre of Asia, and its status was established during the Tang dynasty (A.D. 618-907), when its name was changed from Yüan Chüan (First Spring) to Ansi (West Protecting Garrison). It then became the base from which the Chinese Governor-General controlled the advance of China's conquering armies in Central Asia.

The high city wall commands an outlook over the roads which are still Ansi's only line of communication with the outer world. One of them leads north-west to Urumchi, capital of Chinese Turkestan (thirty-four stages), another south-west to Lob and Yarkand at the foot of the Himalayas (two months' journey), yet another branches south-east through Suchow to Sian in Central China (forty-five stages), and Ansi's north-east aspect looks toward the desert track to Mongolia, beyond which are Paotow and Kalgan (about three months' journey according to season).

All these main tracks are traceable from the top of the city wall, but established custom has decreed that women shall not go there except on special feast days, though on these days they are not only permitted but expected to climb up the steep embankment and walk on the flat promenade which lies at the top. It is then a social function, and the whole city makes merry. Women wear their best clothes, the little girls are gaily dressed and their hair is spiked with artificial flowers. However, being travellers from a very distant land, exception was made in our favour, and we were welcomed to the city wall when only the sentry guard paced the ramparts. It was a toilsome business to climb the steep gradient where steps alternated with a rough path, but it was the only means of reaching the wide walk on the top of the wall from inside the city. The urchins of Ansi got there by another and more exciting way, for the strong wind which is reputed to blow for three hundred and sixty days of each year in this exposed place has swept the loose sand against the outer wall until it has raised a dune the summit of which is almost level with the crenellated parapet. It is stiff work, even for a wiry oasis boy, to climb the sand-hill, but it has become a sports competition among the street boys to race each other and see who can get to the top first. As soon as we appeared above, the children who were bathing in the irrigation canal below sighted us, the bathing-pool was instantly abandoned, and the hot sand-mound was soon dotted with the sun-tanned bodies of a dozen naked youngsters. Up they toiled, almost knee-deep in loose shifting sand, until one by one they reached the top and began to climb the parapet, with bare toes clinging to the worn bricks.

We wished to walk the whole length of the wall, for we felt that this central point of Asia was the right place from which to look out on its historic trade-routes, and the men of the military guard, delighted to hear of our intention, declared themselves ready to escort us all the way and point out the various items of interest both within and without the town. As for the boys, they were not going to miss any of the fun, and so came along too. We knew that the sentries were leaving their posts, but in those days such a common breach of discipline troubled no one, and we were glad of the company.

Looking down from the wall, the city revealed itself in its full decrepitude. Large bare spaces had become the refuse-dumps of the town, and no single building was in good repair. Many of the houses had crumbled away until one room only remained habitable, where, from among the ruins, a faint haze of smoke, curling up an outside wall, showed the opening of a smouldering *kang* fire. The old temples were falling to bits, and the shabbiness of the flaking whitewashed barrack buildings was indescribable.

There was no regularity and no plan left in the town, except at its very centre where the four streets connecting the city gates met at a large covered well, which all the traffic was forced to negotiate. Here, there was a splash of fresh and vivid colour, for the market stalls were grouped round the sides of this large well, and in hot weather the peasants sprinkled their goods with its cool water.

Near the foot of the wall the land was laid out in melon plantations and the fields looked as though they had been paved, for they were covered with large flat stones so that the hot sun-baked flooring should present a surface on which the luscious Central Asian melon would ripen to perfection. Just beyond were vegetable gardens, with here and there a field of cotton where men in indigo-dyed garments hoed the pale yellow soil. The border of the oasis was defined by a line of green which fringed the irrigation canal, and beyond it was arid land the surface of which quivered with the heat. This was the season when the channels were full of water drawn from the Su-lo River, leaving its bed almost dry. One month earlier the river had been dangerous to ford, but now it was an easy matter to cross it.

Looking out over the south gate we saw a few scattered farms, and beyond them a line of bare volcanic hills sloping down to a seemingly limitless stony plain. The only human beings in sight were a few Turki horsemen riding over a faintly defined track which followed the base of those arid hills. They were travelling toward Tunhwang and were probably bound for South Lake and the Lob Desert track to Khotan.

At the south-east corner we stood for a while, and looking ahead I could distinguish a deep furrow in the side of a bare hill, leading to a high plateau above. Hidden in that furrow there lay, I knew, a precipitous path which, following the dried bed of a water-course, led out to Tsaidam and across the Tibetan highlands to distant Lhasa. Over this road red-shawled lamas came and went on their arduous pilgrimages, some of them prostrating their bodies over the whole length of the rough, stony ground, till the skin was torn from their knees and elbows. Tibetan herdsmen also rode down this canyon at a dangerous pace, to barter goods in Tunhwang or in Ansi, and carry back a precious store of barley and wheat to be converted into *zamba*.[1]

Farther east we saw a deeply rutted cart-track which stretched toward China and its fortress gate. A train of twenty large carts was in sight, though it would be long before they reached the city gate. They were great lumbersome vehicles made of heavy wood clamped with iron and piled high with bulky loads packed in wooden cases and huge canvas bales. Some of the carts were covered with a mat awning, in the shade of which a few passengers sprawled, holding on for safety to the ropes which held the goods in place, for the carts lurched heavily from side to side as the wheels were caught by the ruts and stones of the rough road.

"Those are merchants from Central China going to Hami," said the young soldiers. "They are the men to make money. Everything they bring from Tientsin sells well here, and when they go back they carry wool and skins which fetch a big price down there."

My eye was attracted by a distant crumbling wall enclosing a few ruined buildings which had the appearance of a deserted town.

"What is that place?" I asked.

"That is new Ansi," answered one of the boys proudly. "When the Moslems rebelled in my grandfather's time, they destroyed this old town and killed thousands of people, so a new town was built where you see those ruins. Water was more plentiful there than here, but the *fengshui*[2] was all wrong, so the new town kept on taking fire and at last was burnt to the ground."

"That was unfortunate," I said. "How did the fires start?"

"No one will ever know, but when the *fengshui* is wrong strange things will happen. This time it was fire, but another time it might be flood." I knew that this argument was indisputable, for to these boys *fengshui* was that mysterious influence in which the unseen control

---

[1] *zamba*—flour ground from parched grain.
[2] *fengshui*—wind and water, that which cannot be seen and that which cannot be grasped—the geomantic system of the Chinese.

of each man's life and that of every community is centred. They were convinced that no house, grave or site could safely be selected without scrupulous care to see that the *fengshui* was propitious, and I knew full well that any new town where the *fengshui* was even questioned would certainly be abandoned by its inhabitants.

"Does anyone live there now?" I asked.

"No," the child said emphatically, "there is not one family left, and no one would dare to stay."

From the north wall we looked out in the direction of Mongolia. Along this road camel caravans arrive from Paotow carrying cases of paraffin, bales of sugar, woven materials and small-ware manufactured in Peking. When they go back, they are laden with the produce of Central Asia for distribution to the markets of the world—cotton from Turfan, dried fruits, Turkestan carpets and rough blocks of "water stone" in whose matrix precious jade lies hidden.

By the time we reached the observation tower over the north gate it was the hour for the daily hurricane to blow. We saw the dust suddenly caught up in a whirlwind, and in a moment the air around us was thick with sand and grit. The landscape was blotted out, but we knew that we were looking toward the most dreaded of these various desert regions.

"That yonder is Black Gobi," said one of the soldiers. "Every one fears that place."

A herd of little donkeys was just reaching the city gate below us, driven by three burly, top-booted men from Turkestan. "Donkeys from Tu-lu-fan (Turfan)," shouted one soldier, "now we shall have plenty of dried fruit in the town. Tu-lu-fan is the place for sultanas. They cost nothing where those men come from, but they won't give them away for nothing here."

I faced the whirling sand with an impression of utter devastation and loneliness, and as we were enveloped in a cloud of dust I clutched the parapet for support. As the wind subsided a train of carts loomed through the murky air. They were piled high with tin basins and galvanised pails.

"Russian goods, Russian goods," said the young man excitedly. "The road to Siberia must be open again and the Manas River can be forded. Now all our inns will be full up and we shall have great times in the town."

"This must be a dreadful place on winter nights," I said. "Do you keep guard here right through the coldest weather?"

The boy grinned. "We are supposed to be at the look-out, but no one can climb up to see if we are at our posts, and it would be no good to stand here. We should see nothing in a blizzard, so we take shelter and crouch under the rampart. Nothing happens here all through the winter months, for the wind blows incessantly and it is too cold even for robber bands to come out."

We climbed down the steep slope, followed by urchins, and made our way back to the *serai*, thankful indeed for any kind of shelter from the demoniacal blast, but as I shut the broken door of my room and rolled a stone against it to keep it from blowing open, I shuddered, because I knew that within a short time I too should be out on the desert road, shelterless and compelled to press on in face of heat and cold, wind-storms and blizzards. The Gobi had so lured me on and fascinated me with its strange charm that I had almost forgotten its terrors in exploring the unique beauty of its hidden treasures. Its silence had rested me, and its spaciousness had given a sense of expansion to my spirit, but now it sternly recalled me to a realisation of the severity which also formed a part of its discipline.

The walls of the inn-room were unspeakably filthy. Their rough surface was greasy and fly-blown, and near the *kang* was a little niche made to hold the saucer-lamp into which the innkeeper daily poured a spoonful of linseed oil. From its side a stream of dark, shining oil had dripped slowly down until it reached the earth floor, where it soaked through in a dark patch.

On the walls were many inscriptions written by travellers who, like myself, had used this lodging. Some of them were lines of their own composition, unpolished but the expression of a reaction to some grim experience through which the writer had just passed.

> "The wind blows chill, the stage is long;
> Tho' hungry, yet I have no bread.
> Press on, my horse, while still you're strong,
> And take us both to stall and bed."

> "The track is long and danger-fraught.
> In scorching sands a man is caught,
> In bitter cold and deadly frost,
> Many a weary traveller's lost."

Some were proverbs of desert lore:

> "Jewels and gems they are but stones;
> Barley and beans they strengthen your bones."

A long line of battlemented wall was silhouetted against the morning sky

Two men from the South mountains

A desert landmark

The great façade was pierced with innumerable openings

The caves of the Thousand Buddhas

A decorated cave

The walls were frescoed in rich and harmonious colours

One of the decorated ceilings

We reached the three stupas

A grand field for picking up odds and ends

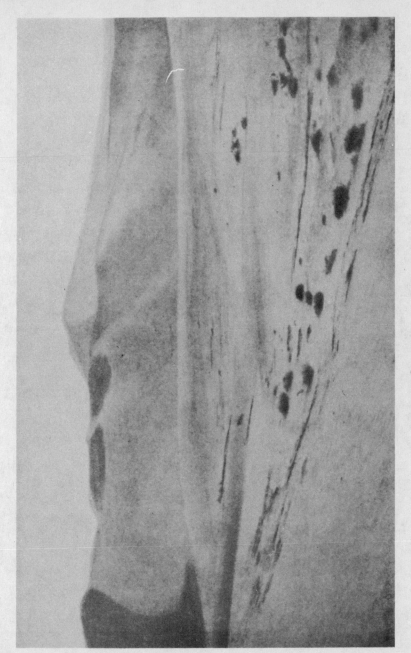

Singing sands

The guardian priest at the Lake of the Crescent Moon

The inn courtyard

Carters—"there's ne'er a good one"

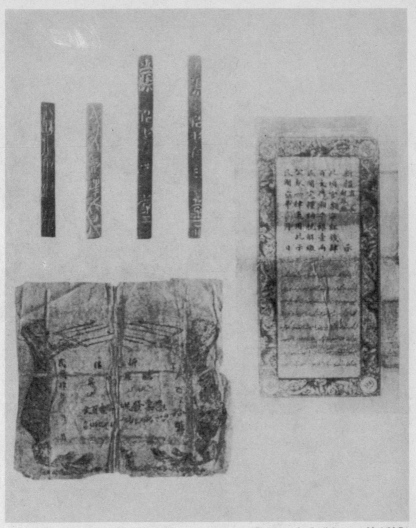

(Photograph by Cecil Curwen, M.A.M.B.)

The currencies of Turkestan

The horns of an ovis poli

Occasionally the quotation was a stanza from classical writings reminiscent of old campaigns and fierce battles with foes beyond the barrier:

> "Hung in the void, the crescent moon,
> Is all that's seen in this wild waste.
> On polished steel of sword and shield,
> The cold dew hangs in icy drops.
> Long must it be ere we return,
> So sigh not, women, left behind,
> Lest you should need to sigh too long."

V

Collecting the Caravan

During the time spent in Ansi we became familiar with the town and with the monotonous routine of its desert-bound people. Every day at a certain hour the wind blew up, whirling sand and powdered stable refuse all over the rooms; every day the wretched inhabitants made their way to market and bought a supply of food, and every day the children of the town went round the streets, basket on arm, collecting horse-dung for the family fire. The only people to require other fuel were the blacksmith, who sent two days' journey for coal-dust to feed the smithy fire, and the baker, who heated his oven with faggots brought from a tamarisk copse two days away in another direction.

The inn-yard was a club for carters and camel-men, and a place of perpetual interest to me. The men were all in the best of humour as they rested and feasted for a few days between the long stretches which allowed for no relaxing of effort. At that time of the year wool was the chief export, and hundreds of camels went eastward to Paotow laden with the huge bales. The camel-men knew all there was to know about that trade, and it was they who showed me how the merchants in the Central Asian markets judged the quality of the wool, not only by the feel and smell of the samples, but through knowing on what pastures the sheep had been fed. No seller's word could be trusted about this, so the buyers would take a handful of the wool, shake the dust from it and know by the feel of that dust if the sheep had grazed on mountain pastures, lowland grass or steppe-land herbage. A real expert could even tell if the sheep had been fed on the north or south slope of the hills.

There was good profit to be made in the wool business, for a bale which only cost four dollars at Ansi would fetch about twenty dollars at Paotow, but the profits of such merchandise only excited the greed of the men who transported it, and by the time they reached the Yellow River market the bales would be most cleverly weighted with the heaviest of the Gobi sand, skilfully introduced between the layers of wool. Camel-drivers, however, were not the only men whose cupidity was roused by the sight of the laden camels, for at regular points on the desert track a customs officer sat in his small tent watching for caravans, on which he would levy the largest sum that he could extort from the *bash*.[1]

Bales of cotton were also carried on camels across Mongolia to the China market, but this line of trade was gradually dwindling. The rule of war-lords first impeded the traffic, and later on a Moslem rebellion in Turkestan made it impossible for merchandise to leave that province. Then Russian buyers established business agencies in the cotton-growing centres, so that when a trade agreement was signed between Urumchi and Russia, most of the raw cotton of Turkestan was diverted to Siberia.

The people of Ansi would have liked us to stay on indefinitely with them, but our quest took us farther, and the hour came when I called in the caravan *bash*.

"Carter Li," I said, "it is time we were off. Make ready for the journey ahead," and I quoted him the proverb which says that no man would send his worst enemy across the Gobi in midwinter or at midsummer.

"Right," he said, "if we leave now it will be better for the beasts. We shall need to carry all we want for ten days, for there is no grain or fodder to be bought all that time."

The corner of the inn-room was soon stacked with foodstuffs. One bag held fifty pounds of flour, another was filled with rice and one with millet. There was a jar of pickled turnip and a wooden box of red pepper mixed with linseed oil. In addition, we were to carry as much crushed peas and sorghum for fodder as the carts would hold. Carter Li came in and out with lists of things which he wanted. We must take medicine for the horses," he said, "for at each stage the water is not only bitter but it is controlled by a chilly principle. The horses will get colic unless they have the greatest care." Carter Li expected me to understand and appreciate this danger to our team, for everyone should know that the great primeval forces are divided into the *Ying* and the *Yang*, the negative and the positive, the dark and the light principles—the

[1] *bash*—Turki word for head: used for the leader of a caravan.

86

dark negative force representing the female, and the light positive force representing the male. To sustain life and health these two must be correctly balanced, and cold water in the desert is too heavily controlled by the chill or shady element.

He asked me for money to buy what was needed, and returned a little later with several packages wrapped in tough grey paper. "This is wormwood," he said. "This is fennel, and here are apricot kernels, rhubarb and ground ginger. I was lucky today and got six ounces of *wutung-lui* (tears of the *wutung* tree)." [1]

"What is that drug?" I asked. I was very familiar with the Chinese *materia medica*, but "tears of the *wutung* tree" was a new drug to me.

He opened the packet and showed me a spongy mass of fungoid growth. "Tears shed by our desert tree the *wutung*," he told me. "The tears congeal to a mass and are broken off and used to dose horses when the chilly water makes them ill. It is hard to get because it is always in great demand, and the price is high."

The next time he appeared it was to demand three thousand cash to pay for a new set of horseshoes and a bag of nails to fix them. Any beast of the team might cast a shoe in the Gobi, and he was too careful a driver to start unprepared for such an emergency. He overhauled the harness, swung a large bottle of linseed oil under the axle, led the beasts to the blacksmith's shop and brought them back strongly shod, then, having seen to all needful for horses and mules, he bothered about little else. As far as he was concerned, we were ready to start.

The carter, however, was not the only person to make preparation, and we also had shopping to do and business arrangements to settle. We must somehow secure sufficient money for the trek, as this was of primary importance to the whole party. It so happened that a local merchant who was shortly travelling home to Hankow was anxious to know if we would take the bulk of his silver dollars and give him a post-dated cheque in exchange. It would be dangerous, he knew, to carry so much money through brigand-infested areas, and he was glad of a chance to transmit it safely to his home, where after three months of travel he would present the cheque and get his money. Because of this unquestioning mutual trust, his special difficulty was met and our own need was supplied.

For so long as we were in China proper the servants were paid in dollars, but after we crossed the Turkestan border, where money values

---

[1] *wutung—Populus diversifolia.* The desert variety is sometimes *kia wutung* or false *wutung.*

were quite different, they were paid in paper taels. The carters, though ignorant of the most elementary arithmetic, always knew to a cash what was due to them, and in which city the exchange from silver to coppers would be most favourable. Each man had a small pigskin cash-box moulded in the shape of a pillow, which he used at night and in which he carried his money, for with his head resting on it he might sleep soundly, knowing that it could not be touched without awakening him.

The number of dollars required for a long journey had to be carefully calculated, allowing a small margin for emergencies, and, apart from silver, there must always be a good supply of copper coins, as innkeepers only allowed a very low rate of exchange on silver, not because the dollar was unprofitable to them, for it was, in fact, the most convenient coin, but because their inveterate greed would not let them lose a chance of grasping a few more coppers if the traveller was in a difficulty.

The money system of the oases was most complicated. The copper coin called by Westerners "cash" was a little smaller than a halfpenny, with a square hole in the centre, and its value fluctuated according to local exchange of silver, but averaged one thousand five hundred cash to the dollar (about one shilling and eightpence). The coins were strung in sections of one hundred and twisted into lengths of a thousand, but this clumsy coinage was being gradually superseded by the ten-cash piece, which was a larger coin with no hole through it. Lump silver was still widely used and was carried in small blocks weighing from ten to twenty ounces or taels. (The value of one tael was approximately two shillings and sixpence.) Local money-shops issued paper notes, some of which represented a value as small as threepence, and in some towns even gamblers' counters made of bamboo or base metal served as currency. In Turkestan, only government-controlled paper taels were in use, and there the quarter-tael note was always called a "puppy dog," because the scroll with which it was ornamented had an outline resembling a Pekinese pup.

A tour of the scanty stalls secured us four boxes of matches, of which each individual stick was so feeble that no one ever attempted to strike it alone, but must use at least three at a time. We also bought one cake of Peking soap and a lump of the Turkestan variety which was made from mutton fat and strong soda. It was a horrible compound, but there was nothing else available with which to wash our clothes. Candles were expensive and poor, but the only kind we rejected with finality was a brand known as "Old Hat." These had a wick which, instead of standing erect, drooped over the edge in a thin winding trail which consumed the wax and left a smouldering line of cotton which really did suggest the flopping brim of a decrepit hat.

The renewal of our wardrobe was an easy matter, for we wore Chinese dress and all we needed was a new pair of ankle-bands to tie in the long cotton trousers, a black scarf to wind round the head, and a pair of cloth shoes. One unlined cotton coat was sufficient for summer wear, and when it turned cold, two such coats skilfully interlined with cotton-wool by an innkeeper's wife made the winter outfit complete. A good sheepskin wrap was a necessity of Gobi travel, for it was needed every night when the cold chill rose over the sand.

Each traveller leaving the *serai* for Black Gobi was warned by the innkeeper of the danger to life of failing to carry sufficient water. "You may miss the way," he would say, "or the beasts may get ill and detain you, and if you carry no water you will be in a bad plight. Many a traveller has lost his life for want of a drink of water."

The tin-smiths of Ansi did a brisk trade in water-bottles, which they made from old paraffin tins. They were finished off with a small tube something like the top of a baby's feeding-bottle. This was to prevent a thirsty man from drinking the water too freely, for by sipping one drop at a time it would go farther. We bought several of these ingenious water-bottles, but the men preferred large gourds scraped free of pulp and seeds and sawn off at the stem. Each member of the caravan had his own provision of the precious drink, and each one was responsible for filling his own gourd and corking it with a dry corn-cob. Turki men always carry a water-gourd and call it a *kabarä*, which suggests a possible origin of the French word "cabaret" for a place of wayside refreshment.

We visited the baker's shop, which was a cramped hovel. The assistant was kept busy kneading dough and cutting it into pieces which he weighed and rolled skilfully into a flat cake, while the master himself presided at the fire of glowing wood-ash over which was slung a cast-iron oven suspended by three chains. By means of a clever device he lifted the heavy cover, laid the dough on the hot-plate, then closed the lid and lowered the oven to the embers. In a few minutes the loaf was ready to be turned, and almost immediately after it came out fragrant, brown and steaming hot. We needed twelve such cakes to be brought round by noon the next day. "Listen to me," the baker said, "if I knead a little oil into the dough it will last fresh for several days, and if I sprinkle fennel seed on the top it will be fragrant and delicious when you eat it with the bitter water. The price will be a little more, but you will be so comforted when you eat it, that you will forget the expense."

The general dealer supplied us with a substantial slab of brick tea, a luxury allowed to the men only when travelling. Provision had to be made for the thirst of long desert stages, which is a craving beyond any thirst known at other times, for it invades the whole body. The last purchase was a basketful of cucumbers which would give a relish to the first few meals, but after that there would be no more green stuff for many a day, unless we should find a crevice among the rocks where wild chives grew.

The matter which took more thought than food or clothing was our supply of Scriptures, for without them evangelistic work would be hampered, and we needed books in the Chinese, Turki, Arabic, Mongolian, Tibetan, Qazaq, Russian and English languages. Wayside encounters were so diverse and so incalculable that we might have to produce Gospels in any of those languages at any moment. Apart from a solid layer of books in the well of the cart, we needed carefully assorted parcels where we could easily get at them. Gobi carters have invented an outside framework attached to the sides of the cart, which provides a flat board on which parcels are laid and secured with a string net. Anything placed in these "ears," as they are called, can be found at once by day or by night.

Long before we reached Ansi the business offices of the Bible Societies in Shanghai, Tientsin and Hankow were posting large consignments to the principal oasis towns, to be held until we claimed them. This involved much forethought, but throughout all our long treks we were always able to produce a copy of the Scriptures in any Central Asian language when it was required.

Packing caravan carts is a work which combines art and diplomacy. The carter exclusively watches the interests of the animals, which he always calls "my beasts" though they are the property of his employer, but the traveller's personal servant, who shares the job of packing, is bound to consider his master's comfort, and side with him against the carter whenever there is a clash of opinions. Thus, packing the cart is the crucial test of the strength of conflicting purposes.

The job of carter's assistant is held by a boy who hopes to learn the trade of caravan *bash*. His is a split loyalty, for his first master is the head carter, but the personal servant, who claims his help in the food department, must be conciliated, and finally the employer, who pays the wages, will certainly dismiss him if he fails to give him satis-faction. Trying to serve so many masters makes his position precarious, and he never stays long in one caravan.

The carter commands his man to balance the weight so as to spare the team, and in order to do this he places large bags of grain in such a way as to barricade the entrance to the cart and encroach on the traveller's sitting-space, as well as completely block his view. The employer protests, and his own servant is bound to take his part, which often leads to high words between the men, but a compromise is generally reached before the dispute has become too serious.

It is of the greatest importance to secure a properly arranged cargo from the start, for once the place has been fixed for grain, food, kitchen utensils, bedding and books, the carter will probably refuse to make any change, and each bundle must go into that same place to the end of the long trek. High winds, curious crowds and nomad stragglers will play havoc with anything which is not strongly roped or padlocked to the cart, and when all is secure it is out of the question to expect any rearrangement until the end of the stage.

In one matter only does the Western traveller insist on having his own way, and here even his personal servant fails to fathom his reason. It is the matter of where the carter's heavy sheepskin coat may be placed. It is the man's travel wrap and sole bedding, and must there-fore be kept close at hand, but for some reason known only to the Westerner, that sheepskin must never be packed where it would touch his own bedding. The carter is always mystified by this unreasonable whim, but the traveller has major reasons for his inexplicable conduct, and in spite of all his care some little detestable creature will almost certainly straddle over to his own covering and torment him the more cruelly because of its cold reception.

At midsummer the travel day begins three hours before sunset, when a call is given and instantly everyone is alert with preparations for the start. Each member of the party has his own appointed work and his individual responsibility. The caravan *bash* gives the word. "Feed the animals," he calls to his assistant, "and give them full measure of grain. There is a hard pull tonight which will take all their strength."

A little later the rhythmic crunch of the creatures' jaws is heard. The grain is dried field peas, coarsely crushed. Were the mules to be fed with unmilled peas, their keen hunger would make them eat too quickly and swallow the feed whole. Uncrushed peas are good enough for easy days in the stable, but of no use to a beast on Gobi stages.

The cook is equally master of the commissariat. No one but himself touches the stores, and he is responsible for seeing that no member of the caravan goes hungry, and that the provisions last out to the end of the trek. While the beasts feed he is cooking, and, for the sake of the good temper and consequent peace of the caravan, he cooks as well as he can. Once a day he will provide the whole party with the popular meal of dough-strings, which he makes by kneading flour and water into a stiff dough. One piece of the lump is cut off to make fine strings for his master, but he knows that the men will grumble if he offers them food with too little substance in it. Finely cut and well-boiled food is for those who sit in the cart, but the man who must walk thirty miles likes his macaroni coarse and rather undercooked, for in this way it takes longer to digest and is more satisfying. For as many stages as possible the employer is served with a taste of fresh vegetable, but when this fails a saucer of pickled turnip is put before him. Carters scorn such flimsy dainties, but delight in a flavouring of garlic, pounded and mixed with linseed oil. Chopped chillies are appreciated by everyone.

As soon as the master's meal is off his hands, the cook lifts the great brass cooking-pot from the trivet which held it over the flame, and shouts the welcome news *"Fan bien-i"* (Food is ready). He has prepared a generous allowance—four large bowls of cooked dough-strings to each one, and the scrapings to the hungriest. If desert rations are poor it is the more necessary to handle them skilfully, and no careless or extravagant cook is tolerated in a caravan. For the next twenty minutes, to the noise of crunching mules is added the sound of sucks and swallows from the feeding men, and no word is spoken until the iron ladle has scraped the bottom of an empty pot.

At last the harness is spread out on the ground in front of each cart, each collar is placed on its own beast's neck and each is backed into the harness and hitched to its own place in the team, which is made up of mules and horses. One animal is firmly held between the shafts, one driven tandem in the traces, and the two remaining beasts harnessed loosely on either side with ropes which attach them to the axle. Handling such a team is a complicated business, and only a professional carter can cope with it.

He uses no reins and drives mostly by word of command, enforced on occasion by a flick from the long whip. Disobedience brings bloodcurdling threats, with swift and heavy punishment from the butt of the whip. If all else fails, the carter will take his mule by the bridle, compel it to look him in the eye, point his finger at it, and describe in lurid language the meat meal which he hopes to enjoy that night—nothing less than mule-flesh dumplings. The mule is a clever beast and knows when it has gone as far as it dare. There will be no more trouble that day, and the carter will have to be content with a meatless supper.

Never until all is ready for the start will the innkeeper produce his bill. He charges three-halfpence or twopence a night per head, for lodging, light and attendance. Stabling is free, for each beast pays for itself by leaving behind a mound of valuable manure which, when sun-dried, is the innkeeper's store of fuel, but a small sum is charged for the parking-space of each cart. In cold weather, if the traveller has allowed himself the luxury of an iron brazier fed with dried desert scrub, the account will run to an extra twopence for firing. The Westerner is considered exorbitant in his demands for water, and the innkeeper's "odd-and-ender" may well have carried three kettles of hot water each day from the kitchen to his room. Why any guest should demand a kettle of water on going to bed and another on rising in the morning remains an unsolved mystery, for no one could possibly want to wash both night and morning, therefore it is only reasonable to demand extra "water money" from those who indulge such a troublesome fad, but the argument always ends pleasantly, and the "odd-and-ender" goes off grinning, for a substantial share of such tips is his recognised perquisite.

THE PLACE CALLED DESERT

I

What the Desert can Supply

To the stay-at-home a map remains merely the thing it was to him in his schooldays, a representation on paper of a section of the earth's surface, but to the man who has travelled, every map assumes a character of romance, and to anyone who has covered the land which it depicts it ceases to be merely a map and all its markings take on a vital significance. The technical lines by which mountains, lakes, rivers or roads are indicated, become pictures which reveal the whole life of that land: on the banks of a great river the tents of nomad colonies spring up; on the island in the lake, which to another is merely a black dot in a patch of blue, there stands out some tall lamasery round which red-shawled lamas pursue their strange activities. The little square which indicates a town becomes a battlemented city through whose massive gates a stream of strange people move in and out, intent on their unknown day's employ, and the stippled surface marked off as desert comes to life and stretches out in boundless dunes among which long caravans move with serpentine flexibility.

Across the map of Central Asia the names of two great deserts are written. One is called Gobi and the other Lob, and the enormous space of nearly six million square miles which they represent never touches a seacoast, and thereby presents a physical phenomenon without parallel on the face of the earth. The spot of the globe which is farthest removed from any sea or ocean is located within its northern portion, and this remoteness from any seaboard, combined with certain characteristics of the land, reduces the amount of rainfall to a minimum. Although this desert area is not without rivers and lakes, these present one peculiarity in that they have no outlet to the sea, so that water-courses which rush down from melting snow-fields in the mountain heights are gradually caught in sand and forced to drain off into salt marshes where they disappear and are seen no more. The arid conditions induce extremes of heat and cold, and the summer temperature may be 115° Fahr. in the shade, while in the same locality the winter recordings will be as low as 20° below zero Fahr. Such varieties of temperature produce fierce winds which sweep across the desert with terrible force, blotting out the sun in a dense sand-cloud and carrying huge quantities of fine sand from one locality to another.

Climatic conditions of such extreme sterility have resulted in a very sparse population, and there are vast areas which can sustain no human life at all, and in which the traveller's track leading from one water-stage to another marks the only line on which man can exist. Throughout the central portion of Asia the average population is said not to exceed one inhabitant to the square mile. Moreover, this aridity is not stationary but increases steadily, and in the course of even a few years the decrease in water-supply is perceptible, and the inhabitants of a very fertile oasis may see the water-level in their wells decline, their ponds drain away, and a whole line of arable land become useless for cultivation. As years go by the effects of evaporation, the increasing depth of saline deposit in the marshes, and the slow choking of lake and river-beds with drifting sand and accumulations of desiccated matter, cause a ceaseless encroachment of desert conditions.

Side by side with vast expanses blighted by desiccation are wide areas covered with stones varying in size from those which form the dark smooth surface of Black Gobi to loose coarse grit or the rounded pebbles of Piedmont gravel. Other parts lie buried under salty clay, or break out into saline efflorescence, the spongy, treacherous surface of which affords no means of livelihood even to the least exacting forms of animal life. All this combines to make of Gobi and Lob the most desolate wilderness that the earth can show.

The only animals found in such regions are those which, either by reason of their strength or their fleetness, are able to cover wide distances in search of food. Among these are wild camels, wild asses, antelopes, gazelles and wolves. The most striking animal of the desert, however, is the wild sheep, called by the Turki *argali*, and known to the West as the *Ovis poli*. It is a beautiful creature, remarkable for the size of its horns, which often measure forty-five to fifty inches in length and fifteen to eighteen inches in circumference at the base and weigh thirty to forty pounds. It covers long distances with incredible speed, and leaps from crag to crag almost with the lightness of a winged being. Wolves, which are very numerous in the Gobi, devastate the herds of wild sheep, and though the *argali* itself is not very often seen, the horns are found in great numbers, scattered on the desert floor, wherever the lovely creature has been torn down and devoured.

Bird life is scarce, but everywhere the approach to water is heralded by the water-wagtail, and there is a small crested, sand-coloured bird which is found at every oasis. The tern seems as much at home in the bird sanctuary of Gobi sands as on the sand-banks of the Norfolk coast. When breeding season comes near it vanishes toward the Arctic regions, following the course of the great Siberian rivers, but a few months later it is back again, skimming the dunes with its rapid, wide-winged flight. In certain low, bare, grey, wrinkled, volcanic hills huge vultures make a home, spying from afar the tired camel which will inevitably drop out of the caravan line and sink by the track not to rise again, or the overladen mule or donkey which is losing strength in the howling blizzard and will soon be frozen to death.

Far overhead Golden Eagles and buzzards outline wide curves in the clear sky, and below them the sparrow-hawk hovers, ready to swoop on any small rodent which has ventured into the open. Among the salt marshes grey herons feed on lizards, and sometimes, where a quiet oasis has a few trees, the branches will be covered with the angular forms of these birds.

There is a yellow burnished snake which lies in the hollow of the sand-ruts. Carters and camel-men fear it greatly, and tell of horses and camels which have died from its bite. They beat the snake to death with their whips or staves, but the impudent little desert lizard is everyone's friend. It lies basking in the sun, but at the approach of man it raises its body from the ground and scuttles away on outstretched legs. Musical tones, such as whistling or singing, will arrest its flight instantly and hold it attentive for as long as the sound continues. In yellow sand its coat is yellow, in grey grit it is dull grey, when the stones on which it lies are shiny black the lizard also is black, and on variegated ground it develops a beautiful protective coat of many colours. Occasionally a much larger lizard is sighted in the sand, but it is so rare that even the naturalists who report its existence have seldom seen it. In many years of Gobi travel I only saw it once. Its bite is commonly believed to be fatal to man or beast, and the Chinese members of the caravan were terrified when it appeared, and chased it with sticks or whips, but it eluded them, taking shelter under a ledge of rock from which they could not dislodge it.

The flat expanse of Gobi is sometimes broken by a declivity where some softer substance has worn away, leaving an upstanding cliff with a road running far below it. From year to year the road is more deeply worn and the cliff becomes higher, until carts pass through a gully and have to pull up to the flat surface on the farther side. These cliffs offer splendid shelter to wild pigeons, which live and rear their young in the deep wind-eroded hollows.

Below the surface of the sand, which is sometimes burning hot and sometimes deadly cold, is a more temperate zone to which all manner of small creatures withdraw and take shelter both from heat and cold. Little hopping and crawling things can be disturbed from their slumber by stirring the ground deeply with a stick. The most fascinating of these hiders is the jerboa, the jumping desert rat, with legs like a miniature kangaroo, a long muscular tail ending in a tuft, and wide-spreading ears which are as fine as an autumn leaf. After sunset the little creature comes out of its hole and will travel for miles with a caravan, leaping from side to side of the track with long agile bounds which easily keep it safely out of reach.

Many aspects of these desert regions are terrifying in their loneliness, but there are certain stretches which surpass all others in power to horrify. One of these is called by the desert dweller the Valley of Demons. It is a stony and sandy gully between forbidding cliffs, and is a short-cut from Turfan to Hami. The fruit-carriers who hurry their wares from the Turfan vineyards to the Hami market take this way, but never without fear. They are hardy travellers, but they will delay neither to eat nor to sleep in the fearful Valley of Demons.

Another place of terror is much farther north, where a short crescent-shaped line of hills rises suddenly on the plain. From the crest of those hills the blizzard crashes with a violence unknown elsewhere. Here many travellers have met death when the dreaded fan-shaped blizzard cloud spreads from behind the summit, and the sudden violence of the wind robs man and beast of any sense of direction, while the perishing cold grips its victims in a deadly embrace.

There is a third area of peculiar terror located in the midst of the Lob Desert, where the site of the ancient Town of the Dragon is located. Old Chinese records describe the region: "For one thousand *li* it is entirely formed of salt, but of salt in a hard and solid state. Here there are mists which rise and clouds which float, and but rarely do the stars and the sun appear. Little is found there of living animals, but there are plenty of demons and strange beings."

All this drought, sterility, climatic hardship, blizzard and hurricane, combine to produce extreme difficulties in the matter of communications. No river is navigable, no railway system is available, and motor traffic, which would be the only remaining solution of rapid land transit, can only be sustained on certain defined routes, and that by dint of very effective organisation. Pioneer expeditions which crossed the desert in motor lorries were obliged to make frequent use of the camel caravan in order to convey necessary dumps of petrol, oil and provisions for passengers. Fuel consumption has to be reckoned at the rate of about four miles to the gallon, and the evaporation of spirit is very rapid. The only reliable means of communication in these sterile lands is, as it has been for centuries, by means of the mule cart, the camel caravan, horseback or pedestrianism, all of which enable the traveller to cover in one day the thirty miles which is the usual distance from one water-hole to another.

In these wildernesses man has not needed to develop his powers of adaptation to changing conditions, for his manner of life has remained stationary through the centuries. Research and excavation show the present-day oasis dweller to be curiously akin to his forefathers, and, in spite of encroaching desiccation, the oases of ancient days seem generally to have been neither larger nor smaller nor more frequent than they are now; in fact, the conditions of life and the means of transport in past times were equivalent to what they still are. The sands have shifted, some wells have been choked and villages have fallen into ruins and disappeared, but other springs have been cleared and the few mud houses which form an oasis hamlet, when they crumble to dust, are replaced by others indistinguishable from them. Successive hamlets have arisen on the same sandy soil to house the traveller today as they housed Marco Polo, Hsüan Tsang, Fah Hsien and, long before them, innumerable generations of wayfarers.

Just as the Central Asian deserts form the largest wilderness area on the face of the globe, so also they are the most varied in character, for they are traversed by ranges crowned with perpetual snows, by barren volcanic hills, and are dotted over with jagged rocks of every shape, size and colour. Their flooring mainly consists of wide expanses of sand or stone-littered plains, but a wealth of detailed variety hides itself under a superficial guise of monotony, and to the close observer each day's march has a definite stamp of individuality. By reason of their vivid and varied colourings these stones are one of Gobi's features of beauty, and sometimes the narrow, faint path passes through a litter of small multi-coloured pebbles, which are rose-pink, pistachio-green, tender peach, lilac, white, sealing-wax-red and black burnished by sand, sun and wind as though black-leaded, the whole, mixed with a quantity of orange-tinted cornelian, forming a matchless mosaic. One of the loveliest rock tints is a true rust, warm and glowing; and there are high jagged peaks of a green shade, so soft that from a distance they seem to be overgrown with lichen, though, actually, there is not the slightest trace of vegetation on them. Other hills are cone-shaped and covered with chips of white porphyry, as though a miraculous snow-storm had left them lightly sprinkled on a midsummer day. Under the bright blue sky and on a variegated flooring, these strange formations give the impression of a real rock garden, that is a landscape garden entirely made of rock.

Though the desert man cares little for all this beauty, and one of his favourite sayings is, "Beauty does not feed a man," yet he allows nothing to be wasted that can be of practical value to him, and the extreme poverty of his resources makes him clever in adapting each product to every possible use. The sturdy desert grass called by the Chinese *gi-gi-tsao* counts as one of his most valuable harvests and is of use to him in endless ways. When still young and tender, if chopped with a big fodder-knife, its green shoots are suitable for horse fodder, but the plant grows quickly and before long its stalks are so hard that even camels pass it by. When it reaches its full height of seven or eight feet it is cut, garnered, and serves many purposes.

In farms which have to maintain the strongest resistance against natural encroachment, the ridge of the dune is cleverly supported by loosely knotted desert grass, and this net-like barrier is most effective in holding back the wind-lashed sand-waves. During the winter months the grass is woven into mats which cover the mud bed, and are also used to line the mud roof of the oasis shack. The same mat, woven in another shape, forms the chassis of the village cart, and also makes its awning. A very long mat forms a circular bin which holds the winter store of grain and fodder. The winnowing-fan used on the threshing-floor for tossing the grain is also made from it, and in the kitchen it is used as a sieve for sifting particles of mud from the wheat. Small children, collecting every scrap of animal manure in and around the oasis for fuel, use a basket plaited from this *gi-gi-tsao*, and the broom with which the innkeeper stirs the dust in his guest-rooms consists of a bunch of the grass, tied round a stick. The carter, on desert stages, fashions from it a makeshift curry-comb to groom his mules, and the only rope or string which the desert provides is grass twisted either coarsely or finely. The planks of the bridge which the farmer and his sons throw across the irrigation canal are held in place by strands of the same grass, and the bridles and halters of horses and bullocks are made from it.

Inside the home the woman at her hand-loom uses a weaver's comb and reed made from the grass, and she also plaits from it a ladle with which to lift dough-strings from the boiling water. The iron cooking-pot is scrubbed clean with a scouring brush of the stiffest stalks firmly tied together, and carefully selected stems, cut to exact length, are used as chopsticks. Over the kitchen stove hangs a grass hold-all in which the woman keeps her primitive cooking accessories, and by stripping off the outer sheath and boiling the pith, a wick for the vegetable-oil lamp is supplied.

During summer heat a curtain made of desert grass, held in place by twisted thread, hangs in the door-frame and keeps out the flies but lets in the air, and the desert nomads make a most charming dado for their tents from the stalks decorated in intricate geometrical patterns with home-dyed and hand-twisted wool. It is also used to weave the hurdles which enclose the lamb, kid and baby-camel nurseries, and serve as camouflage for the encampments.

This same grass is used by the desert child to make his playthings; from it he learns to plait the most entrancing little toys, necklets and bracelets. When the cicada begins to sound its queer tearing call in the great heat, every child cuts the grass to make a tiny cage to hold one of the fascinating tree-hoppers, for in the Gobi the caged cicada is comparable to the caged canary of a Western nursery. The Gobi baby's rattle, too, is a hollow ball of twisted grass enclosing a large bead.

In cases where the dwarf iris is pulped and made into paper, the sieve on which the pulp is drained is made of desert grass, and it is from this sieve that each sheet of paper is lifted to the whitewashed wall on which it is sun-dried. Were it not for the abundant growth of *gi-gi-tsao* on desert steppe-lands the standard of comfort in an oasis home would be much lower than it is now.

When archaeologists examine the walls of very ancient buildings left standing in the Gobi, they find them to be made of alternate layers of clay and fascines. These fascines are composed of vegetable growth which may be either tamarisk, twigs of desert poplar or bundles of desert grass. The bunches of grass cut twenty centuries ago still serve to hold the clay in place and are more lasting than any stronger material could have been.

Another valuable desert product is the excellent charcoal which is burnt from the thickest stems of saksaul (*Anabasis ammodendron*). In large oasis towns, where fuel is very scarce, this charcoal is eagerly bought by wealthy Chinese, who burn it in wide shallow brass basins and seem indifferent to the unpleasant fumes.

From a monetary point of view liquorice (*Glycyrrhiza glabra*) is the most profitable of the desert's wild harvests. The long, flexible and shallow-running rhizome is dug up, sun-dried, cut in sections, and stored on the mud roofs until a camel caravan transports it to Paotow, from whence it is distributed to all parts of the world.

There are many other desert plants of medicinal value, including rhubarb and *ma-hwang* (*Ephedra sinica*). The value of this latter plant has been recognised by Chinese doctors since very ancient times. Sir Aurel Stein, in his excavations among burial sites in the Desert of Lob, found small packets of twigs inserted between the folds of coarse woollen shrouds which on examination were found to be twigs of the *ma-hwang*. In recent years scientific research has rediscovered its active principle ephedrine, which today is so widely used by Western physicians in the treatment of asthma and similar diseases that the supply is not equal to the demand. The Turkis make it the basis of a compound called *naz*, by mixing it with tobacco and lime and pounding it in a mortar. This they chew with the most evident enjoyment.

In oasis towns the walls of Chinese medicine-shops are always decorated with magnificent stag-antlers, and the animal which supplies them often pastures on Gobi herbage. The stag is the accepted symbol of longevity, and the powdered antler is considered a potent drug.

The desert dweller is dependent on caravan transport for his food. Grain is brought to him from distant places, and he learns to do without fruit or vegetable—unless he can beg something from a passing traveller. The desert, however, supplies many accessories to food if he will but search for them. There are swamps which at one time of the year fill up to their highest level with salt water, and at another time are almost dry. There is always a layer of white crystalline salt on the border of the lake which is scraped up and used for cooking. Although salt is a government monopoly, no one can prevent the desert man from filling his bowl and carrying away what he will of the precious commodity, tax free.

Wild chives spring up in furrows, or in fissures between rocks, and have a most delicate and pleasant flavour. The little shoots grow three inches high, fine as blades of grass, and touched with a soft bloom. Carters always know the places where they grow, and are on the look-out for the faint shade of green showing between stones. As soon as they see it they shout "*Ye tsiu-tsai*" (wild chives), and in a moment the caravan is at a standstill and every member is on foot searching for the delicacy, and that evening there is anticipation round the camp cooking-pot of something fresh to give a flavour to the tasteless dough-strings. In a few places the wild carrot is found; its three-inch-long root is of the palest yellow and has the carrot's distinctive flavour. There is also a little green plant known as *ku-ku-tsai* (bitter herb) which, for a short time each early summer, throws out a tender shoot, and children roam about with baskets on their arms hunting for it; when fried or braised it has a pleasant, bitter taste, and a spoonful laid in the centre of each person's bowl of food is reckoned a delicacy.

Sometimes the traveller is offered a meal of scraped *so-yang*, locally always called *so-yen*, meaning "Locked Eyes," and probably so called because of its value as an ophthalmic drug. The plant, which is a *Balanophora*, pushes up through the sand a thick head like a spotted red fungus, and a plantation of *so-yen* looks like a row of painted ninepins. It has a wicked, poisonous appearance, and it must have been a brave oasis dweller who first ventured to taste it. The stem is white and corky, with a texture something like an old turnip, and must be cut low down where it is thick, and then finely shredded. This scraped substance is then rolled in flour, steamed, and flavoured with vinegar and red pepper. We were once asked to share the meal of an isolated family whose only water-supply oozed through the sand and collected at the bottom of a deep pit. For grain they were reduced to a ration of bran, but by mixing this with scraped *so-yen* and steaming it carefully over a fire fed with tamarisk branches the desert woman made a palatable meal, which she generously shared with us. We in our turn taught her how to thank God for daily food.

There is one sand product which finds a place on the Mandarin's table. It is known as "hair vegetable." (*Alga-Nostoc commune var.*) Its appearance is definitely against it, and when the traveller picks up in the loose sand what looks like a handful of black human hair, he would never suspect that it was a pleasant food. A large quantity pressed together looks exactly like a black wig, but soaked, parboiled and flavoured with a little vinegar, it becomes a slightly salted, aromatic and very delicate pickle.

Near the hills, villagers dig up a root which is small, insignificant and dark brown in colour. They call it *chüeh-dẓ*. Each nodule is striated, and when dry the rootlets break into pieces about the size of small beans. Steamed with rice, and sprinkled with sugar, it has a sweet and nutty flavour. Asparagus, known as Dragon-beard, grows to the very verge of arid desert-land. Its foliage is greatly admired, but it is not used for food, and no one except ourselves picked the shoots and ate them.

The plant known as camel-thorn (*Alhagi camelorum*) is the commonest growth of the desert. It bears a pinkish flower and has a soft thorn which hardens as time goes on. In winter the oasis men cut it down and stack it near their shacks for fuel. They burn it in the hollow space under the mud bed, where it blazes and leaves a layer of hot ashes on which horse-dung can be thrown to supply a steady, glowing fire which will last for hours. The tips of this thorn exude a sugary substance which coagulates into a bead, and in the hottest parts of the Gobi the exudation is much greater than in cooler places; it is gathered both for the fragrance of its honey-like taste, and also for its medicinal value. The Central Asian attributes to it the same qualities that the Westerner recognises in glucose, and in remote oases where sugar is almost unobtainable it meets a great need.

The plant *Artemisia annua*, a variety of mugwort, is used to keep away mosquitoes and sand-flies. Its twigs are picked, sun-dried and twisted into ropes which are festooned across the doorway. At sunset the mosquitoes swarm from the salt marshes and the little ponds which the oasis dweller has dug for watering his beasts. They are an intolerable pest, but when the rope is set alight it smoulders for hours, emitting a pungent smoke-screen which keeps the mosquitoes at bay until midnight, when the cold of the Gobi night brings their brief span of life to an end. On the fifth day of the fifth moon a bunch of *artemisia* is still nailed to the door of each house, in commemoration of the order issued by a Chinese general of ancient times who commanded his troops to spare every house which showed this branch of herbage.

A substitute for tea is provided by a plant with small inverted leaves which, curling round each other, form little leafy nuts. When infused in boiling water they provide a refreshing drink, but in different localities various other leaves, especially the small leaf of a stunted willow, are used to make *tisane*.

One of the most valuable desert products is a parasitical growth which is found on the trunk of the desert *wutung* tree (*Populus diversifolia*). Broken off in large hunks it is easily powdered, and, mixed with several other ingredients, is a specific against the dangerous colic to which horses are subject when they drink the desert bitter water. These "*wutung* tears," as they are called, are the veterinary surgeon's most valued drug on desert marches, and are a speciality of the Etzingol area. The hollow trunk of this tree is frequently used as a channel for carrying irrigation water across sand, a length of it fixed on trestles is a manger for feeding cattle, and the thickest part of the trunk, standing upright, serves as a good flour-bin. With its sap Mongolian women make their hair stiff, glossy and easy to dress, and the ash of this same *wutung* wood is used by caravan cooks to raise dough in making bread.

A much stronger form of soda is obtained by baking in a kiln a succulent plant, called by the Chinese *chien-tsao* (glass-wort, *Salicornia herbacia*), until it hardens into semi-transparent blocks, and from this soda, boiled down with mutton fat, a rough, coarse soap is made.

There is even provision in the desert for dyeing cloth. One plant bears a black, shiny berry which the oasis women use in the most primitive way: they collect the berries, crush them and smear the juice over the material. The result is a rather streaky but quite effective black dye, and there are many other plants of which, in some cases the root, and in others the leaf, are used for the same purpose.

Most curious of all is the plant called *sha-mi* (sand millet, *Agrio-phyllum gobicum*). It is the only grain which is indigenous to the Gobi, and it has been known to save the life of a traveller who missed his way and was left without food. The plant grows about two feet high and is one mass of prickles. Hidden among them are small seed-pods, but the plant is far too prickly to be handled, so desert harvesters lay a cloth on the sand round the stem and beat it with rods until the seed drops out. The grain is a small flat disc and requires no further process before being made into tasty porridge; when ground to flour it can be kneaded into a thin cake and cooked on a girdle.

Wherever the sand-particles are bound together with a little soil, there is one plant which thrives and even grows abundantly. It is about two feet high, has a light feathery leaf, and both foliage and flower have the typical pale shade of desert herbage. The flowers are pale yellow, the leaves are greyish-green, and the seed-pods are long, narrow and have a way of interlacing until they are caught together into a tangled lump. The oasis dweller has learnt by experience that with the help of this leguminous plant called *hao-dẕ* he is able both to improve the quality of his patch of ground and also to extend it. He does this very gradually, and the increase of arable land from half an acre to one acre may take many seasons of hard work. To anyone who has watched the process, the building up of a desert farmstead speaks of generations of industry. The farmer cuts the *hao-dẕ* in great quantities and carts it to his land, where he spreads it in a shallow depression on the sand and floods it with some of his precious irrigation water. When it is thoroughly soaked he will add another layer of *hao-dẑ*, and repeat the process. Later he digs the rotting mass into the sand and so provides the first layer of workable soil which, with care, culture and patient enrichment, in time becomes fertile land and produces certain crops prolifically. Whatever the crop may be which the oasis farmer raises, he will always surround it with a border of lentils, vetch, field-peas or other leguminous plants; the only reason he can give for doing so is that his ancestors always did it before him, and therefore, in Gobi farming lore, "it is the custom." So the Westerner by science and research, and the Easterner through centuries of experience, have reached the same conclusion, and each in his own way recognises the value of nitrogenous crops to enrich the soil.

II

An Aerial View of the Spaces

An aerial view of the Desert of Gobi on a midsummer day would show a burning arid waste of dunes interspersed with monotonous rolling expanses of gravel and crossed by occasional ridges of high mountains whose foothills dwindle to low rocky mounds. The whole plain is shadeless and exposed to scorching heat under a pitiless sun. All living creatures seek shelter from its fierce rays and the roads are deserted, for the reverberation of heat makes travel almost impossible.

By night it is quite otherwise, and as darkness falls the desert quickens into life. Scorching heat gives way to a sudden chill which rises from the ground and strikes the traveller with a cold impact which makes him lift his head to catch the warmer upper stratum of the air as a relief from that too palpable cold. Soon that layer too will be permeated by the chill, and he will wrap a sheepskin coat around him in an endeavour to keep warm.

At this hour the observer would see caravans emerge from all the oasis inns and move slowly in various directions. Long trains of two hundred camels, roped together in strings of twelve, stretch out in thin lines over the narrow tracks; caravans of large carts, each laden with a thousand pounds of merchandise, follow one another across the plain; these join up for safety and keep within hailing distance of each other. Pedestrians carrying their own baggage balanced over the shoulder from the two ends of a pole come from many places and look like swinging dots as they move briskly at first, but later settle down to the inevitable pace of Gobi travel.

Half-way through the night all these travellers are seen to halt. This is the moment when caravans moving in opposite directions meet and greet each other. Carters recognise friends from other towns, but there is no more talk between them than is necessary for the passing of needed warnings. Camel-drivers on their immensely long journeys are alert for all unusual sights or sounds, and often carry letters to be handed to those whom they may meet at some halting-place. Pedestrians lay down their loads, rest aching shoulders and drink from their water-bottles, squatting lightly on their heels for a while before they make the second half of the stage. All these men speak but little and there is no easy chat on a desert night journey, nor is loud conversation ever heard; desert talk is always spare, subdued and unhurried, for the spaces teach men to be sharers of their dignity, and to scorn noise and tattle as only suited to the vulgarity of towns. Moreover, in the still air voices carry dangerously well, and silence becomes a cautionary instinct.

The sand deadens the sound of wheels, and camels' soft padded feet move quietly between the dunes. The camp watch-dogs might give a sharp sound by day, but at night they follow at the camels' heels or leap on to the back of one beast and lie there until the halt is called, when they jump down to take on duty. The sonorous, monotonous camel-bell has no sharp clang, but only a deep dull boom, and the rhythmic dip of the camels' neck keeps it in perfect measure. This bell is such a part of desert quiet that it breaks silence without disturbing it. When the great carts draw up for the mid-stage halt, a heavy smell of opium often comes from the pipe of some smoker hidden behind the curtains who lies there listless while the drivers exchange their greeting and then move on again.

Not only humans but innumerable small animals and insects come from their hiding-places as soon as darkness falls. All through the hours of heat they have slept in the tunnelled world which they have burrowed for themselves a few feet underground, and of which the openings are on the sheltered side of many a tiny sand-mound, blown up round the foot of a tuft of camel-thorn or of a low bush of scrub. All through the night the little live things move ceaselessly, silently and invisibly over the sand, and only by chance does a traveller become aware of their presence; after sunrise, however, he sees the sand patterned with all kinds of beautiful markings left by small rodents, beetles, centipedes and other insects which scuttle back to their sleeping-quarters with the first ray of sunshine.

Near the oases an observer might see slinking forms of wolves prowling vigilantly lest a goat or a child should wander from the shelter of the houses, and when some tired beast lags behind the caravan the dark forms gather from all sides to snatch a share of the spoil. Other sinister forms sometimes crouch behind rocks or in gullies—evil men waiting for lonely pedestrians or for some cart which has ventured unattached over the desert waste. The robbers hide themselves at those points on the route where caravans going north must pass just after sunset and where others, travelling south, come in shortly before daylight, for during the grey, twilight hours they will be unnoticed among the elusive shadows.

In the dry desert air the sky becomes a beautiful background for the brilliant stars which hang clear, showing themselves as shining orbs and never creating the illusion of lights twinkling through holes in a curtain, as is the case in dull and murky climes. The Milky Way is not the whitish haze seen in Western skies, but like a phosphorescent shower of myriad spots of light. Night travellers are great star-gazers, and look out over an uninterrupted line of horizon to skies which are always cloudless. The clearness and watchfulness of each planet suggests a personal and friendly interest toward the wayfarer, and Venus has served as beacon to many a caravan crossing doubtful stages.

Of starlight in the desert, Lawrence of Arabia writes: "The brilliant stars cast about us a false light, not illumination, but rather a transparency of air, lengthening slightly the shadow below each stone and making a diffused greyness of the ground." [1] Desert men, accustomed all their lives to that most subtle of all light diffusions, walk freely, even on rough ground, with no other illuminant. The moon, also, is more self-revealing than in heavier atmospheres, and never pretends to be merely a silver sickle or a cradle swinging in the void. She shows her full-orbed sphere, hanging in space, with a varying portion of brilliance outlining her darkened luminosity. With the rising of the moon the desert takes on its most captivating appearance, and through the long hours while she travels from one side of the horizon to the other she has her own way with human imagination, softening all the austere outlines and investing the barest formations with subtle charm. She is a mistress of magic and with one touch can turn the wilderness into a dream world.

[1] *The Seven Pillars of Wisdom*, by T. E. Lawrence.

Over these vast plains old ruined towns, surrounded with more or less decrepit battlemented walls, are scattered. The caravan track enters an enclosure at the place where a city gate used to stand, and leaves it at a gap in the opposite wall where another gate once stood. Inside the enclosed space are ruined walls, and the remains of houses long since destroyed. No one can build them up and use them again, for water has withdrawn itself from these cities of the dead and the old well openings are choked to the brim with sand and eroded matter. The main streets are often quite distinguishable, and even crooked lanes are sometimes recognisable. Silent progress by moonlight through such an ancient ruin vividly stirs the imagination and suggests that these old ruins may well be the haunt, not only of wild beasts, as they certainly are, but also of the ghostly habitants.

Not least remarkable of the Gobi night effects is the dancing magnetic light, which bewilders the inexperienced with its suggestion of men and camps in a region which is wholly deserted. The light flickers on the horizon, appearing and disappearing suddenly and unaccountably; one moment it is there, but a second later it has vanished, and when the traveller decides that it must be an illusion it is back again and yet again. Should he throw off his coat, or a driver touch a mule with his whip, the flash comes quite close, and the garment or the mule's back is streaked with light, and anyone holding a piece of silk, or touching a fur coat, may feel an electric shock. The Mongol poetically speaks of all these magnetic lights as "the Rosary of Heaven," because, through the long hours of darkness, the fires flash and shine like falling beads.

During silent stages when nothing is heard but the soft grind of wheels on loose sand, sound becomes subtly rhythmic and the rhythms resolve themselves into music, harmonising according to the perception of the listener. The muleteer probably hears nothing but a monotonous grating measure, while the more imaginative traveller listens to the rise and swell of mighty cadences, broad melodies and spacious harmonies.

With the rising sun the aerial observer could watch all the caravans reaching their respective destinations at the end of their night's journey. The camels kneel among the sands to have their loads removed, and wide-open doors of oasis inns wait to receive the tired wayfarers who, throughout the night, have covered another thirty-mile stage of the desert road. By divergent ways they come, meeting at the welcome *serai*, and disappear into the darkness and quiet of inn cells to pass the day in sleep.

III

The Charm of Oasis Names

The mere names of Gobi oases are enough to kindle the imagination. They have been given by primitive people and show their reactions to peculiarities of aspect or location, and their accuracy in conveying impressions. For this reason the sound of an oasis name has power to conjure up scenes before the eyes of memory, and to call back the old road and its familiar life. As I hear them the acrid smell of smouldering dung is again in my nostrils, the feel of grit is in my shoes, the sound of a passing caravan reaches my ear, and the sights of oasis life are clear before me, filling me with a fierce nostalgia. It is said that when an old camel-driver leaves the road he must never live where the sounds of the caravan can reach him, for if, by his own fireside, the deep tone of the camel-bell falls on his ear, he will rise and leave home and all, to wander out to the wilderness to which both he and the camel belong. To recall but a few of these names:

ONE CUP SPRING.—That, to me, represents water scarcity at its worst. I see a strip of land too stony for any growth, threatening rocks towering above it, and for all shelter a shack of loose stones laid without mortar, and with a matting roof held down by boulders. A hundred yards away is a hole where bitter water collects. The first driver to arrive finds enough there to water his beasts, but the second party has to wait until more has filtered between the stones at the bottom of the well. There are always quarrels and high words at One Cup Spring, and men watch one another suspiciously lest any take more than his share.

The outline of the landscape is utterly desolate, and there is nothing to relieve the mournfulness of that long ledge of black shale below which there stretches a howling waste so treacherous that, during blizzards, whole caravans have been smothered there in masses of shifting sand and never seen again.

Storms met at One Cup Spring can never be forgotten. I once reached there racing a blizzard which crashed just as our caravan arrived, and for thirty-six hours the drivers could not even get as far as the well to fetch water. Another time when I passed through the inn was lying in ruins, and we spent the night in a dug-out for beasts hollowed from the cliff. This was during a time of rebellion, and at dawn a shot rang out. I thought the brigands had found us, but it was only a poor Mongol, who, in cleaning his gun, had shot himself through the hand. Never in life had he seen anything so clean as the dressings used to bind the wound, and everyone said to him: "In the whole Gobi you could not have chosen any place so good as One Cup Spring in which to shoot your finger off, for where else, on these desert stages, would you have met a travelling *täbib*?" [1]

BITTER WELL HALT.—I see a high plateau, with nothing to mitigate its desolation, stretching as far as eye can see. Three squalid inns lie flat on the sand. The flying grit has been caught by the low enclosing walls until it has piled up so high that it lies level with the roofs and makes a dug-out of the stable courtyard. This is one stage on an important trade-route used by frontier guards on their constant journeys to and fro, and if water fails, the road must be closed. Two innkeepers have given up the uneven struggle for existence, and the third only stays because, by contract with the Government, he is given food in return for keeping the well clear of sand. In their outer life as innkeepers the miserable couple barely subsist, and only in their inner existence as opium-smokers does life count to them for anything. The man watches eagerly to see which of the travellers carries a gourd of sweet water, and his pitiful request is always the same: "Spare me one bowlful of your sweet water. Today I boil the poppy juice and this bitter water would spoil the brew. If you cannot spare a bowlful, then leave me just a cupful. From the kindness of your heart, Lady, spare me this."

On no account would he waste a drop of this soft, healing water on satisfying his thirst; he needs it to boil down the crude juice scraped from the scored poppy-head, and unless he prepares the dope in the right way it will spoil the deliciousness of his drug. A bitter life indeed is that of the innkeeper in Bitter Well Halt.

IRIS WELL.—Behind us there lay a tiring stage over bare sand where the torment of thirst had been aggravated by a tantalising mirage. Suddenly there was a change of quality in the ground, a sense of resistance underfoot, and simultaneously a carpet of blue iris was spread at our feet. There was only just enough clay to hold the roots, but dreariness gave place to loveliness. The dwarf iris plants, with gay blue flowers streaked in a paler shade and touched at the centre with a deep tone, made a brave show. They grew only a few inches high, but

[1] *täbib*—Turki word for doctor.

the sword-shaped leaves were firm and strong, and in this setting the wilderness plantation was a thing of transcendent beauty.

The juice of the fresh iris leaf is unbearably astringent, but when autumn comes and all the leaves lie brown, sun-dried and flaccid, they lose that astringent quality and can be cut and stored for animal fodder. In the very centre of the plantation were three small shacks built of sun-dried clay. The land bore nothing but this wild iris crop, yet the villagers counted themselves lucky, because it provided food for the donkey and kindling for the kitchen fire. How little it needs to make beauty, I thought, and how little to supply a luxury.

EYELASH OASIS.—The approach was by a two days' march among sand-hummocks through a stretch baffling in its monotony and where we feared to lose our way, for every little sand-heap seemed identical with all the others. Nevertheless the caravan had moved ceaselessly in and out of the hillocks, guided by an instinct given only to beasts and to the oasis man who threads his way where all others would be confused.

For two whole days we had met no one, but at sunset on the second day there was a slight rise in the land, and suddenly we stood on a ridge and overlooked a blue glistening river, wide and full of water. On either bank was a fringe of poplar trees, and the name of this place, Eyelash Oasis, leapt into significance.

It was a true expression of artistic understanding in the desert dweller that he should associate the streak of blue gleaming water and the bending poplars with the thought of shining eyes and sweeping lashes.

GATES OF SAND.—This was the very last oasis which tireless Chinese industry had been able to wrest from the ruthless and encroaching Mongolian sands. Beyond this we knew there would be no well, but only pits dug deep in the sand, at the bottom of which some dark brown water might have oozed up and collected. There would be nothing to burn save branches broken from dead tamarisk bushes, and we must carry all we should need with us. How should we ever find our way across this chartless ocean of sand? The camel-driver was not afraid. He jerked the halter, which told the camel to kneel, and bade the riders take their seats. "By day we shall pick up signs," he said. "Others have gone before us, and no caravan can move without leaving some trace behind. If I miss the way, my camels will find it. At night we have the stars and they can never mislead us. Have no fear, Lady, rest your heart. There will be a road."

SANDY WELL OASIS.—In a limitless plain of dim grit was a tiny village street of eight houses, four each side. Five of them were inns, of which three were in ruins; one was a shop which stocked matches, cigarettes, salt and red pepper; one was a shack where the postal courier fed his horse, and where he himself slept; and the last was a shuttered bakehouse which had closed down several years ago. Two minutes sufficed to walk from one end of the village to the other, and at each end the street merged into boundless wilderness. One of the inns was temporarily taken over by soldiers because times were dangerous, and this poor place, though it looked like nothing at all, was reckoned to be of some importance as it stood where two roads met.

Following the direct road I could distinguish the track by which we came and the path by which we must leave, but it was not until I stood with the soldiers at the look-out, on a small mound near the village shrine, that I was able to detect an unevenness in the grit which was like the shadow of a road stretching as far as eye could see toward the west.

"That is the short cut to South Lake, beyond Tunhwang," a soldier said in answer to my question. "We are here to guard that road and stop anyone from entering Turkestan without a permit. Spies and bad characters follow that path in order to evade the frontier guards, but there is no cover and we see them coming a long way off. A strange thing has just happened. Three days ago we were looking out from this post, just before sunset, when we saw something moving on the ground for which we could not account. It had not the movement of a wolf, and we were puzzled. Then one of the crawling figures stood upright, and we saw it was a boy. We went out and found a woman with three children, all nearly dead from hunger and thirst. They are down at the inn, won't you go and see them?"

In a broken-down enclosure, under a matting roof, I found a woman, a boy of twelve, a child of four and a small girl. The woman had a dazed, vacant look, and when we spoke to her she answered in a dead tone, devoid of all expression. From the soldier, the boy and herself, I learnt the details of her story. They had left South Lake, a party of ten people, trekking to Turkestan. "There was my father-in-law, my husband's brother, my husband and our six children," she said. "When we had done three stages we followed a recent camel-track, thinking it would lead us by a short cut, but we walked on and on, meeting no one, and when night came there was no water. My father-in-law went to look for water, but he was away so long that my husband and his brother started out to find him. Not one of them came back, and I was left alone with the children. The baby did nothing but cry, and then it died. I was afraid to let my boy leave me and we waited until we could wait no longer, then we walked on hoping to find the path again. Two more children died on the way. I wrapped them in our bedding and left them on the sand. When we had no strength to walk farther we crawled, and then the soldiers found us and brought us here."

"What will you do now?" I asked.

"I do not know," was her answer.

"One of the guard has gone to Hami to report the case," said the soldier, "and they will certainly send and take her there."

"If only we had not left the road!" she murmured, then relapsed into apathy and became utterly vacant and passive. We left her a share of our road provisions, and at the sight of bread and flour she roused again for a moment, but almost immediately all interest died and her expression became vacant. "We took the wrong road," she repeated, "we took the wrong road."

PIGEON ROCK.—The night stage seemed interminable, but no traveller risked taking it by day lest the beasts' strength proved insufficient for the effort. Moving westward the road sloped downhill, but those who have to take it in the up-grade direction revile each dreary league as they struggle onward. The sun was high when Pigeon Rock came into sight. There were tall cliffs of a pinkish shade towering above; they faced southward and absorbed the burning heat of the sun, reflecting it on the few courtyards which lie at their base. There is no means of avoiding Pigeon Rock, for it holds the only spring of water in a stretch of seventy miles, but the traveller resting there spends a day of misery, chasing an evasive strip of shade round a torrid enclosure until he is thankful, as I have been, to lie in the horses' feeding-trough, since the wall above threw a few inches of shade across it.

The burning cliffs are honeycombed with deep holes in which wild pigeons make their nests. Morning and evening the birds fly in and out, moved by an instinct which makes the whole flock circle and sweep with a purpose like one dominant thought. During the hot hours they hide in the deep, cool hollows where they have their nests. There is no luxury food at Pigeon Rock, and a taste of broiled pigeon flesh would be a pleasant change for the innkeeper. But to trap and eat a pigeon would be contrary to all right feeling, and the oasis dweller's standard of ethics would not admit that a gentle, harmless, self-constituted guest like a wild bird could be deceived, slain and devoured. "The Princely Man," he would say, "is not a betrayer of trust."

The only spring at Pigeon Rock is brackish, and its water parches the mouth, but the old innkeeper has a word of hope which he speaks to every guest who travels westward: "One stage more," he says, "and you reach Inexhaustible Spring Halt. Then you will taste sweet water again."

INEXHAUSTIBLE SPRING HALT.—At last the eight stages of bitter water were over. With inevitable delay for frontier permits, these stages had dragged out to thirteen days of unquenchable thirst in a stony, shadeless wilderness. At dawn I caught the outline of a soft waving mass against the pale sky. It was a tree, with branches moving gently in the morning breeze, and it seemed to me to be the loveliest tree in the whole world. Something within me relaxed, for I knew that the worst of the desert stages were now over.

Seized with a strange excitement I walked straight to the tree and found that it overhung a little sunken pond. Was this also acrid water? Experience insisted that it might be, but a woman filling her water-pot read my thought and smiled up at me. "Our water here is clean and sweet," she said, "take a drink and try it. This is the stage of Inexhaustible Spring, and when the wayfarer tastes this sweet draught he will drink until all the pain of his parched throat and cracked lips is softened and fades away."

"How is it that after so many brackish springs the water here is pure and sweet?" I asked.

The woman lifted her head toward the line of distant snow-hills: "It all comes from the Barkul Range," she said, "and flows direct from the hills to our hamlet. This is the mouth of the *karez* [1] which carries it here. Blessed be Allah who sends the snow and the rain," she added.

MUD PIT HOLLOW.—There was nothing except the name to prepare us for the swamp into which the cart lurched and from which it emerged with difficulty, only to be replunged into a morass and stuck firmly in mud which reached the axle. We thought the carter must have missed his way, but it was not the case. This was, he assured us, the only road

---

[1] *karez*—an artificial underground water-channel.

to the farms of Mud Pit. We were expected, and a village boy was watching for us, ready to help the carter. He had brought a spade to dislodge the wheels, and was soon collecting stones with which to support them while beasts and men made a concerted effort to drag the cart out of the mud. The carter lashed, the boy yelled, and every available man pushed with all his strength on the rims and spokes of the high wheels, while mules strained on the harness. One huge lunge and we came free of the sticky, sucking mess.

When we were safely lodged in the farmstead, drinking tea and chatting with the people, I asked a few questions:

"Is Mud Pit Hollow always like this?"

"Always, excepting in hard frost," said the grinning villagers.

"Some people say that it is the muddiest oasis of the desert," my hostess observed with pride.

"Truly every oasis has some unique feature," I said, and added: "It must make things very difficult for you. Could you not mend the road?"

"We are always doing that, but the morass swallows up all our stones and the pit is as bad as it was before," was the answer.

"How do you get in and out of the village?" I enquired.

"All through the summer we stay where we are, and we only take carts to town during the cold weather when the ground is frozen."

The terrible mud was not due to rainfall, for there was no more here than in the most parched of the desert oases. It came from subsoil water which filtered through sand and collected underground. The tea which was made from it was deliciously sweet and had no brackish flavour.

A village had come into existence at Mud Pit Hollow because irrigation was possible over a narrow strip of arable land. Moreover, there were great stretches of that valuable wild plant called *hao-dz* which makes it possible for the oasis dweller to enrich his lands.

The loveliest sight of the hollow was a field of shining yellow celandine bordered by a ridge of golden sand. I climbed the ridge and saw that beyond it was desert ground again, but with many tufts of camel-thorn and desert scrub. Scattered over the plain was a herd of camels with their calves. The herdsman moved among the beasts, and as he walked he twisted yarn of camel's hair with which to knit socks and caps, or to weave girdles, all of which he would need as he took his beasts across Mongolia to North Shansi. It would be cold then, but now it was hot and the hair was dropping away from the camels' sides in heavy pads. I went over to talk with him.

"This is good pasture," I said.

"That's why we graze the cow camels here," he answered. "The little ones cannot wander far after food."

"How long do you keep them here?"

"About four months, then I shall take them across to Paotow— eight months' journey there and back."

"What goods do you carry?" I asked.

"Turfan cotton and sheep's guts. There is a man at Paotow who buys up all the stuff we can take him. They say the Turkestan sheep have the largest guts of any sheep in the world."

I knew that he was speaking about the casing trade, which supplies many countries, and the German factories in particular, with casings for their largest sausages.

"After that," he went on, "the camels must rest, so we send them to the hillside pastures. My special job is always to stay here with the breeding camels and their young."

We parted, and as he walked away he broke into a high-pitched Mongolian song the lilt of which carried the suggestion of endless distances and of immense spaces.

THE ROBBERS' DEN.—Every wayfarer fears this gorge through the mountains. The overhanging rocks tower threateningly, the road twists treacherously, and every sound echoes through the narrow defile to within hidden caverns where robbers may lurk, watching for defenceless caravans.

The most frightening feature was neither the loneliness nor the stark desolation, but the sinister look of that inn dug-out. All day there had been no sign of human life until a thin spiral of blue smoke curling out from between rocks showed that someone was close at hand. This must be the inn, for there was only one well within many miles.

The entrance was hard to find, for great boulders blocked the way. Then, from behind a crag, an evil-looking man appeared and, seeing us, half turned and called backward to some unseen person.

"Can we have a drink of water here?" was my request.

"Come inside," was the answer, and the man turned and led me to the entrance of his cave-dwelling. Behind the rock was a narrow passage between two boulders, and he bent to enter a low doorway.

Three steps down, and I was in a kitchen built between rock walls. The chimney from which the smoke came was a natural exit, the fireplace was made of big stones, and a nondescript woman hovered near the hearth and stirred the pot. My first feeling was of fear at being entirely at the mercy of these people, then a strange sound asserted itself. It was the weirdest thing, a lilting voice which rose and fell on a sliding scale of quarter-tones. It seemed like a chant of Koranic magic, and was difficult to locate among those rock recesses. What sort of people were these among whom we had fallen? What could possibly be the occupation of this mysterious and terrifying household? One thing was certain, I determined that nothing should keep us there for the night. We would drink our tea, eat our morsel of bread and then away. These people were capable of any evil, and the sinister aspect of their living-place was a symbol of the cruel intentions of their hearts. "Don't unhitch the beasts, we shall push on farther," was the order given to the carter.

We did not pass this way again until several years later, when Turkestan was in rebellion and this thieves' kitchen was known to be the haunt of a nefarious band. This time we were obliged to stay the night, and prayed that a special angel guard might be on duty while we slept through the hours of darkness. The angel of the Lord truly encamped around us, no harm befell us, and we left again in peace, but twenty-four hours later there was murder in that place. News filtered slowly from the desolate ravine, but when the crime became known a squad of soldiers was sent to investigate and to punish the criminals. They never caught them, for when the soldiers got there the caves were all deserted and the terrible robber-band had vanished into deeper fastnesses, where even the desert rangers could not venture to pursue them.

THE PEOPLE OF THE WAYSIDE

I

The Innkeeper and his Shack

THE Central Asian trade-routes are busy thoroughfares where they link large towns, but narrow to a mere track where oases are few and small. Water can be depended on at each stage, but the size and character of the halt is variable, as is also the amount of water available, and its quality. An inhabited oasis may consist of a few shacks, it may be a fair-sized village or it may even be a large town. Occasionally there is nothing to be seen but the circular mouth of a well near which a landmark is raised lest it be missed by the traveller.

Man has a passion to conquer the unconquerable, and that great natural defence called Gobi (Wall of Spears) had by some means to be surmounted. Lack of water was the main problem, so ancient diviners brought their skill to bear on the question. The possible daily stage for man or beast to walk over loose gravel, or shifting sand, was tested and found to be twenty-five to thirty miles, and it was with this in mind that wells were dug and springs released. Whenever the trek was more difficult than usual, by reason of bad road-surface or rising hills, the stage was shortened and the well dug a little nearer. In a few cases, however, the divining-rod failed to respond, so to this day the traveller still has to negotiate the double stage before he can water his beasts. Centuries come and go, but the traffic of the desert path is still the same as when the oasis-makers plied their craft, and whether it be camel, horse, donkey, cart or foot travel, three miles an hour is the accepted pace for the traveller as he crosses the desert.

It is difficult for the Westerner, accustomed to the tempo of modern life and the conditions of its civilisation, to adapt himself to the simplicities of this caravan life which has remained untouched by the pressure of mechanical transport. Yet once he is committed to it he inherits a freedom which he has never known before. His mentality is released from the tyranny of a timepiece with its relentless ticking, and from the dead reproach of its neglect. The flickering needle of a speedometer is not there to urge him to greater effort, and there is no concentration on speed as an objective in itself. He has ample time for observation and nothing of interest need escape his attention. This is the pace for talk, and no desert wayfarer is jarred by the annoyance of a hurried companion nor delayed by the slackness of a fellow-traveller. The human body, having found its natural swing, becomes strangely unconscious of itself and releases the mind to its normal function of transmuting incident into experience. These are conditions in which the wayfarer becomes, according to his own measure, an observer, a philosopher, a thinker, a poet or a seer. He learns to be independent of the calendar, for the moon is his time-measurer. He has no road-map, but his course is true, for the stars are his guide. The tent which is his dwelling goes where he goes, and compels him to a simple rule of life. In bringing his pace down to desert standard he finds that in all worthwhile things he is the gainer, and that his loss is entirely in the realm of the material, the temporary and the ultimately insignificant. Sometimes the thirty-mile tramp brings him to the centre of a stony plain where there is no vestige of vegetation and no visible means of sustenance for any human being. Such land offers no protection, and the blizzard sweeps over these plains with terrific force, but even here there will be a small house built from the stones which litter the ground and always, just outside the inn, is the opening of the well, the water of which, though unpalatable, is life-saving.

In other places there are sand-mounds and the track among them is wide and ill-defined, but at the end of thirty miles it narrows suddenly to a short street between two rows of houses and for the space of one hundred and fifty yards the traveller is in a village. Then comes the illimitable plain again, and the widening road spreading itself across it. In that street there is probably one small spring which has been carefully cleared and is kept free of encroaching sand. From its small basin a tiny streamlet runs with a steady trickle to a larger basin, the border of which is trodden by the feet of beasts. This is where the animals are watered while man drinks at the upper pool.

Overlooking each desert well or spring is a mud shrine which holds a small clay figure wrapped in a little red cotton shawl. This represents the presiding genius of the water-supply, and on either side of the shrine are pasted a few strips of red paper written over with ideographs which ask that the blessing of heaven and earth may rest on the water. In the little mud pot which stands before the figure there is always a pinch of incense ash left from the offerings of passers-by.

The intense isolation of the inhabitant of a small oasis, and the extraordinarily low standard of life imposed upon him, produce a strange mentality. His normal condition is torpor. He sits or lies on his mud bed and thinks of nothing. Only when a traveller arrives does he experience the discomfort of rousing himself, but then, though it may be cold or windy, he must leave the pleasant stuffiness of his bed-living-room, throw off the greasy coverlet which he has drawn over his crossed legs, come into the open and give the service which is demanded of him as innkeeper. The hovel where the last guest slept is still littered with the rubbish which he has left, so water must be fetched and sprinkled on the mud floor and bed. Then the innkeeper takes the besom, made of stiff desert grass tied round a stick, and sweeps until the air of the room is so thick with heavy dust that he is lost to sight in it.

The cleaning is perfunctory, but the rubbish is more or less swept into a corner and the air cleared with water tossed upward toward the ceiling. When the innkeeper once more becomes visible the room is declared ready for the new guest to take possession. This transference of dust from one place to another being the most unpleasant side of innkeeping duties, he shirks it as much as possible, but his meagre living depends on serving guests, and serve them he must.

What he can do inside his own little mud room is less objectionable to him, because he need not be outside in the unpleasant element of fresh air. Indoors he scrapes kindling from the pile of dried desert scrub which is stacked in a dark corner and boils an iron pot of water, while the men who have just arrived borrow his wooden measure and fill it with flour from their own bag. "Make our food," they say.

"Do you want it watery or stodgy?" he asks.

"Stodgy," is the usual answer.

He turns up the ragged cuffs of his old wadded coat, takes a bowl and kneads the flour with water, then quickly and skilfully by reason of long practice he plies his slender four-foot-long rolling-pin, spreading the lump of dough to a large thin sheet of paste. This he folds into many layers, takes a sharp chopper and cuts it into strips which are tossed into the boiling water. When the food is cooked, he ladles it out into bowls with a spoon made from plaited desert grass, and places them on the table, setting a pair of chopsticks by each. Finally, and with a gesture of pride, he puts a small wooden bowl of coarse salt in the centre. This is a concession to style, for, as a matter of fact, the *mien* has been boiled in such brackish water that no further salt will be needed.

The innkeeper knows how to serve out the food so expertly that a good many dough-strips are left at the bottom of the pot, and by established custom what remains there will be his share. He pours them away with the flour-thickened water into a basin kept for the purpose, and hides them quickly lest the hungry travellers demand more than their due. Work, for him, is now over, for the guests will themselves chop sorghum leaves for the beasts' fodder, feed them and then sleep for the rest of the day, leaving again at sunset.

Indolent as the innkeeper seems to be, no traveller is ever able to slip away without paying his bill. As soon as there is a move toward leaving, his room door opens and he appears, blinking, to exact full payment for services rendered. Lodging, attendance and water-money are the three main items of the account, and every copper is wrangled over until the travellers are off; then he shoots the long wooden bar which secures the wide courtyard door and shuffles back to his room to hide his takings in a big earthenware jar. The room which his "guests" used is once more littered with rubbish, but he will leave this to be cleaned until the next visitor arrives and wants to occupy it. My quest led me into many talks with such innkeepers.

"How many years have you been here," I would ask, "and where is the old family home?"

"I am a man from Sian," would be a frequent answer.

"When did you come outside the Barrier?"

"I was born here, and my father before me. My grandfather came here and never returned home." From this answer I gathered that the grandfather had not come of his own free will. It was probably as a prisoner under sentence that he had been escorted to the great gate of Kiayükwan, placed outside it and left to find his own way and make his livelihood as best he could in the dreaded land of exile.

"I expect there is a good living to be made out of innkeeping, for your guests are numerous, and, judging by the way you charge me, I see you make big profits," I said.

"You are joking, Lady," he said. "I only charge you out-of-pocket expenses."

If the life of the oasis man is a sordid one, what is there to be said of his wife's existence? Clothing, which has some place in the thought of nearly every woman, is, to her, absolutely nothing but a protection from cold and a covering for her nakedness. The other incidents of her life are concerned with food and the birth of her children. She knows that her husband has jars of coins buried under the floor of their poor room, but she has never thought of money as a means of securing comforts because there is nothing for which to exchange it. Once a week a caravan carrying Government supplies deposits a bag of flour at the door. This is the subsidy granted to them, in exchange for which her husband is bound to be at his post all through the year, and keep the well from being choked by sand. She has never thought in terms which refer to anything except meals, births and occasional deaths. Her boys may go farther afield, and if they do, she knows that they will never return, but after a time she will become accustomed to their absence and it will not trouble her again.

She herself was the daughter of an innkeeper and born in just such another oasis as this. At the age of fifteen she was handed over as wife to the eldest boy of this home, and served her mother-in-law for many years. Now the old people are dead and her husband is master of the *serai*, which they euphemistically call "The Inn of Peace and Unity." She has not even a chance to buy the printed likeness of the kitchen god at a village fair, so her husband seeks the favour of heaven by inducing a travelling Buddhist priest to write four ideographs on a strip of yellow paper to be pasted on the wall. It reads: "We give thee thanks for thine immense benefits." Big words do not cost money, so the gods might as well be propitiated with something worth while— and, in any case, the priest had to get a free night's lodging. Such are the terms which life has offered her.

With spiritual senses dormant, mental powers arrested and physical demands reduced to the minimum, wherein shall a human being show that he differs from the beasts whose conditions he shares? The charm on the wall was a recognition of some Being whose interest was sufficient to bring him luck or misfortune, and the use of the opium pipe was an assertion of the soul's right to release from the unworthy conditions of this life. The reality of physical comfort could never be his, and even the knowledge of release through spiritual energy was denied him, but the evoking of a dream lay within his range, and by that alone, in a strange perverted way, he declared his freedom from the sordid shackles of his existence and created the dream of the unobtainable.

We had business with such men and women far other than the chaffering over a few coppers on the price charged for kindling. It was a formidable task to evoke the spirit within them, that spirit which apprehends realities of which the illusive dreams are but shadows, and in which dwells the latent power to respond to the call of God. One word might liberate that spirit and make it aware of its inheritance. After a few days spent in the Inn of Peace and Unity, and having declared God's message to its owners, we passed on, leaving that grim oasis for many a long trek. Two years later we reached the spot once more.

A woman who was somehow different met us at the door. It was the innkeeper's wife, and she seemed to be as poor as formerly, but surely she was cleaner and her place was certainly tidier. There was a radical change, however, in her expression and bearing. She held herself differently and her movements had acquired a certain dignity. She led us to her room, and on the wall over the mud bed was a picture which we had formerly given her. It showed a lotus flower opening its pure petals toward heaven though its roots were buried deep in the mud of the pool. On it certain words were printed, words which did not constitute a charm like those written by the Buddhist priest, but which asked a question drawn from an ancient Book of Wisdom. These were the words: "Who can bring a clean thing out of an unclean?" A further sentence suggested the answer: "Create in me a clean heart, O God."

"It was two years on the third day of the last moon since you were here before," the woman said, and, after a pause, added: "I have never smoked opium since then." Seeing the look on my face she continued: "You said that I was displeasing God by doing so, and I could not go on displeasing Him. Yes, I say the prayer every day."

II

The Priest at his Shrine

Even the smallest wayside stage has its shrine, though it is often a neglected one, for the centre of life in the little community is not located where the plaster god sits, but where the life-giving water flows. Every traveller comes to the spring with jar, bottle or gourd, but not all of them will trouble to climb the stony mound on which the shrine is built and place lighted incense-sticks in the dust of the ancient burner. Such wayside shrines are not cared for by any priest, but, apart from these, there are desert temples which in themselves constitute tiny oases, for the well stands in a courtyard surrounded by buildings and is generally shaded by one old tree. A priest always acts as guardian, watching over the water-supply and attending to the temple. He is bound by his profession to perform certain duties, and he is punctilious in his discharge of them. The courtyards must always be well swept, the little heap of desert fuel piled tidily in a corner and the temple gong sounded at correct intervals. Many a guardian secures the help of an assistant, who is left in charge while he himself takes long journeys on foot to populous oases to beg money for the repair and redecoration of the temple. No one refuses him a small contribution, and the begging friar always brings home sufficient for his immediate needs.

On the border of Black Gobi there is such a temple, and it stands alone in a barren waste. The high enclosure wall and the glazed tiled roof are useful landmarks for travellers, and many beg a night's shelter from the blizzard, or crave permission to lie in the shade of a wall through the intolerable heat of a summer midday. It is in the charge of Buddhist monks, and all pilgrims travelling to the sacred mountains of Tibet or of the Altai rest for a time with these servants of the gods, for the priest in charge of a temple must be given to hospitality and grant shelter to all who claim it.

The pilgrim is always an honoured guest, but nowadays many a man on secret service finds it convenient to clothe himself in the grey robe of the Buddhist monk or the maroon shawl of a lama, and not all who wear the monastic garb are true religious devotees. This is known by the authorities, and the religioner is not exempt from suspicion at the frontier station, where his business is carefully investigated by the guards before they allow him to proceed. In the temple it is not so, for there the abbot receives all who come, asks no awkward questions and investigates no visitor's credentials. Such matters lie outside his sphere. No one fears him, and when a deserter from the army asks his assistance he feeds him and helps him on his way, even showing him some small foot-track by means of which he may avoid being caught by army scouts.

Sometimes the peaceful atmosphere of a lonely shrine is rudely disturbed by a squad of soldiers or brigands thundering at the gate and demanding admittance. "Water our beasts," is the order shouted to the guardian, and with extraordinary quiet, calm and self-control the abbot will tell his young disciple to supply the men with what they need, but he is uneasy until they take their departure, for they are intruders and break up the even tenor of his life. When the door is finally shut behind them he will go to his own room, and with the words "Wild men" dismiss the incident and resume his daily round of temple services.

The true pilgrims who frequent these roads are either seekers for further knowledge in matters of the soul, men who desire release from the burden of sin, or those who go to perform vows made in some crisis of life which have to be paid at a distant shrine. Such men follow the steps of the famous pilgrims of old who journeyed across China, passed over these very deserts, and endured amazing trials in order to reach the land in which the Buddha lived and taught, and bring back a more complete understanding of his canon. Since those early days the stream of pilgrims has never ceased. We met with many who were pursuing their way to what they called "the land of the setting sun," hoping, they said, to find God there, and many who were travelling to or from the great Wu-tai-shan, holy mountain of Shansi. The same physical difficulties have still to be met by every pilgrim who would take these long journeys. The stages are the same as those faced by Hsüan Tsang, and there is no amelioration of conditions in respect of water, wind, blizzard or sand-storm. The mental tortures connected with mirage, illusions and the sense of inimical presences may still torment them, and in addition the modern pilgrim may be fired on by brigands and lawless men.

The ancient pilgrims Fah Hsien and Hsüan Tsang can scarcely have presented a more picturesque appearance than does the travelling monk of today. He is recognisable by his loose grey garment and by the distinctive head-dress under which his long hair is coiled about his head. The bundle which holds his possessions is strapped to his back, and in his hand is a long staff. Should he be a mendicant, he carries a begging-bowl of great beauty. It is often made from a section of hollowed vine root, and has been used by generations of friars until its knotted surface is mellowed by human handling to a beautiful, shining, natural polish. Such bowls are highly valued and are handed down from one generation of monks to another, as part of the monastery equipment.

The background of such men is often very remarkable. Some have been dedicated to monastic life by their parents at birth, others during a severe illness as the only hope of saving life, and the aloof, withdrawn gaze of some monks must conceal a deep rebellion against the fate which has made of them beings apart from other men, always shadow-like in the grey garb, and always detached from normal life, though with a strong man's instincts surging within. Others offer themselves as child postulants through being left orphans and friendless. Occasionally a physical disability is the cause of their being received, but a lame, blind or otherwise disabled monk is kept in attendance on the shrine, being unsuited to the fatigues of pilgrimage. Some are meditatives with a longing for metaphysical and mystic learning, and to such, monastic life offers strong attractions. Others again have tasted all that the world can offer them of adventure and of experience before they withdraw to a monastery and adopt the ascetic rule.

Once, in a wayside temple, we talked with such a man as this. The term which the monk uses for the home of his childhood is the same as that by which a married woman speaks of hers, "the mother home," and this man spoke of a "mother home" in Kashgaria, where he was the beloved child of a Turki mother and a Chinese father. After his schooling was completed he left home in order to gratify a lust for adventure, and before many years had passed was a soldier in the army of the war-lord Wu Pei-fu. He shared the brigand's lot of loot, rape and murder, but something within him asserted itself and made him revolt against such a misuse of life. He determined to have nothing more to do with wanton destruction, but to desert from the brigand army and attach himself to a life which was peaceful and quiet. He heard of a temple in which there was a vacancy for a postulant, and joined its community of priests, applying himself with great fervour to the study of the Sacred Books and priestly manuals. In due course he was admitted to full orders, and later was allowed to go on pilgrimage to Holy Mountains and notable shrines. He questioned us closely about the object which had brought us to the temple where he was staying, and the conversation which took place showed that he was not wholly ignorant of Christianity.

"I have heard much about your Jesus," he said, "from a fellow-religious at a large monastery in Kansu." He then told us of a monk who was at heart a Christian, yet discarded neither his monastic dress nor his ascetic rule of life, but spoke of Jesus, the Son of God, to all whom he met.

This late member of a brigand army had been trained in a school where action was centred on destruction, and the Taoist philosophy had appeared to him as a solution of man's inevitable misuse of power, showing him the futility of restless activity. Under monastic discipline he schooled himself to prize and hold fast the central principles of Laodz's teaching: "Emptiness, or freedom from preoccupation, is a condition of receptivity; emptiness is necessary to usefulness." "The thirty spokes unite in the one nave; but it is on the empty space for the axle that the use of the wheel depends. Clay is fashioned into vessels; but it is on their empty hollowness that their use depends. The door and windows are cut out to form apartments; but it is on the empty space in them that the use of an apartment depends. What corresponds to emptiness is freedom from all selfish motive or purpose centred in self."

We talked for long about *Tao* (the Way): *Tao* as understood by the Taoist, and the Way as understood by the Christian; *Tao* the principle of nothingness, and the Way—Light, Life, Completeness in

Christ. Neither the expenditure of energy which characterised the old fighting days, nor his immediate search after the philosophy of negation, satisfied the instinct of pursuit in this man's spiritual exploration.

"You, a seeker for the *Tao*," I said, "have travelled so far in search of it. Have you been successful in finding it?"

"No," he admitted, "I have not."

"Yet you have spent the whole of this day instructing others regarding a way which, according to your own confession, you yourself have not found."

I handed him a book of which the first sentence was: "In the beginning was the Word (in Chinese translated the *Tao*), and the Word was with God and the Word was God." He read this with profound attention, and the talk which developed was prolonged until the stars appeared and the moon shone clear. Suddenly, out of that peaceful silence, a whirlwind swept over the plain and caught the eminence on which we stood, with such violence that tent, bed and baggage were hurled about by the hurricane. In the confusion each one seized something to save it from being carried away in the darkness, the conversation ceased abruptly, and we did not see the pilgrim again. Next morning he was gone before dawn.

III

The Soldiers at the Frontier

Before we left the lonely temple the carters went to the shrine and knelt before the goddess of mercy, seeking her protection on the journey ahead, while one of the postulants struck the iron bell in order to call her attention to this act of devotion. Then priest, postulant and carters stood in a circle while we committed the caravan to the care of the Heavenly Father, and the men were glad, for they believed Him to be a mighty power. The priest escorted us to the threshold of the temple precincts and wished us good luck; we stepped outside, and turning bowed to the old man, thanking him for his hospitality. As we went on our way we heard him close the massive doors behind us and shoot the great bolt.

Our destination was the first important town over the Turkestan border, a renowned oasis, which is called by the Chinese Hami, and by the Turki Cumul.

We had still much to learn regarding caravan life and its accepted code of conduct, and one of my lessons was concerned with the order of everyday greetings. As definite as the exchange of signals between ships that pass on an ocean were the words exchanged between caravans when they met on the seas of sand. The greeting always took the form of questions: "Where are you from?" and "Whither are you bound?" They required an exact answer, and I learnt that no desert traveller mentions the stages which lie between his point of departure and his ultimate destination, the implication being that he left the one solely in order to reach the other.

We had not gone many miles before we met a long train of carts laden with heavy merchandise. Our driver hailed them in the usual way. "Where do you come from?"

"From Kashgar," was the answer. Kashgar was nearly three months' journey westward.

"Whither are you bound?"

"We are bound for Loyang," came the reply. This was a city about two months' journey distant, far away in Central China. That caravan was launched on a five months' trek, but in the outlook of the *bash* nothing was worth mentioning except the point of departure and the place of destination. I thought a good deal about this custom and what might be the law which governed it, and I remembered that in an old book called *The Pilgrim's Progress* John Bunyan makes his pilgrim answer each enquiry in like fashion. "Whence come you and whither are you bound?" was the question Christian was constantly being asked by those who met him. "I come from the City of Destruction and am going to the Celestial City," was his unfailing answer. These were Christian's focal points, and he had left the one only in order to reach the other. Everything which he met by the way was incidental, and I observed that men on great journeys, even in the twentieth century, still feel as he did. The goal is definite and must be reached. Plains, deserts, mountains, small stages, and even large towns, are but incidental to the main objective of the journey.

The desert which lies between Ansi and Hami is a howling wilderness, and the first thing which strikes the wayfarer is the dismalness of its uniform, black, pebble-strewn surface. It seems that any break in the monotony would be a relief, yet when the dark tint changes to a lighter shade and the ground becomes more yielding to the foot, greater difficulty of progress is felt immediately, and when the traveller has spent a few hours toiling in the softer sand he feels again that any change would be welcome. The next stage brings him to an area which he crosses walking on a treacherous crust of crumbling salt, which breaks under the weight of man or beast, releasing a fine powder which flies upward and settles on the skin, making it miserably dry and fissured. Once more he welcomes any relief from the discomfort of this alkaline deposit, but the next change may bring him to deep loose gravel which impedes every step and makes it impossible to keep up the regular pace of three miles an hour.

It is from the middle of such a gravel plateau that the traveller toward Hami sees the outline of dark rocks arise which break the monotony of the plain. Seen closer at hand, these rocks are of a very striking aspect. Some are black and burnished by the constant friction of wind and sand, others are huge boulders of grey granite, with a hue like threatening thunder-clouds, others again are streaked with a vein of glittering white, like petrified forked lightning. Between these rocks is a ravine which extends for several miles and forms the oasis of Hsing-hsing-hsia, which has become the military frontier station dividing the easy-going no-man's-land from the strictly controlled province of Sinkiang, China's "New Dominion."

At one time a man might pass from China to her outlying province without let or hindrance, but the repercussions of the Great European War of 1914-1918 and of the Russian Revolution made the Chinese Governor of Sinkiang feel so insecure that fear drove him to adopt a policy of rigorous frontier control. Passports, permits, local passes and innumerable formalities began to harass the traveller as he moved about, and many Chinese who only gained entrance to Turkestan with difficulty have never been able to secure a permit to leave it again. As the years passed, during which rebellion and revolution shook both China and its New Dominion, the frontier regulations were still further tightened, and caravans often had to spend ten days or more in the unspeakable inns of Hsing-hsing-hsia while messages were exchanged between the Commandant of the garrison and the Governor at Urumchi, whose personal permission had to be secured for each individual to pass on.

Innumerable young men who were travelling on the most legitimate business were seized by the frontier press-gang and forced into the Turkestan army. In the course of many journeys we have seen the pass held by a strong guard of over a thousand troops and at other times we have seen it utterly deserted. On each occasion the place was terrifying—when populated because of the cruelty with which the recruits were handled, and when seemingly empty because of the sense of insecurity from hidden enemies who might be lurking among the great boulders, and of uncertainty as to what lay round the next turn of the defile. Anything might happen in Hsing-hsing-hsia, and every traveller was glad to leave it behind him.

We have stayed in the best inn the place could provide and feasted with the Governor in his *yamen*. We have camped in the open because there was no room in the inn; we have slept in a broken-down shack with scaly scorpions as bed-fellows, and on our last visit we sheltered behind a rock, for the ravine was littered with the bones of dead men and with torn clothing. The human butchers had done their hateful worst and the wolves had done the rest.

On either side of this border defile waterless land stretches out indefinitely, and all the desert traffic is forced through the ravine where a limited supply of brackish water is found. At the approach from the south there stands a great barrier of rock which, splintering under the influence of alternate intense heat and cold, has left the summit jagged into fantastic shapes. Beyond this is a succession of granite crags, and farther on a huge mass of grey rock which appears to block the ravine, but from which the path turns aside, widens for a little space, and then narrows again to a rocky exit through which travel-carts must be dragged over rough slabs of stone.

Such a place lends itself to defence with remarkable ease, and the ingenuity of the garrison has taken full advantage of each natural occasion for camouflage. The splintered rocks have been so handled as to present the effect of armed men ready for defence, and a perfect illusion has been secured with the minimum of trouble. Incidentally, each of these stone figures can, when necessary, conceal a living man armed with a real weapon, and an attacking army can never be sure where the ambush lies. Between the crags which form the ravine are many narrow *couloirs* where parties of scouts can easily be hidden, but the most illusory effect is produced by means of the high grey rock which seems to close the ravine at its narrowest point. It is of precisely the same colour and shade as the Chinese soldiers' grey cotton uniform, and the natural roughness of the stone has been handled with such skill as to make it afford foothold for a large number of men. Every day there was practice, when each man reached his appointed place and there stood motionless. The rock was covered with invisible soldiers, and even the keenest eyes failed to distinguish between the man-like stone and the stone-like men.

The rocky exit on the north side of the ravine is every carter's *bête noire.* Numerous wheels, weakened by long travel and made brittle by the scorching sun, have broken to pieces at that stony spot and left the caravan in a horrid plight. The blacksmith's shop where the soldiers shod their own horses was often called upon to supply nails and a rim of iron to hold the loose spokes together, but such valuable material as iron was given to civilians only as a great favour.

Beyond the ravine there is a famous hill of quartz. Its glittering aspect has given rise to a play upon the name of the gorge, which is properly called The Ravine of Baboons, and a stone tablet records that baboons came there in ancient times to drink of the stream which once flowed between the rocks. By a change of ideograph the name can be read with another meaning and become Starry Gorge. The ravine is now a very dry place, but water-marks on the granite boulders give certain evidence that a river once flowed there. High up among the rocks is the cavern-tomb of the holy Moslem pilgrim who died and was buried there. Unlike that of his companion whose body lay at Moslem Tomb Halt, this sepulchre was hewn out of the rock, but the opening in the floor which showed where the body was laid was similar to the other.

The twelve hard stages between Ansi and Hami offered many new varieties of objectionable water. Sometimes it ran from beneath boulders in a limpid stream, sometimes it lay in a sluggish pool, its surface covered with a repulsive scum; at other times it burst through the soil, and sometimes it was drawn from a well with bucket and rope; but whatever its immediate source, it was always brackish and thirst-creating. Its taste was sometimes that of magnesium sulphate, and sometimes more reminiscent of a copper salt, but it was always unsatisfying and always nauseating.

THE KING OF THE GOBI

I

The Desert Domain

THE Desert of Gobi, like other historic lands, has had its own hereditary king. By the Chinese he was given the title of Wang-ye, but his own Turki people called him Khan. His palace was in the town called Cumul, or Hami, and his domain extended to the frontiers of Mongolia, Dzungaria and north-west China. The wayfarer on a stony desert stage can still see a high boundary stone on which is engraved in Chinese ideographs the statement that this tablet marks the limit of the Khan's dominion. The Khanate was held under the suzerainty of China, and the Khan's hereditary authority was valued by the Chinese Government as a useful check on the turbulent Moslem people who recognised his rule.

The oasis of Cumul is referred to in Chinese history as far back as the first century of the Christian era, and was then known as I-ku. Six hundred years later it was under the domination of the Uighurs,[1] that powerful people whose origin is shrouded in mystery, but who left such strong traces of their civilisation over the wide territory of Central Asia. These were the great oasis-makers who explored and developed the water resources of the Gobi Desert, and their culture, which was of a high order, flourished in the district of Cumul, where their agricultural mode of life raised them above their nomadic neighbours and ensured them an independent and influential position. It was from Cumul that civilising influences spread among the roving steppe dwellers.

During Mongol supremacy this area was part of the portion which fell to Jagatai, third son of Genghiz Khan, and since then it has always recognised the sovereignty of a Khan. Hsüan Tsang tells that in the seventh century he was received there in a Buddhist monastery, and Marco Polo, in the fourteenth century, writes: "The province lies between two great deserts. The people are all idolaters and have a peculiar language. They live by the fruits of the earth which they have in plenty, and dispose of to travellers. They are a people who

[1] Uighur—the name of a Turkish tribe and dynasty which came from the East and ruled in Kashgaria from the tenth to the twelfth century.

take things very easily for they mind nothing but playing, singing, dancing and enjoying themselves." By the sixteenth century, however, a total change of religion had taken place, and Hadji Mahomet speaks of Cumul as the first Mohammedan town he met in travelling from China. At the present time it has both mosques and idol temples in plenty, the former being used exclusively by the Turkis and Tungans, and the latter by the Chinese.

Cumul occupies a geographical position of great strategical import-ance. Like Ansi on the south, so Cumul on the north is a stepping-off and landing place for all travellers who cross the inhospitable tract of Gobi between the provinces of Kansu and Chinese Turkestan. The approach to the oasis is by long and desolate stages, but from the moment that the traveller's foot touches watered land he is in the midst of beauty and luxuriant agriculture, and for several miles before reaching the town the road leads through fields and by farmhouses surrounded with elm and poplar trees. Everything indicates prosperity and an abundance of every product.

Some of the land is cultivated by Chinese settlers and some by Turki farmers. In everything they are a contrast to each other. The Chinese fields are always models of tidiness, where not a foot of land may go to waste, and, thanks to the help of women weeders, there is no appreciable growth of weeds in the fields, nor is any crop considered too trouble-some for cultivation. The Turki farmers are of a less careful and thrifty outlook, and Nature has more of her own way in the lands joining their farms. But they understand how to produce and market the magnificent melons and the grapes for which Cumul is famous.

When we came to Hami we met, for the first time, that particular arrangement of a town which is so characteristic of Central Asian cities, and which allows for people of different races, religions and habits to live close together without disturbing each other. The Chinese Govern-ment offices were enclosed in a small walled city, where officialdom conducted its life according to immemorial Chinese tradition. About a mile away stood the Khan's palace, which was a many-storeyed building with a wide frontage pierced with irregular windows. It held vast reception-rooms and the innumerable suites of private apartments fitted to the demands of Moslem households. Around the palace clustered an untidy mass of low mud buildings, which held the families of those who served the Khan in any personal capacity. Strong, handsome, bare-footed, white-veiled women moved swiftly among the tortuous lanes, and bands of bold-faced children played noisy games in any available space. Apart from these two enclosures was the busy commercial *bazar* where Chinese, Turki and Tungan traders each carried on their specialised lines of business. In this mercantile centre the Tungan element was powerful and the large well-built inns and houses were mostly owned by them.

The Turkis, called by the Chinese *Chantows* (turbaned men), were purveyors of goods from all the South Road towns as far as Kashgar. The poorer among them did the arduous work of collecting merchandise at Turfan, Aksu, Kuche, Khotan and Kashgar, and carrying it by cart or on horseback to the more prosperous merchants at Cumul. These rich retailers spread the gay, attractive goods on a low counter, where they themselves sat cross-legged and chewed *naz*, a vile mixture of dried desert herbage and lime, which the men carried in a tiny polished gourd hanging from the waist. The Chinese of the *bazar* were bankers, pawnbrokers, druggists, cooks, or vegetable and fruit vendors, and a few rich merchants owned handsome shops where all kinds of goods from Peking were displayed.

Near the river was a characteristic settlement of Chinese market-gardeners. They lived in little mud shacks which they built for themselves, and they toiled ceaselessly in the gardens, which they irrigated indefatigably with water from the Narin River. Thanks to them, the *bazar* of Cumul was supplied at all seasons of the year with magnificent vegetables of many kinds. In summer, at sunset, there was buzzing of insects over these gardens, and clouds of mosquitoes rose and spread themselves over the town. The irrigation was controlled by means of a strong sluice, and below it there was a pond, which was used as a bathing-pool by the gardeners' children. On hot, oppressive evenings the boys threw off their scanty garments and dived into the pool, swimming, romping and playing in the water like a school of porpoises. Most of the market-garden labourers came from a locality in the Tientsin area which is particularly subject to flood and other disasters, and Hami is viewed as a providential shelter by these very poor people. Each man who makes good becomes the employer of relatives and neighbours when troubles overtake them and they too have to leave the old home.

When we first came to Cumul, Maksud Shah, the Khan, was already a very old man. When younger, as vassal of the Emperor of China, he was required to visit Peking every sixth year, and on these occasions he was permitted to act as personal servant to the Emperor for a term of forty days. Cumul also sent a yearly tribute to the Imperial Court, which included a consignment of the famous fragrant Hami melons. These can be kept and eaten at midwinter, and were so much appreciated in Peking that the popular saying became proverbial:

"With East Sea crabs and West Sea *hsia* (shrimps)
Stand Turfan grapes and Hami *gwa* (melons)."

The reception-hall of the Khan's residence held many souvenirs of those regal days. It was sumptuously furnished with divans and soft carpets, and contained many beautiful things, but the supreme treasures were the scrolls written by the hand of her Imperial Majesty the Empress Dowager herself. The penmanship showed surprising strength and virility, and great skill in handling the brush, for the "Old Buddha" held her own with both scholars and statesmen. From the palace, visitors were taken to the gardens, which were formed of many orchards, flower-gardens and a beautiful lotus-tank, the inspiration for which had doubt-less come from the sight of the lotus-moats which surrounded the Forbidden City in Peking. There were Chinese landscape-gardens with slender camel-back bridges thrown over running streams, and among the winding paths peacocks swept their trains regally and paraded their magnificence.

A Western visitor once asked the Khan how far his territory extended. With a sweep of his arm he indicated the distant snowy peaks of the Barkul Mountains and all that lay between Hami and the horizon. "All that you see is mine," he said, "and more that you cannot see." The answer was correct, for the mountain slopes of Barkul were his pasture-lands, in the natural fortress of Bardash which towered above his summer palace his word was law, and oases far and near acknowledged his rule and paid tribute to him, but his domain was of that unique character which, in spite of palaces and grandeur, still justified that most strange title—Khan of Cumul and King of the Gobi.

II

The Palaces and Gardens

The King of the Gobi owned three palaces, each of which was situ-ated in a different oasis. The principal residence was in Hami, the summer palace was at Aratäm, and the third palace, occupied by his nephew, was in Lukchun, on the South Road, not far from Turfan.

The Hami palace was the largest of the three and was known to contain the bulk of the Khan's wealth and treasures. The Lukchun palace was of the same design as that of Hami, and within it the various apartments were connected by long and devious passages which led to the numerous suites used by different members of the household.

The Khan of Lukchun had been the representative of the old King of the Gobi, but he had lost his reason and was now closely guarded in rooms at the very top of the palace. His people, from below, might sometimes see their ruler appear on the upper verandah, but he was always surrounded by attendants. All official business was therefore left in the hands of his advisers, but such was the strange reverence of the Turki people for their Khan that, insane as he was, his presence in Lukchun held their loyalty.

An atmosphere of tragedy hung over the whole household, as though the gloom of that mysterious upper storey pervaded it. The women of this madman's harem were numerous. They all dressed in emerald silk and, like other Lukchun women, wore a small, round, embroidered cap, which held the veil in place. Innumerable children ran from one part of the palace to another, laughing, squabbling, crying, complaining and carrying gossip. Every woman in the building had but one concern, and that was to become the mother of a son who would secure to her a permanent place in the harem. They were slaves whose invisible cages were none the less fearsome because the prisoners were fed with luxurious food and wore delicate silken robes.

Each of the wives had her own retinue of servants, but over them all was a head woman attendant. She was very tall and stately, and her grey plaits reached to her knees. By her regal bearing and natural distinction she might have been a gipsy queen. She kept all the serving-girls in order, and was responsible both for the supervision of the harem ladies and for the execution of their orders. It was she who brought us the Princess's invitation, escorted us to the palace, looked after us while we were there and took us back to our lodgings.

She led us through the outer court, past the military guard and under a gateway into an inner enclosure which gave access to the women's quarters. Through a maze of intricate passages she guided us to the rooms of the favourite lady who was expecting us, and after spending some time with her we were taken on to the suite of another wife, and so on, until we were confused by the number of our hostesses. In each room were the same beautiful silk rugs from Khotan, the same sets of metal-fronted boxes burnished in warm tints, the same embroidered satin cushions and the same low tables standing on the slightly raised platform where the princesses, surrounded by their women, sat all day doing the same fine embroidery. The papered window-frames were shaped in graceful arabesques and showed on to the private gardens where the women might walk unveiled. Cups, bowls and teapots stood on every available shelf, and polished brass basins, candlesticks and mirrors gleamed from the recesses.

In each room a *dostoran*[1] was spread and we were pressed to take food from the saucers of apricots, nuts, sweetmeats, grapes, melons and apples, and to taste the round cakes of bread which the hostesses broke and handed to us. Tea, on which there floated fragrant jasmine flowers, was served in azure bowls, and as the month of the *Ramaẓan* fast was only just over, all the special delicacies customary to the season had a place on the table. There were tangles of the finest dough-strings, called *sa-sa*, fried in oil and lying in a crisp confusion on crimson-flowered saucers, dishes of rice steamed with sultanas and sprinkled with sugar, and a custard made of egg beaten up in flavoured water and steamed to a firm substance.

When we sat in the apartments of the harem's immediate favourite, her husband, son of the mad Khan, came in to talk with us. He was interested in all that concerned us, our country, its customs and our religion, and invited us to come as often as we could and see his wives. When he appeared the other women slipped away to their rooms, and with scarcely veiled resentment left the favourite of the hour to do the honours. She, though proud of her distinction, was perfectly conscious that it would not last for long and that the young prince might soon exchange her for another. As soon as he left the room the other women returned, and we spent the whole day with them. We walked in the beautiful gardens and admired the flowers and the white peacocks for which the Lukchun estate was famous. These magnificent birds were the pride of the palace, and when they stood on the parapet or a bridge and spread their tails, or swept their long trains round the flower-beds, this elaborately planned garden made a perfect setting for their sophisticated beauty. As we left the palace we looked up from the outer courtyard at the railed-in verandah and pictured the scenes of irresponsible wilfulness of which we had heard. What stories these royal cage-birds could have told had they been minded to do so!

Years later we met some of these same women again, when war and rebellion had turned them out of house and home. They were then scattered from the palace, which had been destroyed, and had found

[1] *dostoran*—a low table spread with fruits and sweetmeats.

refuge in humble mud rooms with the poor of the land. I think they were happier than when they lived in the Lukchun palace, but I was glad to have seen them there, for, as a Chinese friend once said to me: "If you would understand these canaries, you must get inside their gilded cages."

The third palace used by the Khan of Hami was a summer residence built at the foot of the Karlik Tagh on the bank of a mountain torrent. Its beauty was the subject of much talk, but the grounds were strictly private and it seemed most unlikely that we should ever see them. Only by an unexpected turn of events were we able to do so. During one hot season a long trek in Turkestan brought us to Hami at midsummer, where we found the populace in a state of unrest. Rumour had it that the Khan was very ill and likely to die. The serious character of his illness was, of course, officially denied, but the women retainers at the palace knew the truth, and through them the news spread to the *baʒar* crowd, which was like a hive of excited bees. The men gathered in small groups to discuss the latest bulletin, and everyone looked anxious. One thing only was the subject of daily secret conclaves among the Turki people—the illness of their Khan and the chances of his recovery.

Almost every day some new doctor was called in, but whatever the *täbib* thought, the public announcement invariably declared that the case was not urgent, and that the Khan, though undeniably old, would soon be better. At the issue of each encouraging bulletin the excited talk would subside, but reassuring statements too often gave place to rumours which made everyone fear the worst, and there were many who shook their heads and told of unlucky signs and of unusual portents. The Khan's confidential minister, known as the Tiger Prince, rode here and there through the market-place, busy and anxious, while at the gate of his residence crowds always waited for the last word concerning the sick man.

One day a strange figure passed down the main street. It was that of a tall man with a waxed moustache and a bold impudent eye. He wore smart riding-breeches, high Russian boots and carried a riding-whip. We recognised in him a certain mysterious individual who had appeared in different oasis towns, sometimes dressed as a Mongol, sometimes as a Russian, but who this time was posing as a Hungarian doctor. As he passed through the crowd, men turned and stared and the word went round, "That is the Khan's new *täbib*." Within a few hours of his first visit to the palace reassuring statements were circulated in the *baʒar* and it was said: "The Khan is well again, the foreign drug has cured him." There was a sense of relief in the town, and when the Tiger Prince next rode through the *baȝar* he was smiling and happy.

Yolbas, the Tiger Prince, often had business with the master of the inn where we were staying, and during those momentous days there were long confidential talks between them, in a room of the innermost and quietest courtyard. On such occasions he often called in to see us, and one day he arrived just as the remains of dinner were being removed and the flies were returning to the wall surface for a rest. He looked round the airless room, and said:

"This season of 'Great Heat' is hard to bear in Hami."

"It is indeed very hot," I answered.

"You should go to the hills and rest a time," he said. "You have been looking after sick people day and night, and as long as you stay here you will always be kept busy."

"How could we go to the hills, and where could we stay?" I enquired.

"Well, if you would consider it I will see what I can do for you," was his answer.

A few days later our landlord brought us a message from the Khan himself, to the effect that, as he was not leaving the town this year, his summer residence at Aratäm was at our disposal if we cared to go and stay there.

We gladly accepted, and three days later left on the long road across the oasis and over the dry plain which led to Aratäm. The first stage lay through a stretch of fertile land, divided into farmsteads which were bordered with rows of tall poplars, and with wide-spreading mulberry trees which showed shiny ripe fruit among the leaves. The barley was already cut and the wheat was ripening. As we passed among the rows of field-peas we picked the juicy pods and ate the raw peas. The maize-cobs showed tufts of silky threads, and the sorghum was already raising its feathery panache high above all other field crops. Women in multi-coloured dresses moved among the cotton-plants picking the down from each bursting pod.

We were a larger party than usual, for the Tiger Prince had sent an escort with us, in charge of an equerry who was responsible for our safety, our entertainment and our comfort, and all through the day our cavalcade moved slowly along the narrow path which wound in and out among the fields. At dusk we halted at a farm. We were expected, and several women ran out to welcome us. It was pleasant to be welcomed, it was restful to find food and hot drink ready, and it was good to be among friendly, kind and hospitable people who put us on the footing of friends from the first moment. Next day they were up before dawn, cooking a meal that we might breakfast before we left, and they sent us off with fresh home-made bread for the road. The farm was on the very margin of the oasis, and that day we were on stony Gobi. The morning coolness soon vanished, and the heat grew to intensity, while the burning desert flooring seemed to throb under the fierce action of the sun's rays. There was no shelter and nowhere to rest, so we could only press on. By mid-afternoon a tinge of green became visible and the escort proudly waved his riding-whip in that direction: "Those," he said, "are the trees of Aratäm," but it was dark before we reached them. They marked the extreme southern point of the long strip of oasis, and a few mud houses were scattered among them. Again we were expected, and men were waiting to lead our beasts over the narrow, treacherous bridges and the difficult embankments of the watered land. From one to another the word was shouted: "The Khan's guests have arrived," and women in fluttering veils raced about excitedly, talking and shouting to each other. The men quickly surrounded our escort, eager for the last word about the Khan's health, and when they heard that he was better, a deep murmur of satisfaction went round.

They led us into the house of the headman, and slipping off our shoes we walked in stockinged feet over a soft carpet and sat where huge red satin pillows had been placed to give us support. A low divan table was set before us, on which the *dostoran* was spread. It consisted of thin cakes of baked bread, saucers of Turfan dried fruits, walnuts from the Khan's trees, pine-kernels from the hills overhead and dishes of fresh fragrant mulberries from the fruit orchards. The drink was salted cold tea, pleasant but not thirst-satisfying to a traveller tormented by the drought of a Gobi stage. We watched the restless members of this large household and saw our escort take an important-looking document from his satchel and prepare to paste it on the wall. That document was signed by the Khan, and it related to us. By its royal command we were to be entertained, and in particular must be supplied with fresh meat at each stage of our journey. This was the last official document inscribed by Maksud Shah to his people at Aratäm.

At dawn next day we looked out on the gardens, which seemed to lie close, though they were actually miles away. The oasis was wedge-shaped and hemmed in by grey sand which made a perfect frame for its vivid colouring. Behind the gardens rose the mountain, the base of which was formed of deep red sandstone; overhead stretched the cloudless sapphire sky, and the foreground was made up of many-tinted foliage. The old Khan on his travels had collected many specimens of beautiful and unusual trees, and had them planted by his clever gardeners in the grounds of his summer palace. Through the centre of the oasis the Bardash mountain torrent rushed in tumultuous cascades, dashing between rocks and boulders, and the noisy river gave life and movement to the beautiful scene which was so well fitted to supply a summer retreat for the ancient line of Turki rulers.

We had heard of the great charm of the Aratäm gardens, but when we saw them the unique quality of their loveliness surpassed all our imaginings. Two miles from the first enclosure we entered a winding road between trees of great variety and planted with such skill as to obliterate all suggestion of the gardener's art. Each tree was perfect as to kind and position, for the right one was always in its right place.

The fertility and luxuriance of the vegetation, the gaiety of the dashing stream and the welcoming kindliness of the trees whose boughs hung low under the weight of fruit which they offered to passing way-farers, were made the more entrancing by contrast with that forbidding waste behind.

The cultivated gardens were enclosed, and bordered with high walnut trees whose deep shade gave a shelter from the burning sun, but they were intersected with paths which wandered between plantations of fruit-bearing bushes and of flowering plants, such as the fragrant peony. During the weeks we spent there we wandered freely among eighty enclosures which formed the estate, and each day brought us some new discovery. We feasted on mulberries, on apricots and on the juicy *janästa*, which was a stalkless coral-coloured fruit with both the appearance and taste of a small cherry and which held a pointed stone. It grew on a low bush and, besides being pleasant to eat, was so decorative that the Turki girls picked the sprays to wear in their hair. We passed from one garden to another through small openings in the division walls, sometimes low and half-hidden, but always alluring, such as Alice met in Wonderland, and which we, like her, found to be magic openings leading to further outlooks and to ever more fascinating adventures.

The gardens were watered by means of a network of small irrigation channels, and the gardeners handled the little mud sluices so cleverly that there was no drought anywhere. One enclosure was planted with fig trees and others with pears, with apples or with peaches. The mulberry trees bore so prolifically that it was impossible to gather the harvest, and the ground beneath them was covered with fallen fruit.

It was taken for granted that some social entertainment should be provided for the Khan's guests, and each evening a band of women and girls trooped up the avenue, carrying covered dishes of food for our use and tambourines to accompany the dances with which they proposed to entertain us. As they reached the open space before the tent they fell into procession and passed before us, each one depositing her offering of eggs, bread, doughnuts or fruit.

After this they formed a semicircle round the tent door. Some of the women beat tambourines which were stretched with ass-skin, and others marked the rhythm with a hummed lilting tune, while all the young girls put aside their shoes and, drawing their long sleeves over their hands so as to completely hide them, stepped barefoot in slow, swaying measures to the rhythmic tapping of the tambourines. The dancers were very young girls, and all the small children joined them in this pastoral entertainment.

The low cabins where the gardeners lived were easily climbed, and standing on their roofs we were among the branches of the mulberry trees, some of which bore purple and some white fruit, while others had berries of an attractive pale lilac colour mottled with a darker shade. The flavour of each was different from the other.

Beyond the gardens was a road leading to a series of caves hollowed from the sandstone cliffs, where there were traces of frescoed decoration and remains of stately figures of the Buddha which showed close resemblance to the caves of Chien-fu-tung. These caves were visited by Sir Aurel Stein in 1891, and writing of the approach to the Aratäm gardens he says: "For nearly a mile the road turned and twisted among thick clumps of apple, apricot and peach trees and stately yellow-leaved walnuts. . . . No landscape-gardener in far-away England could have laid out his drive with more cunning, nor could any gardener's art produce such strangely varied, fantastic shapes of trees. Not since I made my way through the terminal jungles of the Niya River had my eyes been treated to such a feast."

The summer palace buildings consisted of one spacious central pavilion with deep verandahs and large airy halls, surrounded by smaller and outlying houses, some of which were only gardeners' cabins. The verandahs of the large hall were covered with beautiful vines, and in the shade of their thick foliage it was possible to escape the heat, even on a summer afternoon. The floors were spread with bright felts and carpets, and large jugs were filled with water and placed ready for hand-washing and ceremonial ablutions. Wall recesses were gay with painted bowls, a varied selection of teacups, many flowery saucers and more teapots than a family could use in a generation.

Following a narrow path up the mountain-side, one day's journey led to Bardash, a small village which held yet another country house belonging to the Khan, but this had not been used for many years. Its site formed a natural fortress and was prepared as a refuge for the Khan's family should political trouble in Turkestan compel them at any time to take flight. Around Bardash were the grazing-grounds of the Khan, and here his enormous herds of cattle and sheep were kept. The old man must often have viewed his possessions, counted his cattle and computed his wealth, feeling confident that so long as he ruled no one would dare to question his power. Yet he must sometimes have felt insecure about the future, and wondered if his young son were strong and experienced enough to hold the reins of government during the crisis which he knew must arise at his death. For this reason he placed increasing confidence in his Chancellor, Yolbas, the Tiger Prince, for Yolbas was a strong and clever man and was trusted by both Tungans and Turkis. Better than Maksud Shah himself, he knew that when the rule must pass to other hands there would certainly be an attempt to abolish the Khanate and bring Hami under the complete control of the Chinese Government in Urumchi. At that hour Yolbas knew that he must be ready to exercise the diplomatic skill which would, if possible, save the Khanate and place the new ruler firmly on his throne, and if that were not possible, would still secure to himself a place of honour and authority under whatever Government was finally recognised.

The days went by and we heard nothing from the outside world, but roamed in the earthly paradise and blessed the kindness of the old Khan in giving us the golden key which opened such vistas of delight. The silence of the nights was only broken by the call of some bird, but one midnight the distant thud of a galloping horse and the sound of a human voice was heard shouting an alarm. As it came nearer we caught the words: "The Khan is dead." Instantly there was a jangle of voices, questions from everyone, and within half an hour horses were saddled and riders were galloping off to Hami. Early next day every man in the place left for the city, and for a whole week we saw only women and a couple of old retainers, too feeble to take the long ride. A spirit of mourning was over the whole place and all the dancing and singing came to an end.

When the men returned they told of a great funeral. The Moslem town at Hami had witnessed obsequies worthy of a descendant of Genghiz Khan. His subjects had come from all sides to honour their dead monarch, and to acclaim his son as successor. They brought all the suitable offerings, and in return there had been largesse on a lavish scale. Every man received a length of cloth for his mourning garments, and purses had been emptied among the crowds. The young ruler could well afford such bounty, for it was known that inside the Khan's palace there was a deep well into which masses of gold and silver were constantly poured to form a reserve treasury fund. The actual location of the well was a carefully guarded secret, but many knew that at the innermost centre of the curiously built palace there was a section always guarded with scrupulous care.

Followed by a vast concourse of his people, the Khan's dead body, wrapped in a winding-sheet, was carried in state to the Mausoleum, where the tombs of his ancestors stood in order. Oblong, pillow-shaped monuments marked the place beneath which each body lay, and down in the crypt was the new opening, prepared to hold the body of Maksud Shah, last of the long line of Gobi Kings.

As I walked in the peaceful gardens I wondered what the future might hold for these excited, turbulent people, so easily deceived and so incapable of balanced judgment. I strolled in and out of the rooms where the Khan and his family had spent so many summers, and through the gardens and summer-houses where there were still so many little intimate things left about, and wondered who would be the next owner of this place. Would the simple vassals be allowed to transfer their allegiance to the rightful heir, or would the long and revered Khanate now come to an end?

In this mood I found my way into a hall where I had never been before, and in it stood the empty throne of Maksud Shah. It was a simple wooden structure raised a few feet from the ground, and its panels were decorated with carvings of the dwarf desert iris. By its side stood the sceptre, emblem of authority. It was from this seat that the Khan was accustomed to meet his people, hear their complaints and exercise judgment on all matters brought to him. It was destined never to be filled again, and that sceptre was not wielded by another Khan. Nazir, heir of Maksud Shah, was soon afterwards taken to Urumchi by order of the Provincial Governor, and there deprived of his liberty. The vassals were swept into a vortex of revolution and many of them were murdered by insurgents. The glorious gardens of Aratäm were soon destroyed by revolutionary bands, the summer palace was burnt to the ground, the fruit trees cut down for firewood, and the whole estate completely destroyed. Only the fortress of Bardash, which lay among the hills, was able to resist every attack and was to prove itself an impregnable stronghold in which rebel armies sheltered and from which no military effort could ever dislodge them.

Some years later I learnt that even the famous Hami melons were gradually deteriorating in quality, and was told that since China no longer had an Emperor, and Hami no longer had a Khan to receive tribute in melons, there was no incentive to growers to vie with one another in producing the choicest fruit.

THE INTERCOURSE OF THE GOBI

I

The Ears of the Gobi

A Chinese friend who was travelling with us toward the town of Barkul told us that Barkul and Pichan were always spoken of as the "Ears of the Gobi." Central Asian speech is delightfully picturesque, and we knew there must be a good reason for this graphic expression.

"The Ears of the Gobi!" I said. "That is a strange description for oases towns."

"You will understand it," he said, "when you get there."

For many days we had been watching the snowy peaks of the Barkul range coming nearer. Those eternal snows were the water-storage from which the fertile land of Hami drew its irrigation, and we were now on the point of leaving the main caravan road to plunge into a maze of stony mounds which must be crossed before we could reach the pass over the lowest part of the long chain of hills. The lake and the town of Barkul lay on the farther side of these mountains, which were the easternmost spur of the Tienshan range and called by the Chinese the Ba-li-kuen Shan. The Turki name for them is Karlik Tagh.

We had been promised a good road all the way to Barkul, but very soon the carters found that we had been deceived and had started on a terrible stage. The old opium sot who was to have guided us through the rocky gorge refused to leave his dope when the hour for starting came, but his little daughter jumped on her donkey's back and volunteered to lead us through a defile which was so blocked with boulders that it was hard to find a way between them. On leaving, she urged us to get ahead with the journey as the way was long and water still distant, then she turned and unconcernedly rode off on a solitary and most forbidding homeward way.

At sunset we had not yet found water and feared that we must have missed it altogether, but after a long search we at last discovered the little depression which the child had described to us, and in its centre was a scummy pool. We camped there for the night, using the only fuel available, which was a small heap of camel-dung left by the last caravan, and early next day pressed on again toward the pass, forcing our way through every kind of difficulty. It was a solitary road, but about midday we heard the sound of a barking dog and knew that there must be a tent not far away. Reaching it we found one family of Qazaqs—nomadic people from the steppes of northern Turkestan—who, when they were satisfied that we came unarmed and had peaceful intentions, received us into the shelter of their good *yurt* and gave us a drink of milk. The men were robust and the women, who were strong and intelligent, wore wimples on their heads. Their clothes were made from the coarsest hand-woven and home-dyed cloth. Their riches consisted of sheep, horses and cows, to which they steadily added by stealing from the flocks and herds of Chinese in the neighbourhood.

After a rest we left the tent, but were soon held up by a snow-storm which came earlier in the season than we had expected. In a short time we were shivering with cold and had to endure a cheerless night on the mountain-side, but even this brought some compensation in the sense of exhilaration which we experienced when next morning the sunrise revealed the beauty of the mountains covered with the glittering, freshly fallen snow.

On the third day we reached the ridge of the watershed, but it proved impossible to drag our travel-carts up the last steep ascent without completely unloading them. Nothing daunted, the drivers rose to the occasion and cleverly extemporised pack-saddles to which they roped the sacks of grain and parcels of goods, and so brought everything in safety to the summit of the high pass. From there a gorgeous panorama unfolded itself before us. The northern slopes of the mountains were clothed with sombre forests of conifers broken by stretches of emerald green pasture-land. Wide patches of blue and purple alpine flowers lay scattered abroad, and glittering snow-fields towered overhead. At our feet was a wide, even, downhill glade, leading through pasture-lands dotted over by flocks of sheep and herds of cattle, to a turquoise blue lake which, although far distant, seemed in that clear atmosphere to be close at hand. Beyond it lay warm-tinted sand-hills. It was nearing sunset and we were uncertain of shelter for the night, but following the easy down-grade we came to a deserted cabin which, though in ruins, served to provide shelter for the party. On the slopes below we could see the distant tents of many Qazaq herdsmen, so that night we made our horses' legs secure with iron hobbling-padlocks, and all through the night we heard them stumbling round the cabin, impatient of their shackles. Nothing except the strongest measures can make an animal safe against the clever wiles of a Qazaq horse-stealer.

The whole of the next day was spent among the pastures of the nomads. These wide-roaming tent dwellers live a life which is governed by the constant need of reaching fresh pasture, and it was this necessity which had brought them so far south as the foot-hills of the Karlik Tagh, where their flocks and herds roamed at large, guarded by herdsmen on horseback. They were a prosperous people and their felt tents conveyed a real sense of comfort, and even a high standard of nomadic luxury. They had great wealth in live-stock and also in pelts, in skins and in wool, and bales of these goods were stacked beside the encampments, ready to sell to travelling traders, who collected such merchandise for firms in southern Siberia.

The Qazaq is always considered by the real oasis dweller as a source of danger to the trade and traffic of a locality, and the peaceable Chinese, who have no means of defence against the raids of a people so strong, so fearless and so aggressive, tenaciously try to hold the area for them-selves.

At one place on the road we were surprised to see a high cross standing out against the sky. It was formed by an upraised pine trunk and a cross-piece, and had been erected in a Qazaq burial-ground. The graves were built up in a variety of structural forms, and there were even little flower-gardens round some of the tombs. They showed intimate signs of being cared for and tended, and with the high cross in the midst the small enclosure looked strangely like a Christian cemetery.

The Barkul valley stretches for fully one hundred miles from east to west and is about thirty miles wide. The southern hills rise well above the permanent snow-line, some of the peaks reaching an altitude of over 14,000 feet, and the whole area, including mountains, basin and town, takes its name from the lake. When we approached its shores we found them to be white with the alkaline deposit of salt marshes, and the lake itself difficult to reach because of the soggy land, but the water, though slightly brackish, was palatable, as it contains only three per cent. of salt. On the farther bank we sighted a herd of the wild asses which are a feature of the valley. The King of the Gobi had rights over these pastures and kept great herds of cattle on the grass-lands, which are renowned for a breed of horses famous for dash and spirit. Though splendid for riding purposes, a carter will not readily use these Barkul horses, as they are too difficult to break in to team-work.

During dry seasons the Barkul Lake attracts all the wild animal life of steppe-land to its banks, and troops of gazelles feed in its neighbourhood. There are innumerable wild-fowl on its waters, and during the days we spent there the sky was always criss-crossed by echelons of flying herons. I can never think of Barkul without the grating sound of herons' wings in my ears.

The town lies in surroundings admirably adapted to the exclusive policy so loved by the Chinese. Protected on the south by the mountain range, it is still better guarded from intrusion by an extensive desert on its northern side. The basin itself is a hollow into which the melting snows of the mountains flow, forming vast underground reservoirs of water on which the agriculturalist and the cattle-grazer can always rely.

The city wall is ancient but kept in excellent repair. Its outline is intended to represent a dragon, and when seen from a height, with the help of a little imagination this form can be recognised, and is a great source of pride to the inhabitants. In a temple just outside the town there is a tablet which was moved there from another temple which is nearer the lake. This inscribed slab is of great historic interest, for it bears the record of a victory gained in Barkul by Pei Tsen, prefect of Tunhwang, over Hu Yen, king of the Northern Hsiung-nu in A.D. 137. This victory records one stage in the long campaign carried on by the armies of the Han dynasty against the Hsiung-nu, or Huns, of Central Asia.

Within the town the spirit of conservatism reigns, and the citizens like to conduct all their business in accordance with the time-honoured traditions of Chinese standards. When entertained by the Mandarin and his family we found that certain customs which had been abolished in China proper since the proclamation of the Republic in 1911 still held good. We were back in the old Imperial days with all the ceremony and ritual strictly observed: the compressed feet of the women, their long finger-nails protected by silver sheaths, their wide-sleeved embroidered coats, the flowing gowns of the men, the old-fashioned tobacco water-pipes which they lighted with a stick of incense, all these things demanded the leisurely actions, the gestures and the courtesies of old-time China. It was a glimpse backward into a former era. Even the shops were entirely Chinese in style, and neither goods from Russia nor gaily coloured wares from Kashgar were stocked. "Foreign goods," was the scornful word with which the mention of all such things was dismissed. The business men were mostly from North China, and even the furniture of the houses was made by Chinese carpenters on the exact pattern used by their ancestors in the towns from which they had migrated.

This completely conservative and exclusive outlook has always been typical of Barkul. Early explorers of Mongolian territory whose travels brought them to its vicinity found no welcome from its officials. Some, such as the Russian trading expedition of 1872, were even refused admittance to the town on the plea that Barkul, though in Turkestan territory, formed part of the Chinese province of Kansu and was therefore not an open area for Russian trade. Other travellers, finding themselves unwelcome and suspect, turned off again to the desert without even entering the town. The gradual alteration of caravan routes has tended to increase this isolation, and Barkul is now much less of a camping-ground for camel traffic between Mongolia and northern Turkestan than was formerly the case.

The colonists of Barkul have been steadily increased by the accession of fellow-clansmen who in times of drought have left famine areas in North China and joined their relatives in this well-watered place. The fame of Barkul has travelled far, and in times of brigandage whole colonies of Chinese refugees have trekked westward and settled themselves on the land, bringing wide tracts under cultivation and achieving a good measure of prosperity. This steady infiltration has been going on for generations, and there is now a long chain of farmed oases among the foothills of the snowy range. Some are on the ledges of the lower slopes, while others stretch over land which has been reclaimed from the desert by irrigation and patient industry. All through the summer beautiful streams of melted snow run in unnumbered rivulets from the glaciers above, and the Chinese, with their genius for farming, have been alert to recognise possibilities in the area. There are unsuspected green fields and fruit orchards hidden in gullies and in every depression where farming is possible.

On the Turkestan side Barkul is cut off by the high mountains, and on the Chinese side by sandy stretches and barren rocky hills so deserted that one traveller records that in twenty-eight marches he only passed one single Mongol encampment. Yet Barkul's inaccessibility pleases her inhabitants vastly. She has one direct road to Hami, but this can only be taken on horseback. The mountain-pass by which we came is so difficult as to prevent all except the most determined from even attempting it, and the long, lonely downland access to the oasis of Tushui on the Kucheng road is now little used even by camel caravans owing to scarcity of water.

There it lies, a secluded town in a fertile valley, looking out toward China, and always alert for news of China and for every rumour from the land of its ancestry. Its inhabitants care nothing for doings in the

West, and Turkestan, though so near, means but little to them. Their messengers come and go to Paotow on the Yellow River, and beyond Paotow to Peking, for that is where the interest of Barkul centres. Isolated, compact, provincial, conservative, uncommunicative and secretive, the town keeps its counsels, but the Gobi has one ear extended eastward across the desert, listening to all that concerns China, and that ear of the Gobi is the town of Barkul. Ever since I stayed there, I have visualised that strange town in the form of an attentive ear, listening, retaining, hearing, remembering, but never telling.

*   *   *

The Gobi's other ear is the Pichan oasis, which lies a full week's journey west of Barkul on the Tienshan South Road. Many a traveller has left Barkul shivering with cold in a late spring snow-storm, and reached Pichan in sweltering heat, for it lies under the bare southern face of a mountain which so reverberates the sun's rays that the people of these oases call that range the Flame Hills.

Between the two ears lies a desolate way across a cup of the hills which was once a forest of tamarisk, but is now a burial-place of dead trees. From this low plain the South Road branches westward and its early stages are very arduous and unattractive. They lead past two lakes called East Salt Lake and West Salt Lake, but these sheets of water, one of which is little more than a pond, contribute nothing to the vitality of the region, for both are unmitigatedly salt. Between them is a ravine which in times of brigandage is a terror to caravans.

On the South Road Pichan is always called Shan-shan. Its right to this name is strongly disputed by the learned explorers of Central Asia, for the original Shan-shan, which is frequently referred to in the Chinese annals, has been clearly located as Loulan, an area of the Lob Desert on the old Silk Road, one of China's ancient trade-routes toward the Western world. On the explorers' maps the town may be marked as Pichan, but by the determinate will of the people Shan-shan it is and Shan-shan it will remain throughout the *serais* of the long South Road.

Every traveller is in a state of expectancy when the final stage toward Pichan is reached, and as we ground our way over the last twelve miles of gravel the carter began to describe the town and the glories of its *bazar*.

"At Shan-shan we shall find all sorts of things on sale," he said, "and from there onwards we shall not need to carry such large supplies.

We shall even find fresh bread at every stage." Then he added, "We must buy in a good stock of Shan-shan red pepper."

"Red pepper!" I exclaimed. "We can get that anywhere. Even the little stalls in the smallest hamlets have pepper if they have nothing else."

"Ah, that is not the same thing as Shan-shan pepper," he said, moving his lips with a greedy sucking sound at the mere thought of mixing that tasty condiment with his bowl of dough-strings. "Shan-shan pepper is famous everywhere," he added. "A little goes a long way, and it will be cheap here though it is expensive elsewhere. The red pepper and dried melon strips of Shan-shan are renowned throughout the country."

"Are the melons here as good as those of Hami?" I asked.

"There are no melons equal to those of Hami," he said, "but the Hami sun will not dry melon strips, and this is the only place where melons can be properly sun-dried."

"Why cannot it be done elsewhere?" I enquired.

"Everywhere else the shui-tu[1] is unsuitable," he said, "and only in Shan-shan is it exactly right. Wait until you taste them."

All he said was true. In this oasis the capsicum was of a quality superior to any that we had tasted elsewhere. As for the dried melon flesh, cut in strips, plaited and pressed, its subtle and aromatic flavour was different from that of all other dried fruits.

When we were still a few miles from the town we stepped over the clear line which divides desert from oasis, and in a moment were surrounded by rivulets which overflowed their banks and ran over the road, so that mules and cart-wheels splashed deliciously through the cool water. Around us were poplars and willow trees throwing patches of shade across our path, and the music of running water and singing birds filled us with delight. The sights and sounds of living and moving things brought intense relief after the deathly silence and immobility of the two Salt Lakes.

Pichan is in every way a contrast to Barkul. It is a fertile oasis surrounded by utter barrenness, and the town consists of one long busy street stretching for more than a mile and teeming with life. The inns were full of people coming and going, and the residents seemed to exist only to minister to the pressing needs of travellers, occupying themselves solely with such trades as supplied the wayfarers' needs.

Herds of donkeys laden with Turfan grapes, dried fruits from Kuche

---

[1] *shui-tu*—the reaction of earth and water resulting in climate.

or bales of raw cotton, were constantly arriving during the day and throughout the night. Lumbering carts from Kashgar brought in loads of coarse cotton goods from western Turkestan, carpets and rugs from Khotan or handsome leather goods, all of which were being conveyed to Hami and from there to the China coastal market. They were met in the Shan-shan inns by the stream of west-bound traffic coming direct from behind the Great Wall, carrying Chinese paper, tobacco, or rolls of satins, brocades and finely woven cotton materials such as Turkestan, for all her wealth in raw cotton, cannot produce. Tungans rode through the *bazar* taking their long trips from Cumul to Aqsu or Yarkand. The crowd was vivid, alive, excitable, talkative, mobile, communicative, impetuous, hurried and quarrelsome. All day long there was jostling, bargaining, shouting and cursing heard from one end of the market to the other.

In Pichan there was none of the cautious, secret curiosity of Barkul. Here everyone was eager for the latest cosmopolitan news, which was brought with extraordinary speed and accuracy, over the Himalayas from India or Afghanistan, or by travellers from Tashkent, Alamata or Samarkand. Down from Kashgar the couriers came, hurrying over the caravan road past Kuche and Turfan, bringing their news to the listening ear of Shan-shan which was oriented toward the West, always interested, always well informed, and always responsive to every repercussion, whether from India, Russian Turkestan or from Europe.

This turbulent ear listens to turbulent news. It hears of riots in Palestine, fierce Moslem demonstrations in India, strikes in far-away Britain and, nearer home, of risings planned by the Tungans, of unrest among the Turkis, of intrigue and occasional drastic purges in Russian-controlled areas.

Proud *Hadjis*,[1] just back from a year's pilgrimage to Mecca, gather interested crowds around them and tell of the pan-Islamic movements which are on foot. It is an old habit of travellers to tell their news at Shan-shan, and everyone is more communicative there than elsewhere. The *Ahungs*,[2] the merchants, the caravan leaders, the donkey-drivers, all gather to listen, then scatter to their daily work, but as they meet near the mosque, buy and sell in the market, or drive their beasts over the trade-routes, like self-appointed news-agents they pass on the information they have gathered to those who will be responsible for its circulation among the masses.

---

[1] *Hadji*—Moslem who has made the pilgrimage to Mecca.
[2] *Ahung*—a term of respectful address used among Moslems.

It is recorded of the great conqueror Genghiz Khan that he once praised a certain general who had refused a bribe by saying to him, "From henceforth you shall be eyes and ears for me." Did some long-forgotten but wise governor appoint officials in Barkul and in Pichan to be his far-extended ears or, not waiting for official recognition, did the people of these two oases take this honour to themselves?

It would need to be a great statesman indeed who could sift the news which reaches these two ears of the Gobi, and exercise such discrimination as to form policies which would enable him to rule with wisdom, equity and strength peoples so different as those of the Tatar, the Chinese and the Mongol strains which make up the tribes of Central Asia.

II

The Languages of the Trade-Routes

No one can travel on these trade-routes without receiving a vivid impression of the varied races, nations and tribes which make use of them. The diversity of physical type alone is enough to suggest the inevitable clashes which occur when men so vigorous, so assertive and so diverse are brought into close proximity. On one side of life only can they find a mutual interest to which each makes a definite contribution and in the making of it discovers a common basis for intercourse and mutual appreciation. It is the *bazar* life of the towns which draws them together and compels them to recognise their inter-dependence. As in the oldest days of inter-tribal relationships, commerce is still the healthy link which establishes friendly relationships between men who, apart from this business intercourse, have but little in common.

The nomad must depend upon the agriculturalist for his grain, the town dweller looks to the nomad to provide him with horses for riding and camels for transport. Chinese competency in the banking business and in money-exchange is universally recognised, while the native of Turkestan is relied on for the quickest transport and it is always he who conveys fruit and vegetables at record speed from one oasis to another. The Sarts and the Noghais from Siberian borderlands are competent to negotiate important deals with foreign firms, and Tibetan and Mongolian hunters supply furs which enable all to face the bitter cold of the Central Asian winter. By means of the hardy traffickers of the Himalayan passes, Indian produce such as precious stones, silk scarves, muslins and laces for women's veils, are exchanged for Kashgarian carpets and rugs, and the artist craftsmen from Peking, seeking jade, depend on the rough Khotan "jade-fisher" to fetch it from the bed of the river.

Thus it is commerce which draws them all together, while diversity of language is the great divider, preventing easy intercourse or exchange of thought between the Chinese and all the Tatar tribes. The two prevailing languages are Chinese and Turki, but each is spoken in a wide range of varied dialects. For official business Chinese is the language most generally used, and from Peking to the border of Siberia, Mandarin Chinese serves the traveller for all necessary purposes, though over a very wide area north and south of Lob Turki is commonly spoken, and Arabic, being the language of the mosque, can be used right across Central Asia.

There is no similarity between the Chinese and the Turki languages. The written language of the former consists of ideographs, thousands of which must be mastered in order to read even simple books, and the calligraphy of which requires great dexterity. Turki, on the other hand, is an alphabetical language, written in Arabic script. Its beautiful and regular construction was described by the great philologist Professor Max Müller as comparable to a tree having innumerable branches, each of which is bowed to the ground by the weight of the fruit which it bears. From one simple root an amazing structure can be built up which imparts every shade of meaning to the original word. The Turki grammar which my companions and I were studying informed us that we need only learn forty-four verb elements by rote, which was encouraging, but when we looked further we met this amazing sentence: "The number of intelligent forms which a single Turki primary transitive verb-root is capable of yielding amounts to not less than twenty-eight thousand." Then despair seized us.

The verbal construction presents such complex tenses as the Hearsay-Compound-Present, which supplies such a form of speech as "I am understood to be doing," and a Future-Present-Potential in which the verb is built up to express "Thou mightest be about doing." In studying this Turanian tongue we detect a "commencement of the process by which the Aryan languages have been polished down and enamelled until they reached their present condition. . . . In Turki it is as though the centuries flowed backwards and we ourselves could watch the process and solve the doubts of the learned as to the methods used." [1]

[1] *A Sketch of the Turki Language*, by R. B. Shaw, F.R.G.S.

This great language is spoken in varying dialects, by the Turki, the Qazaq, the Kirghiz, the Noghai, the Sart and the Uzbek.

As a result of intercourse with such diverse peoples, the Chinese language has undergone a subtle change which has brought it one stage nearer to the more Western speech of the Turki people. Out of the necessity for a *lingua franca* in which business deals can be discussed, considerable simplification in the structure of sentences has been reached, and idiom and catchwords learnt in the desert cause great amusement when used in China proper, where correct and dignified speech is expected. Moreover, as the Chinese who live in the Gobi are drawn from every province of the vast republic, their dialects vary, and a kind of basic language has been evolved which is easier to understand than pure Chinese, which depends so much on the intonation of each word to convey its meaning. Necessity has also introduced a custom whereby when two strangers meet one will say to the other, "My words will relate to farming," or food, or trading, as the case may be, and thus a clue as to what follows is given.

Apart from these two languages, Manchurian is spoken in a small area of Turkestan where Manchurian troops were granted land by the Emperor Chien Lung (1710-1799). They settled around the oasis of Kulja and never lost their native tongue, which meanwhile in their own land of Manchuria was superseded by Chinese. In recent years the study of the Russian language has been introduced into Central Asian schools, and a knowledge of colloquial Russian is spreading rapidly along the main trade-routes.

The division caused by diversity of tongues can be overcome, but the cleavage due to differing religious convictions is fundamental and causes antagonisms too deep to be easily eradicated. The Moslem, whether Turki, Uzbek or Kirghiz, scorns Buddhists for their idolatrous worship, but the man who prostrates himself before a visible god equally despises the Moslem for what he considers his deplorable code of ethics. The Chinese, though he shares the Buddhist faith with the Mongolian and the Tibetan, has no lama system, while the nomads view all religious ceremonies as "lama business."

The demands made upon the Moslem community in regard to purification, food restrictions and constantly recurring religious services inevitably control their whole social system and segregate them from their neighbours. Five times a day they join in public prayer, for one month of the year they take neither food nor drink between sunrise and sunset, they eat only animal food which has been slaughtered under mosque superintendence, and all these restrictions prevent social intercourse with any who hold another creed.

Town dwellers and nomads can have but little understanding of each other's outlook on life. They meet in the *baʒar*, but the nomad dreads to spend a night within the city wall, while the town dweller fears the loneliness of the spaces and desires the comfort of a house and the companionship of neighbours.

These mixed and differing people give a colourful and picturesque appearance to the *baʒar* where they all meet. The nomads are conspicuous by their robustness, and among them the Qazaq women always form an outstanding group. Their intelligent, strong faces are framed with white wimples, and they are alert and interested in all that is happening. The origin of the Qazaqs can be traced back to certain bands of people who left the Turkic Empires of the thirteenth and fourteenth centuries to revert to a nomadic way of life and culture, but the sons and daughters of these steppe dwellers are now absorbing education and beginning to take their part in the administration of their own country, the Republic of Qazaqstan, which is a recognised member of the U.S.S.R. and lies to the north-west of Turkestan, stretching eastward as far as the Altai Mountains.

Another frequent sight in the *baʒar* is the Kirghiz, wearing a pointed cap of bright chintz bordered with lambskin, and a heavy fur coat even though the day is hot. His boots have high heels and he rides a bullock right up to the shop door, shouting to the man inside to come and receive his order. He sometimes carries a hooded falcon chained to his wrist, and as soon as his business is done he is off again to the steppes and to his comfortable tent. He is the descendant of a nomadic warriortribe which gained its independence after the death of Genghiz Khan and firmly refused allegiance to the Russian Empire.

As I stood in the crowd I often saw the shopkeepers saluting tall handsome Noghais, and I observed that they were always addressed as *Bey*, which is a title indicating wealth. These customers bought the best goods on the stall and made nothing of expense. They had come to town on big business, and after long and confidential talk with the leading merchants returned to the Siberian border, where traders would be waiting for their report of the deals they had made.

The Mongol was never in his element in the *baʒar* crowd, and only necessary business took him there. He generally pulled a camel bulkily laden with skins, which he led to a large enclosure set apart as a camel-inn. He mistrusted himself and his own capacity to deal either with the sophisticated Chinese or with the arrogant Turki merchants, both of whom had always cheated him and would do so again. They did not know his language and he understood but little of theirs, yet if the help of an interpreter were sought he would require to be paid by both sides and profits would vanish. The Mongol's broad-featured, weather-beaten face generally wore a slow, kindly smile, but he felt ill at ease among these town folk, and only when he turned his back on them and rode off toward the pasture-lands of Karashar was his native dignity restored. The grass-lands of Karashar are the home of the Kalmuck tribes, but farther east the Torgut Mongol is more frequently met. His forebears once invaded Europe and he is a more assertive man than his Kalmuck brother, though both equally share the nomad hatred of town life.

Occasionally a tall broad-shouldered man, wearing well-cut corduroy riding-breeches, strode down the street, riding-whip in hand. His white shirt-front was scrupulously clean and his bearing distinguished. In deference to Chinese custom, which requires that a rider dismount at the city gate, he led his horse by the bridle, but he was evidently conscious of superiority to the men around him. This was a Manchu from the rich and fertile Ili province. His progressive nature is always eager to seize every educational advantage which will fit him to compete with the most advanced peoples and enable him to hold his own among them.

One strange group of people sometimes appeared in the *bazar*. A man, leading his donkey, would push his way through the jostling crowd. He wore a small cap embroidered with silver thread, and a long coat, unbuttoned and hanging loosely round him. A few paces behind there walked a pathetic figure whose face and form were completely covered with a thick black veil woven from horsehair. Over the head was thrown a long black coat with its empty sleeves hanging at the sides. Something moved vaguely where the arms should be, which revealed this shapeless mass to be a woman with her baby in her arms. It was an Uzbek family party, and illustrated the humiliation of woman and the degradation imposed on her in that Moslem state. Such revolting sights will soon be no more, for the physical release of these captives is being effected by the strong measures introduced with Soviet control.

The home of the Uzbek is in Russian Turkestan and his racial strain is formed of three elements, the Turkic, the Iranian and the Mongol. Many of them are still nomads and living in tribal organisation, but Uzbekistan has been Sovietised since 1924.

At the close of day the common interest which held these incongruous people together loosened its hold, and the crowd separated and fell apart. Nomads urged their steeds to carry them swiftly away from the irksome crowds to the pleasant solitudes; the Chinese put up the shutters of their shops and called the staff together to count the takings and discuss the business ventures of the day, while a pleasant odour of savoury food gave promise of a good meal. The Turki merchant applied himself to the elaborate ritual of the evening hour, then carefully dressed for sunset *namaz*.[1] High above the town a small figure appeared at the summit of the minaret and a sonorous voice proclaimed the unity of God, while in the mosque courtyard prayer-mats were spread and each man prostrated himself toward Mecca, responding in guttural tones to the Muezzin's call to prayer, while the Qazaq, Kirghiz, Uzbek, Sart and Noghai, each on his homeward way stopped and, wherever he might be, knelt and repeated his creed: "There is but one God and Mohammed is His prophet."

III

The Transport of the Gobi

Although the camel caravan is recognised as the best means of transport for valuable goods over great distances, yet, for local journeys or when, owing to the perishable nature of the cargo, time is of great importance, the Turki with his drove of little donkeys is the man. He is met on every road of Turkestan, always hustling his beasts through a cloud of dust and lashing them right and left to keep them up to speed. He is a great burly fellow, dressed in loose clothes which increase his bulk, and his baggy trousers are stuffed into high leather boots. His *chapan* (coat) is tied in with a thick belt, and he wears a round hat with a sheepskin border which mixes with his loose hair to form a shaggy frame to the weather-beaten face. One man, or at the most two, will drive twenty donkeys, riding behind them, shouting incessantly, and never letting them slacken to normal walking-pace.

He mainly conveys melons, early vegetables and fruit—apricots, peaches, grapes and pears according to season—but makes up his load with rolls of loosely woven, undyed cotton. He knows no organisation of travel life, but pushes on from stage to stage with restless energy. When the donkeys must be fed he drives them into an inn-court, tosses

---

[1] *namaz*—Moslem ritual prayer.

the panniers from their backs, carelessly throws fodder into the manger, pulls some hard cakes of bread from his own food-bag and sits down to a meal of bread soaked in tea. Being a Moslem, he will buy nothing from a *kaper* (infidel), so himself carries what he will need to eat on the road. He takes a short sleep while the animals finish their grain, then he flings himself on to his beast's back and urges the drove on for as far as he dare before feeding them again.

The donkeys are small and cheap, so he is careless of life and sacrifices them in large numbers to his passion for speed and his reckless output of strength. He will use dangerous short-cuts over which no other class of transport-man will venture, and in bad weather many beasts die by the roadside. This does not trouble him, and he just lifts the load from the exhausted creature and divides its weight among the others, then pushes on again, regardless of suffering, to deliver the cargo at market, for he has a master as impatient as himself waiting at the other end. He will normally do five full stages in three days and nothing may stand in his way, but when the goods are handed over and he can lodge in a Moslem inn he enjoys twenty-four hours of sheer luxury. There is hot, greasy *pilau*[1] to eat, women to wait on him, and long carefree hours of sleep to enjoy before he starts again on the hectic return journey.

The Chinese method of transport is quite different. Great carts which cross the Gobi link the commercial life of China proper with the raw material markets of Turkestan, and a carter who leaves Kashgar in February will swing through the gates of his Honan home town in August without having shifted his splendidly packed cargo. In the course of this phenomenal journey he will only need to change the axle a few times in order to adjust the cart to the wider desert gauge or the narrowing Kansu or Honan ruts. The widest axle is required between Suchow and Hami, and the narrowest in Honan.

The Chinese transport agent makes constant use of the words *ta-suan*, which mean to compute, calculate, think out, arrange ahead, organise and consider carefully. It represents a characteristic so much admired by the Chinese as to be regarded by them almost as a virtue, and is an integral part of their economy of life. The man who can *ta-suan* gets full value from time, strength, capacity and money, and anyone who has not the intelligence to *ta-suan* is, in Chinese eyes, an uncivilised barbarian. The classic example of *ta-suan* is the incident of a Chinese general who, centuries ago, was sent out with an expedi-

---

[1] *pilau*—Oriental dish of rice with meat and spices.

tionary force to conquer the land beyond the deserts. He sat down to *ta-suan*, and doing so he realised that it might be all too easy to conquer the land yet lose the campaign through inability to feed his own troops. He therefore selected bodies of men versed in agriculture, and sent them ahead with supporting forces to select suitable sites where they must plough and sow, then reap the harvest. If the grain were carefully stored against the arrival of his troops, it would support them through the following year. Thanks to such good *ta-suan*, he carried the campaign to a successful issue.

The Chinese transport system across the Gobi has been built up on the principle of *ta-suan*, and in entire contrast with the native genius of the reckless Turki driver. The distances which make a possible stage for man and beast have been meticulously calculated, as well as the equipment necessary to ensure reasonable ease on the journey. The Chinese understand the art of elimination and how not to encumber themselves with superfluous impedimenta. Before leaving home the Chinese carter has thought out where he can exchange his money to best advantage, what goods can be bought and sold most profitably in each place, and where money invested in an extra horse or mule will bring in most profit. He leaves Central China with large sleek mules for which he himself has paid a good price, but which he sells to rich Tungans at Suchow at tremendous profit, and himself buys rough but desert-hardened beasts. For the return journey he will invest some of his depreciated paper taels in good Turkestan horses, which are very cheap in Dzungaria but fetch a big price in Central China.

By this means his round trip has brought in many advantages apart from the straightforward profit of his hire. In manipulating each exchange, this seemingly simple creature shows himself to be actually a financier of no mean order, and handles the complicated money market of Central Asia like a professional banker. He never allows depreciated currency to be left on his hands, for he has always exchanged it in time for carefully selected goods, and if he has an employer he will stipulate that his wages be paid at the place and in the coin most to his advantage.

The third great transport agent of the Gobi desert is the camel-caravan leader—a *bash*. Owing to his manner of progress across the Mongolian sands, he is often spoken of as a "camel-puller," and anyone who has seen the camel-puller dragging his feet over the long stretches, holding the end of a camel's-hair rope which connects him with the foremost beast of the caravan, appreciates the accuracy of the term.

The Central Asian camel is a very different creature from the fleet dromedary of the Arabian desert. This is the bulky Bactrian species, with two humps forming a natural saddle for riders, and whose caravan training has made its pace slow and steady. From calfhood it walks with the caravan, and the even progress of the long train becomes part of its nature. It is born by the wayside, and for the first few days of its life is carried by its mother in a wooden cradle on her back, but before it is a week old the little angular creature, which seems to be all legs and hump, runs fitfully by her side, always pushing its nose toward her udder. The cradle still serves for an occasional rest and doze, but the young camel develops very quickly, and soon it is learning to follow the trail. Its burden is very carefully regulated to its strength and it is about four years before it carries a full load, but besides its merchandise, the caravan always has a miscellaneous lot of goods to transport, and there is bedding, spare clothes, tent-poles, big iron pots for cooking, trivets and smaller cooking utensils, besides sacks of flour and of ʒamba. Such odds-and-ends are bulky but not heavy, and half-grown beasts can help by carrying some of these lighter things.

The strength of the camel varies according to size and age, but the driver has an unfailing test by which he knows if each beast's burden is suitable to its capacity. When it kneels to be laden it always grumbles, growls and shows resentment, but of this the driver takes no notice. He goes on loading up until the moment when the beast suddenly becomes silent; then he knows that the burden is heavy enough, and nothing more is added. By the time it is four years old the young camel has a wooden pin through its nostril, to which a rope is fastened and by means of which it is controlled and taught to kneel and to rise at a given signal. This pin is a thin peg of wood, sharpened at one end and thrust through the nostril. It is fitted with a wooden or leather washer to avoid chafing the delicate cartilage, and the exact spot for piercing the nostril is carefully chosen. When on march, a fine rope of twisted camel's hair attaches it to the camel which walks immediately ahead. Until the day when it falls out through old age or over-fatigue it lives and moves with its caravan, walking in single file across sandy wastes, and taken away from this life it would inevitably become restless and unhappy. The camel is proverbially surly and resentful, and its only response to friendly advances is a shower of loathsome cud which the creature has regurgitated in its annoyance and sprays over the troublesome human.

It is a slow, heavy beast, but with muscles like steel and amazing powers of endurance which carry it through extremes of heat, cold, hunger and thirst such as no other beast of burden could stand. Its weak point is its *morale*, and it is here that so much depends on its human master. Discouragement is fatal, and it cannot react against over-pressure. When exhausted it loses heart, sinks by the wayside and dies. It is not a clever animal, but there are camels which have the quality which in humans is called the revolutionary spirit, and the caravan leader fears to keep one of these in his ranks, because its instinct is always toward revolt against authority. One such camel will sometimes break up the discipline of a whole train, for, owing to the mass mentality of the herd, even peaceful beasts are suddenly infected with the spirit of revolt and in a few minutes the whole caravan is in utter disorder. Sometimes, without any warning, the leader breaks away, leaving the herd possessed with an unreasoning passion for liberty, and I have seen such a camel racing across the desert spaces with remnants of harness still clinging to its sides. "Let it go," says the driver, "the spirit of madness has caught it and it will race until it falls dead."

With a beast to handle which is temperamentally so ungenial and so unresponsive to human companionship, the choice of a driver is a most important matter. The capacity to handle camels has a certain racial basis, and among the mixed peoples of Central Asia it is recognised that some have these qualities, while in others they are lacking. The Turki, who is a restless, energetic, active being, always on the move and unable to control the impetuosity of his own nature, compels his animals always to travel at top speed. His horse seems to draw vigour from its rider's energy, but the camel refuses to respond to his relentless demands, and soon develops what has been well described as a mood of "fatalistic inertia" which is the despair of a *bash*, for it unfailingly means that day by day, and without apparent reason, some camel will drop out of the train and nothing will avail to induce it to pull itself together and make another effort. On the other hand, the Mongol desert-ranger and his riding camel understand each other completely. At a touch of the halter it turns with him toward something or someone that he has sighted on the horizon, and at a flick of the whip breaks into a loose ambling gait which takes it swiftly over the ground. The Mongolian among the dunes is one with his beast and with the wide desert expanses in which he lives.

The duties of a good caravan *bash*, however, require more mental acumen than the nomad Mongol is able to supply, and any large caravan left under his charge would lack order, system, discipline and attention to detail. The Chinese and some Mongols of northern Shansi, however, have all the qualities necessary for this particular work. They are tall, robust, strong, adaptable and clever, and have brought the organisation of caravan life to a high art. Such men are the product of a long process of mental evolution, and by some mysterious racial atavism they know by instinct all there is to know about desert caravan life. They have imbibed it from observation, tradition, saw and proverb. From infancy they have been with camel-men and cannot realise that there was ever a time when they were unfamiliar with the tones, the commands and the actions by means of which the beasts are controlled. It is a complete mentality, and it is theirs by inheritance. They know how to compute to within the narrowest margin how much grain will be required to feed each guest and each driver, and can tell at a glance which man will be a large eater and which a small one. With a surprising capacity for mental calculation the *bash* will quote prices for men or merchandise with an accuracy which, after the normal rebate on bargaining, leaves the final price fair to the customer and yet with a generous margin for himself. He is a most accommodating host. The guest may, if he so pleases, supply and make his own food, or the *bash* will quote an inclusive price for food and transport over the three months' journey. In the ordinary way the traveller rides a lightly laden camel with his own bedding and fur coat strapped beneath him, but a woman and small child may demand a little more protection from heat and cold, and in this case the *bash* will supply what is known as a camel-litter. It is a narrow wooden box with a seat on which a small Chinese woman can just sit cross-legged with her baby in her arms, but it allows for no change of position, and an equal weight balances the load in a similar box on the other side.

The camel-litter is spoken of in caravan circles as a luxurious way of crossing the desert, and we were often urged to take advantage of its ease. It was doubtless recorded to our credit that we were unwilling to spend extra money on our own comfort, but the fact was that nothing would have induced us to expose ourselves to the torture of being shut up in a small wooden box for long hours of heat and cold, unable to relax a muscle until such time as it would please the *bash* to order the beasts to kneel. Moreover, anyone possessing a gift of imagination could visualise the position of that box if the camel which carried it went mad and ran amuck. Such things have happened before and may happen again.

IV

The Homes of the Desert

It was a liberal education to live as guests in so many and such varied home circles as we did among the oases of the Gobi, where the Chinese, the Tungans, the Turkis, the Mongolians and the Russians each have an entirely different idea of home and what it stands for. Peoples of such widely differing racial strains, yet compelled to live in identical geographical conditions, each construct a home on the traditional pattern handed down by their ancestors, and while these houses in exile are necessarily poorer than the old family homes, the differences which the altered conditions entail are all superficial, while the likenesses are radical.

As nest-building is an ineradicable instinct of the bird, so home-making is a universal urge in the human race, and just as one kind of bird, wherever it is, will build the nest peculiar to its kind, so men of each nation will make a home which is true to type, and which expresses something racially fundamental, even though it be in unfamiliar circumstances and in a place far removed from the land of their birth.

The home of the Chinese, for example, be it in some wealthy city of Central China or in a Gobi oasis, is governed by the same tradition of ancestral control. The tablets stand in the place of honour, and therefore the spirits of those who are gone before are always present. The men and women who use the home today carry on the sacred line of life, and feel responsible to hand it over through others, who in their turn must see that it never fails of a succession. This belief profoundly affects the details of family life, and holds the members of one household together with strands which are not so much woven by affection as by a sense of mutual responsibility within a clan. In the rich home the old grandfather will lead his little grandson by the hand through the flower garden, showing him the dew on the lotus plant and instructing him in the ethical meaning of its purity. In the miserable Gobi shack the flower garden is replaced by a mud "flower wall," made by laying a few sun-dried mud-bricks to form a patterned stand for the onion growing in a bowl and the turnip which has been coaxed to a blossom. Yet round that mud wall the shabby old grandfather also leads a small child, for it is the correct thing to do so, and a Chinese home should have its flower garden, but, failing that, it must have a "flower wall."

At New Year the shack living-room, miserable though it be, is the scene of the most exact rituals when, in absolutely correct order, each member of the family makes obeisance to the elders. The feasts fixed by the Chinese calendar are scrupulously observed, and I have known a man to carry a water-melon for days across the desert in order that at the Feast of the Moon, in the most desolate of wayside stages, he might put an old rickety table in the courtyard and offer the melon, cut in slices, to the queen of Heaven.

The traditions, the rituals, the basic and essential relationships which govern men's intercourse, control the small circle living in such far-away places as rigidly as they control the family which dwells in one of China's great cities. Both act according to principles laid down by ancestors, whose control is so subtle and so little questioned as to leave no room for the spontaneous and the unusual. Such care and decorum in the art of living amounts to a cult, and it is one which the Chinese understand. Let the conditions be ever so degraded and the life of the individual ever so sordid, the little courtyard is still home to him, because he finds there the satisfaction of fulfilling the requirements demanded by tradition of the members of one family, and from this place he hands down to posterity the life with which the gods have entrusted him.

In the home of the Tungan there is neither shrine nor ancestral tablet, but its pattern is as definite as the ancestor-controlled home of the Confucian, only here the scheme of life is ordered by the rules and regulations of the Islamic faith. Five times a day, beginning with the hour of sunrise, the man must prostrate himself with face toward Mecca and recite the liturgy of the hour. He never dares to neglect the endless ceremonial purifications which his religion demands, and for one full month of each year he observes the exacting and rigid fast of *Ramazan*.

The Chinese man is generally satisfied with one wife only, but not so the Tungan, who imitates the prophet in respect of polygamy, and even arranges to keep a family in every town where he does business, that he may be sure of comfort wherever he goes. These different families are kept quite separate and seldom even know each other, but he is the centre round which all the homes revolve, and the whole aim of his women's existence is so to gratify all his appetites that he will desire their services in Paradise and require their presence there. The women live in secluded courts into which no man may ever enter without permission. They dress in black and cover their heads with a black cap or hood, excepting on festive occasions, when they are allowed gayer colours, but if at any time they must pass through a court where men are present, they veil their faces.

It is not unusual for a Tungan to marry a Chinese woman from a Confucian home, and the strain thus introduced has greatly affected the race, but before a girl enters the Moslem household she must submit to the most elaborate purifications in order to cleanse her from any defilement contracted when she was a "pig-eating *kaper*" (infidel). Only after fastings and drastic cleansings may she enter the "clean" household of the husband. The tragedies of the Tungan women and their many humiliations and sufferings have made of them a disciplined and controlled class.

To the Tungan male, home is the place where he moves as lord and master, where every whim is satisfied, where his comfort is everyone's first concern, and where his command is absolute and unquestioned law. To the Tungan woman, home is the place where she is fed and clothed in return for bearing children, and where all that is required of her is entire submission to her husband, and that she put his pleasure before every other consideration. Should he bring home a young concubine, she must show no distress and must discipline herself to be neither quarrelsome nor rude in her relations with the intruder. Decorum is the law of the home and becomes her controlling principle. She moves in and out before her mother-in-law, and among the other wives and their children, a quiet, sad, repressed being. Her only place in the scheme of existence is to be satellite to some man who has bought her for use as he would buy a chattel for his household.

The Turki, though a co-religionist of the Tungan, is in temperament and habits of life entirely different. He seldom marries a woman other than one of his own nationality, and the style of the home is highly individualistic. Nearly the whole floor of the living-room is raised about one foot higher than threshold level, and this higher portion, lavishly spread with coloured felts, is the playground of babies and small children. The number of them is incredible, and in the women's quarters every room has the appearance of a nursery. The children, like their parents, are strong, sturdy, lusty, noisy and quarrelsome, and the atmosphere of the house is restless.

The men live their own separate life of business friendships and convivialities, in which the women have no part and of which they know next to nothing. In contrast with the highly organised Tungan home, the

Turki household has no method at all. When the children are hungry they yell for food, which is instantly thrust at them, and the women do a bit of cooking as they feel the need of it. Baking is the only household duty which demands forethought. Somewhere outside the house is a mud oven of a primitive type, and when there is a big baking on hand all available help is requisitioned to heat the oven, knead the dough, form the flat cakes, moisten them, smack them neatly with the palm of the hand against the inner surface of the hot oven wall, pick them off with a trident and hand out a liberal portion to hungry and greedy youngsters. Many baskets of bread are baked at one time, and the family eat it for several days, whenever the recurrent pangs of hunger demand satisfaction.

A visit to a Turki home is quite unlike a stay in a Tungan house. In the latter all is order, thrift and propriety, for existence has progressed on definite and established lines until it has mastered the technique of orderly conduct. Among the Turkis all is noise and turmoil. Gay clothing, swaying draperies and light muslin veilings combine with the rapid talk of girls and the gutturals of men's voices to fill the air with noise and movement. The Turki hostess only stays quiet for a few minutes at a time. She jumps up, runs away, comes back, calls to her daughter-in-law, slaps a younger child, hugs the baby, runs off to shout to some unseen person, and only spares a portion of her attention to her guests.

A painful feature of Turki home life is the pathos of its unhappy members. There are scorned brides, childless wives daily expecting to be chased from the home, women whose bodies are broken with perpetual child-bearing; the delicate girl-wife victim of rapid phthisis, uncared for and uncommiserated, a child with haunted eyes who knows that marriage with an old man is to be consummated in a few days, or one nursing a limb with a painful tubercular swelling who hears the daily quarrels and discussions as to whether or no she can be married before the man has discovered how ill she is.

The foundation of the Turki home is undisguised gratification of sensuous pleasures. The man comes home to sleep, and all the relationships of the home centre on his use of those hours of darkness. On that score he is master, and tyrannical in his use of power, for the male creation has unquestioned right of dictatorship in the Turki world. He has too many children to be deeply attached to any one of them, and when a child dies its death brings him little sorrow. As to a sick wife, the sooner she goes the better. Family relationships bring him so little of

the chastening which refines and purifies character that it is not surprising that men of the Turki race remain, as their wives always declare
them to be, "mere animals."

The Mongol's home is his tent, and his nomadic life is the expression
of a compelling instinct. A house is intolerable to him, and even the
restricting sense of an enclosing city wall is unbearable. He builds no
house, and is therefore completely free from attachment to a building;
he moves his tent several times each year, and is therefore unattached
to any special locality. He is a child of the desert, and the spaces belong
to him and his roving race. The tent is both attractive and comfortable,
and he shares it with the more delicate of his animals, for on the right
side of the slightly raised portion of the floor where the master always
sits is a space screened off for the use of kids and lambs. Home, to the
Mongol, is the place where he shelters from cold and heat, and from
which he tends his flocks and herds. Above all, it is the place which
holds the family shrine, on which is spread an offering of thirty-six
small brass bowls full of pure water.

Among the Mongols I observed a happy *camaraderie* between the
young married people, which was revealed by the straight, honest, open,
appreciative looks they exchanged, and which showed neither shyness
nor boldness. The wife is generally an excellent horsewoman and an
industrious cattle-herd, and this healthy, bracing, hard life tends to
normality in human relationships. She is her husband's helper and takes
her full share, in fact more than her share, of pastoral work. She is not
his chattel, but his fellow-labourer, and is valued accordingly. Children
are necessary to the family's wealth, but the Mongol lives in and for
the present, and looks neither backwards toward his ancestors nor
forward to his descendants. In fact, so little do personal ancestors mean
to him, that his language has no word for any forebears farther removed
than great-grandfather. Tribal ancestry, however, linking his people
with warriors of old whose memory is a source of pride to the whole
community, has a great place in his thought.

The Mongol lives from day to day, enjoys his life and values his
home—that is the *yurt*, where his few material goods are collected,
around which his flocks and herds are grazing, where his wife shares
his simple nomad life, and where through the family shrine the great
spirit he calls *Tengri* touches his life.

In many oasis towns a few Russian *émigrés* have sheltered and made a home for themselves. They instinctively congregate in one quarter, and though the houses are built of the same mud-bricks and scanty timber as are all the others, the homes which have come into being are of a totally different order from those of their neighbours. As soon as the Western visitor enters the door of the little whitewashed building and steps into a small living-room, he has a sense of something radically different. In the centre of the room is a square wooden table with benches standing round it. Whenever possible the floor is boarded, and all the woodwork is scrubbed daily. The mud walls are whitewashed, and there is always a brick stove made by the man of the house, the front of which is the cooking-stove and the back the woman's bakery, while on the top the bricks are not too hot to make a comfortable bed for the children. By the fireplace are a few home-made wooden stools on which the members of the family sit.

There is no luxury of any kind, but as soon as these people are released from dire poverty and are able to save a little from earnings, the small paper window is replaced with some panes of glass and sufficient pink cotton print is bought to make a curtain which can be drawn across it. By this action the Russian unconsciously expresses the fundamental difference between himself and his Central Asian neighbours.

To the *émigré* his home is a retreat from which he has the right to exclude the curious and shut himself in to enjoy the pleasures of intimacy with his wife and his children. In the houses of the Tungan, Chinese or Turki neighbours, visitors may walk in and out of the open court-yard as they will, but if they wish to enter a Russian's house they find a shut door at which they must knock before they can gain admittance. In the other houses the torn paper windows invite inquisitive or friendly eyes to peep and see what the family is doing inside, but the little pink blind indicates that here this would be an indiscretion.

Unlike his neighbours, the Russian father sits down to meals with his family round the table. Each one will cross himself before eating, and the meal is a family gathering and a natural time for conversation. His Oriental neighbours feed apart and in silence, but Russians retail the day's happenings as they eat cabbage soup and break slices of home-baked bread into it. Nor are these home-makers entirely satisfied until there is a *samovar*, a teapot and painted china bowls to stand on the table, "as it was in Siberia."

To a Russian *émigré* the home would be unblessed without the shrine in the corner of the room, and though he may not have been able to bring the treasured family *ikon* away into exile, yet there will be a card framed by himself and a little oil lamp with a bead of light burning before it.

To these people home is the centre towards which all life converges and for which all else exists. They work in order to support a home, they go out in order to come back to a home, and in that home they relax and enjoy freedom from toil and from the demands of business intercourse.

To the Chinese his home is a link in the long chain which spans the ages, and he feels himself responsible to keep that one link in repair during the time he spends on earth, that the chain be not broken on his account.

The Tungan's ambition is to be master of an establishment which is more prosperous and respected than was that of his forebears. This is why he is so arbitrary regarding his home, and demands so much of his sons and of his womenfolk. None of these must leave a blot on the house which Allah blesses with riches, prosperity and an abundant progeny.

The Turki flings off the conventions and traditions which might restrain him, and in his own home sets out to enjoy to the full the one life which he is sure of, and just so far as this household contributes to that enjoyment, his home is a success.

The Mongol's home is a shelter from the cold wind and blizzard, but when the storm is over he drops the door-curtain behind him and ranges forth across the sands to give expression to his wild nature among the free desert spaces, until the need for shelter calls him homeward once more.

The Russian *émigrés* may have a background of wealth, comfort and culture, but these things belong to their past. In the cruel life of exile there are no such amenities. They uncomplainingly accept the difficult conditions, yet carry with them a sensitiveness which only allows them to feel safe from injury and insult when the door of home is shut.

On the basis of common humanity and as Christian missionaries we found a place in each of these varied homes. With the Chinese we had an understanding born of long years of sojourn in their midst, and of love and appreciation which made intercourse very easy. The Moslem women recognised that we, no more than themselves, were idolaters, and even called us "people of Allah." The Turkis found, perhaps for the first time, women with heart-leisure to sympathise with them in their sorrows and sufferings. The Mongols appreciated our enjoyment of their free, unconventional ways, and the Russian exiles trusted us. Thus we learnt to live in these varied homes among women of many nationalities and to develop, in our nomadic life, the art of being "at home" in a crowded *serai*, a Mongol *yurt*, a Siberian *isba*, a Chinese courtyard, a mud shack, a camel-driver's tent, or the palace of a Khan.

V

The Solitaries of the Desert

The desert atmosphere has a special quality which makes every object in the landscape stand out stereoscopically and with amazing clearness. One traveller very accurately observes: "The air is so clear that there is no perspective," and others have remarked on the surprise which they experienced when, sighting a caravan which they thought was close at hand, they have found that hours passed before it reached them. Trees, walls and landmarks which appear to be but a mile distant are, in fact, half a day's journey away.

This atmospheric peculiarity has its counterpart in the human intercourse of the desert, and in the personal incidents of each traveller's journey. In other surroundings many contacts and happenings might seem too trivial to be remembered, but in the desert the detachment of life from all normal intercourse imparts a sense of gravity to every rencontre, and each touch with human beings is fraught with a significance lacking in the too hurried intercourse of ordinary everyday life.

On the desert track there is no such thing as a casual meeting, for even wayside contacts instantly become significant, and the spot where the meeting took place is for ever associated in the mind of each with that incident. The details of each Gobi journey are recalled as a series of pictures which associate every stage of the road with men and women who were met there, and with unforgettable scenes in which each took part. Just as in a desert landscape the detail of the only cultivated patch on a sandy hillside will stand apart from its grey setting with a brilliance which is like enamel, so these incidents stand out unforgettably against a background which is free from the blurs, the confusion and the turmoil of a preoccupied life. There is nothing hurried in the occasion, but space for such conversation as forms a permanent link between two individuals who will never meet again. Each, in sharing some experience of life with the other, has stripped himself of the trammels of conventionality and the make-believes of artificiality. In such conditions men instinctively speak soberly, never idly nor merely in order to pass the time, but with a sense of living in a world of reality where nothing is trivial. Great journeys do not merely consist in passing over vast spaces, but owe their greatness far more to the human intercourse and knowledge of fellow-men which they involve. It is this which makes them memorable.

Sometimes the rencontre leaves an indelible impression, clear, precise and full of meaning, like a picture composed by a master-hand. One morning at sunrise I walked on a high overhanging bank which skirted an oasis stream. I was out of earshot of the small camp noises, and silence prevailed such as only the desert knows, but the stillness was suddenly broken by a low murmur which seemed to be that of a human voice and appeared to come from beneath the very ground on which I stood. I looked around but could see nothing, so made a wide circuit to reach a place from which I could see what lay under the overhanging bank. When I did so, I looked for a moment on a scene which will ever remain in my memory.

Under the bank there was a low grotto, and in its centre a living, bubbling spring. The face of the small pool was tremulous with airbubbles which rose and broke perpetually on its surface. By the pool there crouched a lama in red cap and maroon travel-coat. With hollowed palms he lifted the cool water and scattered it on the ground, paying homage to the great life-sustaining element. Utterly unconscious of being watched, he performed each minute gesture of the ritual, and I heard the rise and fall of his clear, sonorous mountaineer's voice reciting the liturgies of dawn.

At other times the encounter may take the form of talk with an unseen person. Midway on a tedious Gobi night stage we heard the faint clang of a distant bell which warned us that some other traveller was moving toward us. We could see nothing, but the sound came slowly nearer, and in time one large covered cart, drawn by five mules, loomed from the darkness. The carters exchanged a word, and I called out in Chinese: "Where do you come from?" "From Urumchi," was the answer. There was a movement in the cart and a woman's voice spoke, saying, "Who is there?" The tone showed me that she was not Chinese and I went over to speak to her. "My guest is a

Russian," her carter told me, and when I spoke in Chinese she ventured on a few halting sentences, but when one of us addressed her in French she instantly responded fluently in that language.

The carters sat on their heels and smoked their pipes, exchanging news of the road. The mules stood at ease and rested. I never saw the woman's face, nor did I even ask her name, but under the veil of darkness which enabled us to remain unidentified we talked with great intimacy. She told us of her flight from Russia with husband and child at the time of the Revolution, of their journey across Siberia to Turkestan, of losing all they possessed and of their terrible poverty. When her husband had the chance of a job in Uliassutai they went to that remote place and lived there for some years. She went on to speak of her husband, of his hasty temper and of his impatient handling of the Chinese. "I hate those people, I can never forgive them," she exclaimed. It was evident that this was a woman who had known embittering sorrow and must be met with no easy, comfortable words, but with strong, courageous sympathy. Encouraged by the response, she poured out a tragic story. "The Chinese are so revengeful," she said, "and never forget an injury. My husband was too outspoken and he made one of them lose face. The man said little, but watched his chance to pay him back. He did it through our only child. He was a lovely boy. One day he came in from play and I saw that he was not well. He seemed to be so limp and sleepy that I took him into my arms and nursed him. Then I put him to bed and he was quiet, only unnaturally sleepy. I could not understand it for I had never seen such an illness before, and, of course, there was no doctor in the place. When it was too late I realised to my horror that he was dying of opium poisoning. There was nothing that I could do to save him, and soon he lay dead. That was the work of a Chinese who had been employed by my husband, and that was his repayment for my husband's anger. Soon after this my husband also died, and now I am on my way to Tientsin or to Shanghai. I have no money, but I shall find some kind of work there. My parents gave me the best education that could be had in Russia. I can teach French, German or Russian. I shall surely find something to do, but if all else fails I will do housework."

I saluted the courageous spirit with which this woman faced life, and a future that might terrify anyone. She was undaunted, and there was nothing of defeatism in her heart. The carters moved. "*Tsou, tsou!*" (On, on!) they called, "we must get on." "*Tsou, tsou!*" we responded, knowing that a long stretch lay ahead, but there was still one message to be handed over to this woman which, if she received it, would release her from the torment of hatred which was like a canker in her heart, embittering every part of her existence, a word which might speed her on her lonely way with a sense of care, love and protection. Only a few sentences could be exchanged, but they were vital, as every word spoken in such circumstances must be, and I handed her a New Testament in the Russian language, a book which told of One Who alone could make everything new for her and would be her ultimate defence. This book she took with her into the unknown.

The missionary must be unafraid, easy of access and open to every manner of approach. The Christian caravan must be free to all, at any time. It is the only tent that a stranger dares to approach after dark, but many a desperate traveller, under the shadow of darkness, has come there for help, certain that no fierce dog will attack him nor rifle-shot blaze out at him.

A heavy stage had kept us on the road from dawn until nearly nightfall. Only then did we reach water, and each one went straight to his appointed work in setting up camp. In a few minutes the tent was up, the sail-cloth manger was stretched between the backs of two carts, and a bag of chopped sorghum leaves, mixed with bran, emptied into it for the mules to enjoy. The skilfully laid camp-fire blazed up and a satisfying meal was rapidly prepared.

Darkness fell, and we were wrapt in silence and solitude. Then someone stirred the fire, and as it flamed brightly the light showed the form of a man who had crept silently to within a few yards. It was startling to see the thin, anxious face and the watchful eyes staring at us. A word of challenge rang out: "Who are you? Come and declare yourself." "It is only I, teacher," was the answer. "I have come to beg a dose of medicine for my friend. He is terribly ill."

This was no robber, but a fellow-creature in trouble, and we made room for him and poured him out a bowl of tea. He slid forward, drank the tea and told us that he and his friend were hiding in a cave not far off. The friend had gone down with typhus fever and was delirious, so they could not move on. When he saw the light of a camp-fire he had come over to see who was there, and when he found that it was a party of missionaries whom he had met once before, he knew they would be friendly and help him in his difficulty.

We asked where he came from. In answer he lifted the square of blue cotton that covered his head, and in the flickering light we saw a raw wound where his ear had been sliced off with a sword. Then we knew that this man was a deserter from the frontier garrison fifteen miles away, for the cutting off of one ear was the regulation punishment meted out to a captured runaway. If he ran away once more, as this man was now attempting to do, on recapture he would be flogged so mercilessly that he might die of the wounds. "Why do you hide so near to the garrison?" I asked. He looked at me with a simple honest stare. "My friend and I escaped together, and now he is very ill with fever. I cannot leave him alone, for I must carry water for him and look after him. That is why I came to you for a dose of medicine. Surely you have something with you that will make him well." "If they took you again your punishment would be terrible," I said. "Yes," he answered, "they flog so that you die of it. If my friend were only well again we might escape, but unless we get off quickly, we are lost. I cannot leave him, for if I did so my conscience would reproach me. I must remain with him." He got all he required of medicine, water and food, then vanished into the darkness. Years later we knew that he and his friend both reached safety.

Sometimes we met a fellow-traveller who, far from being tragic, provided us with entertainment by the way. The pitiless Eastern sun was dipping toward the horizon. The long day's march was over and we sat in the courtyard of a Chinese inn which was the only hostelry in a lonely gully. The owner of the inn had saved himself the trouble of building a house by hollowing a few caves from the base of the cliff which shut us in to the narrow defile. Of furniture there was none, but the earth which the excavators threw out had been used to make a mud bed and a little mud table which was of one piece with the bed. The cave was dark and windowless, and I willingly turned my back on its sordid squalor to sit on the doorstep and look out at the more cheerful courtyard where our mules were stirring up the grimy dust as they rolled luxuriously after the hot stage.

Presently I noticed a young boy approach, leading a strange-looking man by means of a short stick, of which each held one end. The man's clothes were ragged, and he had every appearance of extreme poverty. I saw at once that he was blind, yet his face bore the expression of one whose inner being is supplied with some constant and secret delight. His body was broad and well developed, but his bare feet and ankles were the smallest I ever saw attached to so powerful a frame, and he walked with a delicate, mincing tread, as though stepping to the rhythm of a tune that he alone heard.

He sat down on the ground and with a quiet, absorbed air said very simply: "This is the male eagle's call." Then followed a perfect bird-call reproducing the sound so familiar to us in wild mountain ranges. "Now listen," he went on, "the female pitches this note and the little ones in the nest call out thus for their food." Then followed the various cries, each with a subtle change of intonation. He then gave in rapid succession the different notes of the wild pigeon, the pheasant, the magpie, the kingfisher, the water-wagtail and the hoopoe. With complete accuracy he reproduced the travel-call of the wild geese when the birds cleave the air, taking their way to the south marshes. For a full half-hour this beautiful concert continued. The liquid notes, the delicate trills and warbling sounds filled the grimy courtyard with such melody as is only associated with shady woods and babbling streams.

I asked him how he came by so much bird-lore and he replied: "I just listen."

"When did you lose your sight?" I asked him.

"I was born blind," was his reply.

"He lives alone with his mother and she too is blind," the small boy explained. "They are very poor, and when visitors come to the inn I bring him here and so he earns enough to feed them both, but when there are no travellers he and his mother go hungry."

I placed a loaf of bread in his basket and a little string of copper coins, which sent him away delighted at so generous a reward, although it represented merely the value of a few pence in my own country. Darkness was coming on and his young guide took him by the hand to lead him away. Day and night were but a change of word to him, and as he trod his way daintily through the filth of the inn-court his face still gleamed with the delight of artistic achievement.

In what semblance did the country appear to this blind man's inner vision? Was he seeing surroundings as beautiful to the eye as the bird-songs were to his ear? The wretched inn, the dirty yard, the human squalor were nothing to him, whose hearing was always alert to nature sounds, whose movements were measured by some instinctive rhythm, and whose face shone with a rapt absorption in a beauty to which I, and not he, was blind.

Another day brought a meeting with a family party consisting of a man, his wife and a young boy. From the exchange of usual questions and answers we learnt that the father was a juggler from Russian Turkestan and his boy an acrobat. The child alighted from his donkey, and there, on the sandy plain, gave us, with great delight, an impromptu performance of acrobatics, which his father followed up with an exhibition of deft juggling and conjuring tricks. There was a singular charm about the naïve performance, and when it was over we supplied a simple communal lunch of bread and sultanas which was shared by carters, servants, performers and ourselves.

The spirit which blows over the Gobi spaces is a spirit of liberty, yet on a few occasions we made contact with that hideous and revolting thing which has dared to lift its head even in those free spaces—the traffic in women and girls. One day a party of Chinese children reached a halting-place at the same time as ourselves. Their heads were covered with muslin veils, and burly Turki Moslems were hurrying them off to Turkestan, driving their little donkeys at top speed. A few questions and answers revealed the fact that these girls had been bought up in a brigand-infested area of north-west China at an all-round price of a dollar apiece, and were being taken to the large towns of Central Asia. They were children of "infidels," but were now to be made daughters of Islam and the first step was to veil their faces. The children ran to us, chatting of their homes and all they had left behind. They fought down the tears which filled their eyes, accepting the inexorable fate which had befallen them, and when the master of the crowd gave the order, they obediently mounted their donkeys and rode on.

Another day I walked down the narrow street of a small oasis town with impotent rage burning in my heart, for I had met something that afternoon which defiled the spaces and glory of the desert land, something which was an insult to its solitudes and which was only made possible by the vileness of man.

A few hours earlier I had met a young girl near the great tree under which we had sheltered our tent. She was completely out of place in her surroundings, for she had painted lips, plucked and pencilled eyebrows, dyed finger-nails and most elaborately dressed hair—in fact, she wore the complete paraphernalia of the Chinese prostitute. As I spoke with her we were joined by another girl of the same type, and then yet another. They had come from Hankow under escort, and were travelling to one of the large cities in Central Asia. "Come to our inn," said one of them, "there are several more of us there."

I followed her to the *serai*, where a thin, hawk-like woman sat on the *kang*, while yet another young girl standing near her prepared her opium pipe, mixing the drug and lighting the little vegetable-oil lamp ready for her use. Her profession was unmistakable and she eyed me suspiciously and with antagonism, but politeness required that she ask me to sit down, and we exchanged the necessary preliminary remarks. "These girls," she said, in answer to a question, "are my nieces who are travelling with me. We are resting here for a few days, but we expect shortly to move on." I knew that a company of Government troops were also spending a few days in this oasis, and their presence would mean business and provide money to meet the expenses of the further journey.

I learnt something of the girls' history from one and another. They all came from one of the famine areas where stark hunger had driven parents to sell their children when all else was gone. This woman and her gang did regular business in such places and bought girls wholesale. The helpless victims had feared, wept, and then stolidly accepted the sacrifice required of them to save the lives of their parents. "It is the decree of the gods," they would say, and there was heroism in the calm under which they hid agony and offered themselves for the sake of others. There was no escape and they must bear it.

One of them was brazen and callous, but the others were different and longed for home, for parents and for safety. They were frightened of the unknown which lay before them in a strange land and among a people whose language they could not understand. For some it would mean nightly attendance at a city restaurant to entertain visitors after late feasts, and for others, years spent as the concubine of some old profligate.

My words with the "aunt" were few but strong, and when I had finished speaking she made a gesture of impatience and gave a sharp and angry order to the girls to get ready for business. Soldiers were beginning to hover round and she received them affably, taking occasional whiffs of the pipe as she talked with them. I knew that I was dismissed, and I left the place raging to see girls sold to a life which was worse than death. That night the holy stillness of the Gobi was broken for me by that evil thing.

Next morning, while "aunt" was still deep in the stupor of her dope, the girls came again to see us. At this early hour they were weary and dishevelled, their gay clothes were thrown off and the colour was gone from their cheeks. We talked for long, and it may be that a small ray of light penetrated their minds, just enough for them to know that it mattered to God that they were victims of the world's evil. It was a very small ray, but there is no limit to that which one ray of light may reveal.

They soon travelled on and were lost in the life of the larger oases, but they are not forgotten by the women who met them that day, and forces beyond anything they have ever dreamt of are reaching across the desert and touching their lives.

One of the most picturesque encounters was in the streets of a border oasis when the Panchan Lama, who had left Tibet to seek shelter at Peking, passed through with his body-guard. He had crossed the frontier of China at a mountain pass and this was the first town he reached. His armed escort rode to and fro, filling the street with the resonant sounds of mountain calls and rally commands. The horses galloped ahead or wheeled, turned or stood, in instant obedience to the riders, who constantly closed in and circled round a small two-wheeled cart covered with yellow brocaded silk.

Inside that yellow cart sat a figure like a carved wooden idol. A pointed yellow brocade cap covered the upper part of the face, and a cloak of the same material draped the body as idols in the lamaseries are draped. The features were immobile and devoid of personal expression. Long practice in the art of meditation had taught this lama how to obliterate the stamp of personality from his expression. The look in the eyes was remote and he seemed unconscious of the immediate, as though the strange scene of a large commercial oasis town with its main streets crowded with eager, staring, chattering Chinese had no power to summon that latent spirit to consciousness of active life.

The only movement I detected among the yellow draperies was in the fingers of the right hand and in those carven lips. The fingers held a string of yellow beads which dropped slowly one by one as the lips murmured a reiterated *mantra*.[1] This man, so inanimate in the midst of his intensely vital body-guard, claimed the veneration of all Tibet, because he seemed to be so near complete absorption into the passive, the utterly contemplative and the wholly uninterested.

It was in a squalid trade-route town that we first met the Rostoffs. They were Russian *émigrés* and their house stood by a sluggish stream and was reached by a plank bridge. The living-room was large, bare and very clean, for the floor, table and benches were all scrubbed daily. Although they lived in extreme poverty, the atmosphere of the home was cultured, sociable and seemed free of oppressive anxiety. Poverty could not suppress the vitality of these resilient Slavs, just as luxury had never destroyed their power of imagination, and through their years of wealth they had always retained a free unconventionality which now served them in good stead.

---

[1] *mantra*—a sacred text or passage used as a prayer or an incantation.

A barren Gobi range

The sturdy desert grass

The worst of the desert stages were over

A desert road

An old woman of the oases

A child of the oases

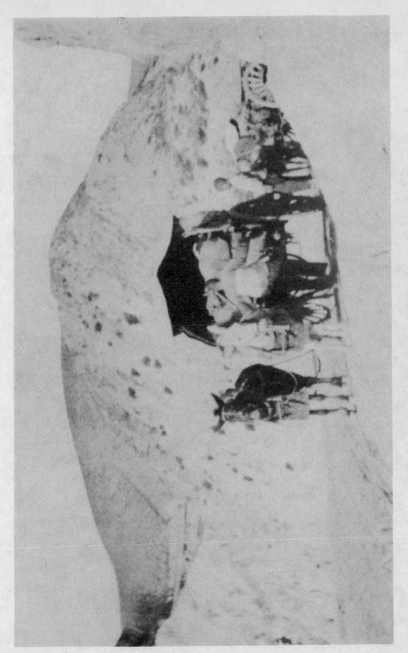

Our caravan near Starry Gorge

One of the Khan's men

A Turki girl

The empty throne of Maksud Shah

Nomadic luxury

A family of Qazaqs

The road between the ears of the Gobi

A Chinese transport cart

The vineyards of Tuyok

The walls of Dakianus

We sat and chatted while Madame poked sticks of kindling into the heart of the *samovar* and blew on them until they crackled gaily; then she carried the urn outside the front door, that the light wind might keep the wood flaming. She took a new loaf of her own baking and cut it into slices which she placed on the table, then she collected bowls and glasses sufficient for her party of guests. The door opened and a tall boy walked in. His face was so handsome and so interesting that I could not take my eyes off him. Monsieur Rostoff made a sign and the boy came to his side: "My son is completely deaf," he said, "but he is very studious and knows French well."

At the tea-table one of us sat next to the deaf boy, and with paper, pencil and the French language as medium of communication a conversation was carried on. The circle was a babel of confused tongues, for some spoke in German, others in Chinese, two conversed in English and the whole talk was bespattered with Russian ejaculations and calls to the younger children. Through it all the deaf boy pursued the silent conversation in French, and he told of the lessons which his father gave him in Russian, in French, and in various branches of mathematics. The joy that he derived from this hidden intellectual life was intense, shut away as he was from all outward form of expression. Under the broad, thoughtful brow his eyes burned with a sombre glow such as I have only seen in the face of poets, yet it was to be his fate never to hear the music of words. Darkness fell, and we bade farewell to these brave Russian people who fashioned happiness for themselves out of such meagre and umpromising material.

Sometimes the occasion of a rencontre has been an offer of hospitality for the night, failing which we should have been left shelterless. It was so on one occasion, when the house was that of a small Turki farmer. His home was part of the outside earth-ramparts of an old ruined town which had been a prosperous place in the time of the Tang dynasty, but was now crumbling to earth, a waterless waste haunted by wolves and other wild beasts. The farmer's home was reached by steps leading down into a small courtyard. He had only one narrow room to offer us, but we crowded into it, thankful for any cover from the storm.

The daughter-in-law of the home was very ill and lay on a small *kang*, in constant and terrible pain. "It is a most mysterious illness," said our host, "she suffers so much, yet there seems to be no cause for it." Enquiry revealed the fact that twelve months earlier she had been thrown from a horse and that her back had been painful ever since.

"Any woman can get over a fall from a horse," he said, "and I cannot think why she has not done so. She has just gone from bad to worse as the months pass, and nothing seems to help her. It must be that an evil spirit is tormenting her and she cannot be well until it is driven out."

Next day there were signs of unusual happenings in the house. The courtyard was swept and tidied as though in preparation for an honoured guest, and soon after dawn several people arrived. First to come were the sisters of the sick woman, then her two married daughters, closely veiled and riding on donkeys. Shortly before midday there was a shout and all the men of the household went outside the front door, bowing low before a weird and evil-looking Mullah.

He and all the others passed into the sick woman's room, and soon the chanting of incantations began. Suddenly a funeral procession appeared in the yard. It consisted of all the relatives and they all wore mourning, while two men carried a bier such as the Moslems use to bear a corpse to the tomb. On that bier the sick woman was laid and covered over with a funeral pall. The bier was lifted by the bearers, and to the sound of a wailing lament she was carried away. Last in the whole procession was a youth carrying a spade and a rope. The cortège walked a mile to where the cross-roads met, and there they waited while the young man lighted a fire and dug a shallow grave. Over that grave the bier was laid, and with many incantations and acts of sorcery a complete funeral was staged.

Finally she was carried back to the house and laid again on her own mud bed. The mourning-clothes were laid aside, the masquerade was over and the devils had been cheated into thinking that the victim was dead. Our unscrupulous host came smiling to our room. "That was a great Mullah," he said. "I paid him handsomely and feasted him too. He says the devil has left her and that she will soon be well." But the exhaustion of the patient, and her groans of pain, gave the lie to all his boastful talk.

THE GREAT TURFAN DEPRESSION

I

The Town of Turfan

THERE is no more interesting oasis on the Asian highways than Turfan, which lies on the trade-route between Hami and Kashgar, and is always called "Turpan" by its own inhabitants. The town lies in a hollow the lowest part of which is claimed to be the deepest dry depression on the face of the earth. To the south the ground sinks to salt marshes, and beyond these to the foot of decayed hills called Kuruk Tagh (Dry Mountains). Writing of this locality, Sir Aurel Stein says:[1] "Along the foot of these Dry Mountains stretched the deepest portion of a great fault trough, descending to close on a thousand feet below sea-level, which forms a most striking feature of the basin. From the barren slopes of the high mountain range to the north there stretches downwards a wide waterless glacis of gravel. . . . Above its foot rises an utterly barren chain of hills thrown up by the same mighty geological dislocation which created the fault trough below it. The forbidding look of this hill chain, glowing red with its bare deposits of sandstone and conglomerate, explains its Chinese name of 'Hills of Fire.'" The barren slopes of the Dry Mountains are destitute of animal life save antelopes, wild camels and hares. The vegetation of their few and widely scattered oases is confined to bushes of tamarisk, saksaul (*Anabasis ammodendron*), reeds, poplars, glass-wort (*Kalidium*), and ma-hwang (*Ephedra*).

To the north of this great undrained basin rise the snowy peaks of the Bogdo-Ola (Mount of God) with an altitude of 22,000 feet, marking the highest part of the Tienshan range in that area. In the centre of these uncompromising surroundings Turfan lies like a green island in a sandy wilderness, its shores lapped by grit and gravel instead of ocean water, for the division between arid desert and fertile land is as definite as that between shore and ocean. Its fertility is amazing, and the effect on the traveller, when he steps from sterility and desiccation into the luxuriance of Turfan, is overwhelming.

The productiveness of this area does not depend on a variable rainfall, which must inevitably result in some uncertainty of crops, but

[1] *Innermost Asia*, by Sir M. Aurel Stein, K.C.I.E.

183

on underground supplies connected with the eternal snows, which have never been known to fail. Such an oasis supports a definite number of families who feed on its produce and thrive by the export of surplus supplies, therefore even one half-acre of usable soil allowed to remain untilled would be a disgrace to its owner, and such neglect would not be tolerated.

The luxuriance of crops in the Turfan oasis is due to the use of a remarkable irrigation technique which is known as the *karez*[1] system. Standing at a height and looking over the Turfan plain, a traveller will see long lines of earth-works on the barren glacis which give the impression of mounds flung up by gigantic moles. The mounds are hollowed in the centre, and closer inspection shows them to be openings leading to a deep underground passage. Far below is a water-channel which conducts the melted snow to the torrid fields which are waiting for irrigation, and the number of openings in one line may be as many as two hundred.

The nearer to the mountain the deeper is the *karez*, and at its start the water may be fifty feet below the surface, but at its final opening it flows almost to ground-level, and is as cool as when it left the hills. Sometimes the water is led into a shallow well, and at others it bursts out and forms a beautiful pool from which the stream is led away wherever it is needed. The *karez* must be kept in constant repair, and until the traveller knows what the long lines of earth-mounds mean he is startled to see man after man emerge from an opening at the top of a mound which he, in his ignorance, probably imagined to be the site of some old grave.

The expense of caring for the *karez* is very heavy, but Turfan produces such phenomenal crops of fruit, grain and cotton that any expenditure on irrigation is justified. From time to time the older *karez* fall into disuse and new ones must be prepared. Wherever there is *karez* water, farmsteads and the homes of agriculturalists will be found, and when the opening is no longer usable the population moves elsewhere. It is an old system of the Persian deserts, and how and when it came to Turfan is uncertain. Early historical records of the district, of which there are many, make no mention of this unique feature, and

---

[1] *karez*. "A subterranean water-course formed by digging a line of wells at certain ntervals on a hill-slope, connecting the bottoms of these wells by small tunnels; as the foot of the slope is reached, the wells get less and less deep till at last the water-course emerges into the open air; in this manner springs at the foot of the hills are tapped and brought to the surface of the land at a lower level. In Eastern Turkestan these *karez* are found near Turfan only."—R. B. SHAW, F.R.G.S.

on the strength of negative evidence it has been surmised that the *karez* system was not introduced until the eighteenth century. Today the Persian word *karez* has become synonymous in Turfan with hamlet or farmstead, and a man will give his address as the inhabitant of such and such a *karez*. It is known, however, that for hundreds of years before the *karez* were mentioned Turfan sustained a large population, and it is therefore certain that there must have been an adequate water-supply. Whether the ruined towns in the vicinity are to be accounted for by the drying-up of old water-courses, or whether wars and a scattering of the inhabitants caused the wells to go out of use through neglect, is still uncertain.

The well water of the town is of such poor quality that no one drinks it, nor can it be used for the washing of clothes; it is only suitable for the daily watering of streets and courtyards, and the purchase of drinkable water is one of the necessary expenses for which every inhabitant of Turfan must budget. There is a stream outside the town, and many Turki boys earn a living by bringing water on donkey-back which they sell to the homes at so much a bucket. The donkeys are saddled with wooden panniers which are filled with water at the stream, and the sale is at the rate of a copper a pail. Each pannier has a hole low down on the side with a wooden stopper, and the boys are very adroit at filling the pails without wasting a drop. They pull out the plug and allow a strong jet to reach the buyer's bucket, but when it is nearly full the plug is forced back, and the flow ceases exactly at the moment when the pail is full but not a drop has overflown. In the hands of an incompetent person there would be mess and wastage, but the Turki child's skill saves both. When the wooden panniers are empty the boys leap to the donkeys' haunches and with shouts and song they race each other back to the stream to fill up again.

During the long summer Turfan is undoubtedly one of the hottest places on the face of the earth, and the thermometer registers around 130° Fahr. in the shade, but it is not hot all the year round and in winter the temperature falls to zero Fahr. The heat is accounted for by its geographical location, which is in a depression watered by no river of any size, and lying below sea-level. Between May and August the inhabitants retire underground, for the mud or brick houses, even though they have deep verandahs and spacious airy rooms, are intolerable by day. In each courtyard there is an opening which leads by a flight of steps to a deep dug-out or underground apartment. Here are comfortable rooms and a *kang* spread with cool-surfaced reed matting and grass-woven pillows which help the people to endure the breathless stagnation of the midday hours; they eat and sleep underground and only emerge at sunset. The shops, which have been closed during the hot hours, are opened by lamplight, and all necessary business is done then, but people avoid the living and sleeping rooms of their houses because they are infested with vermin. There are large and virulent scorpions which creep under sleeping-mats, drop on to the unconscious sleeper from the beams or hide themselves in his shoes. One jumping spider with long legs and a hairy body as large as a pigeon's egg leaps on its prey and makes a crunching noise with its jaws. Another burrows holes in the ground, and its bite is as painful as that of a scorpion. Turfan cockroaches are over two inches in length, with long feelers and red eyes which make them a repulsive sight. All these creatures know how to conceal themselves in sleeping-bags and rolls of clothing, so that man is handicapped in dealing with them. Apart from these virulent monsters, the inns provide every variety of smaller vermin such as lice, bugs and fleas, and each is of an order well able to withstand all the patent nostrums guaranteed to destroy them. On account of these pests the people of Turfan sleep on wooden beds in the courtyards, but the constant watering of the ground results in swarms of mosquitoes, which torment the sleeper almost beyond endurance. The underground conditions of life are not healthy, and the sudden chill of a dug-out striking on a perspiring body results in all kinds of rheumatic troubles; moreover, the cellars are badly ventilated and one phthisical or leprous patient may infect the whole family with the disease.

The natives of Turfan are strict Moslems and builders of handsome mosques, of which there are several in the town. The most striking of these buildings stands to the south-east of the Chinese quarter. It was built by the royal family of Lukchun, and though in its present form it dates only from 1760, yet it was probably erected on the site of a much more ancient building, possibly of Nestorian origin. During the fast of *Ramaẓan* the whole life of the town is altered, as for this one month of the year no Moslem may touch food or drink between sunrise and sunset. During short, cold winter days this restriction merely amounts to a severe discipline, but if it falls in the great heat, when days are long and nights are short, the necessity for drink is urgent and the suffering imposed by abstinence is intense. Wealthy people sleep away the hours of daylight, but labourers, who must do their task in spite of everything, long for the fast to be over. Family meals are cooked and eaten after sunset, and two hours before sunrise, while it is yet dark, warning is given from the mosque by a peculiar drum-tap. All then know that it is time to rise and prepare food, which must be cooked and eaten before the sun is up.

In more sophisticated countries the close of the fast is fixed by the calendar, but in Central Asia it is marked by the first sight of the new moon in the sunset sky. Everyone watches for the first streak of silver, and roofs are covered with people peering into space, each hoping to be the first to give the great news that the faint crescent is visible. As soon as she appears the fast is over, but her presence must be vouched for by at least three witnesses. When this is done the young men run helter-skelter down the roof ladders and back to the homes, where feasts are spread of special dishes; these they eat and enjoy in complete satisfaction, feeling that one more *Ramaẓan* is over.

The *baẓar* of Turfan has a much more Oriental look than that of Hami. In summer the whole street is covered over with reed matting and boughs of trees, to shelter both merchants and buyers from the burning rays of the sun. The earth beneath is always damp, for the young shop assistants are responsible for scattering water many times a day in front of each stall. The Turki shopkeepers, in high leather boots stitched with many colours, and wearing embroidered skull-caps, sit tailor-fashion on long wooden counters, with their goods spread around and a teapot and cup beside them from which they sip pale-green tea.

The dried-fruit market is one of the most varied and certainly the cheapest in the world. The vendor sits amid piles of sultanas of varying quality—the dark, the pale, the golden and the jade-green; these are kept carefully apart, and only the cheapest and commonest are ever mixed. On one side of him are mounds of minute currants, and on the other large, fleshy raisins, with dried black plums and apricots of different kinds, from the cheapest, which have the stones left inside, to the better qualities, from which they have been removed and the kernel folded back in the translucent flesh. There are also piles of sweet apricot kernels, but in this particular fruit the flesh is very tasteless and all the flavour is concentrated in the kernel, which is so sweet as to be almost indistinguishable from the almond; it is used in making an emulsion which is served as a drink at feasts, and when ground, makes excellent marzipan. There are also dried peaches, nectarines and mulberries, piles of shelled walnuts and dried jujube fruit, which is always popular with the Chinese for flavouring and decorating the loaves of steamed bread. Turfan also produces peanuts, but they are small and are not to be compared in quality with those which come from the sandy plains of Honan.

Cotton shares with fruit the first place in Turfan products, and sellers of cotton goods are numerous. They also like to sit cross-legged on low counters, teapot at hand, fanning themselves if the weather be hot with fans woven from dried grass. The frontage of the cotton merchant's store is always decorated with lengths of coarse coloured cotton material, gay horse-cloths and saddle-bags, and flowered squares used for wrapping clothes when travelling. Rolls of bright chintz fill the shelves at the back of the stall. Some of this material is very cleverly dyed, for the women know how to knot little bunches in the length of stuff before it goes to the dyer, so that when it comes back they open it out and find a pattern of flowers or butterflies scattered at regular intervals over the material. The tying of these knots has kept the dye from penetrating to certain places and the effect is charming, with only sufficient irregularity to show that it is handwork.

The Turkestan carpet-weavers practise a family trade, using cow or camel hair in natural and in dyed shades. The boys sit before the hand-loom and weave very rapidly, with no apparent pattern to follow. They are working out the conventional design which has been done by their own family for many generations, for the patterns are traditional and no one would think of varying them.

The Turfan herbalists display a remarkable selection of Central Asian drugs, including gentian, nux vomica, fennel, cardamoms, liquorice root, saffron, ginger, rhubarb, cinnamon, camphor, digitalis, oak-apples, capsicum, aniseed, coriander seed, pomegranate bark, asafoetida, dried poppy-heads, seeds of the castor-oil plant, valerian, juniper, sesame, pine-kernels, stramonium, hyoscyamus, strophanthus and camel-thorn sugar. These and many other drugs are laid out in open wooden boxes at every Turfan medicine-shop.

The silk merchants exhibit skeins of floss silk dyed in every colour, and Turfan silk is highly prized by the women of Turkestan for embroidering caps. Each city has its own characteristic skull-cap, and men from any locality can be recognised by their head-dress. For example, the Aqsu man wears a handsome cap of black velvet heavily embroidered with gold and silver thread, the Hami and Turfan men wear variegated silk embroideries, but the pattern and design is different in each. For ceremonial purposes Moslem men all use a white stitched cotton skull-cap and the more strict followers of the Prophet will never be seen without it. Many women earn a living by making these various caps, which are of excellent workmanship and are all sold in the *bazar*.

The leather merchant has a fascinating display of skins dyed purple, green, blue, maroon and yellow, from which he makes high riding-boots with ornamental stitching in many colours. There are also tiny top-boots to fit small children, for the Moslem boy is dressed exactly as his father, and wears little Wellingtons over which his trousers hang loose and baggy. The convenient trunk used by the Chinese is forbidden to the Moslem, because it is made of pigskin, so the carpenter does a good trade in *sanduks*, which are wooden boxes with a handsome front of metal, hammered in geometrical designs and tinted in green and red.

The melon merchant always claims a big space for his wares on the *bazar* floor. He sits on a mat, surrounded by melons of every kind. The largest and most showy is the heavy water-melon, weighing over twenty pounds, with a glossy myrtle-green rind and a centre of juicy rose-madder flesh, flecked with shining black seeds. These seeds will be collected, salted and dried by fire-heat, after which they have a good sale, for the Chinese love to lighten a social hour by splitting the crisp husks with their teeth and nibbling the thin tasty seeds as they talk. The seller can supply many varieties of firm-fleshed cantaloups, and his customers test them with infinite care in order to select the very best. The degree of ripeness is known by pressure of the finger, but a melon is really chosen by the tone it emits when rapped with a jerk of the forefinger, for there is a reverberation from the perfect flesh which is lacking in any inferior fruit. There is great art in choosing melons, for appearances are deceptive and what looks a tempting fruit may prove tasteless. Even the most skilful buyer cannot be finally certain of the flavour, but if the customer will buy a whole melon, the merchant will scoop a square chunk from the centre and allow it to be sampled. Some of the melons ·are smooth and others rough-skinned, and the flesh is white, greenish, pinkish, or an attractive peach shade, according to the variety. There is one kind in which the pulp is mushy even when the fruit is not over-ripe, and has a perfumed flavour which needs an acquired taste. Some are cut open that passers-by may throw down a coin, seize a slice and walk away eating it as they go, tossing the rind into the gutter, but the more fastidious refuse the piece on which the flies have feasted, though the merchant constantly waves a switch made from a horse's tail to and fro over his wares.

The Turki is a burly man and a voracious eater, and there is always a crowd in that part of the *bazar* where food is sold. One group of men, squatting on their heels, surround the cook, who sells snippets of meat and kidney speared on an iron skewer and grilled over a portable charcoal fire. This grilled meat is very tasty, though generally tough. Another man, who wheels a large barrow covered with a white cloth, offers slices of cold boiled mutton and boiled liver, and not far off is the soup vendor, who sells the broth made from the boiled meat at a copper a bowl. From the bee-hive oven of the Moslem baker come cakes of delicious bread of varying shapes and sizes. This oven is heated with wood, and the unbaked cakes, moistened with a little water, are stuck round the inside wall, where they bake very quickly, so that each customer can carry away bread which is hotter than his hands can comfortably hold.

The favourite dish of the Turki, however, is *pilau*, which is made in a large cauldron from the fattest of the mutton, cut small and cooked with rice, chopped carrots and seedless raisins. There is always a seller of *pilau* in the market, he generally has his stand at the door of a restaurant and is the centre of a buzzing crowd of customers.

Among Moslems a religious ceremony called *nazrä* is observed. It combines charity and hospitality with the acquiring of merit to the donor, and is celebrated in connection with the festivals which accompany weddings, births and circumcisions. On these occasions the host keeps open house for his friends, and crowds of people enjoy his hospitality. Meanwhile the poor of the town congregate at his gate, waiting for the anticipated distribution of food. Each one who receives it is expected to call down the blessing of Allah on his benefactor. At Turfan there would often be hundreds of people gathered at such a *nazrä*, and every day a stream of men and women could be seen coming away from some rich man's door, each carrying a large cake of bread with a slice of meat laid on it.

The *bazar* is always crowded and always noisy. The little city carts which ply between different quarters of the town move quickly, and their drivers shout "*Huish, Huish!*" as they go, a cry which commands right of way. The stream of Turki and Chinese people in the *bazar* only mingles superficially, for, in fact, each keeps separate from the other and follows his own way of life. The Chinese buys at Chinese stalls, the Turki shops among his own people, and the food vendors serve men of their own race. The pleasures and entertainments of Turkis and Chinese are of a different order, for the mentality and outlook of each nation are profoundly different and neither trusts the other.

The Chinese find enjoyment at fairs and theatres and will spend hours in the market-place listening to a professional story-teller. This relater of old tales has his unique place in the hearts of his fellow-countrymen. He stirs their imagination with tales and legends drawn from the early history of China, and makes even the common people familiar with the personalities of long-dead Emperors, the campaigns they carried out against barbarian tribes and the virtues and vices of their wives and concubines. The crowd of listeners which squats round the narrator is largely composed of illiterate men, yet at the mention of one of their favourite heroes, such as Tsao-Tsao, the military leader of the Han dynasty who has become typical of the bold bad Minister of State, every face lights up with a gleam of pleasure. They are never weary of hearing how, two thousand years ago, he crushed the nomad hordes of the sandy desert, became the tyrant of his own royal master, and imprisoned the Emperor in a dungeon while his own daughter was raised to the throne.

Even the simplest yokel sees the point when he hears how Sutai, a politician of the fourth century B.C., found means of warning his sovereign against his love of military aggression by telling him the fable of the mussel and the oyster-catcher. "This morning," he said, "when crossing the river, I saw a mussel open its shell to sun itself. Immediately an oyster-catcher thrust in its bill to eat the mussel, but the latter promptly closed his shell and held the bird fast. 'If it does not rain today or tomorrow,' cried the oyster-catcher, 'there will be a dead mussel.' 'And if you do not get out of this by today or tomorrow,' retorted the mussel, 'there will be a dead oyster-catcher.' Meanwhile, up came a fisherman and carried off both of them. Thus," remarked Sutai, "I fear lest the State should take advantage of your military entanglements to seize both aggressor and victim." This moral application is always greeted with the same measure of approval from the crowd.

The professional letter-writer sits at the door of the Post Office. It is his job to listen to what any particular man wishes to say to his distant friends or relatives, then, using flowery and appropriate terms, to write out the message in the form of a letter to the person indicated. He sits behind a table on which are placed inkslab, a Chinese pen, letter-paper and a pad. The client comes to the side of the table and tells his tale. The writer listens, bargains the price, pulls up his long sleeve, lifts the block of Chinese ink, rubs it very slowly over the inkslab, dexterously applies the brush to the ink, stroking its hair to a fine point, then, with a flourish of his hand, begins to draw beautiful ideographs on the paper.

He tells the parents to whom he has been asked to write that many thousands of *li* separate their son from his honoured parents, that had the said son but been endowed with wings he would fly to them, but not having these, the high mountains and deep valleys which lie between hinder him in fulfilling his heart's desire. He begs the aged ones not to allow anxiety to consume their vitals. He also asks what is the price of grain in their locality, and enquires if the exchange of silver is favourable or otherwise in that distant province. In the very last sentence he inserts a few words regarding the real purpose of the letter, which may be to the effect that their daughter-in-law, his wife, gave birth to a son on the twenty-fourth of the fifth moon, at the hour of the snake. The letter is signed as coming from their "unfilial and unworthy son." The sheet is folded with the utmost care and placed in an envelope which bears the words: "To my revered father," followed by the name in large ideographs, written lengthwise down the centre. The address to which the letter is sent stands high in the right-hand corner, and the name of the place from which it is sent in the lower left-hand space. The address is always in the following order: first the province of China to which it must go, next the district, then the village. When all is complete, the letter is handed to the waiting client, who has heard it read in the presence of a gaping crowd which makes many suggestions and expresses its approval of the writer's art, with free comments.

Another familiar figure in every *baẓar* crowd is the old Chinese Con-fucianist, whose self-appointed duty is to collect any pieces of paper lying about and save the sacred writing from desecration. He carries a pronged picker and puts the fragments of paper into the basket which he carries. He also collects all that is placed in small boxes standing in different parts of the *baẓar* and marked "Receptacles for the respectful collection of sacred paper." All these he takes to the temple to be burnt by the priest.

The most musical sound comes from the Moslem professional musician who sits at the entrance to an inn-courtyard twanging the *dokar*, which is a long-necked guitar with two strings. He sings traditional songs, some of which are love-ballads and some of which are travel-songs.

> "If I would have a red rose blooming
> I must not pluck it in the bud;
> If I want not to fall in love,
> I must not stay in this city."

Or

> "The road to Andijan is sandy,
> None has e'er put sickle to it;
> We are two poor brothers,
> None was e'er so poor as we." [1]

When he strikes the haunting chords which prelude the Song of the Wandering Dove, every wayfarer responds and many will pick up the melody and softly sing it with him.

Above all the noise and shouting there can be sometimes heard a strange, weird, lilting chorus of men's voices. It comes from a band of *kalandars*, a group of strange, dishevelled men with long uncombed hair, dressed in fantastic costumes. One will have iron chains hanging to his arms which he shakes rhythmically as he moves, another will have a frame of hanging discs on which he plays a primitive accompaniment, another will knock pieces of bone together, marking time for the chant. They have sonorous voices, and though many are deformed and some blind in one or both eyes, they are strong creatures and greatly feared, no one daring to refuse their demand for money lest they call a curse down on him. These *kalandars* are a guild of professional beggars, and as they walk they sing old religious songs, always ending with the refrain, "Allah, Allah-hu."

II

The Vineyards of the Flame Hills

The vineyards of Turfan are a glorious sight. They lie to the north of the town toward the base of the Flame Hills, where the denuded sandstone and bare conglomerate is furrowed with narrow gullies. In hot weather the rays of the sun, striking on their barrenness, make the whole hillside quiver as though it were licked by rising flames, and this heat, reflected on watered land, produces a steamy, hothouse atmosphere, which suits the grape-vine admirably. The people who live in the vicinity fear these hills and quote a saying that they are accursed of Allah and that no man who tries to climb their burning heights can remain alive. The vine-growers reckon the crops to be safe from rain,

[1] Turkestan ballads translated by C. P. Skrine. See *Chinese Central Asia*.

193

for only once in the memory of the present generation has rain fallen
during the fruit-ripening season. On that occasion the vintage was
seriously injured, and Central Asia had the unusual experience of being
short of sultana raisins.

In early summer, even before the sheltered vineyards came into
sight, we were conscious of a delicate perfume, exquisite and suggestive
of heavenly things, which came from the flowering vines. During the
summer there was no perfume, but our thirst was quenched by the
juicy grapes to which we might freely help ourselves, and in winter,
when the vines were twisted into small heaps, laid in their shallow graves
and covered with piled-up earth, we still enjoyed their fruit and satisfied
our hunger with sultanas prepared from the sun-dried fruit of the vine-
yard. Every kind of vine flourishes in Turfan, but the most prolific
produce is a small, sweet, seedless variety of grape. It is also the best
fruit for export, and Turfan sultanas are eaten throughout the whole
of North and Central China, in Siberia and in many other parts of the
world. These celebrated vines are cultivated with short trunks and very
long branches which stretch outward in all directions and are supported
by upright posts.

The colour of the dried fruit varies considerably. Turfan sultanas
are of a clear amber colour, those from Tuyok, another grape-growing
area in the Turfan basin, a pale gold, while at Hanchung, a little to the
north of Tuyok, the dried grapes are of a clear green shade, which is
considered the best quality and commands the highest price.

The green of young vine leaves is one of the most brilliant colourings
which nature affords, and the expanse of vivid foliage spreading to the
foot of the blazing hills under an azure sky is a dazzling picture. Among
the vineyards there are spacious buildings, the walls of which are made
of sun-dried bricks laid so as to form a lattice-work which allows every
wind of heaven to blow through. These are known as *chung-chi* or
grape-drying halls, and are only in use for the few weeks in each year
when grapes are being dried, but during that short time they are full
of branched poles, hung over with thousands of bunches of the seedless
grapes. The passage of sun-heated air through the lattice-work is all
that is necessary for the drying of the fruit, but if the bunches were
exposed to the direct action of the sun, both colour and flavour would
be spoilt. The dreaded scorching wind of Turfan is exactly right for
this drying process, and a week or ten days completes it. The *chung-chi*
gleaners carry huge baskets, and into them they collect the best of the
fruit, throwing aside every imperfect raisin. The fallen fruit, which

litters the floor, is then swept up and sold cheaply by the *baẓar* merchant, but the best varieties, which are uniform in colour and are like drops of topaz, amber or sea-green jade, are stored and kept for export.

Wherever human skill and industry can persuade water to flow there are small, garden-like hamlets at the base of the Flame Hills, and in all of them the vine is cultivated, but these are separated by long stretches of stony wilderness. Turfan is the largest oasis, but the village of Tuyok is the most picturesque. At the entrance to the village the road narrows and passes through an old portal into a street where irregular houses border a shallow stream.

Tuyok is quite unlike other Gobi oases, and in its street we could well have believed ourselves to be in a village of Tuscany were it not for the Turki women around us, who laughed, played and chatted in their strong terse dialect as they carried pots and gourds to fill at the water's edge. The source of this mountain torrent lies far back among the Flame Hills and is known as Subash (Head of the Waters). There, amid drought and aridity, is one hollow as green as an English meadow. Small ponds lie everywhere among the grass and overhanging bushes, but instead of being quiet mirrors of the skies, they are always agitated by large air-bubbles which rise from the depths, carrying sand and grit to the surface. Such springs are called "living waters," and through them some deep fount is liberated and released for the healing of arid places. The life-giving stream which runs from Subash reaches Tuyok through a narrow canyon, watering its prolific vineyards and supplying its people with sweet water for all their needs.

Following the path up-stream, we came to where the surrounding cliffs were pierced with tiers of openings, which showed the interior of ruined shrines and cellas, indicating that some early colony of monks had chosen this site in which to establish a monastery. The caves themselves are now far too difficult of access to be visited, but they have been explored by several archaeological experts. Professor von le Coq, by shifting an enormous block of conglomerate, revealed one cell built in Persian style and containing many manuscripts, some of which dated back to the eighth and ninth centuries A.D. Unfortunately many of them were badly burnt or scarred, but he also found embroideries of great beauty, and was charmed by the discovery of a "little reliquary of turned wood, circular in shape, with a lid on the top, tastefully painted in rich tones of red, yellow and blue." Sir Aurel Stein also gained an entrance to some of the caves and writes of mural decorations, of medallions painted in Sassanian style, and of many Chinese text-rolls bearing Uighur writing on the reverse, which he rescued from a welter of crumbling fragments of painted plaster and general débris.

The village of Tuyok is now entirely Mohammedan and holds a famous Moslem shrine, which draws pilgrims from many countries. Behind the mosque there is a very ancient cave-temple hollowed from the rock, but no one is now allowed to visit it. The entrance to the mosque was decorated with the horns of wild animals, yak-tails, and with curiously shaped sticks, locks of human hair, bleached bones and other votive offerings such as are usual at a Buddhist *Obo*[1] but have no place in a mosque. It was still more surprising to find banners dedicated to Buddhist deities hanging inside, but the Ahungs did not seem disturbed when their attention was called to these idolatrous inscriptions, merely excusing themselves on the plea that they could not read Chinese.

This shrine is visited by numerous pilgrims from all over Asia and is the scene of many strange rites which would not be recognised by orthodox believers of the Islamic faith. On one of our visits we witnessed a strange ceremony. It was the hour of evening prayer, and the full-toned singers of the mosque chanted the Koran in loud, sonorous voices. A few Moslem merchants were present. They were obviously men of means, and one of them led a boy of about five years by the hand. At a certain moment the father stepped forward and gave his child over to the Hadji, who picked him up in his arms, chanted a number of sentences over him, then stepped to the opening which led into the deep cave where no one might enter, and, swinging the child in his arms, made as though he would throw him into the cave. He then caught him back, deliberately spat on his forehead, chanted a few more sentences and handed the boy back to his father. This strange ceremony, we learnt, was performed whenever a boy was taken for the first time to that sacred shrine.

When prayers were over they told us the whole story of the ancient tradition which was associated with the strange grotto. According to legend, seven holy men and one little dog lie in an age-long sleep in the depths of the cave. As pilgrims they had wandered over the face of the earth in search of men whose hearts were ready to respond to their appeal for repentance. Thus they came to Tuyok, where, discouraged because there was no response, they entered this cave and lay down to rest until the hour should come when men would listen to their words, leave their wicked ways and turn to Allah. After a thousand

---

[1] *Obo*—a shrine erected in the open by Tibetans or by Mongols.

years they bestirred themselves and came out again, but finding that the world, far from improving, had grown worse, and its inhabitants were more evil than formerly, they turned back to their peaceful retreat. This time, just as the cave was about to receive them again, a little dog appeared and asked leave to follow them. One of the number turned upon it indignantly, saying, "Begone! You are but a dog." "Am I not a creature of Allah?" replied the little beast. Hearing these words, the men acknowledged that they were true, and allowed the dog to seek refuge with them inside the cave. There, with the Seven Sleepers, it rests, awaiting the hour when Allah will awaken them to emerge from their retreat, and welcome the dawn of righteousness in the world.

The keeper of the shrine was a tall, bearded, white-turbaned Hadji, who had learnt the art of impressing every visitor with a sense of privilege at being permitted to see this honoured site. He regarded his own office as one of unique importance and received each pilgrim with dignity and ceremony. He kept a band of hired choristers who would chant a *namaz* for any wayfarer who was prepared to pay the price. At a call from their employer the men ran from their low mud houses and scrambled barefoot up the rock to the mosque cave, where they sat in a circle and raised their voices in a loud chant which echoed from the vaulted roof.

The first time our caravan appeared the Hadji was much interested, for though he had received Western visitors before, he had never entertained Western women. He was always particularly pleased when travellers from distant places came his way, for he counted on substantial reward for his trouble in displaying the wonders of the grotto. His greatest asset was his old *Ma-ma*, who has been exactly one hundred years old each time that we have been to the place. For a centenarian she was extraordinarily agile and ran out to meet us, quite aware that the entertaining of unusual women visitors would bring special kudos to herself. She took us to her own room, arranged pillows on the carpeted floor, spread out her own bedding and insisted that we should rest there during the heat of the day. She called serving-women who brought elegant brass ewers filled with warm water to pour over our hands, and a large brass basin was set on the floor to catch the water which flowed away. By her orders, the girls of the house brought bowls of tea and flat cakes of newly baked bread which she broke and handed to us. With a regal wave of the hand she dismissed importunate visitors, then came and sat beside us, relating in great detail her son's virtues and his devotion to her. She also spoke of the spectre of poverty which always haunted her and the whole family.

Every time a woman appeared at the door she was curtly dismissed with the words, "My guests are very tired and must not be disturbed"; then, as the veiled figure slipped discreetly away, she took up the recital of her own family matters. She told us of the great journey of her life, which was a pilgrimage to Mecca over the Karakoram Pass and through Karachi, which earned her the coveted title of Hadji, and as she talked she handled a rosary made of date-stones which she brought back with her from Arabia. Long years of use had left the stones smooth and polished like mahogany.

At last she left us for a few moments, and, relieved from the restraint of her firm hand, the small crowd which had collected near the door flowed in. For the rest of the day we were the centre of interest and attraction to the whole village, but by reason of being our hostess *Ma-ma* had secured the right of guardianship over us and she dispensed information concerning us, our families, our habits and our business to the interested circle.

"Those two are sisters," she said. "Can't you see that they are exactly alike? That other one is a friend, and they are all three like sisters. They share everything, their money is all in one purse and their food is cooked in one pot. Their country is England; it is just over those mountains, near Hindustan. They are people of Allah."

Before we left, the keeper of the mosque brought us a book in which were the signatures of several noted travellers. He told us how they had sat just where we were sitting, how they had praised his entertainment and enjoyed their stay with him. He was a perfect specimen of the worst type of professional guide. How and where he learnt the tricks of the trade we never discovered, but the old *Ma-ma* of one hundred years, permitted to grace this earth for so long, who needed comforts she could not get, who was so active and so self-denying that pilgrims to the shrine were always her insistent care, appeared on each of our visits and she was always the same, always the "treasured aged one," beloved of Allah and always desperately in need of financial help.

Her son forced kindnesses upon us, but indicated at the same time that recognition of these services should be on a lavish scale. When he handed us the book to add our names to the list of guests, it was with a request for a few words of appreciation. There was clearly an inner meaning to some of the comments written in it, but these were sealed to him, for some of those noted explorers had evidently been smarting under a sense of robbery while their suave host stood over them and begged an autograph.

We wrote our names and spoke of his hospitality, but added a discreet word which might warn others to accept it with caution, indicating that such privileges as a reception by a *Ma-ma* of one hundred years might be followed by a bill proportionate to her exceptional age and her inexhaustible energy. I wonder how old she is now?

III

The Ruined Cities of the Plain

In the course of our journeys we spent many months in Turfan at different seasons of the year, and from there visited sites of great interest, for in whatever direction we travelled we passed ruins of old towns or villages which showed what a large population must once have inhabited this plain. The sense of antiquity was very strong, not only in the Turfan basin but over the whole area which surrounds it, and the ruins we met here were more massive and more extensive than any we had seen elsewhere. At the western extremity of the irrigated land were the remains of an old city, standing high on a raised terrace between two deeply cut ravines in which water flowed. The Chinese call this place Chiao-ho (Between the Streams), and the Turki name for it is Yar-Khoto (Junction of the Yars, or streams). The terrace was covered with closely packed ruined buildings in which it was difficult at first to detect any systematic plan, though gradually a certain outline of design emerged. The villagers of this vicinity were proud of the old place, boasting that these ruins were of greater interest than other and better-known remains, and certainly I saw none of the destruction in progress which has been carried out so ruthlessly elsewhere. Sir Aurel Stein writes that he lacked time for systematic investigation of Yar-Khoto, but the rock-cut grottoes which had evidently served as graves reminded him of the early Christian tombs in desert valleys of Egypt and Palestine, and he connected them with Professor von le Coq's reports of Nestorian remains.

Most imposing of all was the site of a great walled city, the old town of Kaochang, which figures in the annals of the Tang dynasty (A.D. 618-907) as the capital of Central Asia's most important province, distinguished not only by the extent of its political influence, but on account of the high standard of its civilisation.

Accustomed as we were to use more than one name for all Central Asian towns, yet it was unusual to find quite so many referring to one place. Officially it was Kara-Khoja, which is the name of the village which lies near it, but Western archaeologists often use the early Turkish name of Khocho. The Turfan people, however, speak of it as Apsus (Ephesus), a name certainly calculated to arouse interest and curiosity; familiarly it was often referred to as Dakianus, a name of which the derivation, according to Professor von le Coq, can be traced to Decius, Roman Emperor and the persecutor of the Christians. Educated Chinese call it Kaochang, and there is yet another name, Idikut-Shahri (Town of Idikut, the Uighur ruler). Carters and caravan men always speak of it simply as Er-pu (second stage), for they care for none of these ancient associations and only think in terms of road mileage.

This old town with the many names lies east of Turfan. The distance there is not great, but after leaving the oasis the road becomes rough and dreary. At one point we broke the axle of our cart in a very lonely place, and did not know where to turn for help. A moment later, however, a head emerged from one of the circular *karez* openings and a bearded Turki climbed out. He was quite happy to leave his job and come to our rescue, so a mule was unharnessed and both he and the carter jumped on its back and rode away to find a workman. In less than an hour they reappeared with a carpenter surrounded with bags of tools and riding on a donkey. He fitted a new axle to our *mepä* (travel-cart), and in a few hours we restarted our journey.

Next day at sunset we saw a great enclosure-wall rising from the plain, and that night we camped in the shelter of the walls of Central Asian Ephesus. It was already dark when we arrived, and there was no time that night for more than a glance at what lay behind them, but next morning we were up early and ready for an exploration. It lay before us in all its impressiveness, that vast enclosure of two hundred and fifty-six acres, surrounded by a towering wall of stamped clay, twenty-two yards in height. The original openings where the city gates once stood were gaping spaces, but apart from these there were many wide fissures through which entrance could be made, and one of them was conveniently close at hand and served our purpose for entering the old stronghold.

The ruins had the symmetry which indicates a well-planned town, and the outline of the main thoroughfares was easily discerned.

Professor von le Coq suggests that the ground-plan followed the pattern of a Roman castrum.[1] We had seen many other Gobi sites enclosed by massive walls, places which the Chinese spoke of as old Mongol fortresses, but they were rough and clumsy structures, whereas this old city, even in its decay, had a striking stateliness. There was little within the walls to suggest Chinese architecture. In the centre were the remains of the *Padshah's* palace, and around it were handsome *stupas* and high buildings decorated with arched niches. Examination of the ruins has shown that most of these were temples, monasteries, tombs and other edifices for religious purposes. The architecture is mainly of Iranian or Indian character according to whether its use was for Manichaean or Buddhist purposes. When we saw a beautiful brick decorated with the Greek key pattern we realised that the name of Ephesus suited this place well. There was an artistic tradition evident here, which differed entirely from that of the Han or the Tang dynasties which had so strongly impressed itself elsewhere in the Turfan area.

Destruction of the buildings had been going on for a long time, and we saw farmers at work with their pickaxes pulling down the old ruins and probably destroying many relics in the process. The agriculturalists of the district found the old earth valuable for enriching their fields, so they ploughed up the land within the enclosure and sowed crops round the old monuments, but unfortunately the irrigation which is necessary for raising crops is fatal to structures made of earth, to mural decorations and to all other remains which depend on the dryness of desert conditions for their preservation.

The peasants' ploughshares constantly brought treasures to light, and we came away with a seal, an old metal horse, a fragment of an Uighur manuscript, and other small relics. Many beads are collected by children as they play among the ruins, and any old pots which are unearthed are taken into immediate use by the women, to save the expense of buying others.

An old man who walked with us among the buildings showed us a place where, even in his own boyhood, there had been a group of large buildings of which now nothing remained but a pile of ruins. Professor von le Coq heard that only a few years before his first visit in 1906 a peasant, pulling down walls in order to enlarge his fields, had unearthed cartloads of Manichaean manuscripts ornamented with pictures in gold and colours. Being a Moslem, he dared not keep them lest the Mullah should punish him for hoarding infidel books, nor would

[1] *Auf Hellas Spuren in Ost-Turkistan*, by A. von le Coq.

he risk robbery by the Chinese, so he simplified the situation by throwing the whole library into the river.

On the other side of the old town, in the cellar of a temple, a German expedition found the piled-up corpses of about a hundred Buddhist monks, whose cleft skulls and frightful wounds showed that they had been brutally murdered, probably at the time when the Buddhist religion suffered persecution by order of the Emperor. Many of the towers of Dakianus are in the form of Buddhist *stupas*, and there are some vaulted buildings which have been identified as Manichaean monasteries. From one of these Sir Aurel Stein rescued fragments of manuscripts written in Chinese, Brahmi, Uighur, Sogdian and Runic Turki, with a portion of Manichaean manuscript written on parchment which he suggests probably came from Western lands, where paper was not used as it was in the East. The Berlin Museum now holds the best specimens of frescoes and sculpture from Apsus, but inside the farms of Kara-Khoja are many beautiful heads modelled in clay and showing Graeco-Buddhist influence, and we saw some of these standing among unwanted things in tumbledown sheds. Outside the town the plain was littered with pieces of broken pottery ornamented in patterns covering a large range of decorative art.

Such a site as spacious, lonely, silent old Kaochang, crumbling back to dust and wholly undisturbed by the hand of any restorer, has the power to carry the mind back to the days when the town flourished as a thriving centre of culture and civilisation. Many influences contributed to its progress, and these have been traced by the archaeologist. The most evident was that of the Macedonian conquest, which brought the armies of Alexander the Great into Central Asia (327-325 B.C.) and swept the influence of Greek culture right up the old caravan route to the fertile oases at the foot of the Tienshan Range. Men of the disbanded armies soon spread themselves over the land, married the native women, and thus "changed the population to one of mixed nationalities, but of Greek civilisation." I had read so much about racial influences in Central Asia, and learnt so many things from local people in whose homes we stayed, that, as I sat on a mound of rubble and rested in the shade of an old Iranian arch, I seemed to see it all as it once had been, an "entrenched camp standing at the cross-roads of two ancient travel-routes." Those two routes were still in use and I myself was travelling on the one which connected Hami and Kashgar, and had often followed the other over the great Dawan Pass, which to this day provides the best means of crossing the Tienshan Range.

Old Kaochang occupied a strategic site, and in olden times men of many nations and tribes met there. They arrived in a chastened mood, for they had all experienced what has been called the "deep and biting social discipline" of nomad life, and were all subject to the desert's commanding austerities. Such men brought a contribution of new blood and of cultural stimulus to old Kaochang, but it was never more than the old settlement could absorb and use in the development of her unique character. Caravans came over the Eastern trade-routes, bringing silks, porcelain and other goods of delicate craftsmanship to its market, and men from the West, with a background of Grecian thought, helped to transmute craft into culture.

Ancient records of Chinese history make frequent reference to Kaochang, but the name then had a wider application than now, and indicated a whole province. "Kaochang measures 800 *li* (about 266 miles) from east to west," say the Chinese annals, "and 500 *li* (about 166 miles) from north to south; it comprises twenty-one towns. The soil is fertile; wheat and cereals produce two harvests every year; there is to be found there a plant called *peh-tieh* (the white enfolded). . . . It is the custom of the inhabitants to tie their hair into a plait which hangs behind the head." This very early reference to the "white enfolded" cotton-plant shows that Turfan has long been renowned for what is still one of its chief products. That summer day, while sitting on the mound, I looked over the fields where women and children with the braided plaits of which the old historian wrote, filled their great baskets with the fleecy cotton which their menfolk would market in Turfan.

When the heat of the day had passed we wandered in and out among the old ruins and along the paths between them. Many of the buildings were long since levelled to the ground, but fragments of frescoes which still remained represented men with eyes and hair distinctly European in style. It was surprising to find such Western types depicted on these old walls and to learn that it was men of these mixed nationalities who first ventured to give a pictorial representation of the Buddha, and fixed the likeness after the semblance of Apollo. "All the types of classical mythology were brought into the scheme of decoration for Buddhist temples, and this tradition spread through Central Asia, China, Korea and Japan, thus combining the Eastern form of expression with that of Greece." It was this contact and interplay of Eastern and Grecian thought which brought into being that great form of art known as the Graeco-Buddhist school.

Teachers of many religions came to Kaochang, and the early Buddhist missionaries found it such a suitable centre from which to propagate their faith that large numbers of monks congregated in the monasteries. They spent their time translating books from the Sanskrit into Tocharish, the ruling language of these ancient towns, and which is said to have had a similarity to the Armenian, Slavonic and Italo-Celtic tongues. Other religions beside Buddhism left their mark on the old city, which holds the remains of Manichaean monasteries also. The followers of Manes (A.D. 215-273) introduced artistic and scholarly elements from Persia and played an important part in strengthening the connecting link between East and West. Manes himself was drawn to mysticism early in life and declared that he was the last of the prophets. He said that a spirit from Paradise had ordered him to undertake widespread preaching of his religion, so he obeyed and travelled extensively in Iran, India and Turkestan, preaching as he went. When he returned to his native town he was killed by Zoroastrian zealots, but after his death the religion grew and spread, notably among the Uighurs of Kashgaria. He taught a "curious, shadowy, spiritual belief in Jesus Christ, though he did not allow that he had been a man or suffered and died."

The spread of Manichaeism is intimately bound up with the history of the Uighurs, whose creed was described by Robruck, an early Catholic missionary to the Court of the Khan, as "a jumble of Manichaeism and Buddhism with a tinge of Nestorianism."

Manes was not only the founder of the religion called by his name, but was a very fine painter and artist. Manichaean books were beautifully written in a very unusual Syrian script, and decorated with lovely miniatures. Many paintings, frescoes and illuminated manuscripts have been removed from the ruined shrines of Kaochang to Berlin, and all along the foot of the Flame Hills there are still remains of ancient Manichaean monasteries.

Early in the Christian era missionaries of the Nestorian Church brought the enlightenment of Christianity up these trade-routes and, with Christianity, introduced a high degree of culture. They travelled from the Near East over Central Asia and the Gobi Desert, teaching and evangelising as they went. This section of the early Church was called by the name of its leader, Nestorius, who was a native of Germanicia, a city of northern Syria. In A.D. 428 he was made patriarch of Constantinople, but later was pronounced a heretic for his views on the delicate question of the balance of Divine and human natures in the person of our Lord. His contention that the "Virgin Mary could not rightly be called Mother of God, but only Mother of the man Christ," brought him under the ban of heresy, and at the General Council at

Ephesus in 431, Nestorius was formally condemned, deposed and later banished to Upper Egypt, where he died in exile.

The Church which was called by his name sustained above all others the missionary tradition which obeyed the command of Christ to carry the Gospel to all nations, and from the early centuries of the Christian era Nestorians spread abroad and were soon pushing their way eastwards to India and over the Pamirs to Central Asia. "The pioneers were Nestorian artisans who went there for the purposes of trade or found employment among people less advanced educationally than themselves, and in the service of kings, princes and noblemen in the farther provinces of Persia and beyond. The golden age of Nestorian missions in Central Asia was from the end of the fourth till about the end of the ninth centuries. During this period Metropolitan Sees were established at Samarkand, Kashgar, Khitai, Tangut, Cumul and Cambulia." [1]

The Nestorian Church has been described as the most missionary Church that the world has ever seen, and Tatars, Turks, Huns, Tanguts, Mongolians, Yüeh-chihs, Keriats, Uighurs and Naimans were reached by its missionaries. In the very centre of the Chinese Empire there is a decisive, historical, dated record in Chinese and in Syriac called the Nestorian monument, which stands at Sian, one of the ancient capitals of China. While there were no architectural signs of Nestorian influence in Kaochang, yet in Central Asia there are many spiritual traces of the movement left behind in the form of societies whose regulations demand of their members the observance of certain rites, which include the sharing of a symbolic meal of tea and bread. The traditions handed down point to a vague, legendary knowledge of some incidents in the life of Christ, and the secrecy which is required of the members points to periods of bitter persecution which finally stamped out the organised life of the Churches.

A very few years after the death of Mohammed (A.D. 632), the Arabs, carrying the Islamic religion, became prominent factors in the life of Central Asia. Their creed was a militant one and they set out to exterminate other religions and substitute their own. When Islam reached the old trade-routes its followers moved up and down the great arteries, and at the close of the sixteenth century established their first chiefdom in Kashgar.

This religion had come, and come to stay. It was not a constructive force, but a disruptive one, which has always been a cause of revolt and bloodshed. Though not opposed to literacy, Islam in eastern

[1] *Nestorian Missionary Enterprise*, by Rev. John Stewart, M.A., Ph.D.

Turkestan has helped the development of neither art, literature nor ethics, but has rather proved destructive of the civilising influences of neighbourly intercourse, and has established the deplorable tradition of the periodic Moslem rebellions which take place every thirty years.

I walked back to the central spot where the *Padshah's* palace stood, thinking about the *Padshah* or king of Kaochang and how it happened that this province ever had a king, and I remembered that it was China which gave it a royal dynasty through a line of rulers who came from Liangchow in Kansu. That dynasty culminated in its most celebrated King, Chu Wen-tai, who received the famous pilgrim Hsüan Tsang with such embarrassing honours and hospitality that he was obliged to resort to a hunger-strike in order to get free and continue his journey to India. Wen-tai was *persona grata* at the Chinese Imperial Court, where he received the honour of being made a member of the Imperial clan, but in his old age he refused to pay homage to the Emperor or to bow to his dictates. Soldiers were dispatched to deal with him, but when they reached Kaochang they found that he had died of fright before they arrived, so they slaughtered thousands of the inhabitants. When Hsüan Tsang returned from India, the King was already dead, Kaochang, Turfan and other kingdoms had fallen, and China was in control.

The kingdom of Tocharia had become eastern Turkestan, and with the death of Chu Wen-tai came the close of a "charming and eloquent world, a belated survival of earlier races."

IV

The Roadmen of the Gobi

The roadman of Central Asia thinks, lives and acts in terms of trade-routes. He is essentially a man of the road, and from childhood the weave of his thought has known no other framework. His manner of expression, his conversation and his mental outlook centre on "The Road." His talk mainly consists of questions or answers, all of which relate to "The Road." "Is the road open?" he asks. "Is the road peaceful?" "Are there brigands on the road?" If he be a Chinese his farewell is "A peaceful road to you," and if he be a Turki his parting benediction is "*Yol bolsun*" (May there be a road!).

Many of these caravan men spend the whole of their lives on one trade-route, which they cross and recross numberless times, until they know it so well that they can tell if the stones of the road have been disturbed or even if some unusual footprint has been left there by man or beast. Nothing escapes the vigilance of their eyes. They are the descendants of roadmen, and have a long ancestry of caravan guides behind them. The love of "The Road" is in their blood, and if anything keeps them from it they are victims of overpowering nostalgia.

The roads they follow are so old that it is impossible to say when they first came into being, for the origins of caravan trade can be traced back beyond the time of historical records. It was over these trade-

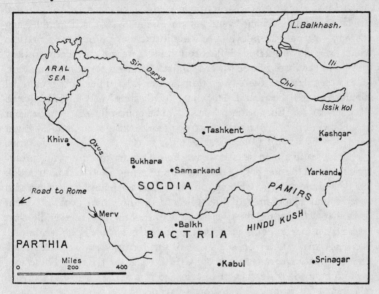

routes that the peoples of the East and West first met on peaceable terms, and learnt many things from each other long before the seas which divided them had been navigated.

These desert highways remain to this day what they have always been, natural flat expanses of arid waste, broken by more or less fertile areas which supply the traveller's final necessity of water, and the main trade arteries stretch out to every point of the compass. One goes northward to the Irtish River, another east to Kalgan, and a third south-east through the province of Kansu, but the road which opened up a highway between the civilisations of East and West, and which connects Hami, through Turfan, with Kashgar, is the one now known as the South Road.

West of Kashgar this road leads on to the Central Asian highland system, which is called the Pamirs, and has an average height of twelve thousand feet. It follows the course of that great river known to antiquity as the Oxus, and now spoken of by the Persians as the Jihun, and by the Turkis as the Amu Darya, which was of such immense importance to the first exchange of civilisations. The earliest inhabitants of the pasture-lands which lie between the Altai and the Oxus, of whom we have any knowledge, were nomad Tatar tribes, of whose manner of life we are not wholly ignorant, for archaeological research has enabled historians to reconstruct their life to some extent.

These Central Asians were not an essentially barbaric people, for at a very early date they developed a highly artistic tradition of decoration which exerted considerable influence both in a westerly direction toward Europe and an easterly one toward China. "Long before the beginnings of recorded history there was transmission and diffusion of cultural stimuli between the near East, where 'civilisation' had its origin, and all other parts of Europe and Asia. . . . The point of special importance in this connection being that most of these exchanges of cultural traits took place by way of Central Asia." [1]

These fearless men seem to have been the first to tame wild horses which roamed the steppes, to use them for driving and, later, to introduce the great innovation of riding on their backs. Many important discoveries and adaptations of life followed on this domestication of the horse. It was among these early steppe dwellers that the saddle was first used, being probably suggested by the shape of the double-humped Bactrian camel. Later on the value of the stirrup was discovered, and later still the advantages of boots over sandals for riding. These last came to be made of leather or of felt, and it is highly probable that the treading of felt from sheep or goat's hair originated among these Tatar tribes. The discovery and manufacture of felt led to important developments in the life of the people, for felt is the material out of which the nomad, to this day, constructs the dwelling which serves him better than any building, because a felt tent is warm in winter, cool in summer, and can be rolled up and moved at will to another locality.

A more radical innovation still, brought about by riding, was the change from the loose skirt-like costume of early times to "that ingenious piece of clothing that we call trousers," and from Central Asia the wearing of trousers gradually spread among all nations and to all parts of the globe.

It was the caravan trade which first linked East and West by

[1] *The Early Empires of Central Asia*, by W. M. McGovern.

the peaceful intercourse of business relationships, and to these ancient merchants the course of the Oxus was the most natural and direct way to guide a caravan from the Tarim basin toward Bactria, or, following the opposite direction, from west of the Pamirs toward the Yellow River. This overland trade found one of its best markets in Rome, for, "as the Romans became increasingly luxurious in their way of life, they developed a corresponding fondness for products of distant places. The short route from Europe to the Far East was that which the Seleucides and their successors wished all caravans to take, that is the way of the Oxus."

Over this trade-route the great caravans moved constantly, eastward and westward, and their interests were irrevocably bound up with the peace and prosperity of the lands they touched. During periods of warfare, when the Huns came south of the mountains and the roads were overrun by armed men, the forces of destruction had their own way and commerce ceased, but so soon as the scene of warfare had shifted to other districts the merchants resumed their accustomed task, reconstructed their caravans, and again carried loads of goods to and fro from one country to another. Then, as now, they visited the most distant lands again and again, until every mile of the road was familiar to them and they had made acquaintances and business connections who received them on a friendly footing everywhere. The instinct of barter, expressing itself through commerce, has been one of the great factors in establishing friendly relations between strong nations, as also in opening up contact between advanced peoples and semi-civilised tribes. "Commerce alone has furnished satisfactory and reliable detail regarding this great way of communication, and it is the itinerary of the merchant prince Titianus which served as a basis to Marm of Tyre and Ptolemy in drawing up the geography of Central Asia."

The benefit to all the peoples connected through the medium of commerce is evidenced by the fact that things which contributed to the progress of civilisation became known about the same time to peoples separated from each other by vast distances. It is a significant fact that from early times the people both of North China and of the Near East knew and used the wheel and the plough, and that in both regions men cultivated wheat, millet and barley. In the second century B.C. China learnt from the Iranian people the cultivation of *alfalfa*,[1] of the grape-vine and of the walnut. On the other hand, Europe owes to the

[1] *alfalfa*—a Spanish name for a variety of lucerne. (Spanish—*alfalfa*, three-leaved grass ; Arabic—*alfacfacah*.)

Chinese the first knowledge of the peach, the apricot, and also of many medicinal plants and their uses. The agricultural system known as the *karez* manner of irrigation was learnt by the inhabitants of Kashgaria from the Persians, and its development in the hands of industrious and peaceful agriculturalists was the means of transforming the Turfan basin from a torrid and sterile land to one of bewildering fertility.

The art of paper-making, which was discovered by the Chinese in the second century A.D., travelled westward over the caravan routes until it touched the Arabs and through them reached Europe. This was followed by the discovery of printing, and again by the far-reaching development of the use of paper money. All these owed their origin to the Chinese, and their transmission from East to West to the quiet, patient caravan life of the Central Asian highways. It was over this same route that the introduction of Graeco-Roman glass into China led indirectly to the discovery of porcelain, for which the Chinese became world-famed. In fact, the porcelain trade was second only to that of silk, which at the time of the Emperor Augustus was already flourishing, and in the centuries that followed attained such proportions that the amount of silk brought from Cathay to the Roman Empire gave its name to one of the trade-routes, which is spoken of to this day as the Old Silk Road. That famous trade-route, which connected Peking with Rome, passed through Loulan and the Tarim basin, over the Pamirs and across Bactria to Merv. Two thousand years ago water was not so scarce in Loulan as it is today, for the land which now is nothing but a salt-encrusted wilderness then had a chain of oasis towns, each of which constituted a small independent state.

At that time the caravan road traversed a series of oases watered by the Tarim River and by an ancient delta now called the Kuruk Darya (Dry River). Of the streams which flow down from mountain glaciers on the Tibetan side, only the Khotan River can now force its way through the terrible sands of the Taklamakan Desert, and that only for a few months of each year, "but within historical times," says Sir Aurel Stein, "a number of these terminal river-courses carried their water considerably farther north." The old road followed the foot of the Nan Shan (South Mountains), passed through Tunhwang to Nan-hu (South Lake) and the Barrier of the Sun, then up a valley-like depression to the north-east and across a dry lake-bed. From here it skirted the Kuruk Darya to Karashar and joined the road to Turfan and to Dakianus, which stood at the cross-roads where the caravan tracks met.

Like other early traders, the roadmen of Central Asia jealously guarded the secrets of their trade-routes and of their merchandise. Though the silk industry gave its name to the road, information concerning it leaked out very slowly. "Silk-weaving Ceres" was the name by which China was spoken of in Rome, but the art of silk production remained unknown until a Chinese princess travelling to the kingdom of Khotan hid some eggs of the silkworm in the folds of her head-dress, and these were hatched out in that district where the mulberry is so prolific. The source of China's silk was then revealed, and Khotan soon became a centre of Central Asian seri-culture, which it remains to this day.

Through the succeeding centuries the life of the trade-routes was subject to frequent fluctuations, and between the middle of the twelfth and fourteenth centuries East and West were brought into much nearer proximity through the invasion of Europe by Mongol hordes under their great leader Genghiz Khan (1162-1227). There must have been long interruption to commerce during the period when these fierce warrior horsemen inexorably spread right across Asia, over Persia into Poland and Hungary, until the Mongol Empire stretched from the Yellow River to the Danube. Yet it was as a direct result of this phenomenal military action that the roadmen of Central Asia first met with cultured European travellers in the Gobi.

Franciscan friars, bound for the Court of the great Khan with an embassage from the Pope or the King of France, were among these pioneers. Then two Venetian merchants appeared, passed into Mongolia, and later returned, homeward bound. After a few years they were back again in company with a youth who was son of the one and nephew of the other. These were Nicole, Maffeo and Marco Polo (1254-1324), who were to become famous among the great travellers of the earth. From that time knowledge of the Far East became an exact thing and was no longer a dim and legendary surmise.

It was, however, left to a Jesuit lay brother from Lahore, Benedict de Goës (1562-1607), to put the final touch to accurate geographical location in the East, by taking an epoch-making journey from India across Asia, and so establishing the fact that the Empire of Cathay across the Gobi Desert, and China the distant land of maritime discovery, were one and the same country. Benedict de Goës died at Suchow, first oasis town of Kansu to the south of the Great Wall, and his body lies in a desert grave. He accomplished his mission, but did not live to complete his great journey to Peking. No monument marks his tomb, only a mound of stones, but his memory survives among those lovers of Gobi traditions who, in the oases, still speak of "the venerable foreigner who was a worshipper of God."

The centuries pass and their generations vanish into the unknown, but the roadman of Central Asia still pursues his steadfast and lonely way. His caravan trade is occasionally interrupted by a revolt of the Moslems or the depredations of a brigand chief and his armies, but these are only passing incidents, whereas his steady labours are the enduring fabric of man's friendly relations, and the recognition of the Divine law of human inter-dependence.

V

The Old Envoys

Every oasis town has its bookmen. They are usually school-masters, and their own intellectual life is nourished solely by the libraries which they own. There is little opportunity of buying new books in the Gobi, but they read and re-read the ancient tomes which record the annals of the Han (206 B.C.-A.D. 220), Tang (A.D. 618-907) and Sung (A.D. 960-1280) dynasties. Talking with such men certain names constantly recurred in conversation, which were those of envoys sent out by Emperors of long-past dynasties with the object of bringing the numerous small states of Central Asia under Chinese rule. These old envoys had their own way of doing things, but some of them were remarkably successful. Understanding the objective of their mission they were not over-instructed in the manner of conducting it. They sometimes spent years on a diplomatic mission, and even then it might fail, but during that time they had gained priceless knowledge of men of other races who lived in strange conditions and viewed things from unusual points of view. The memory of these envoys' initiative, resource, tact and courage has survived in many good stories which have been retold thousands of times among the Gobi oases.

In the days of the glorious Han dynasty the increasing importance of China's commercial relations with Bactria and the Mediterranean provinces made it advisable for the Court to send an envoy empowered to negotiate treaties with the Kingdoms of the West through whose territories the trade-routes ran. The Emperor Wu Ti (140-86 B.C.) appointed Chang Chien for this difficult mission, and he set out under command to make an alliance with the Yüeh-chih tribes[1] against the

---

[1] Yüeh-chih—a nomadic nation which originally occupied the western half of modern Kansu. They were driven out by the Hsiung-nu, first to the valley of I-li, and later to the banks of the Oxus.

common enemy, the Hsiung-nu, or Huns, as they were called farther
west.

This alliance was highly desirable, and the Emperor visualised an
irresistible military movement in which the Yüeh-chih in the west
would combine with the Chinese in the east to crush the Huns and
finally break their power.

Chang Chien set out from Court with a suite of a hundred attendants
to handle this delicate business, but unfortunately, on reaching the
Gobi trade-routes, he fell into the hands of the enemy before he made
contact with the Yüeh-chih, who had meanwhile been forced westward
to the land of the Oxus. For ten long years he remained a captive, but
after this time he escaped, and, viewing the ten years as a mere preliminary
to the commission which had been entrusted to him, he continued his
journey westwards.

On reaching the land of the Oxus, he found the Yüeh-chih so fully
occupied with their own aggressive warfare that they had no inclination
even to consider the overtures of the Emperor of China regarding
another campaign, so, having laid the proposals before them, Chang
Chien himself joined their forces and accompanied them on some
successful military expeditions, in the course of which he learned the
technique of their methods of warfare. When the campaign was over
he started homewards with two followers who were the sole survivors
of his original escort, but on the way was once more captured by the
Huns. This time he escaped after only one year of captivity, and he
finally reached the Court of the Emperor in 126 B.C. after an absence
of twelve years. In respect of his original commission, the expedition
was a failure, but he came back with such an intimate knowledge of
Central Asia, its people and their military strength, its products and its
commercial potentialities, that he became an invaluable adviser to his
Imperial master.

He also introduced to China many Central Asian plants of which
he had learnt the use. All this knowledge which he had so hardly
acquired was too valuable to be wasted, and in 122 B.C. he was sent out
once more, again with orders to negotiate treaties with the peoples of
the north-west. This time, owing to his thorough knowledge of their
outlook, he succeeded in convincing the rulers of thirty-six different
states of the advantage it would be to them to come under China's
protectorate by recognising her suzerainty. These all agreed to pay yearly
tribute to the Emperor of China, while he, in return, was to send periodical
presents to the rulers—the subtle difference being that one was called

tribute and the other was designated merely as a gift. Chang Chien is honoured by Chinese historians with the great title of "The man who made a road," and this is the name by which the oasis bookmen still speak of him.

Another envoy to whom they constantly made reference was General Pan Chao, to whom fell the still more difficult task of consolidating the work begun by Chang Chien. It was easier to effect friendly alliances at such a distance than to sustain them, and during the first century of the Christian era China gradually lost her political hold on the north-west area. For a time the Huns had it their own way, raiding caravans on the trade-routes and pouring down into the Tarim basin. China's political control over the western regions had practically ceased for sixty years when the Emperor Ming (A.D. 58-76) of the Later Han dynasty reopened military operations under General Pan Chao.

This celebrated administrator lived from A.D. 31 to 102. He came from a scholarly family, yet his childhood was spent in poverty, and as a boy he was obliged to earn his bread by hard work. He nevertheless contrived to gain education, and when he was thirty-one years old obtained a small Government post. The pay was meagre and insufficient to keep both him and his mother, so in order to make ends meet he worked as a calligraphist, but the monotonous life of a copyist was hateful to him and one day, weary of the drudgery, he flung down his pen and gave free vent to his feelings. "A hero," he exclaimed, "should not waste his days over pen and ink, but, like the great Chang Chien, he should seek fame in foreign lands."

Fired with this ambition he consulted a physiognomist, who, after scrutinising his features, told him that he had a swallow's beak and a tiger's neck and was therefore destined to fly afar and devour the prey. He returned to his brush comforted, but with his determination strengthened to make a name for himself. Before long he succeeded in becoming attached to an expedition against the Huns which was going to the north-west. Given the opportunity, he soon distinguished himself, and his chief entrusted him with a commission to the King of Shan-shan with orders to secure that state's allegiance to China. On reaching Shan-shan he found that a large body of Huns had just arrived and was camping only a few miles away. His own escort numbered little over thirty soldiers, but by attacking the Hunnish camp under cover of darkness, and ordering his men to make a great noise, the enemy was deceived into believing that he commanded a large force. The result was so successful that he seized the Hun leader, cut off his head, and presented it to the King of Shan-shan along with his terms. The answer was all he hoped for, and this victory led to his being entrusted with further negotiations. The next expedition was to the King of Khotan, who, though himself not unfriendly, was under the influence of the Chief Ecclesiastic, who was inimical and laid plans to murder the envoy. Pan Chao sensed the danger and by a ruse contrived to get the man into his camp. He then seized him, cut off his head and sent it to the King with a request that there be no delay in concluding the negotiations. The effect was immediate, and from Khotan Pan Chao proceeded to Kashgar and on toward Bactria, effecting so many alliances that he could report fifty states as having submitted to China.

In time a new Emperor came to the throne who failed to realise the importance to the Chinese Empire of holding the Gobi trade-routes. He committed the stupidity of recalling Pan Chao, but when, contrary to his own convictions, the envoy prepared to obey the royal command, the rulers of the Central Asian states were filled with consternation. The commander of the Kashgar forces killed himself, and when the great General arrived in Khotan on his way home, the King and the members of his Court clung weeping to the trappings of his horse. "The Chinese envoy is as our father and mother, surely he will not desert us," they cried. Seeing their distress, and realising the defenceless position of these small states in regard to their powerful Hunnish enemies, Pan Chao made the great decision deliberately to contravene the Imperial order and stay where he was. He was too far away to be dealt with, so the Emperor overlooked his disobedience and even sent him a few detachments of soldiers, but by the year A.D. 88 General Pan Chao had raised an army of twenty thousand men with which he defeated the Huns at Yarkand and considerably extended the power of China in Central Asia. He never relaxed his efforts until China was recognised as suzerain by the whole Tarim basin, and in recognition of these services the Emperor gave him the title of Protector General of the Western Regions.

In the year A.D. 100 Pan Chao felt himself to be an old man in failing health. He had served his royal master for thirty years in Central Asia without once asking for leave, but he now addressed a memorial to the throne begging to be called back. The delays were such that two years elapsed before he could leave Kashgar for the Chinese capital. There honours awaited him, but it was too late for him to enjoy them, and within a month of his arrival he died. His true honour was the love and respect of the Central Asian states which he had added to the Empire. In conquering them he had won their friendship and had become their protector against a common foe. By loyal service he gained their confidence, so that to this day Central Asian men speak of him as the model envoy of the Chinese Court.

Within the last hundred years, one man rose to such power in Turkestan that he seemed on the point of making of Kashgaria a kingdom which was to be independent of China. His name was Yakub Beg, and a critical hour of Central Asian history gave him the chance to rise. A great Moslem rebellion broke out in north-west China in 1860 and swept through Turkestan. It coincided with an aggressive movement on the part of Russia toward the Indian frontier, and in the political chaos which ensued Buzurg Khan, Chief of Kokand, moved eastward and in 1865 succeeded in being declared King of Kashgar. Among the officers of Buzurg's army was a clever and audacious youth who had begun life as a dancing-boy but who, through the marriage of his sister to a rich and influential man, was given an opportunity to enter the army and later on rose to the position of commander of the Khan's forces. He cleverly planned the downfall of his Chief, hoping that he might come to the throne in his place. While Buzurg Khan was engaged in the defence of Kokand, Yakub Beg took temporary control in Kashgar, and later on, by a clever trick, persuaded Buzurg to go on pilgrimage to Mecca. During his absence Yakub assumed the title of *Bedaulat*, or Fortunate One, and induced various Moslem states to recognise him as the ruler of Kashgaria.

He was a forceful man and the report of his strong control reached England at a time when the fear of Russian aggression on the Indian frontier was a powerful factor in foreign policy. The matter of an alliance with Yakub Beg came under discussion, and the British Government dispatched a diplomatic and commercial mission to meet him and talk over measures of mutual aid.

The year 1873 found Yakub's nephew and adviser, Synd Yakub Khan, in London and at the Court of Queen Victoria, bearer of messages of friendship from his uncle, and with instructions to gain from the British Government a promise of intervention regarding the attitude of China toward the rebel Government in Kashgar. It is recorded that "his countenance and demeanour won for its possessor golden opinions in English society," but diplomatic moves proved abortive, for China's policy was fixed, and while negotiations between Yakub Beg and the British Government were still in progress he died. How he died is a matter of conjecture. He was probably murdered, but the men of the trade-routes have many strange stories to tell. The most picturesque is, that having prepared two cups of tea, one of which was poisoned and the other innocuous, he left it to the dictate of fate to decide whether he should live or die. Calling his servant, he ordered him to bring a cup of tea from the next room, and the man, suspecting nothing, picked up one and took it to his master, who drank it and fell dead. From this time China's authority was supreme in Turkestan, and under the name of Sinkiang (The New Dominion) it was given the status of a province, with a Chinese Governor resident in Urumchi. There are many small forts on the South Road of Sinkiang which are pointed out to travellers as the forts where Yakub Beg's soldiers successfully resisted the armies of Imperial China.

Conditions of isolation, difficulties of communication and independence of control will always produce leaders of strength and capacity. The pages of Chinese history enshrine the reputation of many men whose virtues and talents have become legendary, but the twentieth century called one man to power in Turkestan who was in true succession of the great envoys. This was Yang Tseng-hsin, Governor of the province from 1911 to 1928.

His handling of men in an hour of crisis was no more scrupulous than that of Pan Chao who enforced his arguments with the present of a rebel's head, but the people of Turkestan liked his robustness, the sincerity of his desire for their prosperity and the directness of his policy. He was called to a difficult post at a difficult time, for war-lords were overrunning China proper, and in areas much more easily controlled than the wide-spreading desert, loot and pillage were rife. Through it all Governor Yang kept his own remote province so well under control that the Gobi trade-routes were safe, and the fact that there were no brigands in Turkestan was a by-word in China.

The population he had to handle was a most difficult one, and only a strong man could hold his own among the conflicting claims of Tungan, Tatar, Kalmuck, Turki and Chinese. Yang Tseng-hsin succeeded in doing it, and all respected him, though among his subordinates he was feared on account of the ruthless determination with which he swept aside any who stood in his way. Many disappeared from public life either because they failed in the execution of their duty or because there was no room for a man who opposed his will.

The frontiers of Turkestan needed careful watching, as Governor Yang knew full well, for first China and then Russia were in the throes of revolution and he was conservative in outlook and dreaded violent and radical change. After 1915 the Cossacks who formerly guarded the

Russian Consulate in Urumchi disappeared, and a guard of the Red Army took their place. Crowds of Russian refugees poured over the Siberian border escaping from Soviet rule. He treated them kindly and with justice, and when the Soviet Consul-General in Urumchi forbade religious services to be held in the little church which had been erected in the Consulate grounds, and said that he intended to convert the building into a propagandist theatre, Governor Yang intervened and refused to allow it. "The church," he said, "belongs to Russian Christians and is to be kept open for their use," and this was done.

He handled China's interests with diplomatic astuteness, and never lost a mile of her territory to an aggressor. When Russia decided to increase her Consulates in Turkestan he acquiesced, but insisted that an equal number of additional Chinese Consulates be opened on Russian soil, so that representation be evenly balanced. He did not greatly strengthen his military defences, for his view was that unless he could have a stronger force than his neighbours it was better not to have one at all, so he trusted to the weapon of diplomacy.

When I met Governor Yang, I understood something of the power he wielded, for he was a most impressive man, tall and stately in his long grey silk gown, and bore himself with the dignity of a Chinese gentleman of the old school. His strong, intelligent, commanding face revealed one who could grasp a situation quickly and deal with it unhesitatingly. He spoke of the difficult problem created by widespread illiteracy, and declared himself convinced that the education of women was essential to the well-being of a nation, suggesting that after my companions and I had completed the journey on which we were launched, we should return to Urumchi and help in organising women's educational work in his province; but the end of his rule was nearer than he thought, and we never saw him again.

Sinister influences were already at work and he knew that enemies were plotting against him. In an endeavour to check them, he changed his former and more liberal policy for new methods, tightening up control on all frontier stations until the entrance to, and exit from, Turkestan could only be effected through his own personal permit. He increased the number of his secret service agents, and consequently his lists of suspects grew. When a plot in his immediate circle was discovered, he dealt with it in a way which is a lasting stain on his memory. He gave a feast to which he invited the conspirators and many other guests, and himself sat down to share it with them, but when the wine was served he left the hall for a moment and returned followed by a soldier. He stood behind the chair of one of the instigators of the plot and had him beheaded on the spot, then repeated the action and another conspirator fell dead, after which he resumed his seat, and the ghastly meal proceeded to its close. It was said in the *baʐar* that Yang bitterly repented this deed, and later the Chinese proverb was freely quoted, "He who murders at a feast, at a feast shall his blood be shed." It is certain that from this time onwards his enemies multiplied, until in 1928 he himself was murdered at a feast by his own Minister of Foreign Affairs, Fan Yao-nan.

Fan, the conspirator, was a cunning, stealthy man, who had been educated in Japan and held very revolutionary views. From the first day they met, he and Yang disliked and mistrusted one another, and Yang insulted Fan by appointing him to a less important post than that for which he had been designated.

When I last saw Fan he was longing to get out of Turkestan, where he felt neither safe nor happy, but the strange, cruel control which made life in Urumchi a nightmare to so many was closing in, and he could not leave the province without the Governor's written permission, nor could he obtain it. Angry, discontented and rebellious, he determined to get free from this sense of imprisonment, and the strain of being himself ignored, insulted and slighted told on his over-wrought nerves. The doom meted out to his colleagues at the famous dinner-party could only be atoned for with blood, and he watched for a chance of revenge. The suitable occasion occurred on July 7th, 1928. Governor Yang was to attend a graduation ceremony at the Russian Language School, and Fan brought in a number of his own men disguised as language school students. At the close of the proceedings, when the feast was served, a signal was given, shots were fired, and Governor Yang fell dead.

Within a few hours, Fan himself was executed by order of Chin Shu-ren, Minister of the Political Department and next in authority to Yang himself. Chin then succeeded the murdered man as Governor, and all the foundations so carefully laid by Yang Tseng-hsin for the stabilisation of Turkestan began to crumble in the hands of this weak, vacillating opium-smoker.

REVOLT IN THE GOBI

I

The Moslem Rising of 1930

THE year 1930 was destined to be a fateful one in the history of the Gobi Desert, for it witnessed the collapse and downfall of the old line of the Khans of Hami, the abolition of their mediaeval Court and the early stages of a rebellion which was to shake Chinese Turkestan to its very foundations. Chin Shu-ren, Governor of Chinese Turkestan, had none of the qualities essential to good rule or wise administration. He was a man beset by fears, alternately too feeble or too harsh, dealing out leniency to the rich and severity to the poor, and showing that combination of tyranny and vacillation which is the most fatal characteristic that an autocrat can possess. He commanded no respect from either his supporters or his opponents, and the Moslem elements in the important oases, always so difficult to conciliate, were only tolerant of his shortcomings so long as their own seat of government was firmly established at Hami under Khan Maksud Shah, a man of their own race, religion and speech, who still held the proud title of King of the Gobi.

During the year 1930, however, this ruler died, and the succession was not allowed to continue as it had done through so many generations, for Hami looked back to the days when Genghiz Khan had included that area in the portion of his son Jagatai. Maksud's son, Nazir, heir to the throne, was summoned peremptorily by the Governor to report himself at Urumchi, and Yolbas, the Tiger Prince, was ordered to appear with him. This was bad news for his subjects, as all knew that Governor Chin was not to be trusted, and no one was surprised when word came from the capital that the young prince had been made a prisoner in his own lodging, and that there were to be many changes in the standing of the Turki people. When Yolbas returned to Hami he left Nazir in Urumchi, and arrived in company with a band of Chinese officials who at once sat down to business and drew up a list of alterations which were to be introduced in the oasis administration.

The subjects of the Khan had often complained hotly of the taxation which he imposed on them, and no one pretended that his court of justice was conducted with unimpeachable equity, but he and his people were one, and they understood each other well. His Oriental style of Court life was appreciated by the Turkis, and the Khan, by virtue of his hereditary title, was unquestionably accepted by them. There was immediate resentment among the populace at the suggested changes, and this resentment became the more bitter when a great display of highly organised officialdom was made.

The whole area of Hami was carefully surveyed and the land redistributed. Three large administrative districts were arranged and given names which dated back to the time of the Han dynasty. The new government was to be wholly in Chinese hands, and the old Khanate system was to vanish. Chinese magistrates were appointed to hear the law cases, and Chinese tax-collectors were to levy the dues and convey them to the capital, where they would be allocated to the respective departments.

The easy-going methods of the old Khan were to be abolished, and the changes were presented to the people as improved measures of justice, but, at the same time, some unappropriated land which the Turki farmers would have liked to use was given to the Chinese, and arrears of taxes from which the Chinese were exempt were demanded from Moslem landowners. Suddenly that dangerous thing so well known to the Oriental as a "breath of fury" rose fiercely among men who had hitherto dealt only with their own Khan, and they unanimously determined on revolt. A telegram exposing their grievances was drafted and dispatched to Urumchi. It was signed by men of every class among the Moslems, and any ruler, seeing it, would know that it represented the views not of a few malcontents but of all, from the richest and most influential merchants of the southern oases to the humble farmers of the poorer districts. No answer came, and that telegram is said never to have reached its destination, but to those who sent it, it seemed to have been totally ignored, and this slight roused profound indignation.

At the same time, one of the newly appointed tax-gatherers, a self-indulgent and uncontrolled youth, insulted the Moslem population of Hami by seducing one of their girls. This scandal set the whole community in a blaze, and on the night of a marriage which was viewed as a crowning insult the sentinels who were appointed to guard the house where the young man lived were attacked and killed, while the mob broke in and murdered the bride and bridegroom with horrible ferocity. Having gone thus far, the revolt had to run its course, led by the excitable, turbulent, bloodthirsty Turkis and backed by the wealthy, astute, calculating Tungans. These two classes of men were in every respect different, but, linked in the brotherhood of Islam, they sank all their differences and determined to wipe out in blood an insult which had been offered to their common creed.

Meanwhile the spirit of rebellion was not confined to Chinese Turkestan, but had spread among the Kansu oases, which lay on the other side of the Great Wall. A very young war-lord had risen to power, and by some personal magnetism had drawn a large army together to follow him. This youth was the son of a certain General Ma, and doubtless inherited some of his father's military genius. The circumstances of his birth were strange. His father had once betrayed a friend, General Li by name, and on the day of the child's birth, as General Ma sat in the courtyard of his house, he suddenly rose to his feet, stared into space and exclaimed, "General Li is here!" As he uttered the words he fell unconscious to the ground, and at the same moment a messenger came to bring him the glad news that the newly born child was a boy.

Young Chung-ying, as he was called, grew up a handsome, elegant, wilful child, who was spoilt by all. It was whispered everywhere that the *kuei* (spirit) of General Li had come to take vengeance on the old General by influencing the son through occult means. When, at the age of fifteen, Chung-ying declared himself to be a military commander, all felt that here was proof positive of spirit control, and from all sides bands of young Tungans responded to his call to arms. His military career became one of such unbroken success that his troops felt he showed more mature military ability than such a child could possibly possess, were it not that he was subject to some mysterious warrior control.

He was a fierce fighter, and terrified north-west Kansu by the violence of his methods of warfare. The only alternative to unconditional surrender was death by the sword, and in one resisting town after another every male over fourteen years of age was slaughtered, boys under fourteen were taken over by the army to be trained as little orderlies, and the young women were left to the pleasure of the soldiers. At Chen-fan, at Yung-chang, at Hung-shui and in other oases he wiped out the male population. In Chen-fan alone he left three thousand corpses lying in the streets. At last no city dared to answer that terrible challenge save by throwing its gates open and by placing its arsenal, food-supply, horses and all else at the disposal of young Ma Chung-ying and his brigand band, until the suffering peasants surnamed him "General Thunderbolt."

Ma Chung-ying's strategy was based on the assumption of the paralysing effect of frightfulness in action, and as a method of temporary invasion it answered his purpose well, but it never served him as a basis of true conquest, nor did he ever establish rule over one single acre of the land which he invaded. His was the method of the locust and the Hun, and his army was always viewed as a plague. It came, it devoured, and when it had passed over, the patient, constructively minded peasants instantly began to repair the damage done to their fields, and to beget sons to replace those who had been swept away in his train.

The army moved on toward north-west Kansu, devouring the country as it went, until it reached the town of Kanchow. This large and prosperous oasis received him with apparent cordiality, and submitted itself to being despoiled by the hungry hordes who rode from village to village and from one farmstead to another, ordering the slaughter of beasts, the transport of grain, vegetables and fuel to the barracks, and levying a toll of forced labour on the young farmers. It was long since the band had enjoyed so much leisure, ease and such abundant food.

After some time it was rumoured that Chung-ying's cousin, Ma Pu-fang, was on his way to Kanchow bearing an important message for the "Baby General," as he was familiarly called by his men. Pu-fang was a commanding officer of the National Army of China, and it was commonly reported that he had brought to his cousin the offer of a commission in the National forces, along with the promise that all his irregular troops would be taken into Government pay and no questions asked. Pu-fang and his body-guard arrived, were given a great reception, and were feasted at the expense of the hard-working, thrifty farmers of Kanchow. Later on the two young men, apparently on the best of terms, went off together to a bath-house, in order to enjoy the refreshment of a hot bath. The attendants soon heard angry tones from within, and before long a number of them were gathered in the ante-room, listening to what was developing into a first-class row between Chung-ying and Pu-fang. Suddenly the bath-house door was flung open and Pu-fang strode out in a towering rage, called for his horse, and leaping on it galloped away, followed by his own men.

Thus, whatever the Government's offer may have been, it came to nothing, and the hour in the bath-house became one of the turning-points in a phase of Central Asian history, for shortly after Pu-fang's exit a deputation of Moslem envoys arrived from Hami at Chung-ying's headquarters at Kanchow. They told of oppression of their people by the Urumchi Government, of the imprisonment of their rightful prince and of an unforgettable insult offered to the Pan-Islamic brotherhood in the rape of a Moslem girl by a vile, infidel, pig-eating Chinese tax-collector. Blood called to blood, and the Hami rebels urged General Ma Chung-ying to come and help in the holy war.

This was a campaign according to "Baby General's" own wild, conquest-loving heart, but there were hard terms to be fixed and the help of a young man who had conquered so many cities of the far north-west and had been offered a commission in the National Army with all the security that this implied, was not easily won. Even the promise of being proclaimed Governor of Turkestan when that province should have been wrested from China and brought under the control of Islam did not bring him to a decision. He remained very hesitant, and though he made definite preparations for a desert journey, he would not commit himself to any course of action. By now he had reached the next oasis, which was the town of Suchow, and every small artisan was busy making tin mugs, kettles and water-bottles out of disused oil-tins, or goatskin bellows for blowing up camp-fires for his army.

Meanwhile two strangers had appeared in Chung-ying's immediate *entourage*. No one knew much about them except that they were Moslems, who spoke of having come from Istanbul; they both had experience of warfare, for both had fought through the European war of 1914-1918, and carried scars gained in that campaign. The younger was a man of action whose army experience at once gave him leadership in military matters. The elder was a graduate of a Paris University, a man who spoke several languages, and whose knowledge of European politics was wide. He remained silent regarding his own personal views, but it was the silence of a man with deep purpose, and of one who awaits the hour appointed by destiny for the pulling down of the mighty.

Both these men bore a personal grudge against Governor Chin of Turkestan. Two years earlier they had hoped to do business in Urumchi and become recognised merchants in its free-trade quarter. They had arrived there with a camel caravan laden with goods in which they had invested their capital, and from which they hoped to draw good profit. Their arrival was reported to the Governor, but Chin, taking no risks with men who were certainly somewhat out of the ordinary, ordered them to be arrested and put in prison. The prisons of Urumchi have never been healthy quarters, and many have gone in who never came out alive. The two Turks did emerge alive, but as men who were financially ruined. Neither of them was a good forgiver, and, on being released, they managed to escape from Turkestan and, hearing of the young rebel Chief, General Ma, they approached him with an offer. Recognising the value of their services, he added them to his staff and they became his military advisers, but with the long view toward ultimate vengeance on Governor Chin.

As the "Baby General" coquetted with the attractions of various offers, the two Turks, as members of his staff, quietly leant their weight to that campaign which threatened the territory of their personal enemy, Governor Chin. Once Chung-ying made an impetuous decision and, turning his back on Turkestan, started southwards toward Ning-hsia, but his Turkish advisers, playing skilfully on his love of flattery, gradually diverted his interest toward the land where their desires lay, and where they intended to execute vengeance on the man who had wronged them. Knowing that he was already on his way south-east, the authorities in Chinese Turkestan breathed more freely, but the Turkish advisers triumphed, and suddenly veering round, the General and his army dashed off toward the desert road to Hami. His crossing of the desert at midsummer with a force of five hundred Tungan cavalry was a daring and strategic feat of military endurance, and when he appeared in Turkestan he was acclaimed leader of the Moslem forces, while the Urumchi Government was taken completely by surprise.

He immediately attacked Barkul, overcame it and promptly equipped his own men with firearms and ammunition from its arsenal. He then advanced on Hami, and besieged it. The Chinese population withdrew from the suburbs and took shelter in the small fortified town which held all the official buildings, and this extraordinary siege lasted for half a year. The small fortress was attacked more than forty times by Ma's army, and his troops used scaling-ladders, tunnelling tactics and every means known to mediaeval warfare, in their attempt to break the resistance of their adversaries while economising their own ammunition.

The defenders of the town were both vigilant and resourceful. They resisted every attempt at tunnelling beneath the walls by using huge bales of raw cotton to block the openings before anyone could get through, and even prepared vats of boiling oil to pour over the besiegers' heads when they attempted to scale the walls, though they themselves dared not waste oil by lighting lamps after dark. The dogs and cats were killed, and the human beings lived on a meagre ration of bran. When they seemed to be at the end of their resources one of the officials remembered the existence of an old and disused arsenal. It had been closed since the days of a certain famous General, Tso Tsung-tang (1812-1885), who had been sent to Turkestan to quell a previous

Moslem rebellion. The weapons found there belonged to a much earlier period of warfare and included large stocks of big swords and of fire-arrows. Armed with these, the beleaguered city was able to keep the enemy at bay. At the end of six months General Ma's limited stock of patience was exhausted, and he declared that this siege of Hami was a futile business and that his army would be better employed in attacking the capital city, so, turning his back on the town, he led his troops toward Urumchi.

When news reached the capital that the siege of Hami was lifted, and the attacking forces were moving toward Urumchi, there was panic in the Governor's *yamen*. Military preparations were speeded up and troops hastily dispatched to intercept Chung-ying. The two armies met half-way, and the Government troops sustained such a crushing defeat at the hands of the rebels that they were almost wiped out. Ma Chung-ying's losses were comparatively small, but he himself was wounded, being shot through both legs. It was his custom to be in the thick of the battle, leading and urging his men on to deeds of valour, but this he could no longer do, and without their mascot leader his followers were lost. Back to Kansu they cantered, carrying the wounded leader in a litter, and taking the desert stages at high speed.

The peaceful inhabitants of the Kansu oases, who had breathed freely since the brigands went westward, were terrified when they reappeared and set up General Headquarters at Ansi. This locality could not possibly bear the burden of feeding, clothing and warming such a large army, so a number of soldiers were drafted off to Tunhwang, which had the name of being a rich oasis. Thus the routine of the food-levy and press-gang squads began over again, with these two cities as centres.

General Ma's wounds gradually healed, and as soon as he could ride again he became restive for further conquest; but the retreat had left his army less well equipped than formerly. The Moslem rebels in Turkestan were still holding out in a few strongholds from which nothing could dislodge them. The fortress of Bardash in the Eastern Mountains above the Khan's summer palace was a magnificent natural fortification. Many took refuge there, believing that, thanks to its rich pastures and the stocks of food stored there, it could hold out to the end—which it did, and in fact proved to be impregnable. It was here that councils of war were held and communications kept open with General Ma by messengers who used a lonely desert track from Barkul.

Ma Chung-ying was, for the moment, not strong enough to respond to the repeated appeals for help from Turkestan, and could only encourage the rebels to hold on. At this juncture, however, he was approached by a Pacification Commissioner from Nanking who arrived at Ansi with an offer from the Central Chinese Government, and this time he gladly accepted command of the thirty-sixth division of the National Army, and this in spite of the fact that sections of his own irregulars were still helping the rebels in Turkestan.

Racial animosity, which is so easily provoked in Central Asia, was actually increasing in violence, and soon Qasaqs, Tungans and Turkis were all involved. Governor Chin trembled behind the triple guard of his nightmare-haunted *yamen*. One defeat of his troops among the hills above Hami was reported, another column of his forces fled in disorder before a band of Chung-ying's men; at Shan-shan the Chinese magistrate and all the Chinese populace were massacred, and although, in retaliation for this wholesale murder, many Moslems were seized and executed, the trouble spread to Turfan and blazed into another massacre of Chinese, with public torture of some very important Chinese officers. Revolt spread beyond all possibility of control, and Governor Chin knew that at any moment the Moslem quarter of Urumchi might burst into rebellion and rise murderously against the Chinese.

The whole province was in a blaze, and the conflagration could not be checked. The South Road was seething with Moslem activity, and the fierce rebels killed and looted at their pleasure, leaving only smouldering ruins behind them. The Governor's untrained and ill-disciplined troops were no match for the lusty, riotous, war-like Turkis, and he soon found that the only men on whom he could rely were the young Russians, sons of *émigrés* to whom his predecessor, Governor Yang, had shown kindness in their great distress, when they were homeless refugees from Siberia. These men fought loyally until the Governor alienated them by his shifty and treacherous ways. At the very time when they were keeping the rebels from the gates of his capital he even refused them necessary military equipment, expecting them to fight on foot, and when compelled to supply them with horses, gave all the best mounts to his Chinese soldiers, leaving only the poorest beasts for the Russians.

At last the Russian troops determined to precipitate a *coup d'état*, and without notice they attacked the Governor's *yamen*, overcame his body-guard, and forced their way into the inner court with a view to seizing Chin and making him a prisoner. At that very moment the

Governor himself, having stripped off his uniform, was escaping over the back wall of his residence disguised as a common soldier.

The Russians were quite open in defence of their action, pleading that the inefficiency of the Governor and the corruption of his chosen representatives imperilled the peace of the whole province. Moreover, they calculated that the time for harvesting and storing grain was at hand, and that if the farmers were not compelled to attend to the crops there would be famine in the land.

Events then moved so quickly in Urumchi that it was hard to keep track of the attacks and counter-attacks, the skirmishes and the retaliations. For some days the streets, especially in the Moslem quarter, ran with Tungan blood. Chin Shu-ren first sheltered near the city, then moved westward, but after a time, uncertain of any support from his own troops, he hesitated and changed his plan several times. Ever a deceiver, he now found himself tricked by the very men whom he had armed to defend him. Finally he went north to Manas and travelled toward Chuguchak, on the southern Siberian border, by motor-lorry. On arrival there he sent his resignation of office to the authorities, then later telegraphed to Urumchi, asking that his personal belongings be sent after him, and then followed up these telegrams with a proclamation condemning the action of the White Russians and declaring that he himself, as Governor of the province, would return to crush the rebels.

However, the Central Government at Nanking on May 5th, 1933, confirmed the document in which he tendered his resignation, and put an end to this vacillation. Meanwhile he was making his way toward Tientsin, travelling by the Trans-Siberian railway. Thus Chin Shu-ren passed out of the land in which he had held the highest official position it had to offer, but Nanking's acceptance of his resignation was only the prelude to further dealings with him, and on arrival at Tientsin he was arrested, tried and condemned to a long period of imprisonment.

Ma Chung-ying, Commander of the thirty-sixth division of China's Government troops, was still at heart the gangster General, beloved by his own men more for his vices than for his virtues. He was born for action, and when the news reached him of protracted Moslem turmoil in Turkestan, his passion for conquest by force of arms was rekindled. He knew that he had only to appear to be again acclaimed leader and chief by his co-religionists, and, forgetful of all obligations to Nanking, he dashed off north-west from Suchow, irresistibly drawn to the fray. The very hour of Chin Shu-ren's eclipse found him once more nearing Hami, and in June, with an army of three thousand men, he had fought his way across the Tienshan Range to Kucheng and made himself master of the North Road.

Urumchi was in no position to offer him strong resistance. From a military point of view it was badly disorganised, and financially it was in a chaotic condition. Governor Chin, with his wild way of getting out of a tight place by printing off a roomful of paper tael notes, had brought the whole country to the verge of bankruptcy. Inflation was already well advanced, and paper money was almost worthless. The only way to overcome the enemy was by means of a diplomatic move so formulated as to flatter Ma's vanity and delude him with fair promises. A deputation was dispatched by Chin's successor, Governor Liu, with the object of seeing Ma Chung-ying in person, and if he consented to the interview, of laying such favourable terms before him as would make him hesitate before attacking Urumchi.

Ma proved more tractable than was anticipated, and it appeared that he was not unwilling to consider the terms which were to be drawn up at Urumchi immediately after the safe return of all members of the deputation which waited on him at Kucheng. These terms were certainly favourable, and offered him some distinct advantages. They were as follows:

1. He was to be Commander-in-Chief of southern Turkestan.
2. His troops were to be counted and enrolled in the regular army of the province.
3. Urumchi was to be responsible for the pay of these soldiers.
4. All magistrates in southern Turkestan were still to be appointed by the Urumchi Government.

On the surface the terms seemed generous, but Ma and his advisers must have seen through them at once. It might be advantageous for him to have his soldiers enrolled with the regular army, but this was outbalanced by the next clause, which made Urumchi responsible for their pay, because in China, more than in most lands, it is proverbial that he who pays, controls. Moreover, if the magistrates in the area over which Ma was to be Commander-in-Chief were of Urumchi's appointing, it was obvious that his freedom of action would be severely limited, and that the secret police would have every facility for reporting on his actions.

At the very moment when these terms were to be sent to Ma by the hand of a responsible delegation, a diversion was created by the unexpected arrival at Urumchi, by air, of a special envoy from Nanking with orders to investigate conditions on the spot, and to draw up a list of recommendations for the Nanking Government.

The civil, military, financial and social conditions of Urumchi were far too complicated to be grasped by any man in the course of a brief investigation, and the envoy, among people of another race, tongue and creed from himself, was out of his element and as it were in a foreign land, though still in a remote part of the Chinese Republic. He knew but little about the Turkis involved in the rebellion, much less could he appreciate their grievances and general outlook on administrative questions. Moreover, Ma Chung-ying had never yet been thwarted, and was not going to be turned aside from his wild career by a rebuke conveyed to him from Nanking. Pacification officers were nothing to him, and the young Chief, with all his brigand band in full cry, advanced on Urumchi. The civil members of his council had advised a bid for a solid post with Government recognition, but his army yelled "*Shah! Shah!*" (Kill! Kill!), and the army had it.

The Government troops, strengthened by the White Russian battalion, soon engaged General Ma's army, and there was a fierce hand-to-hand battle. The Government soldiers were breaking under the pressure of his fierce attack, when they were suddenly reinforced by a column of Manchurian volunteers who arrived at the critical moment. Ma's troops were now hard pressed by this unexpected reinforcement of the enemy, and, as if to complete his defeat, a fierce hailstorm broke over the battlefield. With the strange climatic violence for which northern Turkestan is renowned, the temperature at midsummer suddenly fell to close on freezing-point. Ma's soldiers, in their summer uniforms and shelterless from the storm, were taken badly at a disadvantage and lost heavily in a disorderly retreat.

The next incident took the form of a second *coup d'état* in the capital, and this led to the arrest and execution of certain high officials who were discovered to be plotting against the new Governor. Then followed a period of great political tension. Another power, however, was making itself felt at Urumchi, and it was one of far-reaching influence. For more than two centuries Chinese Turkestan and its fertile oases had been viewed by the Russian Government as an El Dorado, and now the Soviet authorities decided that the time had come for a peaceful penetration of this desirable area of influence. It was a natural field from which to draw various valuable raw products, and also a market which could absorb an enormous amount of manufactured goods. The disturbed condition of Turkestan now laid its Government open to the operation of a bloodless conquest which ended in its virtual control by Russia. It was an hour of crisis. Help the country must have, and she was compelled to seek it at the hand of those who would give it immediately, and without prolonged negotiations. Military reinforcements were speedily forthcoming, and their assistance was paid for by certain trade agreements in which Russia secured the commercial privileges she so much coveted.

In October 1931 a commercial treaty was signed in Urumchi by Slavutski, the Russian delegate, and Mr. Chen, plenipotentiary of the Sinkiang Government, which gave to the U.S.S.R. the right to open trade agencies or offices in all the important towns of Sinkiang and also secured tariff privileges for Russian manufactured goods. It also granted to representatives of trade organisations and to Soviet citizens the right of unrestricted movement for purposes of trade. On the other hand, the Provincial Government of Sinkiang expressed the hope that the Soviet Government would assist them in the organisation of transport, in the development of electrification, in necessary measures for the improvement of agriculture, and would send specialists to Sinkiang to train Chinese citizens in these various departments. Time alone can reveal the importance of this treaty and its far-reaching results.[1]

Ma Chung-ying never slackened his hasty flight until he reached the South Road connecting Hami and Kashgar, where the Moslem was still undisputed master. There he planned to found an empire which would bear the proud name of Islamistan and of which he would be the unquestioned ruler.

Matters, however, took a very different turn from that which he had expected, and this long and fierce Tungan rebellion was destined to join its predecessors on the pages of Chinese history as yet another of the revolts that failed. One by one the oases of the South Road were retaken by the Chinese soldiery, with savage retaliations on the Moslem population. Their homes were left desolate, and the fighting rebels were driven back until they only held the Khotan area, which was one of the most southerly oases on the other side of Lob.

From this time onward the only news concerning Ma Chung-ying which reached the outer world was in the form of rumour. Some said he was still in Khotan, others that he had left, and it was even seriously reported that he had reached London, where he was negotiating with the British Government for assistance. Only after a long period did it become certain that Russia had captured the young rebel and had

[1] See *Journal* of the Royal Central Asian Society. October 1933.

removed him to Moscow, there to be disciplined and trained for some future post of usefulness. What that post may be is still unknown, but it is probable that the world will hear more of this remarkable young man.

A wise old Chinese diplomat, after watching the stormy incidents of Ma's juvenile career, analysed his character in the following words: "Ma has much strength, but he has many weaknesses. He is dreaming of conquering half the world, but past defeats must have taught him sharp lessons. Doubtless he is a prey to secret fears . . . then he is vain. His vanity is so great that it demands tremendous conquests. That is because he is profoundly ignorant and knows no other road to distinction. Show him that peace can bring fame no less than war. Suggest that he is more than a warrior—a scholar, a statesman. Then perhaps he will be glad to find that egotism may be appeased without the risks and inconvenience of slaughter. You never know with such men." [1]

II

Meeting with the Rebels

Travelling during those years of revolt brought us into contact with some of the men who played major parts in the drama. It was often our lot to meet them in unusual circumstances, and we were even detained for a considerable time in the camp of Ma Chung-ying, the brigand Chief. For years before the storm broke there had been rumours of coming trouble, and certain things which we ourselves saw, made us confident that the Moslems meant to carry yet another revolt to its final issue. The commonly accepted tradition in the Gobi that once every thirty years they must rise, produces a strange psychological effect on the oasis dwellers, and as the period draws near they all seem compelled to fulfil their self-predicted destiny. Yet, although the Moslems have produced a remarkable succession of military leaders and show a fierce fighting spirit, they have never been able to wrest the government from the hands of the Chinese, who, when the storm is over, still remain final masters of the situation.

Wise old Governor Yang was kept well informed by his secret agents of what was being said by the conspirators, and as early as 1926, knowing that the time had come to act, he quietly arranged a way of escape for his family and for the transference of his wealth to the security of the British Concession in Tientsin. It was stated in Urumchi

[1] *Turkestan Tumult*, by A. K. Wu.

that his eldest son was shortly leaving for Peking in order to take a further course of specialised study, and under the guise of ordinary travellers' luggage cases of valuables were packed and roped to a cart. The youth, dressed in rough travel clothes, sat with other passengers on the top of the piled-up goods, and so travelled to the Russian border.

It was important that the real purpose of the journey should not be suspected, and we might never have heard of it but for the fact that we boarded the same steamer as he did on Lake Zaisan, and travelled down the Irtish River in his company. Those long, leisurely Siberian journeys, whether by river steamer or by slow train, easily lead to confidential talk, and the young man, released from the strain of the past few weeks, spoke of his anxiety concerning his father and for the future of Turkestan. Where a Chinese official sends his treasure it is certain that he expects soon to follow, and Governor Yang sensed that his time in Turkestan would be short, hence these preparations; but he never lived to reach Tientsin, for in 1930 he was murdered at Urumchi.

No one in Turkestan dared to speak aloud the dreaded word "revolt," but everyone was whispering it, and we had many opportunities of seeing how systematically it was being planned. While officials surreptitiously transferred their wealth to a place of safety, the instigators of trouble were equally persistent in their secret preparations for war. Camels and mules were requisitioned to transport weapons, ammunition and stocks of food over little-used tracks, that they might be stored in mountain caves known only to the few. Steady streams of small caravans carrying ammunition to the mountains came from the South Road, from Tunhwang and across one of the most lonely tracks of the desert route connecting Kansu with Barkul. All these converged on the Khan's summer palace grounds in Aratäm, and the stronghold of Bardash was stocked with huge supplies of food and firearms. Later on the Chinese officials in Turkestan marvelled at the resistance of the Moslem troops, and at the seeming impossibility of starving them out, but the quiet hamlet of Aratäm knew all about it, for the villagers had seen the men who constantly passed through and vanished up the narrow tortuous road which led to the hills beyond. It was in the Khan's garden that we met a party of gun-runners whose camels were so exhausted that it seemed as though they could never take that last uphill stage which led to the mountains; but get through they must, and that quickly, lest they be caught and the plot discovered. In desperation the tired men took flour from our bins and made it into a paste with which they fed the reluctant beasts, then forced them on for the last twenty miles. After that they would be left to die.

There were secret meetings in desert places and decisions made in lonely caves or little-known gullies which meant death to the many and promotion for the few. One morning when the cold chill of night was about to yield before the birth of another day, we surprised such a conclave. We were making ready to start on a long march, so the men had called us before dawn lest we fail to cover the distance by dark. It was a place where the road divided, the upper way leading across an escarpment, and the lower following the plain below. In the uncertain light I saw six mules tethered to the posts of a narrow stone bridge which crossed a dry irrigation channel below, and I dimly detected six men standing by the mules. In a few moments dawn was in control and their outlines could be clearly seen. They were talking earnestly; then one of them, probably a Hadji, turned with face toward Mecca and raised the call to prayer. They all fell down in obeisance, then rose and salaamed with peculiar solemnity. Each man then placed his foot in the stirrup of his mount, swung himself into the saddle, and they rode off, six horses abreast, on the wide plain in the southward direction.

The whole scene was so ominous, and such a strange solemnity hung over it, that I was confident these men's business was no ordinary affair and might be epoch-making in its effect. My instinct was true, but not till later did I know that the six men who rode off on that winter morning were deputies sent to summon Ma Chung-ying to the conquest of Turkestan, and to offer him its governorship as a reward.

Shortly before the outbreak of hostilities we saw the Tiger Prince once more and noticed how his easy, good-natured manner had given place to reserve and caution. He had reason to be anxious, and within a few months he himself was hiding in the Barkul Mountains with a price on his head. He only saved his life through proving himself so useful to both sides that he was chosen as intermediary of negotiations between the contending armies. It was dangerous work, and he went in constant fear of being seized by the Commander of either side. The Khan whom he had served was dead, the dynasty had fallen, and the title of Tiger Prince no longer described him. He knew that he must secure for himself some position in the new order which had come to Hami, so he entered on a career of compromise which eventually made of him the servant of the authorities, one whose duty it was no longer to command, but to obey and carry out orders.

It so happened that we were in the same oasis as Ma Chung-ying and his cousin Pu-fang when the famous quarrel in the bath-house took place. While it was still going on, a small boy came running to our house: "Lady, Lady," he said, "there is a big affair on hand. The two Generals are in the bath-house together, and they are quarrelling furiously." The quarrels of two men in a bath-house did not seem to be any concern of ours, and we paid little attention to his chatter, but later another little news-carrier ran in. "General Ma Pu-fang has come out of the bath-house," he said breathlessly, "and he has called for his horse and ridden away with all his men. The Little General is in a towering rage and no one dares to go near him."

That night the town buzzed with wild rumours and the soldiers expected to be ordered out to pursue Pu-fang and punish him, but gradually the storm blew over and Chung-ying settled down for long enough to revictual and re-equip his men, while his cousin returned to the hilly district from which he came, leaving Chung-ying to go his own way.

A few months later, however, Pu-fang made an attempt to resist his young cousin by seizing one of the oasis towns. We were staying there at the time, and, living under his rule, we found that he was better liked by the people than was his cousin, for he restrained his army from looting and made the soldiers pay for what they used, but he was ruthless in ordering executions wherever treachery was suspected. The prisons were full, while in the cold grey dawn the firing-squads were kept busy with executions. In all these towns there were human jackals following the war-lords in hopes of getting the pickings of their kill, and Pu-fang had no mercy on them.

Mutual abuse between the cousins was a favourite form of expression on both sides, and the towns which they respectively held were posted from end to end with placards attacking the morals of the other side. Chung-ying favoured communistic propaganda, and elaborated the theme of Pu-fang's exploitation of the proletariat. Among the posters were: "Pu-fang, Oppressor of the people." "Pu-fang, Robber of the farmer's grain." "Pu-fang, Devourer of the poor." "Pu-fang's locusts eat the labourer's bread." In contrast to this were the self-laudatory slogans: "General Ma Chung-ying, Deliverer of the people." "Light shines where Chung-ying appears." "May Ma Chung-ying live for ever." Pu-fang's posters, on the other hand, described his cousin as "Prince of adulterers," "Instigator of brigands," "Self-appointed libertine leader," and called him "General Tiger-Head and Snake's tail."

Chung-ying secured a great haul in propaganda literature when he got hold of a roll of unused posters dating from 1927 when some Chinese students were unfortunately fired upon in Shanghai by the municipal police. They were designed by the leaders of the anti-British movement, and showed soldiers in His Majesty's uniform shooting on a Chinese crowd which mainly consisted of women and children. By merely changing the caption, they were made to represent Pu-fang's firing-squads at their deadly work.

Living first in one town and then in the other, we stood with the gaping crowd, and read alternately of Chung-ying's vices and of Pu-fang's atrocities, but all we could feel was loathing of the hateful method of lie-propaganda which practises the art of so confusing men's minds that they have not even the wits to ask themselves if what they are being told is false or true.

Another time while we were camping in the foothills of the Richt-hofen Range, where the villagers were anxious to hear what we had to tell, a whisper suddenly passed from one to another and the crowd which had gathered melted away. Then the village elders came to warn us that a band of Chung-ying's men had been seen marching through the mountain passes and coming in our direction. Within an hour the place was completely deserted. This was a marauding band, caught among the Tibetan mountains, which was being starved out by Pu-fang's soldiers, who guarded the passes and prevented their exit. Their only means of avoiding starvation was to raid the near villages and carry the loot back into the mountains. Although half-starved and almost without ammunition, these men had it their own way among the farms, through deliberate acts of such cruelty as frightened the villagers into yielding to their every demand. Farmers were paralysed with fear, and the womenfolk, wearing their best clothes, would sit all day on the *kang* holding their most treasured possessions, wrapped in bundles, ready for flight. Every hamlet had its spotters, and the alert signal was given by the sounding of a gong. At the first alarm the women jumped on to donkeys and rode to some cave which the villagers alone knew of. When the brigands appeared they found the houses deserted, and they seized grain, fowls, vegetables, sheep and every kind of food, while the owners watched them from distant points of vantage. As soon as the robbers had gone back into the hills the patient, suffering villagers returned to their homes and resumed their normal way of life, but the oases groaned under the heel of the oppressor.

We seemed unable to move without meeting either gun-runners, looting squads of irregulars, or bands of brigands making sporadic attacks on helpless oases. It became a common experience of ours to depart hurriedly at midnight, or before dawn, when we heard the warning signal and the call "Brigands are on the march." A horseman might gallop past shouting the news that there was looting among the farms, or a terrified official might urge us to feed our beasts and hurry away. Once we left an inn a little before some fellow-guests, and met the raiding-party on the road. It was a well-armed band, and the men prodded our bags with bayonets and scattered our luggage on the ground, but when their officer came up he ordered them not to molest us. "These ladies," he said, "are acquaintances of mine, and nothing of theirs must be touched. Ride on elsewhere." They did so, and a little later shot down the people from whom we had just parted at the inn.

Although we suffered less than did many other residents, yet when they wanted lodgings the brigands did not hesitate to turn us out of our quarters at midwinter, to take our best mules and to rifle our medicine-chest. It was this last incident which brought us into contact with Chung-ying's Turkish advisers, the men who played such an important part in the Turkestan rebellion by persistently directing the young General's ambition toward becoming Governor of that province. Later we came to know them well, and had long talks with the one in Chinese and with the other in the French language. They tried to help us, and during a night when the soldiers had leave to loot the town our goods remained untouched because one of the Turks sat with us until after midnight, while his escort guarded our door.

Overtaken by dark we once came to a large farm where we asked for hospitality, and were welcomed to the circle of a simple and kindly household. As we sat round the brazier and ate fried dough-cakes together, there was the rap of a riding-whip on the outside door. Our host and his wife exchanged one anxious look, then he went to unbar the heavy gate. A moment later an officer of the brigand army strode in.

"Measure out five bushels of wheat for my men," he said, "and be quick about it."

"Your men have been here three times already, and have taken everything I have," said the farmer.

"Five bushels of wheat," was the only answer.

"Truly I have not got it," said the old man.

Out came the riding-whip, and the farmer's back was lashed with all the strength of the young soldier's arm.

"How can I give you what I have not got?" our host said with quiet dignity.

The blows rained again on the old man's head and shoulders, and helpless to resist he went to the corn-bin which held the small supply of grain for the family food, opened the little hatch near the floor and swept out all the remaining wheat into the gaping mouth of the sack held open by the brigand officer's retainers. A moment later we heard the clattering hoofs of horses trotting swiftly toward a neighbouring farmstead where the next demand would be made and the same means used to force the farmer to give up what remained of his hard-earned store.

Our host, without a word of anger or of complaint, took off his cotton coat and with his hand felt the weals on his neck and shoulders, then he came and joined our circle round the brazier again. Such is the patient endurance of men who have never seen human rights maintained, the cause of the poor vindicated, nor the rich and mighty brought under a law of equality.

History more often records the brilliant successes and spectacular defeats of contending forces than the effect of war on the common people. No class is more humble nor more suffering than the populace called in China "*lao peh-hsing*" (the hundred-names people). It was among these people of the undistinguished names that we moved, and saw the cruelty of the war-lord system spend itself on them. Like reeds in the blast they bowed before superior physical force, but like reeds they stood again when the blast had passed by, and by reason of their superior moral fibre were able to carry on and endure long after the brutal conqueror was destroyed. Finally it was the meek, not the violent, who inherited the earth.

Later on, Ma Chung-ying's army surrounded Tunhwang and for eight months we ourselves lived under his rule in that Gobi oasis. The town was robbed of everything in the nature of food, goods and money on which the men could lay hands. Silver, however, is easily hidden beneath floors of stamped earth, and the dryness of the land was such that wheat also could be buried for one season without fear of the grain sprouting. Thus the farmer's greatest treasure, seed for the next sowing, was hidden under the sand-hills and kept from the looter. Next to food the most coveted possessions of the oases were the young, vigorous, hardy men, such as the heat, the cold, the sand-storms and the blizzards, the fatigues and the constant hardships of desert life, have trained. From generation to generation these rough, enduring youths have been produced by the natural elimination of the weak, until only the toughest specimens have emerged, able to accept as natural conditions a standard of life which would spell death to any who were not inured to it.

These were the men whom Ma Chung-ying wanted for gun-fodder, and orders were issued to the press-gang to fetch them in from every farm of the neighbourhood, and collect them in Tunhwang city. Every day we saw them being rounded up. The ropes which they themselves had twisted from desert grass were used to tie their hands behind their backs, and to noose their necks in a running-knot. Roped together in droves of twenty or thirty, according to the success of the raid, they were brought to town by captors who rode the horses levied from these boys' own stables. Thrust behind the high palings of temple court-yards, the imprisoned youths lined the barriers, looking out for some passer-by who might belong to their own group of farmsteads and would take a report home that son or husband had been captured.

Out of this rough war-material Ma, the elegant, purposed to form a dashing army. Many of these boys were already slaves of the opium pipe, but there was no indulgence granted on that score by the Commander, and, herded like beasts in a pen, the recruits added the suffering of throwing off a drug habit to the dumb animal terror of being torn away, probably for life, from home, parents, wife and child. Three times a day the squads of new recruits were marched to the drill-grounds, there to begin their training in the army. Later they were drafted to General Headquarters at Ansi, where more intensive discipline awaited them, and, finally, the day would come when the General himself would give them demonstrations of military gymnastics and of riding prowess, for he prided himself on being the most skilful horseman and the best athlete of his own army.

Ma's secret service was efficient and his agents were everywhere listening and reporting to Headquarters any word of treason against his rule. He had a young brother who sometimes appeared in the town, called at various military departments, and talked with the officers in charge, but there was also a mysterious youth sufficiently like Chung-ying himself to pass as his double. When one or other of them came, went and issued orders, only those who were best acquainted with him could be certain whether Chung-ying or his double had been there.

He occasionally heard plain truths about himself, and rumour had it that on one occasion when out walking he met a small child whom he questioned. The boy had no idea who he was, and related the cruelty and infamy of General Ma, who had seized his brother, robbed their farm, and left the family in great poverty. "What do you think of General Ma?" the tall officer asked. "I hate him," said the boy, "and when I grow up I will fight against him." On hearing this the General became quiet and thoughtful, and later on enquired who the boy was. When the incident became known the whole village feared his vengeance, but they need not have been anxious, for instead of punishing them General Ma sent a present to the family. That day he had been surprised in one of his occasional kinder moods.

The man exercised an extraordinary power over his staff officers, who obeyed him with a devotion that was almost a cult. The fiercest men formed a body-guard round this slim, delicate-featured youth, and bowed to his will in all things. He was their mascot, and they believed he would always lead them to victory.

Meanwhile the food-supplies of Tunhwang were rapidly diminishing. The hungry army ate up all the provender as fast as it came in. Peasants who brought vegetables and fruit to market found their baskets seized and carried off, so they soon ceased to come. Sheep were taken from the flocks and killed for soldiers' rations, and every farmer was compelled to yield up his winter store of wheat. The City Magistrate had steadily refused to hand over the stocks of grain which were stored in the great municipal granaries, but one day a peremptory order, backed by awful threats, came from General Ma, directing that a stated number of carts were to be filled with wheat and sent to Headquarters at Ansi. The Mandarin dared not argue the point, and once the gates of the granaries had been opened Ma's men took control, the sound of rumbling carts was heard all night carrying off supplies, and the loot continued until bins were empty and even the floors of the barns swept clean.

Carts, horses, fuel and fodder, all was commandeered, and the luxuriant oasis of Tunhwang became a city of beggars. These filled the streets, pleading for a coin, or even more for a morsel of food. Even well-to-do tradesmen and farmers were reduced to the level of the barest poverty. There was nothing to be bought in the open market, and we, as others, were dependent upon the kindness of some farmer who smuggled a few pounds of flour into our house after nightfall. They knew we should never tell, and it was better for them to sell it to us than to have it levied by the brigands.

Then typhus began to take its toll of victims and the temple entrances were full of men and women muttering in delirium and calling on passers-by for a drink of water to slake their intolerable thirst. Dogs and wolves had a good time outside the north gate, for by ancient custom the bodies of all who died in the roadways were wrapped in matting and buried there in shallow graves.

In the midst of these happenings there came a command for us also, demanding that we present ourselves at the brigand camp, and when we demurred the City Magistrate produced the order which he had received. "You read Chinese," he said; "look at this, and you will see that if you do not obey I have no option but to send you up under military escort." We left on a cold November morning, in company with a band of prisoners, on the four days' hard journey over desert stages before we reached Headquarters at Ansi. The town was entirely taken over by the troops, and it was not easy to submit to the impudent cross-questioning of the boy sentinel at the city gate as we waited for a long time in bitter cold while our arrival was being reported. At last an officer came to take us to our lodging, and the next day we stood in the presence of the young General himself. He had lost the Turkestan campaign through being wounded, and the success of the future military operations depended upon his wounds being completely healed. Having heard exaggerated stories of miracles worked by means of Western medicine, he now summoned us to Ansi and ordered me to complete the cure. Every day we were taken to his room, and the treatment soon gave him such relief that within a short time he was able to ride again. He always treated us with civility and appeared interested in our party, probably owing to the fact that we were the only people who never flattered him and were obviously not afraid of him.

Among the soldiers who were brought to me for treatment were many with wounds caused by the "fire-arrows" discovered in the old arsenal of Hami. These wounds were septic and the flesh was charred as though burned by a chemical. It is known that as early as A.D. 75 a certain Chinese envoy, when in a desperate plight, used phosphorus for poisoning arrows, and by this means overcame his besiegers, and it is not improbable that the old fire-arrows of Hami had been treated in the same way.

In Ma's audience-room I witnessed many strange scenes, watching the callous, flippant youth who enjoyed his exercise of power and was more lenient or more fierce according to the mood of the hour. As I, at a side-table, prepared his dressings, men would be brought in for questioning, who were generally simple peasants, dressed in the home-made coat and trousers of the poor farmer. Their rough, bare feet were thrust into the shoes which the poor man's wife makes with such great labour, and their hair was caught back in a thin short plait. Such a man would throw himself on his knees before the indifferent and supercilious young Chief, who toyed with a hunting-knife and never even looked toward him.

"Spare my son's life, Your Excellency."

"Why should I spare his life?"

"He is my only son, Excellency."

"The boy is disobedient, and my orders are to punish disobedience with shooting."

"I promise he will never do it again, Excellency."

"He has done it once, and that is enough. I do not change my mind, you may go."

The simple fellow bent forward until his forehead touched the raised dais on which the General sat, and the body-guard hustled him away before Ma had time to fly into one of his quick rages and order floggings right and left.

Food shortage at Ansi was acute, at least as far as civilians were concerned, and though on paper we seemed to be well supplied we actually received the most meagre rations. We were daily given an official paper on which was written: "Supply 3 measures of wheaten flour, 1 bowl vinegar, ½ bowl oil, and vegetable sufficient for party, salt and red pepper according to need," signed "Food Controller to His Excellency General Ma Chung-ying."

Our cook took this document to the food office every day, but invariably returned a little later with a sour face, carrying in his hand a small bag of millet and a handful of salt. "There is no flour today," he would say, "and only a small amount of very poor millet, so again it must be millet porridge for dinner."

As soon as Chung-ying's wounds were healed we began to petition for a permit to return to Tunhwang, as life in a military camp was intolerable. Ma's two Turkish advisers gave us their support, for they realised how difficult our position was, and at last permission was given to return to Tunhwang, where we had a certain amount of liberty to go in and out of the city but were forbidden to leave the oasis. We obeyed the order for a time, but all through the hard months that followed, planned an escape, across Gobi, to Turkestan. With this in view we steadily laid aside a tithe of our meagre flour and fodder ration, for unless we could save enough food to take us over ten desert stages it was useless to make the attempt.

After a few months we knew that the time for flight had come, for if our beasts lost their strength through underfeeding, or if the team were commandeered by the military, we should have lost our only chance of escape. One morning, while Tunhwang was taking its early dose of poppy-juice, we left the town, seemingly to call at a neighbouring farm, but as soon as we were out of sight of the guards we turned our mules' heads toward one of the loneliest of desert roads, known only to local men. Unfortunately, it led past the extreme military outpost, where there was a spring of water carefully guarded lest any deserter from the army, parched with thirst, might risk coming there for a drink. We reached the last farm of the oasis unchallenged, and here, to our amazement, learnt that every man from the military post had ridden into Tunhwang a few hours earlier, to join in a looting raid which was timed for nightfall. On we sped, right through the night, and daylight found us once more in open Gobi, released from the hateful surveillance under which we had lived for so long. Each evening we dug a deep pit and kindled a dung fire, keeping it as much hidden as possible, as the glare of a wood fire would be seen many miles away. For two days all went well, but on the third day Chung-ying's rangers saw the impress of our cart-wheels, and following us up, overtook and challenged us. We knew well that General Ma had no mercy on those who disobeyed his orders, and if the rangers had insisted that we return with them to the camp at Ansi, we should have had no further chance of escape, and should have been subjected to the roughest treatment. When these men questioned our right to travel over Gobi, we handed them our large and impressive Chinese passports which bore the great seal of the Chinese Foreign Office. They were wholly illiterate and completely ignorant concerning official documents, apart from those issued by their own General, and it did not occur to them that anyone but himself could affix so grandiose a seal to any permit. They exchanged looks, folded the paper, handed it back, stood to attention and saluted. "Pass on," they said, "and if you get into any difficulty our men will look after you." Then they galloped off toward Ansi, and we passed on, safe for the moment, but knowing that once the incident was reported, desert-rangers might be ordered out to fetch us back. However, they never overtook us, and we reached the Turkestan lines of Government troops in safety.

We still had many dangerous roads to cross, and one week later we narrowly escaped capture by Moslem rebels, for there were bands of marauders attacking caravans among the foothills of the Barkul Mountains, and some of them appeared in our camp one night in a very lonely place. They surrounded us, spoke to each other about taking our beasts,

243

but finally rode off without molesting us. Not until some weeks later did we learn that on the next night these same people captured a party of Russian women, friends of ours, who, unknown to us, were camping near that same place. They held these women as hostages for many months, treating them with great severity and threatening them many times with a violent death. It was two years before they were rescued, and they owed their lives to the fact that they spoke the Turki language well and used their medical skill to help the wounded.

Some months later, when General Ma again attacked Turkestan and threatened the town where we were staying, a Government official brought us secret word of his intentions and urged us, in view of what had happened, to leave while it was still possible. We did so, and by the time Chung-ying reached that locality we were already far away. My last impression of him remains as that of a slender, elegant man, standing in a room of which the walls were hung with every kind of rifle, and surrounded with a body-guard of turbaned warriors, who watched him narrowly as he took from my hand a copy of the New Testament in Chinese, the book which would speak to him in his own tongue, rebuke him and, if he would but repent, convert and remake him. He saluted, I withdrew, and we never met again.

III

Personalities of the Desert

No record of life in the Gobi Desert would be complete without mention of certain typical people who belong to it and form an essential part of its oasis life. These dominant personalities are spoken of much as outstanding members of a clan are talked of in the family circle. They may be liked or disliked, appreciated or criticised, but they are pillars of desert society, an integral part of the communal life which has grown up among desert dwellers, and as such they receive acknowledgment from both friend and foe, irrespective of the tribe or race to which they belong.

Yolbas, the Tiger Prince, Chancellor at Hami, was one of these. He acted as Grand Vizier to the King of the Gobi, but it was a very informal Court and neither the King nor his Grand Vizier made themselves inaccessible to the men whom they ruled. As the Khan grew old and feeble, the power of Yolbas increased and he became the best-known figure in Hami. Everyone looked with favour on him as he rode to and fro, busy with matters of administration, between the palace of Maksud Shah and his own town residence.

There was no trace of Chinese elegance about him. He was powerful and rather clumsy both in figure and in face, with blunt features, a coarse, pock-marked skin, and just enough beard to give him something to stroke when he salaamed. He often wore Chinese dress made from dark-coloured brocaded silk, but he was incapable of looking well-tailored, yet his homely cut added to the impression of *bonhomie* which his whole aspect conveyed. Sometimes he appeared in the plain grey cotton uniform of a Chinese soldier, but in private he liked to wear the Turki *chapan*.

His residence bore the same stamp of simplicity as his person. It was a large house, in the main street, with wide wooden frontage and a long balcony extending under the upper-floor windows. The front door was always crowded with people passing in and out, for everyone had some business with Yolbas or his underlings, and his reception of visitors was simple, unceremonial and genial. He was bi-lingual in the Chinese and Turki languages, and turned from men of one nationality to the other, speaking to each in his own tongue and always as one who says what he has to say and does not tread a cautious path through the diplomatic labyrinth of carefully selected words.

In his official capacity he often had to act with great severity, for disputes between unruly serfs had to be settled by him, and matters relating to taxation were referred to him for arbitration. Though in personal contacts Yolbas was natural, kindly and free, yet in his political life he was faced by serious and growing difficulties, and when the crisis came and rebellion rent the province, his was a most dangerous position, for his sympathies were openly with the young rebel General, Ma Chung-ying, whom he regarded as liberator of the Moslem people. It took all his native wit to make himself so useful to both sides that his downfall would profit neither. Although he had to flee from Hami for a time, and shelter in the rebel fortress, yet, when Chinese control was re-established, in spite of his sympathies, he was reinstated and allowed to retain his old position. The authorities in Urumchi knew better than to dismiss so popular and so influential a man as the Tiger Prince, but they clipped his claws by limiting his power and restricting the sphere of his jurisdiction.

When we were last in Hami, Yolbas still lived in the big wooden-fronted house, and his reception-hall was still crowded with Turki people, but it was no longer he who issued the travel permits and received official visits. He himself was now a man under authority, and under the new régime the best he could hope for was to keep his post and, while still holding the confidence of his own Turki people, avoid giving offence to those who now exercised the real power. The King of the Gobi was dead, the son and heir to the throne was gone, and for Yolbas the glory of Hami had departed.

*   *   *

Scarcely less well known than Yolbas was Wang the Merchant, a typical Tungan, tall, lean and wiry. The Tungans are Chinese-speaking Moslems and have a strange and highly disputed racial descent. The Chinese call them Huei-huei, which can be translated "Returners," and when a Chinese is asked the meaning of that term he has but one answer: "Their ancestors came to this land unwanted and promised to return again to their own place, but they never did so. Therefore we call them 'Huei-huei'—Returners."

As a good Moslem, Wang despised the Chinese for idolaters, infidels and unclean eaters, but he equally scorned the masses of the Turki population, to whom he referred as "wild men devoid of under-standing." He was a man of means who owned *serais* in all the chief oases, and his business had wide ramifications in Turkestan and north-west China. His business headquarters were in Hami, but his brothers moved from place to place and transacted large deals with merchants from China, India, Samarkand, Persia and Siberia.

Wang was a trusted friend and confidant of Yolbas and was consulted by all the important men of Central Asia as representing Tungan interests. He had excellent manners, and conducted his household, as his business, with capacity and conspicuous success. His mother-tongue was Chinese, and this was the language of his home, his children and his womenfolk, but though he spoke Chinese and Turki with equal fluency, in Chinese his intonation was foreign, his vocabulary restricted and his speech mixed with a *patois* interspersed with Arabic words. The construction of his phrases had none of the sprightly idiomatic short-cuts which spring to the lips of the man from China proper and make his speech so terse and unforgettable. Likewise, his Turki talk lacked the racy crispness which constitutes the unique charm of that tongue. His clumsy speech was typical of the Tungan.

As a true follower of the Prophet he gave his sons names from sacred history, and in babyhood they were already Ibrahim, Izak and Izrah, but among the girls very strange names were used, which belonged neither to the Turki nor the Chinese language, but were reminiscent of ancient days before the Moslem conquest of Central Asia. He was an example of all the typical Tungan virtues, industry, frugality, prosperity and clannish benevolence. In building his *serais* he always arranged several small courtyards with convenient suites of sleeping-room and kitchen for use by poor relatives during temporary or even permanent financial difficulty, and when necessary, in addition to lodging, he allowed them a small pension.

By reason of his civic position Wang was highly respected in Turkestan, but, like all Tungans, he was made for revolt and was deeply conscious of racial and religious inadaptability to Chinese rule. The periodical Tungan revolts which devastate Central Asia have their roots in men like Wang the Merchant, and the Chinese Government, while respecting, rightly fears them. We stayed in his *serais* for many weeks at a time, and we became warm friends of the family. His mother was once very seriously ill and we were able to give her some medical care. After her recovery the whole Wang family, with an Eastern and most beautiful expression of gratitude, formally recognised us as now being on the footing of kinship. Never again were we allowed to pay for lodging under the roof of any member of the family, and in very distant cities we constantly found ourselves cared for by some connection of the Hami home.

Wang played a big part in the Tungan rebellion of 1933-1935, and when retaliations began he was a marked man, and his family could not escape vengeance. In a fateful hour his elder son was killed, his second son wounded and disfigured for life, and he himself murdered when acting as spokesman between two antagonistic parties.

The decorous household at Hami was already chaotic and distraught. The women's quarters had been rifled by Chinese soldiers, and the carefully guarded privacy of its inhabitants ruthlessly violated. The old mother died of shock, and Wang's senior wife would not outlive him, so committed suicide. On my last visit the wounded, half-blind Izrah, who had witnessed the murder of his father, told me in a broken voice of the downfall of his home, declaring that the enemies of Allah had brought this tragedy on the family, but he added: "Good and evil will surely be rewarded. If the evil is not yet punished it is because the hour for vengeance has not yet dawned." In those words I detected the first murmured threat of the next Tungan rebellion.

*   *   *

Moving about in the borderland where Mongolia and Dzungaria meet, travel intercourse brought us into daily contact with Kalmuck Mongols. We at once noticed a change in the answer given to the question "Where are you from?" for instead of naming the locality, desert-rangers simply said, "I belong to Shang, the Living Buddha," for they were feudal serfs of the powerful lamasery, and owed allegiance to their lord, the Living Buddha. When I first met Shang Fuh-ye (Shang the Living Buddha) I knew that this was a man whose circumstances of birth were believed to have set him apart from ordinary humanity, for he was more than a lama, and Buddhists held him to be the reincarnation of a spirit which, having attained the goal of *nirvana*, had voluntarily returned to earth to spend a further cycle of lives among men and help them to find their way out of the illusion of sensory things into the realities of annihilated desire.

Living Buddhas, as other men, vary in quality, but the moment I saw Shang Fuh-ye I knew that here was a seeker after higher things, and a man who denied himself pleasures and indulgence from a true desire to rise in the scale of life. He was head of a lamasery in the Altai province and was a man of great influence, receiving the homage of an important tribe and controlling his unruly people in the double capacity of chief and priest. In the early days of our acquaintance we had been able to do him a kindness. He had urgently needed a fresh team of beasts to carry him over the last stages of a three months' journey when his own horses were fagged out with long travel. By using our mules and cart he had been able to overtake and pay his respects to the great Panchan Lama, who was then leaving Tibet for Peking.

On his return he spent some time in the house where we were staying, and we all came to know him well. His was a mind trained in the principles of esoteric Buddhism, and his life was fashioned according to its disciplines. His austere and remote bearing was attractive in its gentleness, but pathetic in that the expression of his spiritual aspirations, though highly trained, was caught in the involutions of a system which afforded no outlet apart from perpetual reiteration of litanies. When this man met the first impact of Christianity his response to it was typical of the earnest Buddhist. Apprehending the beauty of the life of Christ, he at once offered Him unfeigned admiration. The death on the cross he accepted as a fitting end to so perfect a life, lived in conflict with a world of confusion. The vicarious sufferings of the Redeemer were also recognised, but any suggestion of atonement was gently but obstinately rejected. He was sure that only by long-sustained effort could each individual find and follow the upward path of progress. As he read and heard the Gospel narrative he expressed the veneration which it evoked in his inner being, by taking the volume in his two hands and bending over it until his forehead lay on the page of the book. Response was immediate and sincere, but the authority of his long training had disciplined his mind too severely to allow him to accept anything so revolutionary as the declarations which Christ made concerning the way of salvation.

After some time Shang Fuh-ye returned to his lamasery among the Altai Mountains in Outer Mongolia, and many years passed before we saw him again. Meanwhile political moves extended the sphere of Soviet influence over Outer Mongolia and it was closed to missionaries. We were, therefore, never able to use the travel permit which Shang Fuh-ye wrote out for our party in his beautiful script, and which was to secure us safe conduct and hospitality in a dangerous locality. We knew that Russian rule must greatly affect Shang Fuh-ye's position, but though we occasionally received a direct message from him he said nothing concerning himself, but only referred to the books which we had given him and to his desire to learn more about the matters to which they referred.

Several years later we were negotiating a delicate matter connected with local passports in the reception-room of the Soviet-appointed Governor of a Russian-controlled area in northern Turkestan, when the Commissioner's door opened and a stranger was admitted. By his appearance he might have been a Soviet official, for he wore the heavy leather coat and peaked Russian cap which is peculiar to them. A second glance, however, showed the serious countenance and earnest eyes of Shang Fuh-ye beneath that cap. He knew us at once, and under the critical glance of that circle of Russians we shook hands and looked once more into each other's faces. The Governor stared suspiciously when he heard the exclamation: "Is it possible? My old friends the Christian teachers!"

Explanations had to be given, and he told of his visit to our home in distant Kansu and of help given in a time of difficulty. We could say little in that place, but our parting words, "We shall meet again soon," were not to be realised, for although we saw Shang Fuh-ye driving in the town on more than one occasion, he was always under the escort of a Russian guard who never left him. His own Kalmucks had access to him, and one day a message was brought to us by a mutual

Mongolian friend: "Our Fuh-ye greets you," he said. "He cannot visit you at present. He told me to say that he is not at liberty to go where he will, but that he still reads the books which you gave him, and would have desired to ask many questions concerning them."

Lamasery life is now compelled to recognise secular authority, and even a Living Buddha is not free from its control, but no man can fetter the spirit of Shang Fuh-ye nor keep him from thinking deeply of the teachings of Christ, and sometimes sending thoughts of greeting and affection to his "old friends the Christian teachers."

* * *

Although Mr. Sang was a well-known Central Asian character we never met him until we stayed in a *serai* of the oasis town where he lived. He was nominally a retired magistrate, and was certainly a man of means, for his residence was one of the largest houses in the place. He was the head of a big clan, and besides his middle-aged wife there was a young concubine in the home, and many married sons with their children, not to speak of innumerable serving men and women. It seemed quite natural that he should call on us at the inn, and the first time we saw him he merely made all the customary enquiries, adding such polite comments as were required by the occasion. We promptly returned the call, spent a pleasant hour with his womenfolk, and when we left all expressed the hope that we should meet again.

To our surprise Mr. Sang called a few days later, at the unusual hour of seven in the morning. He made himself quite at home in our living-room and rather overstepped the limits of politeness by asking more questions than is customary on such slight acquaintance. The visit left a curious impression and roused an instinct which warned us to be on our guard. The next day he again looked in, just to see if we were comfortable in our simple lodgings, he said, and this time he led a small grandchild by the hand, saying that with our permission he would often bring the little boy to play with a Mongolian child who was with us. Outwardly he was the perfect type of a benevolent grandfather, smiling benignly on every childish wilfulness.

Days went by and Mr. Sang's visits became more and more embarrassing. Sometimes he arrived just as the midday meal was being put on the table, and when, as custom required, we asked him to share the simple fare, he waived all apologies aside, telling us how greatly he enjoyed homely meals. Sometimes he came just as we were leaving the house, and begged us not to change our plans but to let him sit and wait in the guest-room, where he would use the time until our return in reading some of our Christian books. This intimacy we never allowed, and insisted on entertaining him personally for as long as he stayed. One day I was called from the room for a moment, and coming back sooner than he expected, I found him with a Chinese letter in his hand which he had taken from my writing-case. With perfect *sangfroid* he smiled, saying, "What clever women you are to read and write Chinese characters so well." I put out my hand for the letter, but he read it through carefully before he returned it, and offered no apology for doing so.

His interest was extended to all our visitors and included our servants, with whom he lost no opportunity of conversation, even cross-questioning the cook in the kitchen, nor was he in the least abashed when he was pointedly led from the servants' quarters to the guest-room. There was nothing whatever to hide, but his persistent inquisitiveness and too eager interest in our doings made us very reticent. As time went on we discovered that Mr. Sang's true profession was that of municipal spy, whose job it was to find out anything and everything which concerned travellers and visitors to the town, for the purpose of building up their *dossier* at the recently established bureau called Office for the Maintenance of Peace. As his pay depended on the amount of miscellaneous information which he could pick up and report, he could never afford to let any item slip. Conversation now became a battle of wits in which there was much talk but no information was imparted, and we steadily declined his many invitations to spend long hours in his home answering questions about our native land. "You are far too strenuous in your efforts to do good," he often said, "and in my home you could relax, and there would be no one to interrupt our talk."

This business of professional spy kept him busy during the days of intrigue in Turkestan, when many were caught in his net and tricked into fatal indiscretions. In the end the betrayer was himself betrayed, and Sang the Spy was murdered as he had caused so many other men to be slain.

Everyone brought up as he was in the great ethical tradition of the Confucian philosophy should know better than to violate the ideals of "The Princely Man." Also, he should have understood that the desert demands sincerity, uprightness, confidence and true brotherhood of its guests. Mr. Sang had betrayed all these trusts, and when he died no one mourned him.

* * *

The real connecting link between the people of the Gobi oases is the courier postman. On the desert trade-routes by day or by night the jingle of his donkey-bells is heard, and it is always a welcome sound. It serves to give notice of his approach and also frightens away the wolves when he is on lonely and dangerous stages. Over scorching sands, through robber-infested defiles, across swollen rivers or over lonely passes, through summer heat and winter cold, the couriers carry their mail-bags until they throw them down in the large oasis postal office. Here the postmaster's work of sorting, checking, distributing and dispatching begins, which makes of him a centre of information and the arbiter of news.

We had not yet met the postmaster of the important oasis town in which we had just arrived and where we had taken rooms at a central *serai*. Sleeping-bags were lying about, piles of books were stacked on the edge of the mud bed, and bags of food for men and beasts were piled on the floor. We had been travelling all night and were utterly spent. The cook was blowing on the scrub fire to bring the water to boiling-point, for everyone was desperately thirsty. Washing water would do later, but the welcome cup of tea was eagerly looked for by us all.

I sat on the edge of the *kang* lazily watching the carter as he settled the harness, sprinkled water on the wheels, and fed the mules, when, with some dismay, I saw a daintily dressed Chinese appear at the main entrance, looking from one side to the other and evidently trying to find someone who could direct him. I felt sure that this was our first caller, and a moment later the servant came in, holding a large scarlet visiting-card in his hand, which informed me that Postmaster Hu, Stamper of the Skies, was asking permission to present his respects. Encased in grime as I was, sitting on earth and surrounded by earth, I felt quite inadequate to the task of receiving such a dainty visitor as the one I had just sighted, but by the time he reached the doorway I was standing there to greet him. A moment later I was back in my place, sitting cross-legged on the mud bed, and we were exchanging flowery civilities.

The Stamper of the Skies was small and daintily built. He would take no larger size than fours in shoes and sixes in gloves. He wore a dove-coloured silk gown which reached his ankles, and on his head was a round satin cap. On his feet were black satin shoes, and he had picked his way so carefully through the courtyard litter that they showed no trace of mud. This visitor was postmaster at the local office, which was an important one because it was a distributing centre for various lines of communication.

"For many weeks past," he began, "the couriers have been reporting your progress from one place to another, and I knew that you should reach here today. You have had a very hard journey and now you must not hurry away, but rest for a time. I heard from one of my men that you were running short of food on the road, so you must stay long enough to feed up and strengthen yourselves." Then he added: "If you are needing extra money I can supply you with all that you require, and if there is any other way in which I can help, you must be sure to let me know."

It was now my turn to ask questions, and I soon knew a good deal about Mr. Hu's local family circumstances, as well as those which related to his ancestral home in Central China. This frail being was just back from a six months' journey taken in order to convey the body of his father from its temporary resting-place in the Gobi Desert to the family vault in distant Hunan. The coffin had lain in a temple courtyard outside the city, and the son was free of the three years' mourning before he was able to perform this last filial duty which required him to carry the body, by litter, to the home of its forefathers. This recent visit to the land of silks explained the delicate damask gown and general un-Gobi-like attire of our caller.

We were all eager to know if he had any letters for us, for it was two months since we had seen any, but politeness required that he, not we, should broach that subject. Hoping to lead tactfully toward it, I remarked that he must be a very busy man with so many couriers constantly coming and going. "Not really busy," he said, "but I have enough to do"; then he added: "The couriers' loads have been heavier than usual since you started on this journey." Hearing this, I ventured to pursue the subject: "Have they brought any letters for us?" I asked. "Sackloads," was his reply. "There are letters from England, America, Norway, and there is a small parcel from Denmark which looks as if it might contain something to eat. Among the mail-matter there are many Chinese magazines, and as books are scarce here, I opened and read them with the greatest interest. I have passed some on to a friend, but now that you have come, I will get them back for you at once."

I begged that he would not hurry either himself or his friend, and he bowed, then continued: "There was also a parcel addressed to you from Hankow and in it was one single shoe. I was sure that the other shoe must have been stolen in the post, so I sent a tracer to every office on the way, and there will be thorough investigation." This had, in fact, been a dodge of my own to get a pair of sand-shoes safely through the hands of many covetous clerks by having them posted one at a time, but, thanks to the energy of the Stamper of the Skies, it only resulted in an immense amount of work for a number of offices, and a personal triumph for Mr. Hu when the second shoe arrived. I smiled and murmured apologetic thanks for his trouble in tracing it for me.

Before leaving, Mr. Hu asked us all to a meal. The invitation was formulated in a polite phrase, which depreciated the speaker and all that belonged to him. "My wife is a very stupid woman," he said, "and we have to live very simply, but we beg you to come tomorrow evening and share our plain, everyday fare. A cart will call for you before sunset."

We accepted, bowed him to the door, urging him to "walk slowly," and an hour later returned his call. His home held every Central Asian luxury. The *kang* was spread with a thick Khotan silk carpet, tea was poured from a nickel-plated Russian kettle and served in Siberian teacups of a vivid blue, like a Gobi sky. The tea was flavoured with jasmine flowers and came from Hankow. For half an hour we chatted with his wife and played with the child, but only as we were leaving might the subject of letters be mentioned, and that most casually. "Come into the office and see them," said Mr. Hu. In an inner room he showed us three sackloads of mail-matter, which was the accumulation of two letterless months. "Our cart will come and fetch them away," I said, and slowly we bowed ourselves out.

The next day, according to promise, a cart carried us away from our grimy *serai* to the postmaster's house, where a circular table was spread with a delicate feast service, ivory chopsticks, and a vast collection of *hors-d'œuvres* of the most dainty description. For more than two hours we sat and tasted the successive courses of an elaborate Chinese feast. Mr. Hu could command unlimited transport, and by his orders the couriers brought him all the specialities of Central and South China. There were lotus seeds served in thick sweet sauce, fragrant bird's-nest soup, bamboo shoots cooked with rare skill, and a long succession of meat, fish and vegetable courses, ending in a substantial bowl of plain boiled rice, with five dishes of soup and stew. All through the feast Mrs. Hu's chopsticks hovered around, helping us to the best bits, as she urged us to remember the severe strain to which our bodies had been put by the poor food and bad water of the desert, and pressed us not to stand on ceremony, but to eat as though we were at home.

Every time we stayed in the town of which he was so important a citizen, Mr. Hu made it his responsibility to care for us. We always turned to him in any difficulty, and he never failed to help us. On our many later visits we were allowed to share his more simple family meals and spend long hours in his home. When more difficult times came and letters were severely censored and often confiscated, we knew that he did his best for us. On our last visit, an important-looking notice was pinned up in the office over the censor's desk: "It is forbidden to entertain any feeling of animosity toward the censor of mails," it read. I, for one, did not even attempt to obey this order.

The end of the miniature postmaster was tragic. Some years later, when motor lorries began to invade the Gobi trade-route on which he lived, he announced, with pride, that he would now use the lorry for business journeys. He did so. The road was unspeakably rough and the truck was piled so high with merchandise that passengers, perched precariously on the top, were hanging on to ropes to keep themselves from being flung off. While crossing an irrigation canal the bridge collapsed and the lorry lurched to one side. The little post-master was nearly thrown off, but was saved from instant death by the strong hand of a fellow-passenger who seized his frail body and pulled it back to safety. The shock, however, proved too much for him, and in three days he expired.

*　　　　*　　　　*

Every trade-route man of Chinese Turkestan has, at some time, met a cart and its driver, both of which were of a unique character in that land. The cart was small, it rested on low wheels, was covered with a canvas hood and was drawn by a strong team of excellent horses. This cart might attract notice anywhere, for it was built by the British Government for the express purpose of transporting small ammunition to the front line on the battle-fields of France. When the 1914-1918 war was over, a few of these small munition carts found their way into Russia, two of them penetrated into Siberia, and of these one was driven into Chinese Turkestan and put up for sale at Urumchi. It was bought at once by a well-known citizen of that town and used by him to travel on every trade-route of the country. Wherever it was sighted, caravan men said: "There goes the aged preacher of Urumchi," and Chinese travellers alighted from their own carts to offer a respectful salutation to the white-haired man who drove it, but bearded and booted Moslems would often call out: "Well, old thief, are you out stealing other men's religions again?"

Such offensive remarks were not allowed to pass undisputed, for this old Scots missionary was a veteran fighter, and was convinced that his ammunition cart carried armaments more powerful in their effect than those for the transport of which it was first intended. From under the canvas hood there would emerge a tall, loose-limbed figure, and a gentle, courteous voice would rebuke the Turki for his unmannerly speech, but the conversation would soon pass on to matters of sin and how men can be saved from its power. The respect of the Moslem was deeper than his antagonism, and when the two men parted each went his way wishing well to the other.

The twentieth century was only a few years old when this Aberdonian trekked to Urumchi from north-west China. He saw the strategic importance of the town, so made it his home and the base from which to itinerate over the whole of Chinese Turkestan. Frontiers were loosely held in those days, and he often penetrated into' Siberia unchallenged, and roamed among the Altai Mountains and Kobdo. The South Road to Kashgar knew him well, he was a familiar figure in Hami, in hot weather he crossed mountain pasture-lands to Kulja and beyond toward Alamata, and in cold weather he took short-cuts which could only be used when snow supplied drink for men and horses. The nomads of the steppes were his friends, and the Mongolians of Karashar welcomed his visits.

In the room which he built for himself in Urumchi was a collection of books which he valued very highly, for these would help him to give to each of the peoples of Turkestan a translation of the Bible in their own tongue. All the time which he could spend in Urumchi was given to this important work. The Bible was his constant companion, and he was seldom seen without a copy of it in his hand.

He never revisited his native land, but lived the life of a single, lonely alien. Renowned Western travellers sought his advice, and envied his intimate knowledge of unknown localities and scattered tribes. Best informed of Europeans on Central Asian matters, he was trusted by all, for no one had ever known him to commit an indiscretion or divulge a secret. He fitted into Central Asian life as few Westerners could have done, and had his place among the outstanding personalities of the Gobi. In a land of political intrigue and light morals he held a course of impeccable rectitude, and the men of Turkestan, observing his transparency, the honesty of his dealings and the truthfulness of his speech, bore testimony to his character. When he had driven past on some high-road the caravan *bash* would put up his thumbs in a gesture of approbation, saying: "There goes a good man. If British men are all like that, then Britain must be a great country."

HIGHWAYS AND BY-WAYS

I

Trekking on the By-ways

"The passion for the high-road—the safe, dull, well-known high-road—
is deeply ingrained in every Asiatic," and persuading the *bash* to take
a by-way is as difficult as coercing the mules to leave the ruts. Studying
maps and listening to caravan talk soon makes a traveller familiar with
desert highways, but it is only the pressure of some difficulty which
takes him to the by-ways. On one occasion we were ready to leave
on the stage from Kiayükwan to Moslem Tomb Halt, with uncompromising desert before us, when a friendly villager warned us that
brigands were close at hand. It seemed that there was no possible way
of escape, until he told us of a small track to the north of the Great
Wall by which we could thread our way through narrow gorges and by
little known hamlets, and emerge four days later at Jade Gate, where
we should rejoin the highway. We had not previously even known
of this bypath, but all turned out to be as he had said, and this was
how we came to the Gully of Wild Asses and to the oasis of Flowery
Pond.

A German professor, geologist to a scientific expedition, had recently
spent several weeks camping in a ravine near by, and when we reached
the first hamlet we heard many stories regarding the nature of his unusual
interests.

"What that man seemed to like best was collecting stones," we
were told.

"Why, he would give us money in exchange for any which he
fancied," said one man.

"I suppose he came from a country where stones are very scarce,
and that made him think a lot of them," said another.

"He told us that this gully was once at the bottom of the sea, and
showed us fish-bones which he had hacked out of the rocks, but we
knew all about that sea before he came here, because the last bit of it
still remains," added yet another.

"Where is that?" I asked.

"Only two miles off, in the very centre of that plantation of desert
grass toward the south," was the answer. "Would you like to see it?"

I was glad enough to see anything so interesting as the last drop of the Gobi Ocean, and the whole group of men and women who were standing by came along too. We all plodded through a rough growth of scrub, until we came to the brink of a small sunken pond.

"There you are," said one man triumphantly. "That is the last of the great sea, and the water is so deep that no one has ever fathomed it. Now watch," he continued, and taking his long shepherd's staff he plunged it into the water and churned it vigorously. In a moment the pond was alive with fish darting in all directions. "When this was an ocean, the fish were very large," he said, "but now there is no room for them to grow to full size."

The next place where we camped was Flowery Pond, and from the last drop of the great ocean to that oasis was a difficult way, though every few miles we found some hollow at the bottom of which a mere shade of green herbage showed that the place was not permanently waterless. At one desolate spot was a stone tablet which bore the inscription *Hsi-pei ta lu* (The Great Road to the North-West). Had it not been for this landmark, I could never have guessed that we were crossing an old and now disused travel-road.

Flowery Pond (Hwahaitz) was an area of which everyone knew the name, though few ever reached the place itself because of its isolation. It boasted a small surrounding wall standing four-square, a pond which was never completely dry, and some arable land which partially maintained the population. The men fetched donkey-loads of wheat from Jade Gate, but the women practically never moved from their own homes. The name of Ing-pan (military garrison) has clung to this small place ever since the wars of the Han dynasty, when it was the only spot in ninety miles of desert stretch where a garrison could find water.

West of Flowery Pond the by-way led into dreary wastes where we skirted a disused channel, choked by desiccation, on the other side of which was a caravan route little used, even by camels, on account of water scarcity. It was there that the pilgrim Hsüan Tsang is thought to have turned his horse's head back toward China and, for a few hours, to have abandoned hope of ever reaching the lands of the west.

Then the character of the country changed and we crossed ten large gullies which must have been cut by deep rushing water. The banks between the gullies were precipitous and dangerous for our brakeless carts, but below was tall grass and rich pasture where contented cattle fed. From the last of the gullies we turned into Pulungchi, called by the Mongols Bulungir. This vast enclosure was an abandoned town eleven hundred yards square and surrounded by city walls still in fairly good repair, though each one of the old gates was now nothing but a gap in the wall. There was space to shelter thousands of families, yet the inhabited portion was reduced to half a dozen shabby inns, built up round a couple of wells from the débris of crumbling ruins. As late as the seventeenth and eighteenth centuries Pulungchi was still a military camp of the Imperial Chinese garrison, and when China sent armies to conquer territories in the far north-west, they made a strong base at Pulungchi, but when the campaign was over, Gobi, which had been held at bay for a short time, took back what belonged to her, and the place was left the more desolate because of the traces of human habitation.

We left the old camp on another by-way which led to yet another deserted town called So-yang, and if Pulungchi was a lonely place, So-yang was much more desolate, for the sand had fallen on its ruins and drifted into every sheltered corner, till it lay under a smothering pall from which a *stupa* rose up as the one distinctive landmark. Its most unusual feature was a double east wall, probably erected as protection against the terrible winds, and in one part of the enclosure there were massive walls which Sir Aurel Stein thinks may have been built to protect the cemetery, or abode of the dead. Coins found on the site would indicate that So-yang was inhabited until the time of the Sung dynasty (A.D. 960-1127).

Nothing could be more effective for the preservation of old litter than a covering of dry sand, and there was so much of it that, to this day, no one need ever leave So-yang empty-handed. Pots, seals, penstands, beads and vases of glazed pottery can still be picked up when high winds have shifted the sand-drift, for the old site was evidently abandoned in haste by people who fled, leaving their valued goods behind them. Travellers write of this place as So-yang, but locally it is called "So-yen city," from the two ideographs meaning "locked eyes," which is a name for the edible plant which grows there in abundance.

Not far off is Ta-shih, a by-way town in which a few inhabitants have struggled so bravely against desert encroachment that, in the main, they have kept the enemy at bay. The storerooms of the Ta-shih people are furnished with many stoneware pots dug out from sites within the town, but the habitable houses are few as compared with those which have disappeared in the sand-drifts. On the left bank of the Ta-shih River are ten small cave shrines hollowed out of the conglomerate cliff, which are called locally "The Smaller Thousand Buddha Caves," and the frescoes which they contain are said to date from the period of the Tang dynasty (A.D. 618-907).

From Ta-shih a steep hillside path descends to old Kwachow (City of Melons), which is now an impressive ruin but must once have been a great fortress. Its walls are of stamped clay, enclosing a rectangular space measuring one-half by one-third of a mile. It is said to have been finally reduced to ruins in a Moslem rebellion.

On another by-way we came to a place known locally as "King To-lo's Camel Town." The massive mud walls are one mile in length and one thousand four hundred and sixty yards in width. One solitary family lived within the enclosure, and the well they used was so deep that only with the help of a donkey could a bucketful of water be drawn. The rope, after passing over the windlass, was attached to the little beast's harness, and it was made to walk straight ahead until the bucket appeared at the well-opening.

It was a by-way in the area of Turfan which brought us out at Lama Town, marked on the maps as Lamchin. In olden times it held a settlement of lamas, but they have long since disappeared, and the present inhabitants are fanatical Moslems. A young Christian schoolmaster, convert from Islam, received us there in his home, and took us to see the tombs of his ancestors, who were all *Imams* [1] of the Islamic faith. Under his direction we followed the course of a stream which we crossed and recrossed, stepping from one low bank to the other, then turned and took an uphill road to a stony waterless plain bordered with a high earthen cliff. The long row of Moslem tombs stood beyond the stony plain, at the foot of the cliff, and behind them were small mosque buildings. One of these was of special interest, for it was used as a shelter for holy men wishing to observe a forty days' fast. Each year someone was expected to volunteer for the ordeal, and when he entered the cave it was blocked and sealed, leaving only a small opening through which one pitcher of water was passed at sunset. The cell held a mud *kang* and had a floor of beaten earth, and in the ceiling was a small circular opening. For forty long days the only occupation of the fasting man was to say his ritual prayers and to enumerate the ninety-nine attributes of Allah. In the centre of the cell lay a little heap of ninety-nine dark grey Gobi stones, left by the last man who had occupied it. I stood there awhile and let my imagination picture the stones falling ceaselessly through forty long days from the weakening fingers of this man who

[1] *Imam*—religious teacher attached to the mosque.

knew all the ninety-nine names for God but had never learnt the one which would have changed everything for him—God is love.

The story is told of one holy man who fasted forty days but waited in vain for release, as the *Imam* forgot him and never came to break down the mud plaster which sealed the door. By virtue of his merit the faster was able to raise his body from the earth and escape through a small aperture in the ceiling to a second cave, from which he reached the open. He then walked across the plain and sat down to meditate upon the strange fate which had sent him, a man from Arabia, to wander in the terrible Gobi Desert. Resting his head on his hands he was given a vision of Mecca, and rising, he immediately collected suitable stones and with them built a model of the Prophet's tomb.

We too walked across the stony plain to see this replica of the tomb in Mecca. It was kept in perfect order and stood as a desert witness to the Islamic faith, for every time the *buran* disturbed the stones they were carefully replaced. The tombs on this Gobi plain were marked by white transverse stones laid across grey uprights. White stones are commonly used to convey directions to desert travellers; sometimes they show where a water-hole may be found, and the white ideographs can be read from afar against the black background. We ourselves used white pebbles to bring to the notice of travellers the declarations which are found in the sacred Scriptures, and many a wayfarer has read words of our Lord, such as: "Jesus said, 'Come unto Me . . . and I will give you rest,'" written in stones, and near by has found a small book weighted down and protected with larger stones, which explained the meaning of the words.

On our way back from Little Mecca, a friend invited us to rest and drink a cup of tea at his house. He earned a living by making soap from mutton fat boiled down with an alkali which he got from burning Gobi plants in a kiln. The mixture was boiled in a huge cauldron, then poured into a row of small bowls, and when cold, turned out like little pies. This soap found a ready market in the *bazar*, being both cheap and strong, but when used for washing clothes it produced no lather and its effect on the skin was disastrous. Nevertheless, this soap factory was the pride of Lamchin.

Following by-ways in such areas introduced us to many varieties of insect life which thrive and multiply in the hot sandy soil. No sooner had we put up our sleeping-tent among the Flame Hills than the dust would be stirred by the movement of little ticks which became uncannily aware of our arrival. Unless discovered in time, they climbed up our outer garments until they found a shelter in the hair on the nape of the neck, then swiftly, quietly and painlessly burrowed under the skin and began to exercise their vicious blood-sucking habits. In a few hours they were fattening and swelling, and soon grew so large that it was almost impossible to dislodge them from under the skin. Horses and mules suffered too, for they developed symptoms known as "sweating blood." When hot, their coats streamed with red trickles caused also by ticks which grew until they burst the skin and released jets of blood. Camels were preyed upon by the largest species, which were nearly two inches long and capable of growing to a considerable size. In the hottest season the most careful drivers on the South Road put their horses and mules into loose trousers to protect them from the torment of mosquitoes and other virulent creatures.

The path leading back to the main track took us through a dry and dusty fissure of the Flame Hills, overlooked by two sets of seven rocks called the *Yet Kiz* and the *Yet Oyol* (Seven Maids and Seven Youths). Some wayside stones among these hills bore ancient inscriptions in circular Uighur script, and at one place the road was blocked by a large detached boulder of red sandstone, carved on two sides with representations of Buddhist scenes. It was called *Tamguluk Tash*.

On the south side of the hills we emerged near the beautiful little village of Sirkip, where, standing in an open space surrounded with houses and gardens, was the lovely tower for which it is famed. This terraced shrine rises from a base of stamped clay which is forty-eight feet square and ten and a half feet in height. Above the base are six terraces, each of which is a little narrower than the one immediately below it. There was formerly a seventh storey, and probably a final superstructure also, though of this nothing is now left; each side is ornamented with seven niches, some of which still contain figures of the Buddha. Even in its present broken condition the tower is over fifty feet in height and dominates with graceful stateliness the low village which surrounds it, but when the great structure stood complete its beauty and symmetry of outline must have made it a unique Gobi landmark on that road near the Flame Hills.

The by-paths of Gobi certainly led us to unique places and to the homes of unusual people, but our carters were always happier when we came back to the familiar high-road. When the track led across desert wastes where sand-hills or hummocks covered the plain, nothing would induce them to take what seemed to be a quick cut, for if they left the main track there was no means of distinguishing one path from another, and any deviation would have been dangerous. Even on safe by-paths there was a sense of discomfort at having left the deep ruts over which the carters of past centuries had driven their teams in safety. The by-way held the threat of the unknown and might produce some new experience—a thing to be dreaded by a man of fixed ideas, who only desired to move as did his ancestors in past centuries. It was easier so, the ruts were ready-made for him and he needed only to keep within them. But I felt otherwise, and when I could induce the *bash* to venture on an unknown way I welcomed the new experience and listened unmoved to his complaints and reiteration of the old proverb which declared that in all circumstances "the old is better."

II

Etzingol Camping Grounds

The eastern Gobi merges into Mongolia, and whereas the western desert has no indigenous population but is inhabited by settlers of mixed races, the eastern side is claimed by nomads whose tradition is that of hunting, herding and flitting.

It is a region so vast that the encampments are as widely separated by sands as islands on the face of an ocean are by water, but wherever there is steppe or grazing land, there the Mongol comes, spends a season, feeds his flocks and herds, then rolls up his tent and moves on to fresh pastures. The Gobi winds clean up the place which he has soiled, the pastures which his flocks have cropped grow greener than ever, and Nature promptly repairs all the mischief he has done to her clean orderliness.

The nomad loves every stretch and dune of his rolling spaces, but in the whole of eastern Gobi there is no locality which compares for charm and nomadic comfort with the beautiful banks of the river called by Mongols the Etzingol. It dashes down from the far distant Tibetan ice-fields, through a long chain of fertile oases, cutting its way through the sand and making of the whole area a coveted camping and grazing ground, for it supplies clear sweet water sufficient for man and beast, at every season of the year, and the Mongols live by its bounty.

In Chinese territory this stream is called the Black River, and is a source of riches to many colonies of Chinese farmers before it ever touches Mongolia, for the Chinese are past masters in the art of irrigation and calculate the value and use of water to the last bucketful.

In summer, when snow melts rapidly, the Black River becomes a roaring torrent which carries earth, rocks and boulders before it, and the surface of the water is kept in a constant turmoil of swirling eddies, cross-currents, whirlpools and natural weirs with a strong backwash. The noise and movement are so bewildering that a rider or driver when fording the river easily loses his bearings, and all through the hot season it takes a heavy toll of human life. The main stream flows on over stony ground until it reaches the sands of Mongolia, and even here Chinese industry has, by dint of ingenious labour, reclaimed some scanty strips on either bank and converted them into arable land, but beyond the place known as Gates of Sand there is no more cultivation and the river, now called by its Mongol name, Etzingol, divides into two branches of equal size called Oboengol (Obo River) and Dondorgol (Middle River). Between them is a raised bank, and on this level plain, impeded by the sands, the streams slacken, sometimes flowing between erosion terraces, sometimes dividing into deltas, and finally losing themselves in the twin lakes Gashun and Sokonor. Thus, after conquering the stony obstacles of its earlier course, the river is overcome by the smothering sand and finds a grave in the dreary swamps of a Mongolian waste.

Between the oasis called Gates of Sand and the Twin Lakes there is a unique camping-ground. The desert poplar thrives there to such an extent that the banks of the river are dotted over with small copses which form at some seasons of the year a leafy shelter from the burning sun, and at others are golden woods of enchanting beauty. The desert poplar (*Populus diversifolia*), which is also called the unequal-leaved poplar, bears two kinds of leaves at one time; those on the new growth are narrow and lancet-shaped like the willow, while those on the older branches are broad and tooth-edged. The Chinese name for this strange tree is *wutung*. Hardy as it is, and able to endure both cold and dryness, it is yet the very first tree to feel the touch of autumn, change colour and cast its leaves. For this reason the Chinese have chosen to make the *wutung* symbolic of sadness, and the eldest son of a family should lean on a staff cut from the *wutung* when he follows his father's coffin in the funeral procession. The bark of the tree carries masses of spongy growth called the "tears of the *wutung*," doubtless because of this association with sorrow. These trees rise to a height of seventy-five feet, and the branches, meeting overhead, form dignified arched alleys. The patches of woodland are as symmetrical as though they had been planted by hand, and the edge is a clear-cut line with no straggling growth.

Along the borders of the river are plantations of willow and dense growths of tamarisk half-smothered in sand. Farther back are clumps of saksaul (*Anabasis ammondendron*) which the Chinese carry away on camels and burn for charcoal, and there is also abundance of liquorice growing around the wooded belt, which is of a particularly fine quality.

As elsewhere in the Gobi, the ruined remains of large cities are proof that considerable colonies of people were once able to live where human life cannot now be sustained for lack of water. Marco Polo records: "When you leave the city of Campchiu (Kanchow) you ride for twelve days and then reach a city called Etzina which is toward the north of the verge of the Sandy Desert; it belongs to the province of Tangut. The inhabitants live by their cultivation and their cattle, for they have no trade." The ruins of this ancient Etzina, now called Khara-Khoto, still lie among the sands beyond the Etzingol.

Sir Aurel Stein very graphically describes the effect made on him by this old ruined city: "It was a striking sight, the most impressive that I have ever seen on true desert ground, this dead town with massive walls and bastions, for the most part still in fair preservation, rising above the bare gravel flat which stretches toward it from the river bank. A conspicuous *stupa*, of distinctly Tibetan appearance, crowned the big bastion of the north-west corner." In the time of Kublai Khan (A.D. 1216-1294) this was a busy city and a calling-place for caravans travelling toward Karakoram, where the great monarch held his Court. "At Etzina," says Marco Polo, "you must needs lay in victuals for forty days because when you quit it you enter on a desert which extends for forty days to the north and on which you meet with no habitation nor baiting place."

The present-day Mongols of the Etzingol area belong to the Torgut tribe and are comparatively recent arrivals, being a section of the vast company which trekked back to Mongolia in the eighteenth century, from Russian camping-grounds on the banks of the Volga. There are records to show that as early as the second century B.C. the Yüeh-chih were using the Etzingol grazing-grounds, but later the Huns drove them out and held the land, until the Uighurs in turn forced the Huns westward through Central Asia to beyond the Tarim basin. When the Uighurs were finally dispersed, the kingdom of Tangut was established on the Etzingol. For two hundred years from the early eleventh century A.D. Tangut extended its rule throughout north-west China, but at the end of that period the Mongol hordes, under Genghiz Khan, moved westward and the land of Etzina served his armies as a highway toward the conquest of Asia. About the year A.D. 1225 the great Genghiz finally overcame the Tanguts and remained master of the whole region. To this day men of the Etzingol use the term Kara Tangut (Black Tangut) in speaking of certain tribes.

The nomads of this vast area are in every way a contrast with the settlers of Turkestan. The man of the trade-route always covets to own a piece of land and a house in which to live with his family and to establish a line of descendants. In nomad-land the spaces belong to the tribes, and the Mongol rides over them singing and shouting, free as the air he breathes, tied to no building and confined by no walls of city or of home. He belongs to the desert and the desert belongs to him. Travellers passing through it are his guests: they cannot command an innkeeper's reserves on a business footing of payment for services rendered, as they can on a trade-route, but are entirely dependent on the tent-dwellers' goodwill and kindness.

The Mongol is hospitable beyond all thinking, but ruthless in reprisals on any who abuse that hospitality. When ranging over the desert he may leave his tent unguarded and will put a box of parched corn and a skin of milk at his door that any who are in need may help themselves, but death would be the penalty were anything else in the tent to be touched, nor could a robber hope to escape, for the traces of his footprints would certainly be detected by the desert-rangers' eagle eye.

We went to the Etzingol at the invitation of its Prince. A message had reached us from this elderly Chief, whose health was failing, to the effect that, having heard of us as itinerant missionaries, he asked that one of our journeys should include a visit to the territory which he controlled. His encampment was three weeks' journey away from where we were staying, and close to the twin lakes, Gashun and Sokonor. The river, which is full and impassable for many months of the year, had to be forded, and its quicksand bed made of that a perilous undertaking. There were immense stretches of sand to cross in which only a desert-born man could be sure of his way, and there were trackless tamarisk forests which in their baffling sameness could be most treacherous of all. On that journey we nearly lost our mules in the quicksands, and also had the terrifying experience of feeling that we were lost in a maze of tamarisk hummocks from which it seemed impossible to extricate ourselves. Nothing could be more baffling than to follow a twisting way in and out among bushes the lower half of which were buried in sand-mounds and wholly indistinguishable one from the other. We walked for hours on a narrow path which

wound its way round and round the hummocks and never led out anywhere. The sun was near setting before we emerged into lighter
brushwood and found an outlet. The smaller tamarisk tangles, which
were from eighteen to twenty feet in height, served as hiding-place for
nomad tents, but only those who knew how to read the indications
could find the encampments. The men were alert to look for pieces
of cotton hanging as though caught accidentally on a branch of tamarisk,
for such happenings are no accident in such solitary places, and should
another indication confirm the first, and a wisp of sheep's wool or a
few threads of red cotton catch the eye, they would know that we were
nearing tents. Then the barking of fierce dogs would be heard, and
shouts from men who had become aware that someone was at hand.
One more turn among the tamarisks and we were faced by tall Mongolians, each with a gun slung on his shoulder and the handle of a hunting-
knife showing above his high leather boot.

Then we stood still with hands open and arms thrown away from
our sides, showing that we were unarmed and totally unable to defend
ourselves, for we carried neither gun, whip, nor even a stick, and our
gesture showed both our friendliness and our trust in those to whom we
came. Instantly all fear vanished and the men were calling to their
womenfolk to come out and receive us. These warm-hearted children
of the steppes took us into their tents, held our hands, patted them,
fingered our clothes and gave us a hearty welcome. The tents were
built upon a framework of light wood covered with thick felt which the
women had trodden out from the wool of sheep and goats and which
gave effective protection against both heat and cold. An opening was
always left in the centre of the roof, but it had a covering of felt which
could be rolled back at will so that smoke from the open fire could find
its way out.

At a word from the men the fierce dogs crept to one side, but when
the women lifted the heavy and beautifully quilted door-curtain to
invite us inside, I stepped in backwards, keeping my eye on one huge
mastiff which was, I knew, longing for a bite from my leg. Inside the
tent was a really comfortable home. Dyed felts covered the floor, and
all around stood lacquered boxes, while facing the entrance was a table
on which stood rows of small brass bowls full of clear water. This
was the family shrine where the precious element of water is daily offered
by the Mongol to his god. Beyond the fire of smouldering camel-dung
was a slightly raised seat, reserved for the master of the home, and we
sat on the floor round the embers while one young woman ran off to

milk the camels and another threw tamarisk twigs on the fire and coaxed it to a flame, then heated the milk in a large iron pot into which she threw a lump of brick tea and a pinch of salt. The first cup of tea was served at the shrine, then we took ours, and with it ate pieces of milk cake made by heating the rich camel's milk so slowly that the cream formed a thick crust which could be lifted from the pot, dried and eaten like a biscuit.

The standard of manners required when mixing with these primitive people was exact and binding, and any breach of etiquette would create immediate hostility and suspicion. For example, had any member of our caravan walked into the tent with a whip in his hand the whole colony would have been antagonised, or had one of us remained standing at the entrance in such a way as to dominate the tent there would have been no welcome for us. Had anyone been so indiscreet as to touch the cooking-pot in passing, we should have given the gravest offence, and our very attitude in sitting was controlled by custom; one knee must be kept flat on the ground while the other was raised, for this is the rule a guest must observe in an Etzingol home. These seemingly arbitrary regulations are not merely the trivial ways of polite society but fixed tribal customs, and behind each there is some reason connected with possible treachery or with a danger always present in unprotected nomad life. For a guest to be careless of a regulation, or unaware of its existence, is an unpardonable offence.

Being received on a friendly footing in a Mongolian family is to be given the freedom of a circle which is wider than that of the strong, robust, fearless, but childlike nomads themselves, for there is a larger family which includes the flocks and herds which are a real part of it. Inside the tent is a place reserved for the new-born lambs and tiny kids which are the playmates and pets of the children. The camel-nurseries are just outside, and are surrounded by palings of dried desert grass, for the baby camel is born at midwinter and needs some protection from the rigours of the Mongolian storms. Within their enclosures these grotesque little creatures gambol with an angular awkwardness which is very captivating. When their mothers are out to pasture they must be hand-fed, and this is done by means of a feeding-bottle made from a bullock's horn pierced at the tip and adapted to a leather teat perforated with a small hole.

From one encampment to another we followed our quiet course, sharing for a while the life of a primitive culture which had overlapped from a previous age—this wandering life of the steppes which is the basis from which modern civilisations have been developed. The people of the Etzingol knew nothing of present-day civilisation and its complex problems arising from capitalism, centralisation, housing, employment and education. The sky, the air and the natural produce of the land were their inheritance and sufficed for all their needs, nor did the lapse of time bring them any sense of pressure. We too, for these few months, luxuriated in being free from the bondage of all organised occupations. No postal courier penetrated nomad-land, and no news of the outside world reached us, so we, who had been caught in the complicated processes of modern life, chose for a time to forget the lapse of the long centuries and willingly returned to the conditions of our ancestors, glad to be primitive with the primitives and nomad among nomads.

We enquired our way as we went, and the directions were always localised by an *obo*: "To the west of the *obo*," "North of the *obo*," "Half a day's camel stage beyond the *obo*." Each conspicuous summit was crowned by one of these strange structures. Branches of poplar and tamarisk had been dragged up the steepest rocks to make a rough framework for the landmark. A coarse red banner showed from afar, locks of hair fluttered from the sticks, and in the hollow nest of the shrine all sorts of strange things, such as stones, fossils or shells, were left as an offering to the traveller's guardian spirit, but after we had visited an *obo* it also held copies of the Gospels—the pilgrim's true guide—in the Mongolian language.

At last, one day, we emerged from a sandy belt on to a green pasture. Herds of beasts were grazing at will and mounted herdsmen galloped among them, whirling their short-handled whips and shouting exultantly. This was the entrance to the vast pasture-lands which were reserved for the Prince's herds of horses and cattle. Directly we were sighted, the herdsmen veered their mounts in our direction, and we were soon surrounded by excited men, eagerly questioning our right to be there. From them we learnt that the old Prince, at whose invitation we came, had recently died, and that the new head was a usurper who seized the Chieftainship, with all the tents and all the riches of the old Prince.

Next morning we sat in the tent of this bold supplanter, and with the help of his Chinese interpreter we talked with him of many things. We were not the only guests that day, for behind the raised dais on which the Chieftain sat, stood a lama who had just returned from a journey into Soviet territory. The Chieftain's simple mind was bewildered by two irreconcilable assertions which simultaneously claimed his attention, and both of which were new and foreign to his thought. One concerned the Mongolian New Testament which we had sent ahead and of which he turned the pages as we talked. The first great proposition which faced him was a call from God to repentance: "God commandeth men everywhere to repent." The other word was a denial of the existence of God, and a declaration by the strange lama that religion was the weapon of imperialism and the dope of the people. This was a shattering announcement to a man whose activities, questionable as they might be, had yet always taken him to the *obo* to seek the favour of a god. "No God? Then what of *Tengri*?" he asked, "the Being who controls all life and all the spirits."

That day, in the audience-tent, the destiny of the Etzingol tribes seemed to be outlined before our eyes. In the hands of a powerful and astute Government all spheres of influence are rapidly and skilfully explored for purposes of propaganda. Young boys would be claimed for school-life and their outlook cleverly biased, amplifiers carrying the voice of a Moscow broadcast might speak in the tents of Chieftains, and the conversion of fearless herdsmen into dashing cavalry could be easily effected. This might well be the future of the Etzingol nomads.

III

The Winding Road

There is one caravan route which occasionally brings a merchant from Paotow or the Temple of the Larks to the banks of the Etzingol River. It is called the Winding Road, and most of those who use it are straightforward business men, dealers in pelts, camel's hair or liquorice, but now and again it brings a man whose object it is to disappear from his native land and never be heard of again. Such men often have a strange background, and they travel under an assumed name and on fictitious business. Sometimes there is even a price on their heads. The Etzingol camping-grounds are an attractive place to the mock nomad, for there is good profit to be made in handling barter and exchange among people who are so elementary in methods of commerce as these Mongols. Such enigmatic guests generally join the caravan at a small halting-place, and hope for a free passage by acting as cook's helper or junior puller. The *bash* is not deceived, nor is he surprised if, before the journey's end, they fail to report when the camp moves on, and are never seen again. If any comment is made he will merely remark, "To every man his own business," and dismiss the subject.

A strange chain of circumstances brought us in contact with such an exile. We were drinking camel's milk and eating *ʒamba* in a Mongol tent one day when a man lifted the door-curtain, stepped inside, and, according to Mongol custom, exchanged snuff-bottles with the host. After this correct greeting the stranger sat down and was given a bowl of milk, while the interrupted talk was resumed. Our host was eager to know something of our country, and asked many questions regarding its King, its customs, its people, and regarding certain strange inventions the wonders of which had been reported to him. "Was it really true," he asked, "that there were carts which flew in the air?" He knew that one horseless cart sometimes crossed Mongolia, but he had heard that it often refused to move, and that camel-caravans, though they travelled more slowly, might overtake the huge monster where it lay stuck in a rut. He had heard of the "iron road" at Paotow, but had never himself seen it, nor had he any wish to do so, for, as he said, "In this country camels are best." He spoke fairly good colloquial Chinese and expressed admiration of our easy use of that language, to which we replied that before we came to these parts we had already lived for many years in Central Shansi. At these words the new arrival looked sharply in our direction, then turned away and continued his conversation in Mongolian about the business which had brought him there. It was quite clear that his interest had been arrested, but we were used to being the centre of notice in such a group and thought little of it. Presently he turned and spoke to us in Chinese, and it was evident that, though dressed as a Mongol, this was his native tongue and his intonation was that of Shansi. "From which part of the province did you come?" he asked. I mentioned the name of a city where we had lived for many years, but he said little more and soon took his departure. Later in the day we met him in other tents, and he always asked us a few questions in Chinese and always left us hurriedly.

Next day we were watching baby camels at their frolics in an enclosure near one of the encampments when a rider broke through the tamarisk thicket, tied his horse to a branch of the growth, and strode toward us. It was the same man again, and he was evidently well known here too, for he joined the family group like an *habitué*. Once again he spoke: "You said that you came from Shansi. Do you know many of the towns?" he asked. "We know most of them," I answered. We then talked of that province, of its various localities, its progressive Governor and of its prosperity, but again he broke off abruptly and chatted in Mongolian with the family, drank another bowl of salted tea, saluted, leapt on his horse and rode off.

Two days later we stood in the *yurt* which housed the head lama of the Etzingol. It was a handsome tent and richly furnished with all the goods which indicate nomadic wealth. The brass and copper kettles were of the largest and heaviest description, the bowls were made of polished wood rimmed with silver, and the *ʒamba* boxes were lacquered in golden-bronze tints. The raised portion of the tent floor was larger than usual, and on it was placed a long, low table spread with the complete paraphernalia of ecclesiastical usage. There was a filigree jug of holy water, a bunch of peacock's feathers with which to sprinkle the worshippers, rosaries to mark the recitation of mantras, a bell to sound at rhythmic intervals, a little hand-gong and a small prayer-wheel, an effigy of the thunderbolt, a wooden crab, a hammer with which to strike it, a conch which is blown to assemble the lamas, and most important of all, a vase which held bamboo slips inscribed with answers to the prayers of those who wished to fix a lucky day for some undertaking. There were also many brass bowls filled with butter, and a brazier in which to offer it as a burnt-offering. Behind the lama was placed the great cockscomb head-dress, kept in readiness for ritual occasions.

Facing the temple furnishings sat a man of such an evil countenance that he might well be accustomed to hold intercourse with dark forces. He was draped like an idol, in yellow and deep red brocade, and never ceased from muttering the one sentence: "*O mane padhme hum*" (O thou precious jewel in the lotus). He had been saying it so perpetually and for so long that his chin was moulded by the words into a strange shape. He never took his hand from the beads, and the muttered prayer persisted during every break in the conversation.

Several times the door-curtain was lifted to admit a Tibetan or a Mongol who knelt to receive the lama's blessing, and among them was the same sham nomad whom we had already seen so often. He made an obeisance to the lama, who sprinkled him with holy water, then sat down on the ground near me, and while my companions continued talking with the lama he began to question me again about the district of Central Shansi, its towns and its villages.

"Do you know Peach Bloom Farms in the Eastern Hills?" he asked. "The village is not far from the town where you lived."

"I know it well," I said.

"Do you know the Li family who live there?" he asked again, his face tense with interest.

"I do," I replied, "and I have often stayed in their home."

When he asked that question I immediately realised to whom I was speaking, but I think that I succeeded in so controlling the expression of my face that he suspected nothing. Now that I held the key to his identity, the striking likeness of this Mongol to my old Shansi friends, the Li family, was unmistakable. He listened intently, and I spoke as naturally as possible of the young daughter-in-law and her child, and of the death of the old parents. Though I sat in the Mongolian tent and talked with this mysterious stranger, actually I was more vividly conscious of standing in a Shansi courtyard at Peach Bloom Farms, where a young woman was pouring out a strange story which concerned her dead husband. I knew her well, for she had been first a pupil, then a student, under my care, and it was natural that she should speak to me in her perplexity. The boy to whom she was betrothed had been a firebrand of revolutionary activity from schooldays, and after the marriage, while the young bride cared for his parents, he went off to a distant town, where he became involved in a political plot. It was discovered and he was arrested, condemned to death and executed. Later on, the rough coffin holding his body was brought home and buried at Peach Bloom Farms among the family graves.

"A week after his funeral," the young widow was saying to me, "I came to the grave to mourn for my husband, and there I found a girl dressed, like me, in coarse white mourning. She crouched at my husband's grave, wailing for the dead. I had never seen her before, and I asked her who she was and where she came from. She only said, 'I have come to wail for my brother.' 'You are mistaken,' I replied, 'this is our family grave and my husband was buried here not long ago.' She only shook her head and rocked to her wailing. I was frightened and ran home. There I found a stranger talking to my parents. He said that when my child's father was condemned to death many tried to help him to escape, and a few hours before the execution a man was found who sold his own life for a large sum of money and let himself be shot in his place. That stranger said: 'The coffin which is buried in your field does not hold the body of your son, but of the man who took his place, and his sister has come here to wail so that his spirit shall not be among the neglected dead. As to your son, he is alive, but he has fled to a distant country, from which he must never return to China.'"

Sitting in the lama's *yurt* I thought of the old parents, of the girl who was neither wife nor widow, and of the grave which held the body of the man who had parted so carelessly with his life. I looked into the face of this mock Mongol and he gave me one searching glance. We both understood, but even at this distance from his home it was better not to say more, though I knew that I was speaking to the fugitive son, and he knew that I knew. He rose, gave the lama a final *kowtow*, turned to us with a Chinese salutation, and left the tent. He did not cross our path again, but his persistent inquisitiveness had not escaped the notice of our vigiliant Chinese servants. They knew nothing of our side of the story, but took an opportunity to tell us that this man was no Mongol, but a Chinese fugitive, disguised and hiding in the forests of the Etzingol.

WITHIN THE GREAT WALL

I

The Passing of an Era

FROM Etzingol to Turfan, from Spring of Wine to Chuguchak, we had spent long years in following trade-routes, tracing faint caravan tracks, searching out innumerable by-paths and exploring the most hidden oases. Wherever we heard of some side-track which led to a hamlet, or even an isolated home, far from the main roads, there we went to deliver our message. Five times we had traversed the whole length of the desert, and in the process we had become part of its life. The caravan men knew us, carters hailed us as old friends and oases dwellers welcomed us to their homes, reminding us with touching accuracy of the date of our last visit. In every Gobi temple which we had touched the priests now owned a copy of the Scriptures, and in some of the most remote places the schoolmaster would show his respect for Christianity by marching the boys to the preaching tent, where he ordered them to listen attentively, and never forget a word of what was said.

The merchants of the larger towns reckoned on our visits, and there was always a murmur of pleasure when our travel-carts rolled in at the city gate and through the *bazar*. Innkeepers treated us as valued clients, and it would have been a great offence had we moved our custom to a rival firm. "Here's the Gospel back again, back again, back again," was the rhythmic lilt which hailed our arrival in innumerable hostels where we stayed. Teaching, preaching, healing and imparting the good things of the Good News, we had spent ourselves ungrudgingly. From morning till night, and if needs be from night till morning, we had bought up opportunities, and in doing so had made the strangest contacts. Princesses and beggar-maids were alike in the circle of our friendship, and our purpose was that no one should meet us without becoming conscious of the Lord Whom we represented. Our first reception in a town had sometimes been inimical, even to the point of being stoned by Moslem antagonists, but on a second visit the hostility was generally less, and finally there were always some people who made friends with us.

A tent, a cart or an inn-room was our only home, our guest-room, preaching-hall, dispensary and bookshop. The problem was how to

Tombs built in Persian style outside Dakianus

A brick from Dakianus

A lonely desert grave

(*Photograph by a Chinese.*)

Ma Chung-Ying, aged 23

The city gate at Tunhwang

(*Photograph by a Chinese.*)

Yolbas the Tiger Prince

A stony by-way

Objects picked up at Dakianus and So-Yang

The tower of Sirkip

Mongolian sands

A Mongol woman at her tent door

Camels on the winding road

An old Tibetan woman

The sands were furrowed with deep ridges

A red-robed lama

The acolyte at the temple

keep ourselves supplied on trek with enough Scripture portions to meet the demands of those who thronged the bookstalls. It was only once in years that they had the chance of turning over such piles of books and selecting those which roused their interest, so at fairs and at festivals the crowds carried away thousands of brightly bound gospels, many New Testaments and numerous other books relating to the Christian faith. Large posters designed by Chinese artists which declared the commandments of God and the precepts of Jesus now hung on the walls of town houses, village farms, innkeepers' quarters and even of Confucian temples and Buddhist shrines. It was necessary to carry books in seven different languages in order that the Mongol, the Chinese, the Turki, the Tibetan, the Manchurian, the Russian and the Arabic-reading *Ahung* should each be supplied with the Gospel in his own tongue.

For long years we had travelled through heat and through cold, but now the immediate job was done, and our faces were once more set toward the fortress of the Great Wall, the starting-point from which we had set out. The homeward trek lengthened into months of travel, and as we went we became increasingly aware of a definite change in the bearing of the people. There was an anxious look on the stolid faces of the camel-drivers whom we passed, and though they would commit themselves to nothing definite, they dropped a whispered hint to our carters, warning them to keep on the side-roads and to avoid touching certain towns.

As we left the stretches where we had been only tent dwellers and came once more to the land of inns, we found that inn doors were kept closed instead of being wide open as formerly, and that innkeepers peeped suspiciously through a crack to see who we were, and only when they recognised us unbolted the door. This time the word which passed from lip to lip was "Communists are on the march," and everywhere the word provoked a reaction of horror. The main road was almost deserted, and when we reached Tomb of the Moslem oasis the look of the place was so abnormal that I slipped over to talk with the man at the little shop and ask him the meaning of it all. He would not speak aloud, but whispered: "Every woman and child has left the place." Then, taking me to the back of his small house, he pointed up among the hills.

"Do you see a black spot below the line of fir trees and a little to the west?" he asked.

"Yes," I answered, "I do."

"That is a cave," he said, "and they are all hiding there. Every night after dark we go up, taking food with us, and some of us spend the night there to protect them. Reports of the road are very bad, and there is surely worse trouble coming."

"What is it of which you are all in such terror?" I asked.

"Bands of Communists from the Southern Provinces," was the answer. "They have been chased up north by Government troops. We have never had them before, and people say that they are cruellest of all the irregular troops for robbing the peasant of his food. "But," he added, "they won't find much here to steal. Those caves up in the hills are good hiding-places for us and for our crops. There are so many caves and we know our way about them so well, that we are not afraid of anyone attacking us up there."

I knew that he spoke the truth, for I was once taken to see such a hiding-place, and I found the earthen cliff honeycombed with caves, partly natural and partly excavated by generations of fugitives hiding from robber-bands. All the caverns were connected by narrow passages or *couloirs*, and in the innermost recesses chimneys had been cut and mud fireplaces built on which huge cauldrons of porridge could be boiled, sufficient to feed whole villages of refugees. The perilous life which these men's ancestors had lived since the days when the Huns devastated their lands has preserved a great heritage of the hiding instinct, and only by using and cultivating this have they avoided extermination.

We decided not to risk taking the stage to Kiayükwan through Gold Washers Halt by night, and left Moslem Tomb in the grey dawn so as to get in by nightfall. It was dusk when we first sighted the high turret of the fortress, and everyone gave a shout of joy, for if the Chinese leave their homeland with a sigh they re-enter it with a cheer, but when we came into full sight of the gate we saw that the towers which had been a Gobi landmark for centuries were broken down, the brickwork of the fort was defaced, the great portal through which the carts once rolled in and out was shut, bolted and locked, and only the small side-gate was open. There was no military guard to greet us, for the men of the garrison had vanished and the barracks were in ruins; nothing was left of the houses but crumbling walls. The only people who had remained were two families of the old residents now living in dug-outs. The desolation was complete and I wandered up and down the streets like an uneasy ghost, picturing the horrors which had brought about this devastation. "Where," I asked, "was the Governor, and what had become of his garrison? What had happened to the women and children, and all my old friends?" The old man in the dug-out answered my questions with a terrible story of battles, of slaughter and of reprisals, but these derelict people, though they lamented the Kiayükwan that had been and now was no more, accepted with deadly submission the inescapable decree of fate. "*Muh-yu fah-dẓ*" (man can do nothing) was the sum of their philosophy.

On reaching Suchow we were challenged by suspicious and unfriendly soldiers, who tossed our bedding-bags down in the dust, searched them for firearms, and then roughly ordered us to drive on. We bumped through the crooked city gate into the main street, and there we heard the people all around us exclaim, "The teachers have come home again." They spoke truly, for here at Suchow was the house and the home in which Gobi evangelism had been planned. Here were the friends with whom we were linked by a chain stronger than the ties of flesh and blood—the spiritual bond of vital union between fellow-Christians. Here we should find the comfort of a spacious room and the luxury of a door which we might sometimes shut. Here too was an abundant supply of soft, sweet water, and facilities for a standard of cleanliness beyond anything we could maintain on trek. Clean bodies, clean clothes, a clean kitchen from which we could banish the flies, a clean living-room with whitewashed walls—in a word, privacy and cleanliness: these were the only final luxuries which had preserved their attraction for us. So many things which might seem necessities to those in easier conditions had dropped out of life without leaving a regret, nor could they ever count for much with us again, for the valuation of living conditions had been readjusted to a scale which overturned the accepted use of the words necessity, comfort and luxury.

II

A Journey of Memories

We were back in Suchow, the city often called by its most ancient name Chiuchüan (Spring of Wine).

It was the first town within the Wall to welcome travellers, and was a place of military importance, for the Minister of Defence was stationed there. This was an old-established office, and according to the archives, the first Commander to hold it was appointed to Spring of Wine in 115 B.C. How we loved its landmarks, its distinctive pagodas, its stately trees and its wide streets. Looking up at the glittering scooped ridge of the ice-fields in the South Mountains I truly sang for joy, and when I stood again in the summer pavilion where the actual Spring of Wine gushed upwards in a pond surrounded with green reeds, I thought of the weary days behind when only bitter water had been our portion. This water was so delicious that it seemed like new wine in its power to revive and refresh exhausted travellers.

The walk home led through Jade Street, which was roughly paved with refuse jade from which the core had been extracted. Here men of the ancient guild of jade polishers still lived and, using the most primitive tools, made wine-cups, bracelets, inkslabs and balls of jade for scholars to roll in the palms of their hands and so keep the fingers supple for writing. Our house stood near the west wall, which, according to the decrees of the geomancers, must never be pierced by a gate, for Kiayükwan, more than twenty miles away, had been declared Western Portal of Suchow, and it was believed that should any ruler dare to cut an opening on that side, floods would pour in and destroy the town.

Then I came back to the room where the map of Turkestan and the Gobi Desert was once more nailed to the wall. How differently I viewed that map in former days, when the trek was being planned. My comrades and I had then studied it so carefully, measuring distances and calculating mileage. Dictionary in hand we had searched out the meaning of each complicated ideograph which indicated the name of an oasis. With what eagerness we questioned any travellers who had covered the ground, noting all they told us regarding conditions, landmarks and the character of each locality. What was then insatiable curiosity had now become accurate knowledge and solid experience, and the map was no longer a mere cartographer's diagram, but a living thing, and each name conjured up a town of distinct individuality. How different, each from other, were these widely spaced oases, and what strong characteristics they each had developed. Unlike the huddled towns of thickly populated countries, whose peculiarities are merged into general features, each desert oasis had its unmistakable identity, just as human beings brought up in conditions of isolation gain in personality what they lose in adaptability. The course of our various journeys was outlined in red, and my eye followed the marking, through the portal of the Great Wall, right on to the border of Siberia. The oases were dotted over that red line as beads are threaded on a scarlet cord, and each evoked a unique picture.

There, at the start, was Yümen (Jade Gate), so small and so exclusive.

The light turrets which decorated its city wall gave an architectural individuality to the town, which its inhabitants transmuted into conscious superiority, holding themselves slightly aloof from other places, though they would never break the laws which bound them to courtesy and hospitality. After our first visit we never again arrived at Yümen in dusty and travel-stained clothes, but instinctively tidied ourselves before we reached the city, and noticed that carters and servants did the same. Something in the spirit of the little town required it of us, and the tidy, bright *baʐar*, grouped round the entrance of the Mandarin's house, would have politely rebuked our shabbiness. On a whitewashed wall facing the *yamen* a large map of China and her dependencies was painted in place of the customary tiger, and this, in itself, gave a touch of culture, even to the market-place.

The name Jade Gate has historic associations, for during the days of the Han dynasty, Jade Gate Barrier was already a renowned outpost of the Chinese Empire. There has been long dispute concerning its location, but the people of Yümen still argue that since the name is the inheritance of their town, the site also may well be theirs. "Who," they say, "could show a better claim?" Discussion on the point is dismissed with the Chinese phrase " *Yu tamen,*" which may be translated "They say. What do they say? Let them say. It is immaterial." The town does not stand on an eminence, yet the unbroken stretches around produce a strange effect, due perhaps to some mirageous illusion, and standing by the turret I always had a sense of being nearer to the blue sky there than anywhere else on earth.

Following the line of the desert road, my eye travelled on to lonely, desolate Ansi, which has nothing to compensate for the forlornness of its barren surroundings and the devastation of its ceaseless winds. The West Protecting Garrison is an ambitious name for this vast enclosure, so sparsely built over with shabby houses into which their owners creep, seeking shelter from the desolating blasts of the Gobi *buran.* No one lives in Ansi by choice, and all who must of necessity do so complain bitterly of their lot. Its storms are proverbial, its houses are miserable, its cold is perishing and it has no fuel. Ansi greets its guests with sand-tornadoes, racks them with dung-laden whirlwinds, and speeds them on their way with dusty blasts which choke nose, eyes and throat with nauseating grit.

My eye caught the word Tunhwang, and I remembered how conscious its people were of being custodians of Gobi's art galleries and of being entrusted with the matchless jewel of Crescent Lake. From there the

line curved toward demon-haunted Lob, where strange voices lure the
unwary traveller from his path. I shuddered and looked away to Black
Gobi, past the sombre ravine of Hsing-hsing-hsia and beyond the
sordid low-crouching shacks of the small water-stages, to Hami, the
Cumul of the Khans, which was as colourful an exit to the long desert
stretch as Ansi at its entrance was drab.

A picture of the women of Hami wearing flowing robes of blue, green,
purple and scarlet, and carrying water from the well in warm-tinted
shapely gourds rose before me. Hustling crowds thronged the *baᶻar*,
where noisy merchants bartered their wares, and carts, camels, donkeys
and bullocks forced their way through the streets. I saw it as it was
when the palace of the Khan, lofty and proud in its gardened enclosure,
still stood in the midst, but the outstanding landmark of Hami was
the blue-tiled cupola of the Royal Mausoleum, pride and glory of the
Turki populace and tomb of dead Khans.

Beyond Hami the track led to Tsi-kio-king, the Seven-Horned Well,
which stands as sentinel where north and south trade-roads divide, each
taking its own way on one or other side of the dividing mountain range.
The old well watches the South Road disappear over a dismal gravel
plain toward the burning oases of the Flame Hills, and the North Road
enter the narrow tortuous defile which cuts the Tienshan range of
mountains in two. In times of peace Seven-Horned Well was a dreary
hamlet, but in war-time it became a strategic desert outpost from which
soldiers guarded three main arterial roads toward Turfan, Hami and
Urumchi. It has been the scene of fierce Gobi battles, and its sands
have many a time been reddened with blood and littered with the bodies
of men and carcases of horses. Every invader covets its strategic position
and knows of its tamarisk growth, which, though smothered by sand,
will supply abundant fuel for his army.

Both north and south trade-routes were marked in red, for we had
trekked them both many times. The southern road kept south of the
mountain range, past East Salt Lake and West Salt Lake to Turfan, and
over the steep Dawan Pass to Urumchi. The northern road, however,
led through a jagged cut in the Tienshan where, for a long nine-hour
stage, a narrow and almost level path wound with innumerable turns
between great bare crags and lofty granite cliffs, emerging at last on the
Dzungarian plain.

This route led past the little town of Mu-lei-ho, which might well
be called Shansi Over-Sands. Though the snowy peak of the mighty
Bogdo-Ola towered overhead, I was always under a strong illusion when

there of being in a small town of distant Shansi, for all around I heard the speech, the calls, the idiom and the tones of that far-away place. The Shansi family which received me was subject to the discipline, the restrictions and the rigid traditions of that most conservative province, where heavy dignity and assumption of superiority by sole virtue of age formed the groundwork of social intercourse.

Every important business house of Mu-lei-ho was the branch of a Shansi firm, and every few years each *employé* was entitled to some months of leave, which were arranged according to rules of strictest convention. The young man must return to his old home dressed in good clothes, wearing satin shoes, a satin cap on his head, and reclining in a cart like a prosperous merchant, but when the few months of holiday were over he must take the journey back on foot, wearing rough shoes and a poor man's cotton suit. Convention decreed that a son should only leave his parents' home through stress of poverty, and that, having left it for reasons of filial piety, he must make good, so whatever the true circumstances, he always returned with outward signs of affluence. On leaving again for his distant job, however, he must appear to have given all he had to his old parents, and be returning to his business as poor as before. Facts, truth and reality might go to the winds so that the conventions be not contravened. Mu-lei-ho truly is Shansi Over-Sands.

To the north of Mu-lei-ho the word Kucheng (Ancient Town) was written. Speculators congregate in this industrial centre and large fortunes are built up here, but only to be spent elsewhere. Business interests are jealously guarded in the Ancient City, and each prosperous merchant is careful to gather young men of his own clan round him, lest any of the money he makes should profit outsiders. Shansi bankers, Honan copper-smiths, Szechwan tailors and Kalgan furriers transact their business here, dispatching and receiving numberless caravan-loads of merchandise, but Kucheng has no interest in Turkestan beyond that of grasping her riches, and if Barkul and Pichan are called the "Ears of the Gobi," Kucheng might well be likened to its greedy, grasping hand.

A name in heavier type indicated Urumchi, renamed Tihwa, City of Enlightenment, by a Manchu Emperor of China, but it might more fitly have been called The City of Dark Intrigue. Capital of Chinese Turkestan, seat of the provincial Government, location of the U.S.S.R. Consulate, it is a centre of every political faction. The town has no beauty, no style, no dignity and no architectural interest. The climate is violent, exaggerated, and at no season pleasant. During the winter there are constant heavy snow-storms, but the snow must not be allowed to lie on the flat mud roofs, lest at the first thaw the water should leak into the houses. It is therefore shovelled wholesale into the streets, and trodden by the traffic to a hard, slippery surface, which makes walking extremely difficult for several months of the year. During the winter householders find it convenient to throw all sorts of rubbish into the street, where the constant falls of fresh snow cover up the garbage, but when the thaw sets in the mess is indescribable, and the town stinks. For one month of the spring, and one of the autumn, the mud-pits in the roads are such that beasts are sometimes lost in them, and only the most athletic men can go on foot, as progress involves leaping from one stepping-stone to another. The summer heat is even worse than the winter cold, and the dirty, dusty roadways are filled with jaded, unhealthy-looking people.

Urumchi's shopkeeping class lives to make money, and its official class lives for promotion. Nothing draws men to the place but the prospect of good business or of political advancement, and the sordid streets are typical of its sordid civic life. In government circles friendly social intercourse has become impossible, as any visitor might be an informer. A secret report can always command a price, and promotion often depends upon supplying it, therefore no man trusts his neighbour. For such reasons as these no one enjoys life in Urumchi, no one leaves the town with regret, and it is full of people who are only there because they cannot get permission to leave and may not leave without permission.

No one has troubled to develop the natural resources of the locality. On one side of the town a wide river flows, but the water it supplies has to be laboriously carried in pails to the houses of the people and there paid for. There are coal-mines in the vicinity, but they are worked so casually, and transport is so badly organised, that delivery is uncertain and it is not unusual, in the coldest weather, for fuel to be unobtainable. A few miles outside the town is a plain where sulphur-springs bubble from the earth. This should be a valuable asset to any locality, and handled with normal intelligence the springs could be used for thermal baths, but the natural hot water is mainly used by women who take their washing to the streams in order to save firing. While mothers do the family laundry their small children play at setting fire to the little jets of sulphurous vapour which break through the soil. For bathing purposes there are only two sheds, with a couple of tanks of more than questionable cleanliness, where the halt, the blind and the lame seek healing.

Towering above Urumchi is the matchless snowy peak of the Bogdo-Ola, Mount of God. Its lower slopes are clothed with pine forests and carpeted with wild flowers and mountain strawberries, and in its recesses it hides rushing torrents, quiet lakes and dashing waterfalls. There could be no more perfect place for a summer resort, but a personal permit must be obtained from the Governor by anyone who wishes to go there, and it is therefore only accessible to the favoured few, while the people of Urumchi have to endure the damp stuffy heat of the town all through the summer.

It is a striking contrast. On the one hand the slopes of the Mount of God, a perfect paradise of purity and beauty, and on the other the man-made slum city at its foot, a slough of iniquity and misery—yet the only possible and easy connection between the two is banned by man's folly.

To the north of Urumchi I passed over the words Manas and Hsihu, the grain-markets of Turkestan, but when I saw the word Dubugin on the map, a strange picture rose before me. This was the market of the Mongols, and the wandering people of the Altai nomads who paced its streets presented the most fantastically dressed crowd that I had ever seen. Robes of brilliant brocade and coats of embroidered satin were fastened with buttons of solid gold, held by elaborately woven girdles and hung over with heavy silver chains, strings of cornelian beads, embossed ornaments and polished brass amulet-holders. No head-dress was too extravagant for Mongols on holiday, and the gaudiness of their footgear matched the eccentricity of their hats. Their high leather boots were made of skins dyed scarlet, purple or maroon, with stitchings of brilliant contrasting colours, and the handle of each man's long-bladed hunting-knife showed above them. Gleaming ebony plaits framed the broad, flat-featured faces of the women, and made a solid base for the brocaded, silk-embroidered caps which suited them so well.

Up and down the street these Mongols tramped, carrying a weight of clothes that would hopelessly impede weaker people. They talked noisily and were as completely free from self-consciousness as children, and, like children, were fascinated by the showy goods on the stalls. The merchants had studied Mongol taste and displayed gleaming brass kettles, large brass wash-hand basins, brightly painted crockery, gay horse-trappings, heavy silver neck-chains, snuff-bottles, thumb-rings and hair-ornaments studded with coral. Every man carried off a huge slab of brick tea stamped with decorative Mongolian writing and made of tea-leaves compressed to the solidity of a real brick. The Mongols had valuable exchange in their heavy satin purses to offer for all they wanted, for these people of the Altai traffic in gold-dust, and when they shook it into the scales they commanded the best of the market. I never wearied of the streets of Dubugin and of watching the giant children of the Altai at their play.

The next town on the map was Chuguchak. It is the terminus of the desert trade-route and is also called the City of Seagulls, but seagulls are not the only migrants which follow the course of the great Siberian rivers southwards to Chinese Turkestan, only seagulls are free to come and to go back, while the human migrants must be exiles for life.

At Chuguchak the Russian *émigrés* have introduced just that touch of ease to life which marks the difference between East and West. The roads are wider, and are bordered by shady trees. In poorer homes the mud walls are whitewashed and in the richer they are papered. The standard of cleanliness is higher, and Chuguchak boasts the luxury of a Russian bath-house. The Siberian baker not only makes the ordinary loaf, but will sometimes bake a tray of buns or of *brioches*, and Siberian honey, mountain-strawberry jam and fruit-flavoured sweets can sometimes be bought.

Inside the neat homes a board flooring has replaced trodden earth, and the Chinese *kang* has been superseded by wooden bedsteads, tables and chairs. Knives and forks are used instead of chopsticks, and the sound of a bubbling *samovar* is a summons to sociability. When snow comes, home-made sleighs appear, drawn by Siberian ponies whose shaggy manes brush the drift as they gallop past.

Here Sunday is observed as a day of rest, worship and festival by the Christian Russians. Each one wears his best clothes, and the women's print dresses and kerchiefs are spotlessly clean. In the little wooden church the service and the singing are an unrestrained expression of religious fervour which is a balm to sad hearts. The *émigrés* are within sight of their fatherland and love it passionately, but they may never return there. Whenever they meet the talk is of Russia, and soon they break out into sad folk-songs which reveal the intense longing of their hearts. Only when fresh refugees arrive do messages from the old home reach them, and then the news is nearly always tragic. Chinese customs are gradually retreating, and shrinking before the more forceful and progressive standards of these Russian people, and the City of Seagulls is rapidly becoming a Siberian town outside the borders of the Soviet Union.

IN THE CHAPEL OF MEDITATION

Where the Gobi taught in Parables

THE journey of memories was over, the wings of imagination were refolded, and I was back in the quiet room from which we had set out on these long wander-years. It was here that our few belongings were packed in boxes and stored away that we might be free from the tug which a home gives, even though it be but a hired room. We had heard a call, we had visualised those Central Asian trade-routes with their cities, villages and hamlets, we knew that some Christian women must go to the people who lived in them, and we were glad to be the women chosen for the job.

Far from being impoverished by the sacrifice, we now realised something of the wealth which had been added to life, and the enrichment of thought and experience which had come through all the inevitable detachments, as well as by the contacts and incidents of the way. As teachers of others we went forth, but as disciplined learners we came back, having found that the desert was gracious to us and that it "lavished liberty upon us in the far-flowing vastness of its solitude." The old desert fathers held that solitude is a thing to be earned, and on our long slow journeys we knew that we were earning it.

All through these years we had been, as it were, hiding treasure in a field, and now that we had come into possession we must dig it out, make it our own, and appropriate its value by use. All too soon we should be back among the crowds who, understanding nothing of its purpose, would measure the whole journey in terms of an adventure. They would certainly be interested and they would question us, but when we replied they would be seeing it all from such a different point of view that the undertaking, as we viewed it, would remain incomprehensible to them. Their lives were organised on an intricate pattern involving constant and delicate adjustments; ours was baffling by its very simplicity. It might be that after a time spent in an atmosphere of sophistication I, for one, should cease the mental struggle for expression, and no longer try to convey my deeper thought about these desert experiences. In the end I might lock the door upon myself and even throw away the key. Lest that should finally happen, it was imperative that I now review my riches, appropriate them and make them irrevocably mine. The time, the mood and the place for such a retrospect must all be fitting. The time must not be delayed, for the mood was present, and as to the place, the Lake of the Crescent Moon would supply me with a Chapel of Meditation.

*   *   *

I saw no change in the lake among the dunes, for there was nothing there to fix the passage of time, and the Abbot and his assistants followed such an even tenor of life that days, months and years slipped by unnoticed, marked only by the monotonous procession of the seasons. My two companions and I were the only guests at the rest-house, and the Abbot understood at once that we had come for quiet after the long pilgrimage, and gave us our choice of the rooms. "You can rest here," he said, "visitors are few these days, for all are busy in the fields and no one will disturb you."

That evening I walked round the margin of the lake. It was full moon and the place had that intense quality of stillness which is peculiar to moonlit nights. The clear-cut ridge of the high dune, reflected in the water, divided its surface transversely, leaving half of it dim and showing the remainder bright with a silvered reflection. Where the pavilion steps dipped to the water's edge there was a faint sound of lapping wavelets, and here I sat for long, stilling my heart to a calm which would be in accord with the outer quiet.

The daylight hours at Crescent Lake, though not quite so silent as the night, were no less tranquil, for the blue heavens above, the reflecting lake below, the encircling sand-hills, the quiet rest-house, and complete absence of news from the outer world, combined to create an atmosphere where solitude brought thought to fruition, and in which it was possible to review the events of the past years. The simplicity of the guest-house did not supply a chair, so I scooped out the sand to make a restful seat for myself and reclined on its soft, yet resisting surface.

I thought myself back to those days so long past when, turning away from the ordinary conditions of busy life in a Chinese city, I had set myself to learn the habits of those who dwell in deserts. Released from a whole round of trivial activities which were an inevitable part of normal life, I immediately came into a new environment. No neighbours would now be concerned about me, none of my friends would even know where I was, and henceforth my place would be with a moving caravan. In that hour I felt as detached as an early mariner must have felt when his small sailing-vessel lifted anchor and set off alone across the boundless ocean. My course would now lie over a sea of sand, and as the seafaring man stands at the prow of his vessel and looks across the trackless waste of waters, so I stood on a small desert eminence and looked over the boundless plain.

My first feeling had been a sense of liberation which was intoxicating. I threw up my arms as if to take flight, saying: "I have the freedom of the spaces and I can go anywhere"; but even as I looked, my eye caught the faint trace of a scarcely perceptible line leading across the waste and I realised that this was the desert foot-track, a path trodden out through the ages by countless wayfarers. The dust-storm might cover it over for a time, but its ancient foundation would slowly and surely re-emerge. As I looked at the path I became conscious that never before had my feet been held to so narrow a way.

Between the high banks of the old cart-road on the other side of Kiayükwan I was safely enclosed, and the age-abiding ruts of the highway made it impossible for me to lose my direction. But on this foot-track I was free and uncontrolled; yet it was a matter of life and death to leave the faint path so lightly traced by the feet of those who had been treading it for generations. It needed great care to keep to that one line, so illusive that at a distance I questioned if it were a road at all, and only as I followed it step by step was I aware that there was something different on that one line from the surrounding sandy space, something which showed that others had walked there before me. Many had left it, and their bleaching bones witnessed to their folly. I saw that the desert is not a trackless waste but a wilderness with a path through it, and that where the traveller finds no sign of a track he has missed the way and the only hope of life for him is to retrace the line of his own footsteps until he rediscovers the path at the point where he stepped aside from it.

Just because I had the whole desert spaces to myself, and there was no compulsion to keep me in the straight and narrow way, the greater was the need for vigilance. To keep my feet to so exacting a path while my eyes were sweeping such limitless horizons, this was discipline. I was free to enjoy the spaces and the liberty, everything was mine, but enjoyment was only possible so long as my feet kept steadfastly to the one track. If I once left it, confusion and anxiety, leading to terror, would be my fate. Was this what Christ meant, I wondered, when He spoke those severe words: "Narrow is the way which leadeth unto life"? If so, then I began to see that the acceptance of a severe rule of life is an integral part of the absolute freedom which is theirs whom He makes free.

Another form of discipline also met me. In the old days of easy travel, how often I broke the stage at the half-way house. "Unhitch the beasts, we will go no farther today," was a common order; but on these great journeys, being committed to my stage, I must make it through heat, cold or blizzard, from early dawn till dark or even through the night. There could be no turning back, nor was any provision made for the procrastinating, the slack, the feeble or the purposeless traveller.

As time went on the charm of wide plains, the sweep of distant horizons, the austerity of silence and solitude, increasingly attracted me. Long uneventful stages were not now something to be endured as a necessary means of reaching a goal beyond the tedious waste, but were desirable in themselves, and I ceased to crave for rapid transit which would obliterate the spaces by mechanical means, for these very spaces now meant so much to me that I valued them intensely for their own sake. Night travel, which had been rather terrifying at first, became a spiritual and mental refreshment. For the first time in life I was in a position to "consider the heavens" from the hour when the too dazzling sun sank below the horizon until it reappeared to blind me once more with the confusing glitter of the mirage.

Desert dwellers have keener sight than other men, for looking out over wide spaces has adjusted their eyes to vastness, and I also learnt to turn my eyes from the too constant study of the minute to the observation of the immense. I had read about planets, stars and constellations, but now, as I considered them, I realised how little the books had profited me. My caravan guide taught me how to set a course by looking at one constellation, to check the progress of the night by observing the shifting position of others, to recognise the succession of morning and evening stars, and to observe the seasons by the place of Orion in the heavens. The quiet, forceful, regular progress of these mighty spheres indicated control, order and discipline. To me they spoke of the control of an ordered life and the obedience of a rectified mind which enables man, even in a world of chaos, to follow a God-appointed path with a precision and dignity which nothing can destroy.

My guide also taught me another lesson, and that was how to walk by starlight. At first I stumbled and hurt my feet among the stones, but I saw that he walked as quickly, as securely and as freely by night as by day. Then I realised that he had used his daylight powers of sense to train the more subtle instinct which served him in the dark, and gradually I too learnt the art of training and then trusting my instincts until I also felt secure in the clear darkness, which is the only darkness that the desert knows. I remembered a wise word spoken by an old prophet concerning a man who was faithful and obedient yet who walked in darkness and had no light. Surely, like the desert way-farer who walks securely by starlight, that man had learnt obedience and quick response in days of normal experience, and when dark hours came he walked confidently, his heart stayed upon God and relying on the certainties which he had proved in the hour of clear vision.

I recalled my early fears when the uncanny loneliness of the night made me shudder as I realised the utter isolation of our solitary way. We had embarked on an enterprise of which our most experienced Chinese friends spoke only in terms of warning; the natural shrinking from such loneliness, however, soon became a thing of the past, and those particular fears ceased for ever directly I realised that they were but the mock armaments of a foe with no power really to hurt, but who, as master in the region of fear, tries to dominate through frightening suggestions.

If, as those soldier-boys at Kiayükwan had so confidently declared, the Gobi is the haunt of demons, then the night should have been the time when their presence was most real, yet in fact it was more by day than by night that the word *kwei* (demon) was on the driver's lips, and most often it was the desert dust-spout which provoked it. However breezeless the day, somewhere on the horizon a slender spiral of sand would rise, move, circle, walk across the plain, leave the earth and vanish in the sky. Sometimes the whole desert floor was alive with them. At a distance they seemed insignificant, but close at hand they were fearful in their cyclonic force. Travellers call them dust-spouts from their likeness to an ocean water-spout, but the desert dweller, certain that these waterless places are peopled by *kwei*, calls them dust-demons. The pillar of sand gives the impression of an invisible being daintily folding a garment of dust round its unseen form. Some whirl from left to right, and some from right to left. "This one is the male and that one the female *kwei*," said the men; "you can distinguish them by the way they fold the dust cloak around them, right to left or left to right; see how they come in pairs."

The couple came gliding across the plain in our direction, then suddenly turned aside, passing quite close, yet enveloped in such a narrow whirlwind that the curtains of the cart scarcely moved, though we saw sand and stones lifted high from the ground. A laden camel can scarcely resist the full force of a dust-spout, and when I was caught in the fringe of one, it nearly swept me off my feet.

The scientific mind of the Westerner studies the phenomenon with a view to understanding the atmospheric conditions which cause it, but the oasis man who lives and dies among desert scenes believes that waterless places are peopled by spirits who desire to be reclothed with flesh. "The best for the demon," they say, "is when a living human will let himself be possessed, but, failing this, the *kwei* uses the dust from which flesh is made as cover for its nakedness."

The spirit which agitates the long night hours uses fear as its weapon, but the demon of noon is the demon of discouragement. When the chill of night is dispelled by the sun's rays the heat quickly grows in intensity until the midday hour brings unutterable weariness to every member of the caravan. The landscape itself seems to take on a metallic and inimical aspect, and every hill and boulder is rimmed with a yellow aura which gives a hard and repellent outline to the unfriendly scene. The expectant joyousness of the morning start has faded away, pleasant anticipation of the journey's end is still too far ahead to be any consolation, and although half the stage is accomplished yet there is as much still to cover as lies behind, so the half-way line brings no sense of exhilaration. This is the moment when the noonday demon has power to transmute physical exhaustion into such weariness of spirit as drains all joy from service, leaving only stern duty to issue orders. Inertia invades beasts as well as men, and it is useless to urge flagging powers to greater effort. This, however, is no new difficulty to the caravan *bash*, and experience has taught him how to meet it. A halt must be called and a pause allowed in which to release tension and recover poise. In the desert there can be no rest without escape from the direct rays of the sun, the glare and the scorching heat, therefore some shade must be secured. The shadow of a rock is best, but where there is no rock there may be a man-built landmark made of desert clay, which throws reliable shade. Sometimes there was only the plain and its uncompromising nakedness, then the desert guide taught me how to use the shadow of my own cart and seek refuge between its high wheels. A brief period of rest for man and beast sent the caravan on its way renewed in strength and courage. The noonday demon had been overcome by recognising the noontide right to relax.

The still days when dust-demons walk abroad are good for caravans on the march, but sooner or later the time comes when the camels, alert as a barometer to atmospheric changes, show signs of uneasiness and become restive. The driver knows the indications and scans the horizon for signs of the coming storm, then moves among his animals, tightening ropes and securing packs. Before long there is a distant roar, and a cloud like rolling smoke with a livid edge advances and invades the sky, blotting out sun and daylight; then suddenly the sandstorm breaks on the caravan. No progress is possible and human beings shelter behind a barrage of kneeling camels from the flying stones and choking sand. When such a blinding storm is in progress there is no indication by which to find the way, and the only safe course is to stay still until it has exhausted itself by the surcharge of its own violence. It is a stirring of earth's surface which blots out the light of day, robs the atmosphere of its purity, blurs the outline of tracks and landmarks and takes all sense of direction from men, making them helpless to use even their natural powers of orientation. It cannot be overcome by resistance, and those who dissipate energy in fighting it will inevitably be exhausted by its fury. The camel-driver is too wise to waste strength in fight and, following the instinct of the camel that kneels in order to offer less resistance, he learns to shelter till the terrible blast passes over. Such a storm will not last many hours, and as soon as it has spent itself the sun reappears in a serene sky, the violently disturbed sand and stones sink to their own place, and the caravan can continue its journey.

Had I been without an experienced guide I should certainly have been deceived when I first heard that strange illusory voice calling for help, of which so many travellers have spoken.

"Halt," I said, "there is someone calling!"

"There is no one calling," said the *bash*, "and there is no reason to halt."

"Cannot you hear?" I persisted. "Someone is calling from among the dunes."

"Never listen to those voices," he replied. "It is not a man's cry, and those who follow it may never come back to the caravan. We must push on." He urged the beasts forward and refused to listen. As he trudged ahead he spoke again: "Those voices are heard all over Gobi, but are worse in the Desert of Lob. One night when I was travelling there I got separated from my caravan. I heard a shout and the sound of camel-bells which I tried to overtake for hours. Then the moon rose and I saw there were no recent tracks of camels, so I halted, and turned back, but something held me and the voice still called. At last, with a great effort I retraced my steps to where I could see the tracks of our camels leading off in another direction. It was a strange experience, but as soon as I was on the right road those devilish voices ceased, and by midday I caught up with the caravan once more. They nearly had me that time, as they have had many others."

"What then," I asked, "are those strange voices which I heard?"

"The people of Lob call them *Azghun*," he replied, "and say that it is a *kwei* which lives among the sand-hillocks and sometimes takes the form of a black eagle. If travellers listen, it leads them away to waterless places where they perish."

Dust-demons, phantom voices with their insistence, always trying to turn travellers out of the way—it sounded so fantastic that at first I was inclined to dismiss it all with an incredulous smile, but something in the subconscious arrested me, and I repeated aloud those words: "When an evil spirit has left a man it roams about in the desert, seeking rest." I had to acknowledge that they were spoken by the only One Who really knows, so I thought on those words and kept silence.

It seemed as though the pastime of those demons was to make sport of the few lonely human beings who ventured into the desert, by encircling them with every manner of deception.

By night, lights which were like flames from a camp-fire played on the horizon, but no one has ever located them or come any nearer by following them. Watching my two companions walking ahead of the caravan one day, I was amazed to see four people where I had believed there were only two. My eyes saw something which my reason refused to accept. I overtook them and there were but two: I dropped back, and again there were four. Thus do the refractions of desert light shake confidence in the powers of discernment and call for a new standard of discrimination in which things seen with mortal eye are not to be relied upon, whereas the things which are relied on may be contrary to the evidence of the senses.

Mirage is the desert traveller's constant companion and his perpetual torment. As soon as the sun is high above the horizon, the sand begins to glitter like water and appears to move like wavelets, while the clumps of camel-thorn look like tall bushes or stunted trees, and seem to be set by the edge of a lake. All through the day this illusion persists, and not until near sunset does the mirage vanish, the sand cease to glitter, and the landscape show itself for what it really is, a dull grey surface. Even the old traveller must never reckon himself free from the snare of illusion. On one occasion we were to spend a night in a Qazaq tent, but it was autumn, and the coarse desert-grass grew rank and hid the encampment. In the late afternoon the carter gave the cry: "*Dao-liao!*" (We have arrived), and, sure enough, there were the tents, the herds and the pasturing flocks. A man hurried on to prospect, and we urged our tired beasts to further effort. In an hour's time the tents, herds and pastures, though still there, were no nearer, and when darkness fell the voice of our man was heard shouting: "We are lost! I cannot find any *yurts*. We must stay here till morning." In the straight clear light of dawn we saw the plain in its true aspect; there were no tents, no cattle and no water in sight. Not till the following sunset did we reach the encampment.

How terrible if in this realm of illusion where that which seemed real was not true, and where true things appeared false, I were left to find my way without a guide. Never could I hope to disentangle the web of deception, and free both mind and sense from its impalpable net. In the desert I learnt to detect some of the illusions which constantly surround me on the greater journey of life, and to depend for direction on the wisdom of Him Who is my unerring guide.

*   *   *

Without water the desert is nothing but a grave, and is useless either as a dwelling-place or even as a high-road for the living. If the traveller's food is poor he will go hungry, if his road is long he will be weary, if his lot is hard he will be lonely, but to all these things he can become inured. No one, however, can be inured to thirst. When the craving for water assails a man he will forget all else in his frantic search for it, knowing that life itself depends on finding it, and that failing it he will soon be the victim of delirium, madness and death.

When a traveller first starts out to cross the desert he is inclined to take water for granted, and though the old innkeepers warn everyone to carry it, he may refuse to listen and prefer taking a risk to being burdened with a water-bottle, but once that man has experienced the torture of thirst his outlook is changed, and nothing will induce him to start upon any stage without a supply.

As the long hours pass, the burning sun seems to sap the moisture through every pore of the skin, until thirst is not only felt in the dry throat and cracked lips, but throughout the body, and as the days of rationed water go by, the whole system, tormented by a craving which becomes more and more urgent, calls out for the sight, the smell and the feeling of moisture. Sometimes the sunset hour brings a caravan to a lonely spot where a water-hole should be found but is hard to detect. All members of the caravan dismount and hunt for the small depression, perhaps marked only by a stone. It is so easy to miss, and once darkness has fallen it would be impossible to locate it. Then a shout is heard, "Water, water!" and all run to the spot to quench their desperate thirst.

The mirage has been a decoy to many thirsty men. I myself, when I first saw a lovely lake with trees standing on its farther bank in mid-Gobi, urged the drivers to push on and reach it quickly, but the *bash* only smiled and spoke indulgently, as one might speak to an ignorant child: "That's not water," he said, "that's glitter sand—dry water." That lake was but a mirage, and the farther we went the farther it receded, tantalising our thirst with its falsity.

I was caught by another deception to which weary wayfarers are subject, and this time it was not "glitter sand" but the brackish water of the salt desert. The sparkle of the limpid spring was irresistible, but when I ran toward it, certain this time of the water's reality, the same gruff voice cautioned me: "Drink as little of that water as you can," it said. This time I cared for none of his warnings, for I had found real water and would enjoy it to the full. I soon learnt that the *bash* knew better than I, for the more I took of this water, the more parched I became. It was brackish—neither salt nor sweet. Not salt as sea-water which drives to madness, nor sweet like spring-water which heals and refreshes, but brackish, leaving thirst for ever unquenched. I drank my fill, and came again, but I was thirsty still.

This experience made me wary of all desert waters, and when I came to the oasis of Ever-Flowing-Stream, though the water looked so tempting and so cool in the little grotto under the shady trees, I was shy of it, for other water had looked cool and tempting too. I tasted it cautiously, but here there was no deception and it was a stream of sweet, satisfying quality. This was *karez* water and came direct from the eternal snows of the distant mountains. Through a deep underground channel it had crossed the torrid plain, and when it emerged at the place where I stood it was as sweet, as cool and as pure as when it left the foot of the glacier, nor would the stream run dry so long as the snow-clad hills remained and the channel was kept unchoked.

Occasionally I heard a desert spring spoken of as "living water," and when I saw one I understood the expression. Its vitalised energy was so irrepressible that from the depths of the water-hole it pushed upward and broke on the surface in shimmering bubbles. Those who draw from such a living spring always speak of it reverently and as of something akin to the divine. The pilgrim prays there at break of day, the Buddhist erects a shrine in its vicinity, the Moslem goes to it for water of purification, and when I stood and looked into the moving depths I better understood the question asked of Christ, "Where do you get living water?" and the answer He gave: "The water I give becomes a spring, welling up to eternal life."

It is water which marks the stage, and only where there is water are there human habitations. The people who live there may be terribly poor, but though poverty-stricken and sordid, their houses are homes and their hamlets are oases because water, which is an essential of life, is accessible to them. These men of the water-holes had another supreme need beyond that of bread and water, for man does not live by these alone, and though I could not bring to them life's normal amenities yet I was there to offer each one that living water for which his spirit craved.

I sat for long hours in my sand-chair by the Crescent Lake and reflected on the teaching of those desert experiences, the illusive mirage, the tormenting bitter water, the sweet water of the *karez* channel and the invigorating water of the living spring. Then slowly the lovely lake at my feet recaptured my attention, seeming to say, "Now consider what lies before your eyes." So I dismissed all thought of desert rigours and yielded myself to the charm of the moment.

The whole scene, from the brilliant glazed-tiled roofs, the light loggia, the golden sand, the silver trees, the fringe of green sedge, and the delicate hues of wheeling pigeons, was reflected in the still water as sharply as in a mirror. An acolyte came to the water's edge, stooped, filled a bucket with lake water and turned back toward the temple. The scene had an unreal quality which held me motionless as though a movement on my part might shatter the spell and disperse its beauty like a dream. Overhead the great dunes towered threateningly. "Why," I asked, "why was this lake not long since buried by these encroaching sands? Why does its fragile beauty last when the whole configuration of the landscape is changed by obliterating sand-storms? Towns and villages have vanished in a wilderness of death and desiccation, yet this lake remains and no one has ever seen its water margin low. What is the secret of its permanence and of the unseen source from which it draws such plentiful supplies that drought has no effect on it?"

At that moment I saw one of my comrades walking over the crest of the hill, ploughing a deep furrow in the sands as she went. From the summit she slid down the face of the dune, and as she did so I heard the sands sing, then she walked to the guest-house and passed through the door, leaving the whole line of her path, from the top of the hill to the lip of the lake, profoundly disturbed. The sands which, before, had not shown one wrinkle were now furrowed with deep ridges, but, as I watched, I saw their surface slowly but surely smoothed out again till, gradually, every mark was obliterated. The ceaseless winds of God were at work and, as always, they blew off the lake and upward toward the crest of the hill. By some mystery of orientation the lake was so placed that every breath which stirred the encircling sand-mounds blew upward and lifted the drift away from the water. I picked up a handful of sand and threw it downward, but the breeze caught it and blew it back in my face. This, then, was the secret of this exquisite lake's permanence—its exposure to the upward-wafting winds of God, and its deep unfailing source of supply.

"Do you understand this picture of one who has attained what you seek and reached the goal of your desire?" something within me said. "In the midst of threatening danger this lake lifts its face heavenward, reflecting as in a mirror the glory of the sky. It is not withdrawn from the terrible sand which constantly threatens to engulf it, its position is always perilous and it lives dangerously, but every time the sand threatens, the winds of God are there to protect it, and no harm touches it. This is why its peace, its purity and its serenity can never be destroyed. Surely the parable is clear—it is the pure in heart who see God."

The sight of a red-robed lama walking in my direction called me back to the immediate, and I rose, greeting him, then sat down and talked with him, first of his long pilgrimage and later of the search for God which urged him to such an arduous undertaking. Walking back together toward the guest-house we met the guardian of the temple, who appeared strangely agitated. "Look," he said, "did you ever see anything like that?" He pointed to a curious triple halo in the sky. The three rims of light spread a diffused radiance, and we all stood and watched the strange atmospheric effect. "This is a terrible omen," said the priest, "a sign of awful happenings, and of trouble coming such as the world has never known. Alas, alas for this world!" Too profoundly disturbed to say more, the old man turned off to the temple shrine to burn incense and seek to pacify the anger of the gods.

Next morning the lama, carrying his little bundle, passed on his way toward Tibet. With my companions I walked once more round the lovely lake, gazing till every detail of its beauty was impressed on my memory. Then we said goodbye to the priest, walked to the foot of the great sand-hills, stood there for a moment and gave one last backward look, then waved a long farewell to the lovely lake, and rode away.

EPILOGUE

THE old Abbot knew how to read portents into the signs of the heavens, and this time his prophetic utterances were amply fulfilled. News of the triple halo and its ominous interpretation spread all over the Gobi. Something terrible must be about to happen, men said, and happen it did. Japan invaded China, armies began to march, and in time the whole world was encircled by a zone of war. Lonely, silent, unmoved, Gobi had stood apart from the turmoil, but its isolation could not be maintained and a gang of technicians soon appeared among the oases. They tested bridges, measured gradients and marked for blasting rocks which had strained the axles of innumerable carts and proved the skill of their drivers through the centuries. When they passed on, heavily laden lorries thundered down from the Siberian railhead, for munitions were needed in China and the old desert trade-route was the direct road by which to convey them. The trucks carried war material, some of which had come by way of the Old Silk Road, along the banks of the Oxus, and southward over those Gobi trade-routes which my companions and I had covered so often on our missionary journeys. New conditions required a new name, and the main artery through Turkestan was soon spoken of as The Red Highway. A new era of Gobi life had begun.

Meanwhile political intrigue stopped traffic between Turkestan and India, while Russian agents diverted the export of raw materials and controlled men's comings and goings. Innkeepers in water-hole hamlets stared to see men who had no need of their services drive top-heavy trucks past their shacks, asking of them not so much as a drink of water, and very quickly the *serais* became useless, small oases were abandoned, and innkeepers withdrew to larger centres.

In the large towns rough paving-slabs were replaced by the macadamised surface of a motor road, and the old inns, unable to compete with the tawdry travellers' quarters known as "Hotel Marco Polo," closed their doors which had welcomed so many generations of Central Asian travellers. Government officials were no longer housed in old and dignified *yamens* but in jerry-built, stucco-fronted erections where the 'allo, 'allo, of telephone operators dominated all other sounds.

Picturesque Central Asian crowds ceased to depend on Hadjis back from Mecca or upon itinerant Indian merchants for news of the outer world because, hidden among the battlements of the city wall, was a loud-speaker which blared out information as issued by the Propaganda Bureau of Moscow. Young men were recruited for military service, schools were reorganised on a Western pattern, and even in such conservative places as Turfan boys in scout's uniform marched through the streets to the strains of a local band. The best scholars of each district went to Russia for higher education and there learnt not only to march but also to think in step with their instructors.

Women who had been like slaves in the harem and might never venture out unless veiled, now found themselves freed from this control under the protection of new laws which recognised them as human beings having equal rights with their menfolk. Even young girls joined in processions with the boys and dressed in uniform, marched unveiled and unabashed singing songs of emancipation

"From the burning eyes of a million souls flashes one steadfast will,
Ye brown-skinned women, haste to the work. Unveiled ye weave the dawn's red glow."

Simultaneously the organisation of the secret police spread a network over every oasis town, and the beautiful simple hospitality of desert communities withered, poisoned by the fear of some guest's betrayal. Nomad people evading interference withdrew to their steppes, fearing lest their liberty be curtailed and the order to house them in model dwellings be enforced.

Journeys from one oasis to another were now covered too swiftly to admit of the quiet thought and meditation of night marches. The majestic silence was shattered by the roar of machines and the hooting of motor-horns, while wayside intercourse was made impossible by the din of shouting drivers and the agitation of harassed passengers. Mud shacks became mounds of rubble, and wells which had been dug by the ancient Uighurs soon filled up with sand. Even the heavens were invaded and Gobi dwellers looked up one day to see "winged dragons" roaring across the sky. The lorry-drivers laughed at their consternation and said: "Those are flying carts and are piloted by men."

The inviolate spirit of the desert withdrew before such an unmannerly invasion. Is it only concealing itself in some still unexplored waste, to return when the turmoil is over? I hope so, but I fear not, for machine-minded men are now in control, who discuss the Gobi in terms of profit and loss, and propose to lay iron rails across it and commercialise its ancient sites.

They may conquer the desert spaces and shatter its silences, but they can never capture its magic charm, and those who have been disciplined and instructed by its austerity still find that the elusive spirit of the desert can call them at will, to roam again in the Gobi that once was.

KEY TO OASIS NAMES

Ansi	West Protecting Garrison.
Chang-liu-shui . . .	Inexhaustible Spring Halt.
Chiuchüan	Spring of Wine.
Hsing-hsing-hsia . . .	Ravine of Baboons or Starry Gorge.
Huei-huei-pu . . .	Moslem Tomb Halt.
Hwahaitz	Flowery Pond.
Kiayükwan	Barrier of the Pleasant Valley.
Kotzyentun	Pigeon Rock.
Kucheng	Ancient Town.
Kushui	Bitter Well Halt.
Kwachow	City of Melons.
Malienking	Iris Well.
Maomu	Eyelash Oasis.
Matishi	Horseshoe Temple.
Nan-hu	South Lake.
Ni-ko	Mud Pit Hollow.
Shachow	City of Sands.
Shamen	Gates of Sand.
Tsikioking	Seven Horned Well.
Tunhwang	Blazing Beacon.
Yangkwan	Barrier of the Sun.
Yümen	Jade Gate.

AUTHOR'S NOTE

THE perennial problem of how best to convey to the English reader the pronunciation of Chinese names has been considered by the Author who, in order to avoid confusion, has adopted the system of Romanisation used by the Chinese Post Office.

MILDRED ALICE CABLE (1878-1952) was born and brought up in Guildford, the daughter of a draper. She first felt the call to missionary work when she was still in her teens, and, with the aim of becoming a medical worker with the China Inland mission, she studied science at London University. In 1901, after the Boxer Rebellion, Mildred Cable joined Evangeline French (1869-1960), a well-known missionary, in Shansi province in China. They were later joined by Eva's sister, Francesca (1871-1960), and together the Trio (as they became known) ran a school for girls in Hwochow, which soon grew to over 200 pupils. They were in China in 1911, when the last Imperial dynasty fell and the last Emperor was deposed. In 1923, four years before Chiang Kai-Shek became China's leader, they received permission to preach to the nomadic tribes of the Gobi Desert. They were the first Christians to go to the region since the sixth century, and in the next fifteen years they travelled huge distances in Central Asia, and crossed the Gobi Desert five times, wearing Chinese dress, preaching, distributing translations of the scriptures, learning local dialects, and gaining the respect and devotion of the people. The Trio left China in 1936, during the Sino-Japanese war, a few years before the Chinese Revolution of 1939, and returned to Britain where they continued writing, lecturing, and working for the British and Foreign Bible Society.

Together with Francesca French, Mildred Cable wrote over twenty books, including *Through Jade Gate and Central Asia* (1927), *Something Happened* (1933), *A Desert Journal* (1934), *Towards Spiritual Maturity* (1939), and *The Gobi Desert* (1942), which was widely acclaimed, and received an award from the Royal Central Asian Society. Later books included *Dhina, her Life and her People* (1946), and *Journey with a Purpose* (1950). Mildred Cable died in Dorset in 1952, aged 74.